BRITISH
TRADE UNIONISM

VOLUME I

BRITISH
TRADE UNIONISM
Select Documents

N. ROBERTSON

and

K. I. SAMS

With a Foreword by
GEORGE WOODCOCK
C.B.E.
Sometime General Secretary of the T.U.C.

VOLUME I

ROWMAN AND LITTLEFIELD
Totowa, New Jersey

© Basil Blackwell 1972

All Rights Reserved. No part of this publication may be
reproduced, stored in a retrieval system, or transmitted, in
any form or by any means, electronic, mechanical, photo-
copying, recording or otherwise, without the prior permission of Basil Blackwell & Mott Limited.

First published in the United States 1972
by Rowman and Littlefield, Totowa, New Jersey

ISBN 0-87471-098-7

Printed in Great Britain

CONTENTS

VOLUME I

FOREWORD   *by George Woodcock* C.B.E.   vii

PREFACE   ix

INDEX TO DOCUMENTS   xiii

PART I: INTRODUCTION—THE TRADE UNION
          MOVEMENT 1914–1969   1

PART II: DOCUMENTS   31

  Section I   Objectives and Functions

    COMMENTARY   33

    DOCUMENTS   42

VOLUME II

  Section II   Structure and Organisation

    COMMENTARY   278

    DOCUMENTS   283

  Section III   The State in Industrial Relations

    COMMENTARY   413

    DOCUMENTS   422

APPENDIX: DEVELOPMENTS IN 1970   567

GENERAL INDEX   599

FOREWORD

It is more than forty years since Walter Milne-Bailey published his selection of documents illustrating the objects, the practices and the organization of British trade unions.

In those forty years there have been some quite striking changes in most of our institutions. If changes in the trade unions have not been as conspicuous as in other institutions, that is all the more reason for the publication of a selection from more recent material showing the extent and the nature of the changes that have, in fact, taken place.

One change, generally recognized, is the greatly increased strength and authority of the unions, individually in industry and collectively within the State. To some extent this is a natural consequence of the much improved economic, industrial and social conditions and the more direct involvement of governments in industrial affairs in the post-war years. But it must to some extent also be the result of internal changes in the unions—different policies, better organization, more intelligent and efficient administration.

Inevitably, the greater power of the unions has revived and sharpened the old arguments about the rights and responsibilities of trade unions to society as a whole as well as to their members.

The documents have been selected in order to illustrate the attitudes and activities of trade unions and trade unionists on these and on all other issues affecting trade unions. The work is intended mainly for teachers and students but everyone interested in trade unionism or industrial relations will find it a useful work of reference.

GEORGE WOODCOCK

PREFACE

A proper understanding of the British trade union movement requires reference to be made to original sources; only thus may a true insight into the nature of the subject be acquired. A case in point is provided by the increasingly important role of the State in industrial relations, and the consequential publication of extensive legislation and official commentary. Many original sources (official or otherwise) are, however, not readily accessible. A most impressive collection of documentation was provided by W. Milne-Bailey in his book *Trade Union Documents* (London, G. Bell, 1929), but although this work is still of considerable value, the passage of time has diminished its applicability. The purpose of these volumes is to present a selection more relevant to current circumstances. It is hoped that the work will be found useful to students and teachers in supplementing a number of the introductory studies of British trade unionism which have appeared in recent years.

The work is divided into two Parts. Part I consists of an Introduction which surveys the salient features of British trade union development between 1914 and 1969. This Introduction is not, of course, a complete history; it is intended to provide a general outline of events so that the documentary material may be seen in perspective. The choice of period is somewhat arbitrary; however, there are grounds for supposing that the stage for modern British trade unionism had been set by 1914.

Part II consists of three Sections and an Appendix. Section I treats of the objectives and functions of British trade unions, Section II deals with their structure and organization, whilst Section III is devoted to the State in industrial relations. Each of these three Sections opens with a Commentary which establishes a framework for the documents which follow it. The Commentaries also to some degree supplement and elaborate upon particular aspects of the Introduction comprising Part I; some repetition proved unavoidable, and, it is trusted, will be excused. The Appendix deals with certain developments in 1970. It had originally been intended to deal with events up to the end of 1969, and with this object in mind the work was virtually completed by the spring of 1970. However, 1970 witnessed changes judged to be of such importance as to warrant the inclusion of further material. The Appendix therefore consists of a brief Introduction surveying some of the events of 1970, followed by a Commentary and certain documents, the chief of which relate to the Industrial Relations Bill introduced by the Conservative Government in December 1970; the version quoted is that brought from the House of Commons on March 25th 1971.

It is suggested that the reader should bear the above framework in mind when consulting these volumes. In general it would be advisable to consult the relevant Commentary before reading a particular document or group of documents. The documents within each Section and in the Appendix have been arranged according to their subject matter. Each document has been assigned a number, and is referred to by this number in the appropriate Commentary. The reader will be enabled to follow this classification by examining, in Volume I, the Index to Documents. Since certain of the documents contain material which is relevant to other than the main themes under which they have been classified, the General Index, in Volume II, should also be consulted on particular topics.

The word 'British' has been used as a description of Great Britain and Northern Ireland; most of the material has relevance to the trade union movement throughout the United Kingdom. However, no attempt has been made to illustrate such peculiarities as attach to the systems of industrial relations in Scotland and Northern Ireland, or to indicate variations in the application of legislation in these countries.

Since the purpose of these volumes is to provide insight into current British trade unionism, the bulk of the material selected for reproduction was published within the last fifteen years. In certain cases, however, where necessary for the balanced development of a particular theme, earlier matter has been included.

Limitations of space have required rigour in the choice of material. Many documents have been excluded which, although undoubtedly interesting, were judged to be of limited value in obtaining a rounded view of the nature of British trade unionism. The problem of selection arose in a particularly acute form in Part II, Section II, dealing with the structure and organization of individual unions. It was decided to concentrate illustration upon a relatively small number of unions which seemed important either by virtue of their size, their prominence in trade union affairs, or because they appeared to be reasonably representative of certain categories of organization. A similar problem was posed in Part II, Section I, with regard to collective agreements; in this case only those agreements were included which were important in their own right or illustrated salient features with particular clarity. It should perhaps be stressed that there was no intention to produce a collection of readings. Nonetheless, on a few occasions extracts from the works of recognized authorities have been used when these seemed particularly apposite.

The themes chosen for development called for differing approaches to the problem of compilation. For example, Part II, Section III, is devoted, *inter alia*, to incomes policy and the attempts of the State to foster increases in productivity. In these instances documents were selected which trace the development of State policy over the past thirty years. However, other subjects did not lend themselves to this approach. For example, the analysis in Part II, Section II, of the structure and organization of individual unions was judged best undertaken by a survey outlining the position in the latter half of the 1960s. Such documents as were derived from an earlier period were included only when necessary to illustrate particular points. Again, in Part II,

Section III, there is a survey of what is called 'the traditional role' of the State in industrial relations. This role has been examined as it had evolved at the end of the period, and in the main has been illustrated by legislation which was in force in 1969. In other parts of the work an endeavour has been made to combine elements of the historical and the contemporary approaches.

As far as possible the text of each document has been allowed to speak for itself. Nonetheless, footnotes have been inserted where it was considered that part of a document warranted further explanation. In a very few cases the documents contained their own footnotes; these have been reproduced in italics.

The texts of the documents originally appeared in a variety of typographical styles. There seemed to be no advantage in attempting facsimiles of the originals, and the style of the text of the documents and of such headings and sub-headings as they contain has therefore been standardised. In quoting legislation containing various Parts the Part titles are reproduced only when reference is made to a Part in the text. Typographical errors in the original material have been corrected.

Concern with a substantial time period poses an obvious problem in that names of institutions change, and, indeed, some institutions disappear through amalgamation with others. As regards trade unions, the name of the union given in a document title is that which obtained at the time of the publication of the material quoted; however, earlier and subsequent names have been included either in the Introduction or, where more fitting, in footnotes to the appropriate documents. Where Ministers or Government Departments are mentioned they are identified by their titles at the time of publication of the relevant material.

The process of editing is indicated in three ways. Where a substantial amount of the original material (for example a paragraph or more) has not been included its omission is indicated thus

.   .   .   .

Where material has been omitted from within a sentence, the omission is indicated by . . . and where the omission is made after the close of the sentence the indication . . . follows upon the full stop which closes the sentence.

The compilation of these volumes was facilitated by the generous assistance of many persons. The project was largely financed by a grant from the Nuffield Foundation, and we wish to express our gratitude to the Trustees. We were given valuable advice and aid in many stages of our work by Mr W. J. Blease, Northern Ireland Officer of the Irish Congress of Trade Unions. We were helped on particular themes by Senator N. Kennedy, Irish Regional Secretary of the Transport and General Workers' Union, and by our colleague Mr J. B. McCartney. Other colleagues gave generously of their time; Mr W. J. Vennard helped at many stages in the preparation of material, and Mr H. Booth and Mr J. M. Horgan gave valuable aid in proof correcting. We are extremely grateful to the staff of the libraries of our own university, of Nuffield College, Oxford, and of the Trades Union Congress where we were very greatly helped by the personal interest taken in the work by the Librarian, Mr E. E. Brown. Mr H. L. Schollick and Mr G. Woodforde of Messrs Basil

Blackwell and Mott Ltd gave wise and kindly advice on many matters concerning the preparation and presentation of the book. Mrs J. Brown and Miss I. Dougherty provided expert typing assistance.

We wish to express our grateful thanks to Mr George Woodcock, the former General Secretary of the Trades Union Congress, for his kindness in contributing the Foreword.

We also wish to express our grateful thanks to the large number of persons and institutions who willingly gave us permission to reproduce material. We offer our grateful thanks to the following authors and their publishers: Professor H. A. Clegg, Mr Rex Adams, Mr A. J. Killick, Dr W. E. J. McCarthy and Basil Blackwell and Mott Ltd; Professor H. A. Turner and The Political Quarterly Publishing Co. Ltd; Mr A. I. Marsh, Mr A. Shonfield and Her Majesty's Stationery Office. We wish to acknowledge our substantial debt to the following organizations: the Amalgamated Society of Woodworkers, the Amalgamated Union of Engineering Workers, the Association of Scientific Technical and Managerial Staffs, the Draughtsmen's and Allied Technicians' Association, the Electrical Electronic and Telecommunication Union–Plumbing Trades Union, the National and Local Government Officers' Association, the National Union of Boot and Shoe Operatives, the National Union of General and Municipal Workers, the National Union of Mineworkers, the National Union of Public Employees, the National Union of Railwaymen, the National Union of Vehicle Builders, the Post Office Engineering Union, the Society of Graphical and Allied Trades, the Society of Technical Civil Servants, the Transport and General Workers' Union, the Union of Post Office Workers, the Confederation of Shipbuilding and Engineering Unions, the General Federation of Trade Unions, the International Confederation of Free Trade Unions, the International Transport Workers' Federation, the National Federation of Construction Unions, the National Federation of Professional Workers, the Printing and Kindred Trades Federation, the Chemical Industries Association Ltd, the Confederation of British Industry, the Engineering Employers' Federation, the National Federation of Building Trades Employers, the Shipbuilders and Repairers National Association, the British Furniture Trades Joint Industrial Council, the Chemical and Allied Industries Joint Industrial Council, the National Joint Committee for the Scottish Baking Industry, the National Joint Industrial Council for the Electricity Supply Industry, the British Steel Corporation, the Co-Operative Productive Federation Ltd, the Electricity Council, the Esso Petroleum Company Ltd, the Gas Council, Imperial Chemical Industries Ltd, the National Coal Board, Upper Clyde Shipbuilders Ltd, Robert Davies and Co., the London School of Economics and Political Science, the Bristol and Bath Productivity Association, the British Productivity Council, the International Labour Office, and the Labour Party. We are particularly grateful to Her Majesty's Stationery Office and to the Trades Union Congress.

All errors of fact, interpretation and presentation are, of course, the responsibility of the Editors.

The Queen's University
of Belfast
May 1971

N. ROBERTSON
K. I. SAMS

INDEX TO DOCUMENTS

SECTION I OBJECTIVES AND FUNCTIONS

Objectives

1 The traditional view

1.1 Webb, S. J. and Webb, B., *The History of Trade Unionism*   42

2 The legal view

2.1 Trade Union Act 1913   43

3 Statements by individual unions

3.1 Amalgamated Society of Woodworkers, *Rules*   43

3.2 National and Local Government Officers' Association, *Constitution and Rules*   45

3.3 Association of Scientific Workers, *Rules*   46

3.4 National Union of Boot and Shoe Operatives, *Rules*   47

3.5 National Union of Mineworkers, *Rules*   49

3.6 Post Office Engineering Union, *Rules*   50

3.7 National Union of Railwaymen, *Rules*   50

3.8 Union of Post Office Workers, *Programme, Rules and Standing Orders*   51

3.9 Transport and General Workers' Union, *Members Handbook*   51

3.10 Association of Scientific, Technical and Managerial Staffs, Advertisement in *The Times* 1968   53

4 Statements by the Trades Union Congress

4.1 General Council of the Trades Union Congress, *Interim Report on Post-War Reconstruction* 1944   54

4.2 Trades Union Congress, *Trade Unionism*   55

COLLECTIVE BARGAINING

5 Definition

5.1   Ministry of Labour, *Industrial Relations Handbook*   56

6 Bargaining rights

6.1   International Labour Conference, *Freedom of Association and Protection of the Right to Organise* 1949   57

6.2   International Labour Conference, *Application of the Principles of the Right to Organise and to Bargain Collectively* 1949   58

6.3   *In Place of Strife: A Policy for Industrial Relations* 1969   60

7 Legal status

7.1   Trade Union Act 1871   62

7.2   Royal Commission on Trade Unions and Employers' Associations 1965–1968, *Report*   62

7.3   Industrial Council, *Report on Enquiry into Industrial Agreements* 1913   63

8 Conventions

8.1   Court of Inquiry into a Dispute between the British Transport Commission and the National Union of Railwaymen, *Final Report* 1955   64

8.2   Court of Inquiry into a Dispute between the National Federated Electrical Association and the Electrical Trades Union, *Report* 1953   65

9 Industry-wide and workplace

9.1   *Model Constitution and Functions of a Joint Industrial Council*   65

9.2   Royal Commission on Trade Unions and Employers' Associations 1965–1968, *Report*   68

10 Procedural

10.1   Chemical and Allied Industries Joint Industrial Council, *Constitution* 1967   69

10.2   Engineering and Allied Employers' National Federation and the Trade Unions, *Agreement: Procedure—Manual Workers* 1955   70

10.3   Marsh, A. I., *Disputes Procedures in British Industry*   74

10.4   Shipbuilders and Repairers National Association and Confederation of Shipbuilding and Engineering Unions, *Memorandum of Agreement: Procedure for Dealing with Demarcation Disputes* 1969   75

11 Substantive

11.1   Chemical and Allied Industries Joint Industrial Council, *Schedule of Wage Rates and Working Conditions* 1967   77

12 Widening of scope and content

PRODUCTIVITY BARGAINING

12.1 Transport and General Workers' Union and Esso Petroleum Co. Ltd, *Memorandum of Agreement: Refinery, Fawley* 1960   84

12.2 *Productivity Bargaining* [Royal Commission on Trade Unions and Employers' Associations, *Research Papers* 4 (1)]   88

12.3 Chemical Industries Association Limited and Associated Trade Unions, *Joint Agreement on Principles and Procedures of Productivity Bargaining* 1968   92

FIXED TERM AGREEMENTS

12.4 Engineering Employers' Federation and Confederation of Shipbuilding and Engineering Unions, *Memorandum of Agreement: 40-hour Week and Related Matters* 1964   94

12.5 Association of Supervisory Staffs, Executives and Technicians, *Are Long-Term Contracts Good?* 1964   97

REDUNDANCY PROVISION

12.6 Gas Council, *Scheme with regard to compensation in the event of redundancy* 1963   99

12.7 Chemical and Allied Industries Joint Industrial Council, *Schedule of Wage Rates and Working Conditions* 1967   101

FRINGE BENEFITS

12.8 Electricity Supply Industry, *Agreement relating to the terms and conditions of employment of Industrial Staff* 1968   102

CHECK-OFF ARRANGEMENTS

12.9 Electricity Supply Industry, *Scheme for the Deduction of Trade Union Contributions* 1967   104

13 The efficacy of industry-wide agreements

13.1 National Board for Prices and Incomes, *Pay and Conditions of Service of Engineering Workers* 1967   105

13.2 National Board for Prices and Incomes, *Payment by Results Systems* 1968   105

13.3 National Federation of Building Trades Employers, *Statement of Evidence to the National Board for Prices and Incomes* 1968   106

14 The 'two systems' of industrial relations

14.1 Royal Commission on Trade Unions and Employers' Associations 1965–1968, *Report*   108

15 Reconciliation of the 'two systems'

15.1 Royal Commission on Trade Unions and Employers' Associations 1965–1968, *Report*   109

SAFEGUARDING AND INCREASING EMPLOYMENT OPPORTUNITIES

16 Restrictions upon entry into employment

16.1 McCarthy, W. E. J., *The Closed Shop in Britain*   112

16.2 National Joint Committee for the Scottish Baking Industry, *National Working Agreement* 1966   113

16.3 Royal Commission on Trade Unions and Employers' Associations 1965–1968, *Report*   113

16.4 *In Place of Strife: A Policy for Industrial Relations* 1969   117

16.5 British Furniture Trade Joint Industrial Council, *National Labour Agreement* 1968   118

16.6 Engineering and Allied Employers' National Federation and the Amalgamated Engineering Union, *Memorandum of Agreement: To Provide for the Temporary Relaxation of Existing Customs* 1956   119

17 Control of the use of labour

17.1 British Furniture Trade Joint Industrial Council, *National Labour Agreement* 1968   120

17.2 Royal Commission on Trade Unions and Employers' Associations, *Evidence: The Shipbuilding Employers' Federation*   121

17.3 *Restrictive Labour Practices* [Royal Commission on Trade Unions and Employers' Associations, *Research Papers* 4(2)]   124

17.4 National Board for Prices and Incomes, *Wages, Costs and Prices in the Printing Industry* 1965   126

17.5 Committee of Inquiry into the Port Transport Industry, *Final Report*, 1965   127

17.6 *Restrictive Labour Practices* [Royal Commission on Trade Unions and Employers' Associations, *Research Papers* 4(2)]   129

17.7 Royal Commission on Trade Unions and Employers' Associations 1965–1968, *Note of Reservation by Mr. Andrew Shonfield*   130

17.8 Royal Commission on Trade Unions and Employers' Associations 1965–1968, *Report*   131

USE OF THE STRIKE

18 Definitions of 'trade dispute' and 'strike'

18.1 Trade Disputes Act 1906   133

18.2 Trade Disputes and Trade Unions Act 1927   133

18.3 Contracts of Employment Act 1963   133

18.4 Royal Commission on Trade Unions and Employers' Associations 1965–1968, *Report*   134

19 The right to strike

19.1 *European Social Charter 1961*   134

20 Union strike procedures

20.1 Society of Graphical and Allied Trades, *General Rules*   135

20.2 National Union of General and Municipal Workers, *Rules*   135

21 Statutory restraints on strike action

GENERAL

21.1 Conspiracy, and Protection of Property Act 1875   136
21.2 Emergency Powers Act 1920   136
21.3 Trade Disputes and Trade Unions Act 1927   138

CLASSES OF INDUSTRY AND PERSONS

21.4 Conspiracy, and Protection of Property Act 1875   139
21.5 Electricity Supply Act 1919   140
21.6 Trade Disputes and Trade Unions Act 1927   140
21.7 Merchant Shipping Act 1894   140
21.8 Police Act 1964   141
21.9 Aliens Restriction (Amendment) Act 1919   142

METHODS EMPLOYED

21.10 Conspiracy, and Protection of Property Act 1875   142
21.11 Trade Disputes and Trade Unions Act 1927   142

22 Statutory safeguards for trade unions

22.1 Conspiracy, and Protection of Property Act 1875   143
22.2 Trade Disputes Act 1906   144
22.3 Trade Disputes Act 1965   145

23 Social security and strike action

23.1 Employment and Training Act 1948   145
23.2 Ministry of Social Security Act 1966   145

24 The 'strike problem': the inter-war years

24.1 Provisional Joint Committee, *Report to Industrial Conference 1919*   146
24.2 Joint Committee, Trade Union Representatives, *Memorandum to Industrial Conference 1919: Causes of and the Remedies for Industrial Unrest*   150
24.3 *Message from the Prime Minister*, May 1926   151
24.4 *Message to all Workers*, May 1926   151
24.5 Trades Union Congress, *Official Bulletin No. 5*, May 1926   151
24.6 Conference on Industrial Reorganisation and Industrial Relations, *Interim Joint Report* 1928   152

25 The 'strike problem': the post-war period

SIGNIFICANCE

25.1 Royal Commission on Trade Unions and Employers' Associations 1965–1968, *Report*   154

CAUSES

25.2 Royal Commission on Trade Unions and Employers' Associations, *Evidence: Transport and General Workers' Union*   156
25.3 Royal Commission on Trade Unions and Employers' Associations 1965–1968, *Report*   157

xvii

25.4 Royal Commission on Trade Unions and Employers' Associations 1965–1968, *Report* 160
25.5 *In Place of Strife: A Policy for Industrial Relations* 1969 162
25.6 General Council of the Trades Union Congress, *Announcement of June 18, 1969* 164

BENEFIT AND WELFARE PROVISION

26 Importance in union functions

26.1 Trades Union Congress, *Trade Unionism* 165
26.2 National and Local Government Officers' Association, *About Nalgo* 166

27 Conditions governing payments

27.1 Amalgamated Society of Woodworkers, *Contributions and Benefits* 167
27.2 Transport and General Workers' Union, *Rules* 169

28 Variants in benefit provision

28.1 Transport and General Workers' Union, *Rules* 1968 171
28.2 Transport and General Workers' Union, *Rules* 1962 171
28.3 Draughtsmen's and Allied Technicians' Association, *Rules* 172
28.4 National Union of Boot and Shoe Operatives, *Rules* 172
28.5 National Union of Public Employees, *Rules* 172
28.6 Society of Graphical and Allied Trades, *Rules* 173
28.7 National Union of Railwaymen, *Rules* 174

29 Variants in welfare provision

29.1 Royal Commission on Trade Unions and Employers' Associations, *Evidence: Electrical Trades Union* 175
29.2 Transport and General Workers' Union, *Report, 1966: Education* 178
29.3 National Union of General and Municipal Workers, *Rules* 181
29.4 Transport and General Workers' Union, *Report, 1966: Legal Department* 182
29.5 Post Office Engineering Union, *Rules* 185

30 Levels of expenditure

30.1 Transport and General Workers' Union, *Report and Balance Sheet for the year 1966* 186
30.2 Chief Registrar of Friendly Societies, *Report for the year 1968, Part 4: Trade Unions* 187

SHARING IN CONTROL OF INDUSTRY

31 Objectives

31.1 Trades Union Congress, *Trade Unionism* 188

32 Radical forms

32.1 Unofficial Reform Committee, *The Miners' Next Step* 1912 190
32.2 *Prospectus of Guild of Builders* (*London*) *Limited* 1920 192

33 Co-operation and co-partnership

33.1   Co-Operative Productive Federation Ltd, *General Rules for an Industrial and Provident Productive Society* 1966   196

33.2   *Imperial Chemical Industries Ltd, Employees' Profit-Sharing Scheme* 1966   200

34 Nationalisation

34.1   General Council of the Trades Union Congress, *Trade Unionism and the Control of Industry* 1932   203

34.2   General Council of the Trades Union Congress, *Interim Report on Post-War Reconstruction* 1944   204

35 Joint consultation

35.1   Union of Post Office Workers, *National Rules and Standing Orders*   206

35.2   Sub-Committee on Relations Between Employers and Employed, *Interim Report on Joint Standing Industrial Councils* 1917   206

35.3   Committee on Relations Between Employers and Employed, *Supplementary Report on Works Committees* 1918   209

35.4   Upper Clyde Shipbuilders Limited, *Joint Consultative Scheme* 1968   210

35.5   *Constitution of Colliery Consultative Committees* 1968   215

36 Worker directors

36.1   Trades Union Congress, *Trade Unionism*   218

36.2   National Executive of the Labour Party, *Industrial Democracy* 1968   219

36.3   British Steel Corporation, *Group Boards and Employee Directors* 1968   222

37 Contemporary views

37.1   Confederation of British Industry, *Evidence to the Royal Commission on Trade Unions and Employers' Associations*   223

37.2   *In Place of Strife: A Policy for Industrial Relations* 1969   223

POLITICAL ACTIVITIES

38 Purpose and methods

38.1   Trades Union Congress, *Trade Unionism*   224

39 Legal conditions

39.1   Trade Union Act 1913   226

39.2   Trade Disputes and Trade Unions Act 1927   227

39.3   Chief Registrar of Friendly Societies, *Trade Union Act 1913: Model Rules for Political Fund*   230

40 Finance

40.1   Chief Registrar of Friendly Societies, *Report for the year 1968, Part 4: Trade Unions*   233

41 The individual union and political activity

41.1 Transport and General Workers' Union, *Report 1966: Political* 234
41.2 Royal Commission on Trade Unions and Employers' Associations, *Evidence: Amalgamated Engineering Union* 236

42 Relationships with the Labour Party

42.1 Labour Party, *Constitution and Standing Orders* 238
42.2 National Executive Committee of the Labour Party, *Report* 1970 242
42.3 *Labour Party Conference Report* 1968 244
42.4 Trades Union Congress, *Trade Unionism* 245
42.5 Trades Union Congress, *Incomes Policy* 1967 246
42.6 *Trades Union Congress Report* 1960 248

SERVING AS AGENCIES FOR COMMENTARY ON CONTEMPORARY ISSUES

43 The individual union

43.1 *Electron* July 1961 250
43.2 Cannon, L., *Automation* 1968 251

44 The Trades Union Congress

44.1 *Trades Union Congress Report*, 1937 252
44.2 General Council of the Trades Union Congress, *The International Situation* 1939 253
44.3 *Trades Union Congress Report* 1933 254
44.4 General Council of the Trades Union Congress, *Promotion and Encouragement of the Arts* 1961 256

INTERNATIONAL ACTIVITIES

45 Purpose

45.1 Trades Union Congress, *Trade Unionism* 257

46 The individual union

46.1 Amalgamated Engineering Union, *Rules* 258
46.2 International Transport Workers' Federation, *Constitution* 259

47 The Trades Union Congress

47.1 International Confederation of Free Trade Unions, *Constitution* 263
47.2 International Confederation of Free Trade Unions, *Report on Activities 1965–69* 268
47.3 International Labour Organisation, *Constitution* 269
47.4 International Labour Organisation, *Declaration concerning Aims and Purposes* 272
47.5 General Council of the Trades Union Congress, *Report to Congress 1967: Section F International* 274

SECTION II STRUCTURE AND ORGANISATION

THE INDIVIDUAL UNION

Structure

48 Classification of union forms

48.1 Clegg, H. A., Killick, A. J., and Adams, Rex, *Trade Union Officers* 283

48.2 Turner, H. A., *Trade Union Organization* 285

49 Debate on industrial unionism

49.1 National Union of Public Employees, *The Challenge of New Unionism* 1963 286

49.2 *Trades Union Congress Report* 1926 289

49.3 General Council of the Trades Union Congress, *Trade Union Structure and Functions* 1964 290

50 Advantages of amalgamation

50.1 General Council of the Trades Union Congress, *Trade Union Structure* 1965 291

51 Problems of large unions

51.1 Royal Commission on Trade Unions and Employers' Associations, *Evidence: General Federation of Trade Unions* 292

52 Trades Union Congress Policy

52.1 General Council of the Trades Union Congress, *Organisation by Industry* 1927 294

52.2 General Council of the Trades Union Congress, *Interim Report on Trade Union Structure and Closer Unity* 1944 296

53 Statutory regulation of amalgamation and transfer of engagements

53.1 Trade Union Act Amendment Act 1876 298

53.2 Trade Union (Amalgamation) Act 1917 298

53.3 Societies (Miscellaneous Provisions) Act 1940 298

53.4 Trade Union (Amalgamations, etc.) Act 1964 299

Organisation

54 Conditions of membership

STATUTORY REGULATION

54.1 Trade Union Act Amendment Act 1876 300

54.2 Police Act 1964 301

54.3 Trade Disputes and Trade Unions Act 1927 302

RESTRICTION OF CHOICE OF UNION

54.4 Post Office Recognition Committee, *Report* 1952 302

54.5 Court of Inquiry into the dispute between the British Steel Corporation and certain of their employees, *Report* 1968 303

54.6 London Passenger Transport Board, *Statement* 1946 305

ENTRANCE REQUIREMENTS

54.7   Transport and General Workers' Union, *Rules*   307

54.8   Electrical Electronic and Telecommunication Union–Plumbing Trades Union, *Rules*   308

54.9   Draughtsmen's and Allied Technicians' Association, *Rules*   311

54.10 Race Relations Act 1968   312

54.11 General Council of the Trades Union Congress, *Trade Union Rules* 1969   313

OBLIGATIONS OF MEMBERS

54.12 Electrical Electronic and Telecommunication Union–Plumbing Trades Union, *Rules*   314

55 Administration

GENERAL PATTERN

55.1   National Union of Railwaymen, *Rules*   315

SHOP AND BRANCH ORGANISATION

55.2   Society of Graphical and Allied Trades, *General Rules*   320

55.3   Post Office Engineering Union, *Rules*   320

55.4   Electrical Electronic and Telecommunication Union–Plumbing Trades Union, *Rules*   321

DISTRICT, AREA AND REGIONAL ORGANISATION

55.5   Amalgamated Union of Engineering and Foundry Workers, *Rules*   324

DELEGATE CONFERENCE

55.6   Post Office Engineering Union, *Rules*   327

EXECUTIVE COUNCIL

55.7   Transport and General Workers' Union, *Rules*   330

ORGANISATION OF PARTICULAR GROUPS

55.8   Transport and General Workers' Union, *Rules*   333

55.9   National and Local Government Officers' Association, *Constitution and Rules*   336

55.10 Electrical Electronic and Telecommunication Union–Plumbing Trades Union, *Rules*   338

56 Union officers

CONDITIONS FOR OFFICE

56.1   Electrical Electronic and Telecommunication Union–Plumbing Trades Union, *Rules*   338

SHOP STEWARDS

56.2   Amalgamated Union of Engineering and Foundry Workers, *Rules*   339

56.3   Electrical Electronic and Telecommunication Union–Plumbing Trades Union, *Rules*   341

56.4   Royal Commission on Trade Unions and Employers' Associations 1965–1968, *Report*   343

BRANCH OFFICERS

56.5   National Union of Railwaymen, *Rules*   344

SENIOR OFFICERS

56.6   National Union of Vehicle Builders, *Rules*   346
56.7   National Union of Railwaymen, *Rules*   348

57 Rules revision procedure

57.1   Transport and General Workers' Union, *Rules*   352

58 Disciplinary procedure

58.1   Amalgamated Union of Engineering and Foundry Workers, *Rules*   354
58.2   General Council of the Trades Union Congress, *Trade Union Rules* 1969   358

59 Finance

59.1   National Union of Railwaymen, *Rules*   359
59.2   Chief Registrar of Friendly Societies, *Report for the year 1968, Part 4: Trade Unions*   363

60 Criteria for new principles of rules

60.1   Trades Union Congress, *Trade Unionism*   363
60.2   Post Office Engineering Union, *Evidence to the Royal Commission on Trade Unions and Employers' Associations*   364
60.3   Royal Commission on Trade Unions and Employers' Associations, *Evidence: Electrical Trades Union*   365
60.4   Royal Commission on Trade Unions and Employers' Associations 1965–1968, *Report*   368

JOINT ORGANISATION

61 The case for joint arrangements

61.1   Royal Commission on Trade Unions and Employers' Associations, *Evidence: Amalgamated Engineering Union*   370

62 Arrangements to secure common services

62.1   Draughtsmen's and Allied Technicians' Association and Society of Technical Civil Servants, *Report on the Relations between D.A.T.A. and the Society of Technical Civil Servants* 1964   372

63 Co-operation through industrial negotiating bodies

63.1   Electrical Trades Union, *Trade Union Structure—Relations With Other Unions* 1964   374

64 Federal organisation based on industry

64.1   National Federation of Construction Unions, *General Rules*   376
64.2   Confederation of Shipbuilding and Engineering Unions, *Rules*   379
64.3   Printing and Kindred Trades Federation, *Rules*   384
64.4   Confederation of Shipbuilding and Engineering Unions, *Report* 1969   386

65 Federal organisation based on class of worker

65.1 National Federation of Professional Workers, *Constitution and Rules*   387

66 Federal organisation based on type of service provided

66.1 General Federation of Trade Unions, *Rules*   389

67 The Trades Union Congress

67.1 Trades Union Congress, *Rules and Standing Orders*   393

67.2 Trades Union Congress, *Trade Unionism*   401

67.3 *Trades Union Congress Report* 1969   407

67.4 Trades Union Congress, *Relations between Unions* 1964   409

68 Trades councils

68.1 Trades Union Congress, *Model Rules and Standing Orders for a Trades Council* 1969   410

SECTION III THE STATE IN INDUSTRIAL RELATIONS

THE TRADITIONAL ROLE

69 Restrictions on the employment of classes of person

CHILDREN

69.1 Education Act 1944   422

69.2 Children and Young Persons Act 1933   422

69.3 Education Act 1918   423

69.4 Employment of Women, Young Persons and Children Act 1920   423

YOUNG PERSONS

69.5 Mines and Quarries Act 1954   424

69.6 Factories Act 1961   425

WOMEN

69.7 Mines and Quarries Act 1954   425

69.8 Public Health Act 1936   425

70 Promotion of the employment of classes of person

70.1 Disabled Persons (Employment) Act 1944   425

70.2 Race Relations Act 1968   427

71 Regulation of production methods

HARMFUL SUBSTANCES

71.1 Factories Act 1961   427

71.2 Agriculture (Poisonous Substances) Act 1952   428

EXCESSIVE WEIGHTS

71.3 Factories Act 1961   429

OPERATIONAL COMPETENCE

71.4   Mines and Quarries Act 1954   429

72 Regulation of terms and conditions of employment

CONTRACT OF EMPLOYMENT

72.1   Contracts of Employment Act 1963   430

HOURS WORKED

72.2   Children and Young Persons Act 1933   432
72.3   Hours of Employment (Conventions) Act 1936   433
72.4   Young Persons (Employment) Act 1938   434
72.5   Factories Act 1961   436
72.6   Coal Mines Regulation Act 1908   438
72.7   Transport Act 1968   439

HOLIDAYS

72.8   Young Persons (Employment) Act 1938   440
72.9   Shops Act 1950   440
72.10   Factories Act 1961   442
72.11   Holidays with Pay Act 1938   442

WORK ENVIRONMENT

72.12   Offices, Shops and Railway Premises Act 1963   443
72.13   Agriculture (Safety, Health and Welfare Provisions) Act 1956   446
72.14   Merchant Shipping Act 1894   447
72.15   Mines and Quarries Act 1954   448
72.16   National Insurance (Industrial Injuries) Act 1965   449

PAYMENT OF WAGES

72.17   Payment of Wages Act 1960   451
72.18   Checkweighing in Various Industries Act 1919   452

MINIMUM WAGE REGULATION

72.19   Wages Councils Act 1959   452
72.20   Trade Boards Act 1909   456
72.21   Trade Boards Act 1918   457
72.22   Agricultural Wages Act 1948   458
72.23   Agriculture Act 1967   460

73 Regularisation of employment and provision for unemployment

73.1   Employment and Training Act 1948   460
73.2   Dock Workers (Regulation of Employment) Act 1946   461
73.3   National Insurance Act 1965   462
73.4   National Insurance Act 1966   463
73.5   Redundancy Payments Act 1965   464

74 Promotion and extension of collective bargaining

74.1   Coal Industry Nationalisation Act 1946   466
74.2   Fair Wages Resolution of the House of Commons 1891   467
74.3   Fair Wages Resolution of the House of Commons 1909   467

74.4   Fair Wages Resolution of the House of Commons 1946   468
74.5   Sugar Act 1956   468
74.6   Cotton Manufacturing Industry (Temporary Provisions) Act 1934   469
74.7   Conditions of Employment and National Arbitration Order 1940   470
74.8   Industrial Disputes Order 1951   473
74.9   Terms and Conditions of Employment Act 1959   477

75   **Maintenance of industrial peace**
75.1   Conciliation Act 1896   478
75.2   Industrial Courts Act 1919   479
75.3   Munitions of War Act 1915   480

76   **Pending changes in the traditional role**
        WAGES COUNCILS
76.1   Royal Commission on Trade Unions and Employers' Associations 1965–1968, *Report*   482

        LABOUR TRIBUNALS
76.2   Royal Commission on Trade Unions and Employers' Associations 1965–1968, *Report*   484

THE NEW APPROACH

Attempts to Improve Productivity

77   **Statement of policy**
77.1   *Statement by the Chancellor of the Exchequer: Increased Production in Industry* 1948   486

78   **General provision**
78.1   Anglo-American Council on Productivity, *Final Report* 1952   487
78.2   British Productivity Council, *The Objective* 1953   490
78.3   Bristol and Bath Productivity Association, *Constitution*   491
78.4   National Economic Development Council, *Growth of the United Kingdom Economy 1961–1966*   491
78.5   Industrial Training Act 1964   492

79   **Particular industries**
79.1   *Statement by the President of the Board of Trade: Industrial Organisation (Tripartite Working Parties)* 1945   494
79.2   Industrial Organisation and Development Act 1947   495

80   **Individual firms**
80.1   Engineering and Allied Employers' National Federation and Shipbuilding and Engineering Unions, *Memorandum of Agreement: Constitution of Joint Production Consultative and Advisory Committees* 1945   499
80.2   National Joint Advisory Council, *Joint Production Committees* 1947   501

81 Trade union attitudes

81.1   *Trades Union Congress Report* 1953   503
81.2   General Council of the Trades Union Congress, *Statement on National Productivity Year* 1963   504
81.3   *Trades Union Congress Report* 1966   505
81.4   General Council of the Trades Union Congress, *Trade Unions and Automation* 1956   506

Incomes Policy

82 1941–1945

82.1   *Statement by His Majesty's Government on Price Stabilisation and Industrial Policy* 1941   509
82.2   *Employment Policy* 1944   510

83 1945–1951

83.1   *Statement on the Economic Considerations affecting relations between Employers and Workers* 1947   512
83.2   General Council of the Trades Union Congress, *Reconstruction and Transition* 1947   512
83.3   *Statement on Personal Incomes, Costs and Prices* 1948   513
83.4   General Council of the Trades Union Congress, Special Committee on the Economic Situation, *Recommendations* 1948   514

84 1951–1961

84.1   Court of Inquiry into a Dispute between the Engineering and Allied Employers' National Federation and the Confederation of Shipbuilding and Engineering Unions, *Report* 1954   515
84.2   *The Economic Implications of Full Employment* 1956   516
84.3   Court of Inquiry into a Dispute between the Engineering and Allied Employers' National Federation and the Confederation of Shipbuilding and Engineering Unions, *Report* 1957   518
84.4   Council on Prices, Productivity and Incomes, *First Report* 1958   518
84.5   General Council of the Trades Union Congress, *Council on Prices, Productivity and Incomes* 1958   520

85 1961–1964

85.1   Council on Prices, Productivity and Incomes, *Fourth Report* 1961   520
85.2   *Statement by the Chancellor of the Exchequer: The Economic Situation* 1961   522
85.3   Speech of the Chancellor of the Exchequer, *Incomes and Productivity* 1961   523
85.4   *Incomes Policy, The Next Step* 1962   524
85.5   *National Incomes Commission* 1962   526
85.6   General Council of the Trades Union Congress, *National Incomes Commission* 1962   528
85.7   National Incomes Commission, *Scottish Plumbers' and Scottish Builders' Agreements of 1962*   530
85.8   National Incomes Commission, *Agreements of November–December 1963 in the Engineering and Shipbuilding Industries*   531

86   1964–1969

86.1   *Joint Statement of Intent on Productivity, Prices and Incomes* 1964   532

86.2   *Machinery of Prices and Incomes Policy 1965*   534

86.3   *Prices and Incomes Policy 1965*   537

86.4   Trades Union Congress, *Productivity, Prices and Incomes* 1965   539

86.5   *Prices and Incomes Policy: An 'Early Warning' System 1965*   540

86.6   *Prices and Incomes Standstill 1966*   543

86.7   Prices and Incomes Act 1966   545

86.8   *Prices and Incomes Standstill: Period of Severe Restraint 1966*   551

86.9   *Prices and Incomes Policy After 30th June 1967*   553

86.10   *Productivity, Prices and Incomes Policy in 1968 and 1969*   554

86.11   *Productivity, Prices and Incomes Policy After 1969*   558

86.12   National Board for Prices and Incomes, *Productivity and Pay During the Period of Severe Restraint 1966*   561

86.13   National Board for Prices and Incomes, *Productivity Agreements* 1967   562

86.14   National Board for Prices and Incomes, *Productivity Agreements* 1969   563

APPENDIX   DEVELOPMENTS IN 1970

87   Changes in the traditional role

87.1   Merchant Shipping Act 1970   572

87.2   Equal Pay Act 1970   574

88   The new legalism

88.1   Industrial Relations Bill 1970: Explanatory and Financial Memorandum   576

88.2   Industrial Relations Bill 1970   585

PART I

INTRODUCTION—THE TRADE UNION MOVEMENT 1914–1969

CHANGES IN THE ENVIRONMENT OF INDUSTRIAL RELATIONS

A variety of environmental changes influenced the growth and development of British trade unionism in the period 1914–69. Certain of these were of particular importance.

An impressive change took place in the general level of unemployment. It has been estimated that, from the 1880s down to the First World War, unemployment averaged about 5 per cent.[1] In the inter-war years, the average rose to 13 per cent; as will be seen from Table 1 (p. 26), unemployment exceeded 20 per cent in the years 1931 and 1932. Between 1945 and 1969, almost continuous 'full employment' was experienced, the unemployment rate averaging 1·9 per cent, and exceeding 3·0 per cent in only one year.

Substantial changes occurred in the economic organisation of society. Old industries, products and industrial areas declined and new ones arose. Changing technology removed the premium on some skills and occasioned demands for new types of labour, whilst the scale of production increased and monopolistic arrangements among firms became common.

The period encompassed a striking increase in the economic activities of the State. Two developments were of particular importance for trade unions. Firstly, the State became paymaster of a growing proportion of the labour force, both directly, through the expansion of central Government services, and indirectly, as a result of a massive extension of public ownership of industries. Secondly, attempts to maintain full employment and, thereafter, to reconcile this objective with those of economic growth, price stability and balance of payments equilibrium, forced the State to a more active role in the general management of the economy. By the 1960s, this second development had led to ambitious attempts to control the labour market.

A marked change can be discerned in the attitudes of employers towards trade unions. In 1914 there still existed much outright hostility, based on fears of the unions as possible centres of revolution and a doctrinaire belief in the merits of *laissez-faire*. With experience of modern trade unionism, this attitude was modified to one of guarded tolerance. By the late 1960s, most employers were prepared to give positive encouragement to the unions as agencies capable of improving, rather than hindering, industrial efficiency and of simplifying managerial responsibilities.

Albeit indirectly, the period brought a significant change in the legal

[1] See Beveridge, W. H., *Full Employment in a Free Society* (London, George Allen & Unwin Ltd, 1944), p. 72.

position of the unions. They had emerged in the face of the intense hostility of the law. By 1914 considerable success had attended their struggle against irksome legal restrictions; however, further restraints, introduced in 1927,[1] were not removed until 1946. After 1946, unions were once again regulated by a series of laws which had been designed to protect and encourage the development of a weak movement with special disabilities. Given the vastly increased strength of the unions after the Second World War, a position was reached which many commentators considered to be unduly preferential to trade unionism. This complaint became more urgent in 1969 when it appeared that additional legal advantage was likely to be conferred pursuant to the *Report*[2] of the Royal Commission on Trade Unions and Employers' Associations, 1965–1968.

Such changes as have been outlined had important effects on the rate of growth of trade unions, their objectives and functions, the forms of organisation which they adopted, and the beliefs and attitudes which they evolved.

GROWTH AND DEVELOPMENT OF TRADE UNIONISM

1914–20

By 1914, the stage for modern trade unionism had been set. Membership of unions in Great Britain and Northern Ireland rose from 1·6 million in 1892 to 4·1 million in 1914. Viable forms of organisation and methods of operation had been evolved, and, after many vicissitudes, a satisfactory legal status had been attained.[3] During the years 1914–20 an impressive degree of development and consolidation was achieved, bringing the trade union movement to a position of unprecedented strength.

Stimulated by a strong demand for labour during the war years and the post-war boom, trade union membership rose spectacularly to 8·3 million in 1920 (see Table 2, p. 27). Progress was achieved in many other directions. Structure was improved by important amalgamations of unions and the creation of new federations; of particular significance was the formation of the Iron and Steel Trades Confederation in 1917,[4] and of the National Federation of Building Trades Operatives in 1918. Amalgamations were considerably facilitated by the Trade Union (Amalgamation) Act 1917.[5] Joint

---

[1] By the Trade Disputes and Trade Unions Act 1927, repealed by the Trade Disputes and Trade Unions Act 1946.   [2] (Cmnd. 3623) 1968.

[3] In broad terms, when acting in contemplation or furtherance of a trade dispute, unions were immune from action as criminal or civil conspiracies, and, if also acting in accordance with their rules, they and their individual officers were immune from action in tort.

[4] The Confederation, and the British Iron, Steel, and Kindred Trades Association, a trade union also formed in 1917 and intended to become the sole union for the industry, became practically indistinguishable.

[5] By the 1917 Act, unions might amalgamate provided at least 50 per cent of their individual memberships voted, and a majority of at least 20 per cent was recorded in each. The Trade Union Act Amendment Act 1876 had required the consent of at least two-thirds of the members of each participant.

arrangements of a less formal nature were also developed. Thus the miners, dockers and railwaymen concluded a 'Triple Alliance' for mutual support in industrial disputes.

Bargaining strength, of course, was increased directly as a result of the development of larger unions and improved structures. Other circumstances worked less directly to the same end. The Trade Boards Act 1918 widened the scope of general statutory wage regulation;[1] special provision was introduced for agriculture under the Corn Production Act 1917. This underpinning of rates in badly organised trades freed union resources for other purposes. By the operation of the 'Fair Wages Resolution',[2] which required Government contractors to observe wages and hours 'not less favourable than those commonly recognised' by employers and unions, an extension of State trading during the war and post-war periods had similar effects.

Developments in social legislation also strengthened the bargaining position of the workers. A limited scheme of unemployment insurance, introduced in 1911, was slightly extended in 1916 and made general in 1920.[3] A scheme for sickness insurance was also established in 1911.[4] Apart from obvious direct benefits, an indirect advantage in economy of resources again accrued.

The procedures of collective bargaining were extended and regularised. In particular, there developed a trend away from localised, single-trade agreements, towards national arrangements covering whole industries and encompassing all classes of manual worker. The evolution of national unions had been one contributory factor. Another was the experience, during the war, of industry-wide arbitration awards. The Trade Boards, covering whole industries, also gave pointers. The formation of national 'Joint Industrial Councils', recommended by the Whitley Committee,[5] brought industrial bargaining in its train.

In the light of subsequent developments, particular importance attached to an appreciable increase in the unions' political influence. Although the 'Khaki Election' of 1918 disappointed the hopes of the Labour Party, which between 1914 and 1918 increased its membership from 1·6 million to 3 million, the number of Labour Members of Parliament was raised to 57, as compared with 42 after the 1910 Election. More important, however, the Party's revised Constitution of February 1918 established it as a true Socialist party, pledged to secure the common ownership of the means of production, distribution and

[1] The original legislation, the Trade Boards Act 1909, had applied to four 'sweated' trades only. The 1918 Act could be invoked in respect of any trade where the Minister of Labour considered that 'no adequate machinery exists for the effective regulation of wages'.

[2] Adopted by the House of Commons in 1909. A previous Resolution, of 1891, had required the payment of wages such as were 'generally accepted as current'.

[3] National Insurance Act 1911, National Insurance (Part II) (Munitions Workers) Act 1916, Unemployment Insurance Act 1920.

[4] National Insurance Act 1911.

[5] The Committee on Relations between Employers and Employed, under the chairmanship of the Rt. Hon. J. H. Whitley. Set up in 1916, in response to alarm at isolated examples of serious industrial unrest, the Committee published five reports in the years 1917–18. Between 1918 and 1921, 73 Joint Industrial Councils and 33 'Interim Reconstruction Committees' were constituted. The Committees were of a less formal character than the Councils, and were considered appropriate for industries where organisation was not yet sufficiently developed; 14 of these were in time reconstituted as proper Councils.

exchange, and to promote popular control of industry. The ideological and operational relationships between the Party and the trade union movement were thus made more explicit, and the bonds between them stronger. In fact, 49 of the Labour Members of the 1918 Parliament were trade union sponsored.

During the war, and for the first time, the unions acquired a considerable measure of public prestige. Loyal co-operation was given by the great majority of workers. Compulsory arbitration[1] (involving the banning of strikes and the imposition of legally enforceable awards), dilution, and restrictions on the movement of labour were all accepted, and the unions joined with employer and Government representatives in various measures designed to preserve industrial peace and to increase production. An increased participation by the State in the affairs of industry was dictated by wartime needs, and this brought greater involvement of the unions.

Related to this growth in power and prestige, the unions acquired a significant degree of acceptance, certainly by the Government, but also by a rising proportion of responsible employers. A firm underwriting of this position was provided by the Whitley Committee, which gave unambiguous endorsement to the desirability of strong organisations on both sides of industry as a prime requirement for good industrial relations. The national Joint Industrial Councils were intended to embrace not only collective bargaining but also joint consultation, and opened possibilities for the development of some feeling of joint concern for the well-being and progress of industries. The Committee had also strongly recommended the formation of 'Works Committees' to provide joint consultation in individual establishments.[2] A further recommendation of the Committee led to the foundation of an 'Industrial Court'[3] to which industrial disputes could be referred for arbitration with the consent of the parties, provided domestic machinery had failed to achieve a settlement. Use of the Court's facilities thus implied recognition of unions by employers, and the existence of joint arrangements, even if only of a limited sort, between the two sides.

Power, prestige and acceptance brought confidence. In some sectors, great militancy ensued. Thus unofficial movements among engineering and shipyard workers, and miners, were associated with attempts to promote "workers' control" through 'syndicalism'. By this system, those employed in particular industries would take over and administer the means of production; if necessary, the change would be effected by persistent striking. In this connection, the success of the Russian Revolution was not without significance. Militancy of a more official sort produced isolated strikes during the war, and, more frequently, in the immediate post-war period.[4] As will be seen from Table 3 (p. 28), the incidence of strikes, and their severity, rose markedly after 1916. In the circumstances of the time—a trade boom and continued participation by the State in the control of some important industries (e.g. mines and railways)—the unions achieved considerable success by industrial

[1] Under the Munitions of War Act 1915.
[2] Between 1917 and 1922, more than 1,000 such Committees were established.
[3] Under the Industrial Courts Act 1919.
[4] Police strikes in 1918 and 1919 showed the spread of militancy to unusual quarters.

6

action. The miners, dockers and railwaymen, backed by the threat of their Triple Alliance, proved particularly effective.

The State reacted in accordance with the new attitudes. In 1919, an Industrial Conference of unions and employers was convened, at which a Joint Committee was appointed to report on the causes of industrial unrest. The Committee recommended the creation of a permanent National Industrial Council to consider, and advise the Government on, national industrial questions. Worsening relationships made the proposal still-born. Traditional attitudes then prevailed. The Police Act 1919 made repetition of striking in that quarter unlikely. The Emergency Powers Act 1920 empowered the Government, in appropriate circumstances, to take steps necessary to secure continuance of essential services and the safety of the public. The stage was set for industrial conflict.

1920–39

In the light of progress in the preceding decade, the trade unions faced the post-war years with optimism; this was to prove short-lived. The breaking of the post-war boom brought set-back and disillusion. By 1921, the general unemployment rate had risen to 12·9 per cent, and pressures for wage-cuts forced a series of disastrous strikes and lock-outs, the extent of which is clearly illustrated in Table 3 (p. 28). A lock-out in mining in March 1920 led to the invocation of the Triple Alliance, and the dockers and railwaymen announced their intention of striking as from April 16th. On Friday April 15th, 'Black Friday' as it came to be called, this support was withdrawn; the Alliance, put to the test in unfavourable circumstances, had collapsed. In a succession of disputes in the next few years most of the major unions suffered crushing defeats. And the worst was yet to come.

The failure of the Triple Alliance added urgency to the search for more effective means of securing joint action in industrial disputes. One answer was felt to lie in the Trades Union Congress which, more than fifty years after its foundation, still had little real co-ordinating power. In 1921, however, its Constitution was radically altered. The old executive, the Parliamentary Committee,[1] was replaced by a much more powerful body, the General Council, authorised, among other things, to promote co-ordinated action in industrial disputes.

The new powers of Congress were soon to be put to the test. In 1925 a further reduction in miners' wages was proposed, and T.U.C. support was promised should a lock-out occur. A general stoppage was avoided at the last moment only by the Government offering the industry a subsidy for nine months to enable the wage-cuts to be deferred. In 1926, reductions were announced, rejected by the miners, and a national lock-out advertised as from May 3rd; a repetition of the T.U.C.'s threat proved unavailing. On May 4th, workers in a variety of industries—in particular, transport, iron and steel, and printing—were duly called out in what has popularly been known as the

[1] The name of its executive reflected the main purpose of Congress to date, namely, to exercise a watching brief on legislation affecting trade union and working-class interests.

'General Strike'. The T.U.C. had not the authority, the skill, the funds, or even perhaps the will to conduct such a struggle. The State was armed with the Emergency Powers Act. Given these circumstances, and the prevailing economic situation, there was no chance of success. On May 12th the 'second line'—consisting of engineering, shipbuilding, etc.—was to have been called out. On that day, however, the T.U.C. gave the order to return to work. The miners, now isolated, struggled on for some six months, but had eventually to resume work at considerably reduced wage-rates.

The failure of the General Strike heralded a period of demoralisation for the trade union movement. With economic conditions continuing to worsen—unemployment reached a peak of 22·1 per cent in 1932—membership fell steadily, and in 1933, at 4·4 million, was only slightly above its 1914 level. The unions learned that much of the prestige and acceptance they had enjoyed when strong was ephemeral. Employers were impelled to press for wage reductions. The Government seemed basically hostile to the unions by virtue of its conduct during the General Strike, and by the subsequent promotion of the Trade Disputes and Trade Unions Act 1927. This Act made illegal 'sympathetic' action of the sort which had been employed in the Strike, forbade civil service unions to have political objects or to affiliate to outside unions or federations of unions (e.g., the T.U.C.), and contained provisions designed to restrict the political activities of all unions.[1] The strains placed on unemployment relief by the depression led to the hated 'means test'. Disappointment attended the unions' political activities. Although Labour Governments, albeit minority ones, held office in 1924 and 1929–31, they achieved little to advance working-class interests. Failure of experiments in 'Guild Socialism', a less extreme form of "workers' control" than syndicalism, disheartened those with aspirations towards industrial democracy. While for most the attractions of the Russian example had long since evaporated, Communist-dominated minority movements[2] engendered dissension and bitter struggles within the labour movement, individual unions, and the T.U.C.

From these disillusionments and set-backs there developed a bitterness and militancy some part of which, forty years after, survives. The older union leaders remember those days, and their recollections have formed part of the training of the young.

The later 1930s brought some improvement in economic conditions. Trade union membership recovered, although even in 1939, at 6·3 million, the 1920 peak had not been regained. Determined efforts were made by some union leaders and employers to promote a happier atmosphere. These had begun as early as 1928, when the 'Mond–Turner Conversations'[3] were held. The discussions were designed to secure some *rapprochement* between workers and employers after the disaster of the General Strike, and were aimed at evolving

[1] Specific 'contracting in' was required of individuals wishing to pay any political levy; this reversed a requirement of the Trade Union Act 1913 which had hitherto regulated the political activities of unions.

[2] Such as the National Minority Movement and the National Unemployed Workers' Committee.

[3] A series of conferences between some employers led by Sir Alfred Mond, the chairman of Imperial Chemical Industries Ltd, and the T.U.C., of which Mr. Ben Turner was the chairman.

a policy of joint responsibility for industrial prosperity. Unsupported by the central employers' organisations, and meeting considerable hostility from certain trade union leaders, the Conversations led to few concrete results; but it is likely that they enabled the participants to view their mutual problems in a broader perspective and with less ill-feeling. Although little reconciliation was achieved with Conservative Governments, and indeed grave differences developed on vital questions of domestic economic policy and international relationships,[1] the continued widening of State participation in industrial affairs required that the unions be increasingly consulted, and, by virtue of the Fair Wages Resolution, their 'recognised' wages and hours observed over an extended area. Experiments in public ownership had directly beneficial effects. Thus, for example, the London Passenger Transport Act 1933 created a Negotiating Committee and a Wages Board to facilitate the settlement of disputes between the Transport Board and the unions concerned.

In spite of the set-backs of the inter-war years, some positive achievement could undoubtedly be claimed. Thus the structure of trade unionism was improved. There had been a trend towards fewer and bigger unions, which were increasingly centralised as to authority, operated more and more in a national rather than a localised way, and possessed considerably greater financial resources than had ever been acquired by the pre-war organisations. Among the more spectacular amalgamations were those accompanying the re-constitution of the Amalgamated Society of Engineers in 1921 as the Amalgamated Engineering Union, the formation of the Transport and General Workers' Union in 1922, and the creation of the National Union of General and Municipal Workers in 1924. Existing federations achieved further consolidation and new ones appeared. Unionism among white-collar workers made progress. The T.U.C., as a result of the re-organisation already described, improved its claims to be regarded as a representative body; its activities in inter-union disputes, especially over claims to organise particular groups of workers, added further to its reputation.[2] Communist-dominated minority movements, although they continued to exist, no longer offered a serious threat to official leadership.

With improved organisation came improved methods. Collective agreements now applied to a substantial proportion of the working population, and these agreements were increasingly national in their coverage and comprehensive in the classes of workers included. Depressed economic conditions, forcing the traditional craft unions to relax skill requirements for membership in order to counter low-wage competition, had made an important contribution to this trend. In several trades, Joint Industrial Councils had survived and prospered, and had helped promote improved bargaining machinery and improved industrial relations generally.

[1] For example, remedies to be adopted for deflation and attitudes to be taken towards the development of Fascism. Events were to prove the trade unions' ideas on both scores to be considerably more sensible than those of the Governments of the time.

[2] The position regarding inter-union disputes was considerably eased as a result of the adoption by the 1939 Congress of certain principles for delineating spheres of influence between unions and handling practical problems arising. The 1939 Congress was held at Bridlington, and the statement of the principles is popularly known as the 'Bridlington Agreement'.

Although little of direct benefit had resulted therefrom, political action had at least helped to produce Labour Governments and to leave the Party with 154 Members in the House of Commons after the 1935 Election. And, in no small measure due to trade union pressures, legislation had been enacted designed to improve the workers' position in a variety of ways. For example, special protection was given to workers in industries facing particularly serious economic problems. Thus the Agricultural Wages (Regulation) Act 1924 re-introduced a system of the Trade Board sort.[1] The Road and Rail Traffic Act 1933 made the issue of licences to public carriers conditional on the payment of 'fair wages', and the Road Haulage Wages Act 1938 introduced what was, effectively, a Trade Board system to that industry. By the Cotton Manufacturing Industry (Temporary Provisions) Act 1934, statutory backing was given to minimum conditions established by voluntary collective bargaining in the trade. The Holidays with Pay Act 1938 empowered all statutory wage regulation authorities to prescribe paid holidays up to one week per year; at the time, paid holidays for manual workers were rare. Finally, various pieces of legislation were enacted to improve the health, safety and welfare of the working population; of particular significance were extended restrictions on the employment conditions of children, young persons and women.[2]

Progress was also achieved in the sphere of international trade unionism. An International Federation of Trade Unions, consisting of representatives from national organisations, had been formed in 1913; the British unions were represented by the T.U.C. The Federation was re-formed after the war and, during the inter-war years, made substantial progress, providing a valuable medium for the exchange of ideas on industrial, social and economic questions; of particular concern was the threat to world peace developing in the late 1930s. Complete international solidarity, however, was not achieved, the Russian trade unions, and Communist unions in other countries, maintaining a rival organisation, the Red International of Labour Unions, formed in 1919.

Parallel to the I.F.T.U., and in many cases ante-dating it, were the International Trade Secretariats, representative of unions in particular trades in various countries. These also made progress, although a somewhat uneasy relationship was maintained between the Secretariats and the I.F.T.U. Representatives of the Secretariats attended congresses of the Federation, with the right to speak but not to vote, and special joint conferences were also held. However, the Secretariats never quite became reconciled to the restriction of their right to take decisions without first consulting the Federation.

1939 ONWARDS

Wartime conditions gave a great stimulus to trade unionism. Membership

[1] The Corn Production Act 1917 had been repealed in 1921 and a voluntary, and largely ineffectual, system for wage regulation introduced.

[2] For example, Employment of Women, Young Persons and Children Act 1920, Children and Young Persons Act 1933, Hours of Employment (Conventions) Act 1936, Young Persons (Employment) Act 1938.

rose from 6·3 million in 1939 to 8·8 million in 1946, thus exceeding the 1920 peak. No post-war slump was to follow on this occasion. Unemployment averaged less than 2 per cent over the years 1946–69, representing a sustained level of national economic activity never before achieved. In these favourable circumstances, membership continued on an upward trend, exceeding 10 million in 1964, and reaching the highest total ever recorded—10·3 million—in 1969.

The trend towards fewer and larger unions was accelerated;[1] between 1939 and 1969, the number of unions fell from 1,019 to 508. Particularly notable amalgamations produced the National Union of Mineworkers in 1944 and the Union of Shop, Distributive and Allied Workers in 1947. A later wave of amalgamations produced the Society of Graphical and Allied Trades in 1966, the Amalgamated Union of Engineering and Foundry Workers in 1967, and the Electrical Electronic and Telecommunication Union–Plumbing Trades Union in the following year. In 1969, agreement on amalgamation was reached between the Amalgamated Society of Woodworkers and the Amalgamated Society of Painters and Decorators, the new union to commence operations as from January 1970. The traditional craft unions increasingly relaxed their membership requirements, and in the process increased their memberships. Prior to the amalgamation of 1967, the Amalgamated Engineering Union, with 1·1 million members, had become the second largest union in Britain. White-collar unionism, in membership terms, made spectacular progress. By 1966, the National and Local Government Officers' Association was the fifth largest union in the country. The white-collar unions also engaged in important amalgamations, for example, those producing in 1968 the Association of Scientific, Technical and Managerial Staffs, a militant and extremely effective union of highly-qualified persons.

Federations also improved their coverage and effectiveness. For example, the Confederation of Shipbuilding and Engineering Unions was greatly strengthened in 1947 by the accession of the Amalgamated Engineering Union, the largest single union in the industry. In 1969, with 26 member unions and an affiliated membership of 1·9 million, the C.S.E.U. was by far the largest of the federations. Other less formal working arrangements between unions came to play an important role, a revival of interest in Joint Industrial Councils contributing to this process.

Growth in trade union membership, and the tendency of white-collar unions to affiliate, increased the strength of the T.U.C.; concentration of membership in larger organisations added to its operational efficiency. The social and economic needs of the times made high level consultation between Governments and the trade union movement essential, and so encouraged the acceptance of the T.U.C. as a spokesman, both by the unions themselves and by the State. The great debate on incomes policy, to be described below, further emphasised the role of the T.U.C.

Improvements in the structure of the movement were not, unfortunately, paralleled by the changes in internal organisation which the increased size and heterogeneity of units almost certainly demanded. Some of the outwardly

[1] Easement of the legal requirements for amalgamation, by the Societies (Miscellaneous Provisions) Act 1940, and the Trade Union (Amalgamations, etc.) Act 1964, facilitated the process.

impressive amalgamations of the 1960s left the constituent unions to all intents and purposes autonomous, operating their own rules and methods of organisation. One manifestation of deficiency in internal organisation was the difficulty which many unions found in maintaining effective relationships with members at workshop level, and in particular with their shop stewards who, in circumstances of full employment, acquired greatly increased power and influence. In a large number of industries, the stewards' authority far exceeded that of full-time officials. However, attempts were made to adapt by increased use of 'trade group' organisation for particular classes of member, and, if only because of greater memberships in certain firms, of branch organisation based on workplace rather than, as hitherto, on place of residence. By the late 1960s, certain of the larger unions, such as the Amalgamated Engineering Union, the National Union of General and Municipal Workers, the Transport and General Workers' Union, and the Electrical Trades Union, were undoubtedly making efforts to evolve more modern and efficient organisational systems. Most unions, albeit belatedly and after much prompting by the T.U.C., had become aware of the shop steward problem and of the need to make organisational changes appropriate to incorporating stewards more closely within the formal administrative system.

The wartime alliance with Russia brought a revival of interest in Communism, and a substantial growth in Communist Party membership. The stability of certain unions was impaired as bitter internal struggles developed between official leaders and Communist-inspired minority groups.[1] However, before lasting harm was occasioned, political developments in Eastern Europe brought a rapid decline in the Communist Party's fortunes, and in its disruptive influence in the national trade union movement.

Increased membership and improved structure brought greater bargaining strength. Other factors contributed, if in more indirect ways. Thus the extended participation by the State in the affairs of industry, and in particular the major nationalisation programme of 1945–51, produced in a widening sector of the economy an employer particularly ready to recognise and to negotiate with trade unions.[2] The effect was cumulative, for similar responsibilities were placed on firms wishing to do business with public enterprises. The Fair Wages policy, increasingly adopted also by local authorities, had similar effects; a new Resolution of 1946 required the observance of 'fair' wages, hours and conditions generally and the recognition of the freedom of workers to belong to unions.[3]

[1] A celebrated article, 'Communism in Trade Unions', published in *The Times* of February 9th 1948, claimed that, of 15 unions with memberships of 100,000 or over, Communists and their supporters had sufficient representation on executives to control or dispute control of 4 (with an aggregate membership of more than a million), and had appreciable influence on 6 (with an aggregate membership of over 3 million). Total trade union membership at the time was 9·4 million. The powerful Electrical Trades Union, with a membership of approximately 250,000, remained Communist-dominated until 1961, when the case of *Byrne and Chapple v. Foulkes and Others* effectively ended Communist control. See p. 19, footnote 1.
[2] The nationalisation statutes, in fact, made this obligation explicit.
[3] Fair terms and conditions were now defined as being not less favourable than 'those established for the trade or industry in the district where the work is carried out by machinery of negotiation or arbitration' to which the parties were properly representative organisations.

Statutory provision had also contributed to increased bargaining strength. The Wages Councils Act 1945 considerably widened the scope of existing Trade Board legislation.[1] Additional provision was also made for particular industries, for example, the catering industry, and existing regulation extended, for instance, in agriculture.[2] By 1965, Wages Councils and other statutory wage regulation authorities embraced over $3\frac{1}{2}$ million workers.

The effectiveness of collective bargaining was also enhanced, indirectly, as a result of the re-introduction of compulsory arbitration by the Conditions of Employment and National Arbitration Order (Order 1305) 1940. Under the Order, it was possible to require employers to observe 'recognised terms and conditions' of employment, effectively those established by voluntary collective bargaining. Similar provision was retained in the Industrial Disputes Order (Order 1376) 1951. When Order 1376 was finally revoked, the Terms and Conditions of Employment Act 1959 continued a procedure for enforcing 'recognised terms and conditions'.

The insecurity of the employment relationship had always been a cause of weakness in the workers' bargaining position. However, the Contracts of Employment Act 1963 required that most workers be given written contracts not later than 13 weeks after engagement. Upon continuous employment of 26 weeks, a specified period of notice, varying with length of service, was required to terminate the contract. Rates of payment during notice periods were also specified. The Redundancy Payments Act 1965 gave added protection by providing payments, related to length of service, for most workers becoming 'redundant' after a minimum of two years' employment.[3]

Social legislation of various sorts also contributed to increased security, by establishing the principle of unrestricted financial support, as of right, in genuine cases of unemployment, injury or sickness.[4] Indirect benefit accrued in that the unions, who had previously devoted a large proportion of their resources to such ends, were enabled to use these resources for other purposes, including bargaining. A similar effect attended the introduction of general entitlement to free legal aid by the Legal Aid and Advice Act 1949.[5]

Consequent on greater bargaining strength came an extension of collective bargaining and the improvement of bargaining machinery. The tendency

[1] Councils could now be set up either on the Minister of Labour's own initiative, where he was satisfied that voluntary machinery for wage determination was inadequate or 'was likely to cease to exist or be adequate', or when he received a claim made jointly by representative organisations of workers and employers to the like effect. Councils were given the right not only to fix minimum wage rates but also to specify statutory minimum *remuneration*. They were also empowered to serve as representative consultative bodies in industrial matters generally. The 1945 Act, together with other statutory wage regulation, was consolidated in the Wages Councils Act 1959.

[2] By the Catering Wages Act 1943, the Agricultural Wages (Regulation) Amendment Act 1940, the Agricultural Wages Act 1948, and the Agriculture Act 1967.

[3] The motives behind this Act were not completely altruistic, for the Government hoped that it would also improve labour mobility.

[4] Of particular importance were the National Insurance Act, the National Health Service Act, and the National Insurance (Industrial Injuries) Act, all passed in 1946, and the National Assistance Act 1948.

[5] Free legal assistance to persons of limited means had been available for centuries in Britain, but only in some courts and to a circumscribed extent.

towards national and comprehensive agreements was continued.[1] The high economic activity of the war and post-war years brought a revival of interest in Joint Industrial Councils and similar bodies, and by the mid-1960s some 200 were known to exist. By 1969, most major industries maintained joint organisations approximating to the Whitley pattern. Under the general cover of national agreements, advantage was taken of full employment circumstances to negotiate for superior terms at local level in a variety of industries.[2]

The content of agreements also changed. Some traditional items tended to disappear or to be given diminished emphasis. Thus much less weight was attached to detailed regulation of apprenticeship ratios, demarcation, and the conditions under which systems of payment by results might be employed or overtime worked. Agreements instead began to cover such matters as redundancy and promotion, and, in some few cases, 'fringe benefits' such as retirement pensions, sick pay, and the provision of social, recreational and educational facilities. Paid holidays had become standard practice. A particularly important development of the 1960s was the incorporation of clauses whereby wage increases were made conditional upon changes in work practices, designed to improve productivity; agreements of which this was the prime purpose came to be called 'productivity agreements'. Changes of a more procedural nature included 'closed shop' arrangements, and provision whereby union contributions were collected by a 'check off' system, the appropriate amounts being deducted by employers from wages. A further departure of some significance was the specification of time periods, for example, three years, for the currency of agreements.

In the post-war period, the unions also considerably increased their political influence. Majority Labour Governments held office in the years 1945–51 and again after 1964; around 150 Labour Members were union-sponsored in the Government formed in 1966. Among the more obvious manifestations of political influence was legislation which directly improved the legal position of the unions. Thus the first post war Labour Government repealed the Trade Disputes and Trade Unions Act 1927;[3] the restoration thereby of 'contracting out' both increased the financial support available to the Party and further consolidated its relationships with the trade union movement. Another enactment of a Labour Government removed doubts which had arisen regarding trade union immunity in tort.[4] The nationalisation statutes of 1945–51, as already mentioned, gave specific encouragement to the unions concerned. However, the passing of a considerable volume of legislation

[1] In 1965, the Ministry of Labour listed some 500 pieces of negotiating machinery at the national level, including statutory wage fixing bodies, for manual workers alone, cover ing some 14 million out of a total of 16 million in employment. On the other hand, it was estimated that less than 4 million non-manual workers out of a total of 7 million were included in such arrangements. See Royal Commission on Trade Unions and Employers' Associations, *Written Evidence of the Ministry of Labour* (London, H.M.S.O., 1965), p. 19.

[2] This trend did not always secure the blessing of official union leadership, causing problems for them, and for the economy, which will be discussed below.

[3] By the Trade Disputes and Trade Unions Act 1946.

[4] The Trade Disputes Act 1965. The celebrated case of *Rookes v. Barnard and Others*, 1962 had put the matter in doubt. See p. 19, footnote 3.

favourable to the working class in general, and the trade unions in particular, gave ample evidence that effective influence was not confined to Labour Governments. It was a Conservative Government, for example, which passed the important Offices, Shops and Railway Premises Act 1963, contributing thereby to substantial improvement of physical working conditions in those sectors, and the Trade Union (Amalgamations, etc.) Act 1964, which further facilitated amalgamations among unions.

During the Second World War the unions did much to regain and extend the prestige they had enjoyed in the years 1914–20; with enhanced standing went a greater degree of acceptance, at all levels, by Government and employers. Compulsory arbitration, including prohibition of strikes and lock-outs and legally enforceable awards,[1] 'dilution' and direction of labour were all accepted, as was a measure of wage restraint.[2] Even more than in the First World War, the unions became involved with employers and Government representatives in all sorts of measures designed to further the war effort. At national level, the T.U.C. joined with representatives of the British Employers' Confederation[3] in the National Joint Advisory Council, set up in 1939 to advise the Government on matters in which employers and workers had a common interest. Close co-operation was maintained with the National Production Advisory Council for Industry, established in 1941 to serve as a forum for Government consultation with representatives of both sides of industry. A willingness to collaborate in promoting industrial efficiency and well-being brought a revival of interest in Joint Industrial Councils having joint consultation as well as collective bargaining in their functions. At the level of the individual plant, 'Joint Production Committees', designed to foster joint concern with efficiency, were formed in many industries.[4]

These trends were maintained in the post-war years. Continued economic difficulties led successive Governments to call for union co-operation. Compulsory arbitration under Order 1305 continued to be accepted until 1951, and a significant degree of wage restraint was observed between 1948 and 1950. Although similar policies attempted by Conservative Governments in the period 1957–64[5] were consistently opposed, largely on the grounds that other

[1] By the Conditions of Employment and National Arbitration Order (Order 1305) 1940.

[2] A White Paper of 1941, *Price Stabilisation and Industrial Policy* (Cmd. 6294), while stressing that free collective bargaining should continue in wartime, called upon both sides of industry to do all that they could to prevent the cost of living from rising. Between 1938 and 1945, wage rates rose by 50 per cent, earnings by 77 per cent, and retail prices, thanks in part to price controls and subsidies, by only 49 per cent.

[3] Formed in 1919. In 1965 the Confederation joined with the Federation of British Industries and the National Association of British Manufacturers to form the Confederation of British Industry.

[4] By 1944, it has been estimated that there were 4,565 such Committees in the engineering and allied industries alone. See Worswick, G. D. N. and Ady, P. H. (editors), *The British Economy, 1945–1950* (Oxford, Clarendon Press, 1952), p. 122.

[5] These policies included: (a) in the period 1957–61, the operation of a 'Council on Prices, Productivity and Incomes', charged with the function of keeping under review changes in prices, productivity and the level of incomes; (b) in the years 1961–62, an appeal for a voluntary 'pay pause', and the restriction of the rate of increase of incomes to 2–2½ per cent per annum, the rate then considered to be consistent with price stability; (c) in the period 1962–64, a 'National Incomes Commission', to which the Government could refer wage agreements for an opinion as to whether they were in the national interest.

15

forms of income were not similarly constrained, the T.U.C. in December 1964 joined with central employer organisations in a 'Joint Statement of Intent on Productivity, Prices and Incomes', pledging co-operation with the newly-elected Labour Government in improving industrial efficiency and evolving viable price and income policies. The setting up of a National Board for Prices and Incomes in April 1965 was similarly endorsed.[1]

In the post-war years, increased participation by the State in the affairs of industry brought new opportunities for invoking trade union co-operation, and this was willingly given. The T.U.C. was a constituent of the United Kingdom section of the Anglo-American Council on Productivity, set up in 1948 to promote exchange of information relevant to productive efficiency, and of the British Productivity Council which succeeded it in 1952. In 1962 the T.U.C. became a member of the National Economic Development Council, founded by a Conservative Government to consider the whole question of the growth of the economy.[2] Following increased concern with economic planning on an area basis, the setting up of regional Economic Planning Councils provided further opportunities for participation. Membership of the Central Training Council, established under the Industrial Training Act 1964, opened yet another avenue for T.U.C. collaboration.[3]

Individual unions were similarly involved. In the years 1945–47 they collaborated in tripartite 'working parties' set up to investigate efficiency in various trades, and, thereafter, in the tripartite Development Councils set up in four of them.[4] Economic Development Committees, associated with the N.E.D.C. and designed to promote efficiency in particular industries, provided similar opportunities for participation. At local level, unions joined in the activities of the local Productivity Councils associated with the British Productivity Council. In individual firms, many unions responded to the Government's appeal, made in 1947, for a revival of Joint Production Committees, and, in others, more informal joint consultation procedures were successfully developed;[5] the right to joint consultation seemed to satisfy most unions' aspirations regarding "worker's control".[6]

Other developments added to trade union reputation. Although no funda-

[1] The Government could refer to the Board, for an opinion as to consistency with the national interest, increases in prices or incomes. As regards wages and salaries, a 'norm' of 3–3½ per cent was indicated as a permissible annual rate of increase; increases above the 'norm' were to be allowed only in specified special circumstances.

[2] With its functions largely superseded by the N.E.D.C. and the Department of Economic Affairs, established in 1964, the National Production Advisory Council for Industry, an earlier body in which the T.U.C. had participated, was wound up in January 1965.

[3] The broad purpose of the Act was to establish Industrial Training Boards for particular industries, financed by levies on firms, to provide or secure the provision of appropriate training.

[4] These Councils were formed under the Industrial Organisation and Development Act 1947 and, financed by levies on firms, were to provide means for 'improving and developing the service to the community by industries'. Only two—the Cotton Board and the Furniture Development Council—achieved any real success.

[5] By 1957, it was estimated that all the largest firms in manufacturing industry had some form of consultative machinery. See Royal Commission on Trade Unions and Employers' Associations, *Written Evidence of the Ministry of Labour* (London, H.M.S.O., 1965), p. 24.

[6] Hopes attached to nationalisation had, like those vested in earlier, more radical, methods proved mainly disappointing.

16

mental change was effected in basic objectives and functions, the interpretation placed on these was undoubtedly less restrictive. Thus less importance was attached to devices designed to restrict entry to a trade (e.g., rigid apprenticeship ratios, opposition to dilution) or to limit output (e.g., restriction of payments by results schemes and overtime working, insistence on demarcation). Productivity bargaining was welcomed in many situations. Perhaps the most significant change of all, however, appertained to the use of the strike. Although, as will be seen from Tables 3 and 4 (pp. 29–30), strikes had become decidedly more frequent, they were on average shorter and smaller; moreover, they had become relatively less common over questions of wages and hours.[1] The proportion of strikes which were unofficial, and therefore not authorised or supported by the unions, had risen considerably.[2] Over the years 1940–65 there were few official national strikes of any significance. The unions were abandoning the strike as a device to be used on a large scale for bargaining purposes.

By the early 1960s, increased prestige and a greater degree of acceptance, by Government and employers, allied with a growth in strength and effectiveness, had placed the unions in a position of unrivalled power and influence. Although advantage had been taken of this position to achieve substantial improvements in the economic and social conditions of the working class, it had not been abused. Partly in consequence, the general state of industrial relationships had been transformed beyond recognition, and the bitterness and hostility which had characterised the inter-war years had been largely expunged.

In the field of international trade unionism, matters had proceeded less smoothly. The operations of the International Federation of Trade Unions had been effectively suspended on the outbreak of the Second World War. With feelings of international solidarity still strong, considerable enthusiasm attended the formation of a new World Federation of Trade Unions in 1945. However, the powerful American Federation of Labor, unwilling to associate with unions from Communist countries, did not join. In a very few years, conflict began between Communist and non-Communist members. In 1949, the T.U.C. and the American Congress of Industrial Organisations withdrew, and, together with the A.F.L., initiated the establishment in 1949 of a rival International Confederation of Free Trade Unions, to be composed of 'free and democratic trade unions'. The central organisations in most other democratic countries soon affiliated to the new Confederation, and the W.F.T.U. became essentially a Communist organisation.

---

[1] The causes of strikes in two historically similar periods, 1911–25 and 1927–47, have been compared. It was found that the proportion due to 'basic' causes (wages and hours) fell markedly from 69 per cent to 54 per cent; that the proportion due to 'frictional' causes ('employment of certain classes or persons', 'other working arrangements, rules and discipline') increased sharply from 22 per cent to 39 per cent, and that the proportion due to 'solidarity' causes (matters of trade union principle, 'sympathetic' strikes, etc.) fell slightly from 9 per cent to 7 per cent. See Knowles, K. G. J. C., *Strikes—A Study in Industrial Conflict* (Oxford, Basil Blackwell, 1952), p. 234. More recent statistics confirm this trend; over the period 1960–65 the percentages of strikes falling under these broad heads were approximately 49·5 per cent, 46 per cent and 4·5 per cent.

[2] From some 50 per cent in the late 1930s to 95 per cent in the mid-1960s.

With ideological conflict resolved, the I.C.F.T.U. made impressive progress; by 1969 it had a membership of some 63 million, drawn from 95 countries. Regional machinery was established, and effective liaison with the International Trade Secretariats was achieved through a joint Consultative Council. The Secretariats themselves made substantial progress, and by 1969 numbered 17 with 44 million members. While no less jealous of their independence of any central organisation, they achieved, through their permanent co-ordinating committee, some measure of common action.

In 1969, however, the international movement demonstrated once again its capacity for self-disruption. The influential American Federation of Labor–Congress of Industrial Organisations[1] withdrew, reducing membership of the I.C.F.T.U. to little over 50 million and its income by one-fifth. Exception had been taken at the apparently sympathetic consideration being given to independent membership for the United Automobile, Aerospace and Agricultural Implement Workers of America (U.A.W.), which had disaffiliated from the central association. While it seemed likely that the quarrel would be satisfactorily resolved, the U.A.W. application being rejected in November 1969, the incident provided evidence that the international situation was by no means yet completely peaceful.

PROBLEMS OF THE 1960s

CAUSES

The favourable situation at which the British trade union movement had arrived was not destined to continue. By the mid-1960s, prestige had markedly declined, and the state of industrial relations in several important industries had deteriorated alarmingly. A variety of factors contributed to this turn of events.

Employers, struggling with labour shortages and rapid changes in methods of production, showed mounting exasperation at certain work practices enforced by many unions. A rising incidence of strikes, and in particular unofficial strikes, and the apparent inability of unions to control either their shop stewards or their rank and file memberships in the workplace, added further problems for management, both directly as regards industrial relationships, and indirectly in the matter of profitability of enterprises. For much the same reasons, Governments, increasingly reliant on control of the labour market as a means of combating inflation in a full employment economy, found themselves baulked in their efforts to induce improvements in productivity and to secure the implementation of policies designed to prevent excessive rises in money incomes. Public opinion, kept constantly if not always accurately in touch with such opinions through the mass media, began to share them and to react against the unions. Further hostility was aroused by much publicised cases of victimisation,[2] Communist activity in

[1] Formed in 1955 by the joining of the two previously separate central organisations.

[2] For example, the case of *Bonsor v. Musicians' Union* 1956, arising from the expulsion of a union member for persistent failure to discharge arrears of subscriptions. The plaintiff

18

unions,[1] etc. There had developed a growing feeling of resentment, shared by many employers and politicians, at the power supposedly wielded by the organised working classes. This found frequent expression in a complaint at the 'privileged' legal position of the unions,[2] a complaint which the Courts seemed prepared to endorse.[3]

The unions themselves were encountering problems. Thus there was some truth in employers' claims that control of the shop floor situation was being lost in some industries. While formal administration had become increasingly centralised, there had occurred a marked transfer of *actual* activity and authority to the shop floor, to which the unions had been slow to adjust. This process, dating from the time of the Second World War, was contributed to by a variety of factors.

Firstly, there were changes in the industrial environment. Full employment, and keen competition for particular classes of labour, prompted employers to offer terms and conditions superior to those of national agreements. Rapid change in methods of production posed problems requiring essentially workshop settlement. The growth of new industries, and significant changes in old ones, accelerated the development of multi-union representation in individual firms, and further increased the need for local working arrangements.

Changes in the structure, organisation and methods of the unions were also important. The trend towards larger and more heterogeneous unions, and the tradition of national agreements, made it increasingly difficult to accommodate the needs of particular workshop groups or to deal expeditiously with disputes concerning them. Some decentralisation of authority, informally if not formally, was therefore forced on the unions. In addition, larger unions found it increasingly difficult to maintain communications with—and control over—localised groups. This prompted the appearance of less formal leadership and methods of operation.

Again, there had developed divergent attitudes within the movement. As trade union leaders assumed increasingly 'responsible' patterns of behaviour, a gap opened between them and the rank and file members. The latter, retaining more traditional views, sought unofficial leaders, more responsive to their immediate needs, from among their own number in the workplace. In

[1] For example, the case of *Byrne and Chapple v. Foulkes and Others* 1961, in which a Communist minority, controlling the senior offices and the executive of the Electrical Trades Union, was held to have engaged in fraudulent conspiracy to manipulate the results of Union elections.

[2] See p. 4, footnote 3. That collective agreements were not legally enforceable was also a ground of complaint.

[3] In the case of *Rookes v. Barnard and Others* 1962, the House of Lords held that individual union officers might be liable in civil action for having used 'intimidation', such as a threat to strike in breach of contract of employment, to force an enterprise to dismiss a non-unionist. Most labour lawyers did not believe that such an action could succeed, and were baffled by the verdict. The Trade Disputes Act 1965 was intended to remove this newly discovered liability.

was thereafter unable during the remaining years of his life to practise his profession. It was eventually held by the House of Lords that, in this expulsion, the Musicians' Union had not observed the due processes of their rules, and substantial damages were awarded.

more affluent circumstances, the defensive urge which previously secured loyalty to the union was increasingly replaced by the more immediate loyalties arising from the work situation.

Finally, there was the more positive role of the State in industrial relations, and, in particular, its concern with improving productivity and influencing rates of increase in wages. Both developments clearly focused greater attention on the shop floor, productivity for obvious reasons, and wage considerations because earnings, if not wage-rates, were increasingly determined there.

While most unions were aware that there had been some shift in the locus of operational authority, few would have agreed that harm was thereby occasioned. There were, however, other more widely felt anxieties. Thus some unions were concerned at the harm caused to the repute of the movement by what they considered to be 'misapprehensions' held by employers, Government and the public, and were eager that these should be corrected. Other unions believed that the current system of industrial relations failed to provide them with a role in the affairs of industry which accurately reflected their contemporary power. One manifestation of this view was a revived interest in direct forms of "workers' control", both the T.U.C. and the Labour Party contemplating schemes for industrial democracy which would include workers' representatives on the boards of enterprises.

By the mid-1960s there had developed a widespread belief in the need for a reappraisal of the British system of industrial relations. The decision to set up a Royal Commission on Trade Unions and Employers' Associations in April 1965 was therefore greeted with considerable enthusiasm by many sections of opinion, albeit for diverse reasons.

A further decline in the prestige of the unions was to occur while the Commission was sitting. Attempts to enforce incomes policy led to friction with employers and the Government, and to angry and militant behaviour by the unions. The course of events was as follows.

Just before the September 1965 Trades Union Congress, with voluntary methods palpably failing to contain wage increases within the 3–3½ per cent norm, the Government announced its intention of strengthening incomes policy by the introduction of an 'early warning system' for proposed wage and price increases. These would have to be formally reported, and no further action would be allowed the parties concerned pending investigation, and, where thought necessary, reference to the National Board for Prices and Incomes. Faced with this development, the T.U.C. hurriedly proposed an alternative plan whereby Congress itself would introduce a 'vetting' system for wage claims by member unions, the implication being that the criteria of the Board would be applied. The scheme was accepted on a trial basis and duly initiated. However, the Government did not withdraw its plan for at least permissive legislation, and an appropriate Bill was presented in February 1966. When a General Election was called in March the Bill lapsed.

Little opportunity was afforded for assessing the new T.U.C. scheme. With both wage rates and earnings continuing to rise rapidly, and confronted by a serious deterioration in the balance of payments, the re-elected Labour Government announced a 'standstill' in prices and incomes in the six months to December 1966, followed by a 'period of severe restraint', during which increases should occur only in special circumstances, in the first half of 1967.

Legislation duly followed in the Prices and Incomes Act of August 1966. By Part I of the Act, the N.B.P.I. was re-constituted on a statutory basis (it had previously existed by Royal Warrant), and both its terms of reference and its formal powers were extended. The controversial aspects of the measure came in Parts II and IV, to be current for 12 months from the passing of the Act. Part II, if invoked, provided the Government with powers to enforce a 'standstill' on particular wage or price increases for what was effectively a maximum period of four months. Financial penalties were provided for defaulters. If Part IV were activated, the Government would have powers to direct that specified prices or wages should not be increased without the consent of the appropriate Minister, and also to reverse price or pay increases implemented since July 1966 and felt to be unjustified. Financial penalties would again apply.

The T.U.C. had given grudging support to the new policy, although it represented an unprecedented degree of interference with the processes of voluntary collective bargaining and, a most significant departure, introduced financial sanctions. The T.U.C.'s actions were based on the belief, fostered by the Government, that the policy would remain voluntary and that Parts II and IV of the 1966 Act would not be invoked. Massive opposition was developing within individual unions. With neither 'standstill' nor 'restraint' obtaining universal recognition, the Government in October 1966 activated Part IV of the Act. Trade union hostility now became general and open.

It had been expected that the controversial Parts of the 1966 Act would expire in August 1967, with a return thereafter to a voluntary system based on the joint operation of the N.B.P.I. and the T.U.C. vetting scheme. However, with serious economic difficulties persisting, the Prices and Incomes Act of July 1967 continued the currency of Part II, not so far activated, for a further 12 months and extended the maximum 'standstill' period to seven months. In August 1967 Part IV of the 1966 Act lapsed, and Part II was activated. Under the Prices and Incomes Act of July 1968, the maximum 'standstill' period was extended to 12 months. These provisions were due to lapse in December 1969. However, once again the Government had a change of mind. In December 1969, it was announced[1] that Part II of the 1966 Act, in its original form, would be continued until December 1970. It was also intended that the N.B.P.I. should be merged with the Monopolies Commission[2] in a Commission for Industry and Manpower. Trade union anger at what seemed clear breaches of faith by the Government was natural, and was given ever more plain expression. By the time the Royal Commission reported in June 1968, relationships between the unions and the Government were in a critical state. At the same time, the incomes policy debate had led to worsened relationships with employers and a serious decline in the public reputation of the unions.

[1] In a White Paper *Productivity, Prices and Incomes Policy After 1969* (Cmnd. 4237) 1969.

[2] The Monopolies and Restrictive Practices (Inquiry and Control) Act 1948 established the Monopolies and Restrictive Practices Commission, re-titled the Monopolies Commission under the Restrictive Trade Practices Act 1956. In broad terms, the function of the Commission was to consider whether monopolies or oligopolies operated in ways contrary to the public interest.

SOLUTIONS

The Royal Commission's main thesis was that most of the contemporary problems of industrial relations derived from conflict between two 'systems'. On the one hand, there was the formal system, represented by the behaviour of official institutions (trade unions and employers' associations) and the industry-wide collective agreements which they concluded. On the other hand, there was the informal system, generated and sustained in the workplace by the employees, their shop stewards, and managements. The informal system gave rise to factory-level agreements which, for substantial numbers of workers, determined operative conditions relating to pay levels, work methods, grievance procedures, etc. Such agreements, improvised and often unwritten, lay largely outside the control of the national officials of unions or employers' associations, and consequently had developed in piecemeal fashion. The result was disorder in workplace relationships and in pay structures.

The situation was deleterious to the progress of society. Thus uncertainty in the face of arbitrary action, and in particular unofficial strikes, impaired the effectiveness of management and led, in the cause of uneasy peace, to the acceptance of inefficient and high-cost methods of working; unofficial strikes, of course, had also directly harmful economic effects. Managers and workers had become reluctant to initiate or accept change and innovation. Distortion of the relationships between wage rates and earnings, and between pay and productivity, had added to the Government's difficulties in controlling the economy.

Although the unions were not considered blameless, the main responsibility for this situation was placed on management who, concerned to attract and retain labour in times of full employment, had abrogated much of their duty and authority in industrial relations.

The Commission rejected various proposed remedies. Thus the notion of a special tribunal, empowered to outlaw particular restrictive practices, was discarded because of the difficulties of isolating the anti-social aspects of such practices and of enforcement. Suggestions regarding compulsory 'cooling off' periods for impending strikes, compulsory strike ballots, extension of arbitration, and legal enforcement of collective agreements were also rejected. The reasons given included the over-riding desirability of preserving voluntarism, the satisfactory nature of present less formal but more flexible machinery, and (again) problems of enforcement. Only very modest legal changes were recommended. Thus the Trade Union Act 1871 should be amended to enable consenting parties to conclude legally-enforceable agreements.[1] Unofficial strikers should lose the protection conferred under the Trade Disputes Acts 1906 and 1965 on those inducing breach of contract in industrial disputes. Immunity from action in tort, available under the 1906 Act, should be limited to torts committed in contemplation or furtherance of a trade dispute.

With more restrictive solutions rejected, the Commission's main prescription followed fairly obviously. Conflict between the two systems had to be removed. This required an acceptance of present trends and of the importance

[1] The 1871 Act had specified that agreements between unions and employers' associations were not legally enforceable.

22

of factory-level arrangements. Collective bargaining needed revision to induce greater formality into negotiations, agreements, and the conduct of those responsible for them. Therefore industry-wide agreements should be limited to what they could effectively regulate (e.g. the lengths of the standard working week and of annual holidays), and should set guidelines for acceptable company or factory agreements.

The main responsibility for deterioration in the system had been placed on management; so was the onus of initiating reform. The Commission recommended legislation obliging undertakings of a certain size (initially those employing at least 5,000 workers) to register their agreements with the Department of Employment and Productivity, or, if they had no agreements, to explain why. In time, smaller enterprises would be required to register.

The Act should also provide for the establishment of a Commission which, on receiving references, would investigate and report on problems arising from the registration of agreements. It would also make inquiries into the general state of industrial relations in an industry or in a company, having particular regard to factors preventing the conclusion of effective factory-level agreements. The recommendations of the Commission should not initially be compulsory, although this policy might be reviewed in the light of experience.

The Royal Commission made a variety of ancillary recommendations, designed to facilitate the translation to, and the operation of, the new system. Since success would depend on strong and effective trade unions, it was recommended that they should be encouraged to improve their structure, organisation and methods. Trade unionism should be strengthened indirectly by making illegal in contracts of employment any requirement that persons should not belong to trade unions. Powers should be available to force employers to recognise unions. In a situation of increased trade union strength, a substantial degree of protection for the individual would be required. The Commission thus recommended compulsory registration of unions, this procedure to include the obligation to observe model rules regarding admission, discipline, disputes with members and the conduct of elections. An independent review body should be available to hear complaints from persons refused admission to, or expelled from, a trade union. In order that unrest in the new system be minimised, perennial—and largely unnecessary— sources of disputes should be eliminated. Thus legislation should proscribe unfair dismissals, compulsory unilateral arbitration should be available when it could contribute to sound collective bargaining (e.g. on issues such as failure of an employer to recognise a union or to bargain in good faith), statutory minimum terms and conditions should be enforceable where approved forms of collective bargaining were failing to prosper, and the rights of the State to initiate fact-finding inquiries and promote conciliation in disputes should be extended.

The new system should also facilitate relevant aspects of national policy. Thus improved utilisation of manpower should be encouraged by more realistic training programmes and better training facilities. The unions should be encouraged to display a more flexible attitude towards late entry, dilution of skills, etc. Assuming the need for incomes policy to continue, legislation should be introduced placing on all arbitrators an obligation to take the

23

requirements of the policy into account in their deliberations; they should also be encouraged, contrary to British tradition, to give reasons for their awards.

Finally, the Commission called on both sides of industry to inculcate changes in attitudes appropriate to inaugurating, and ensuring success for, the new system.

The Labour Government's intentions were revealed in a White Paper *In Place of Strife: A Policy for Industrial Relations*, published in January 1969.[1] The Commission's analysis and prescriptions were accepted in broad terms. There were some differences in emphasis. Thus, as regards analysis, the Government was decidedly more circumspect on the extent to which the localised, informal system had either superseded, or come into conflict with, the national, formal system. And a much more cautious approach was adopted in the matter of restructuring the system of industrial relations to accord with the needs of incomes policy; for example, the Commission's suggested changes in the nature of arbitration were tacitly ignored.

There were differences also in prescription. Some of these were merely in detail; for example, registration was to be restricted to procedural agreements, and slight changes were suggested in the duties of the new Commission on Industrial Relations (the C.I.R.). Others were of more significance. Thus reorganisation of the trade union movement would be facilitated by a Trade Union Development Scheme, administered by the C.I.R., under which grants or loans could be made to individual unions, federations, or even the T.U.C. for such purposes as improving trade union research services, training shop stewards, employing management consultants, etc. The bargaining efficiency of trade unions would be improved by legislation enabling them to obtain from employers information about their companies likely to facilitate negotiations. A further contribution would be made towards the elimination of unnecessary industrial disputes by provision for the reference of inter-union recognition quarrels to the C.I.R., which would be entitled to rule that one of the unions should be excluded from recognition. A new Industrial Board, with members drawn from the panels of the Industrial Court, would have power to enforce penalties on defaulters on either side. A statement that experiments in the appointment of workers' representatives to boards of undertakings would be welcomed, and that appropriate changes in company law would be considered, represented a more positive attempt to foster the necessary changes of attitude in industry. Somewhat ironically in the light of the Government's subsequent failure to press an alternative, more vigorous scheme, the Commission's recommendation that unofficial strikers should lose legal privileges was rejected.

In some important respects, the Government's recommendations went well beyond those of the Commission. Thus legislation would empower the Secretary of State for Employment and Productivity to delay impending strikes when he believed a serious threat to the economy was involved. He would have the right to require a secret ballot in official strikes and to enforce a 'conciliation pause' of up to 28 days' duration in strikes which were unconsti-

1 Cmnd. 3888.

tutional or in which for other reasons adequate joint discussions had not taken place. Financial penalties, to be collected if need be by attachment of wages, would be provided. In addition, collective agreements would be made legally binding, but only by the wish of the parties concerned, and by express statement in such agreements.

At this, a mounting volume of hostility towards the Government finally broke loose. Although the T.U.C. tried to preach restraint, for most unions this attack on the cherished right to strike could not be countenanced. Threats of industrial unrest if the policy were pursued were freely made.[1] The Government found little support in other sectors. Many employers, right-wing politicians and sections of public opinion complained bitterly at the Government's continued refusal to introduce mandatory legalisation of agreements and comprehensive restrictions on strikes.

With the whole traditional relationship between the unions and the Labour Party in jeopardy, the Government withdrew. The justification was a promise by the T.U.C. to amend its Constitution so as to enable the General Council to intervene in serious unofficial strikes and to discipline unions which refused to carry out subsequent directives. The manœuvre regained little support from the unions; it engendered even greater hostility in the ranks of the disappointed critics.

Few positive results attended the new policy by the end of 1969. The C.I.R. was established, the T.U.C. duly amended its Constitution, and an Industrial Relations Act was promised for the 1969–70 Parliamentary Session. On the other hand, the Labour Government had lost favour with both sides of industry. Having added opposition to strike legislation to that already directed against incomes policy, the unions were regarded with considerable disfavour by some sections of public opinion. Whether this unpopularity would prove temporary, or whether it would impel Governments to respond with policies which constituted a serious permanent threat to the independence of the British trade union movement, remained a matter of speculation.[2]

[1] Some were carried out. On May 1st 1969 ('May Day'), token unofficial strikes caused serious stoppages of work in the national newspapers, the docks and car factories.
[3] See Appendix for later developments.

Table 1. Percentage unemployment in Great Britain and Northern Ireland, 1914–69

Year	Percentage unemployment	Year	Percentage unemployment	Year	Percentage unemployment
1914	3·3	1933	19·9	1952	2·1
1915	1·1	1934	16·7	1953	1·8
1916	0·4	1935	15·5	1954	1·5
1917	0·6	1936	13·1	1955	1·2
1918	0·8	1937	10·8	1956	1·3
1919	2·1	1938	13·5	1957	1·6
1920	2·0	1939	11·6	1958	2·2
1921	12·9	1940	9·7	1959	2·3
1922	14·3	1941	6·6	1960	1·7
1923	11·7	1942	2·4	1961	1·6
1924	10·3	1943	0·8	1962	2·1
1925	11·3	1944	0·7	1963	2·6
1926	12·5	1945	1·2	1964	1·7
1927	9·7	1946	2·5	1965	1·5
1928	10·8	1947	3·1	1966	1·6
1929	10·4	1948	1·8	1967	2·5
1930	16·0	1949	1·6	1968	2·5
1931	21·3	1950	1·5	1969	2·5
1932	22·1	1951	1·2		

Note: Because of definitional changes, figures before and after the years 1921 and 1947 respectively are not strictly comparable.
Source: Series given in *The British Economy: Key Statistics 1900–1970* (London, Times Newspapers Ltd, 1971).

Table 2. Number of trade unions and trade union membership
in Great Britain and Northern Ireland, 1914–69

Year	Number of unions	Membership (000's)		
		Males	Females	Total
1914	1,260	3,708	437	4,145
1915	1,229	3,868	491	4,359
1916	1,225	4,018	626	4,644
1917	1,241	4,621	878	5,499
1918	1,264	5,324	1,209	6,533
1919	1,360	6,600	1,326	7,926
1920	1,384	7,006	1,342	8,348
1921	1,275	5,628	1,005	6,633
1922	1,232	4,753	872	5,625
1923	1,192	4,607	822	5,429
1924	1,194	4,730	814	5,544
1925	1,176	4,671	835	5,506
1926	1,164	4,407	812	5,219
1927	1,159	4,125	794	4,919
1928	1,142	4,011	795	4,806
1929	1,133	4,056	802	4,858
1930	1,121	4,049	793	4,842
1931	1,108	3,859	765	4,624
1932	1,081	3,698	746	4,444
1933	1,081	3,661	731	4,392
1934	1,063	3,854	736	4,590
1935	1,049	4,106	761	4,867
1936	1,035	4,495	800	5,295
1937	1,030	4,948	895	5,843
1938	1,021	5,128	926	6,054
1939	1,019	5,288	1,010	6,298
1940	1,004	5,494	1,119	6,613
1941	996	5,753	1,412	7,165
1942	991	6,151	1,716	7,867
1943	987	6,258	1,916	8,174
1944	963	6,239	1,848	8,087
1945	781	6,237	1,638	7,875
1946	757	7,186	1,617	8,803
1947	734	7,483	1,662	9,145
1948	735	7,648	1,672	9,320
1949	726	7,613	1,661	9,274
1950	715	7,573	1,670	9,243
1951	710	7,706	1,775	9,481
1952	723	7,797	1,792	9,588
1953	721	7,749	1,779	9,528

Table 2 (*continued*)

Year	Number of unions	Membership (000's) Males	Females	Total
1954	707	7,753	1,808	9,561
1955	698	7,868	1,863	9,731
1956	678	7,866	1,902	9,768
1957	678	7,929	1,889	9,818
1958	675	7,789	1,850	9,639
1959	668	7,756	1,868	9,623
1960	664	7,884	1,951	9,835
1961	646	7,905	1,992	9,897
1962	626	7,860	2,027	9,887
1963	607	7,859	2,075	9,934
1964	598	7,936	2,143	10,079
1965	583	7,973	2,208	10,181
1966	574	7,890	2,221	10,111
1967	555	7,724	2,246	9,970
1968	533	7,713	2,321	10,034
1969	508	7,841	2,460	10,302

Note: Membership figures have been rounded to the nearest 1,000; the sums of the constituent items may not, therefore, agree with the totals shown.
Source: Annual surveys of trade union membership published in the *Ministry of Labour Gazette* and, latterly, the *Employment and Productivity Gazette*.

Table 3. Stoppages of work due to industrial disputes in Great Britain and Northern Ireland, 1914–69

Year	Number of stoppages	Number of workers involved (000's)	Number of working days lost (000's)
1914	972	447	9,360
1915	672	448	2,970
1916	532	276	2,370
1917	730	872	5,870
1918	1,165	1,116	5,890
1919	1,352	2,591	36,330
1920	1,607	1,932	28,860
1921	763	1,801	82,270
1922	576	552	19,650

Table 3 (*continued*)

Year	Number of stoppages	Number of workers involved (000's)	Number of working days lost (000's)
1923	628	405	10,950
1924	710	613	8,360
1925	603	441	8,910
1926	323	2,734	161,300
1927	308	108	870
1928	302	124	1,390
1929	431	533	8,290
1930	422	307	4,450
1931	420	490	7,010
1932	389	379	6,440
1933	357	136	1,020
1934	471	134	1,060
1935	553	271	1,950
1936	818	316	2,010
1937	1,129	597	3,140
1938	875	274	1,330
1939	940	337	1,350
1940	922	299	940
1941	1,251	360	1,080
1942	1,303	456	1,530
1943	1,785	557	1,830
1944	2,194	821	3,700
1945	2,293	531	2,850
1946	2,205	526	2,180
1947	1,721	620	2,400
1948	1,759	424	1,940
1949	1,426	433	1,820
1950	1,339	302	1,380
1951	1,719	379	1,710
1952	1,714	415	1,800
1953	1,746	1,370	2,170
1954	1,989	448	2,480
1955	2,419	659	3,790
1956	2,648	507	2,050
1957	2,859	1,356	8,400
1958	2,629	523	3,470
1959	2,093	645	5,280
1960	2,832	817	3,050
1961	2,686	771	3,040
1962	2,449	4,420	5,780
1963	2,068	591	2,000

29

Table 3 (*continued*)

Year	Number of stoppages	Number of workers involved (000's)	Number of working days lost (000's)
1964	2,524	873	2,030
1965	2,354	869	2,930
1966	1,937	531	2,400
1967	2,116	732	2,780
1968	2,378	2,256	4,720
1969	3,116	1,656	6,930

Notes: (a) the figures relate to stoppages beginning in each year;
  (b) the figures for workers involved include those indirectly involved;
  (c) the figures for working days lost are rounded to the nearest 10,000.
Source: 1914–36, *Abstracts of Labour Statistics*; 1937–69, *Annual Abstracts of Statistics*.

Table 4. Stoppages of work due to industrial disputes in Great Britain and Northern Ireland, 1911–65; averages over certain periods

Period	Average number of stoppages per year	Average number of workers involved per stoppage	Average number of working days lost per stoppage
1911–18	905	862	11,757
1919–21	1,241	1,699	39,618
1922–28	493	985	56,951
1929–39	619	555	5,592
1940–45	1,625	310	1,223
1946–54	1,735	246	1,076
1955–65	2,505	267	1,030

Notes: (a) See notes (a) and (b) to Table 3.
  (b) Statistics relating to industrial stoppages are subject to bias by the effects of large-scale disputes in particular years. So that trends may be more accurately identified, the following stoppages have been excluded:
  1926—the General Strike (1·6 million workers involved, 15 million working days lost);
  1955—strike in engineering and shipbuilding (1·07 million workers involved in a one-day 'token' strike);
  1957—strikes in engineering and in shipbuilding (800,000 workers involved, 6·15 million working days lost);
  1959—strike in printing (120,000 workers involved, 3·5 million working days lost);
  1962—strikes in engineering and shipbuilding and in rail transport (3·8 million workers involved in one-day 'token' strikes).
Source: As for Table 3.

PART II

DOCUMENTS

SECTION I

OBJECTIVES AND FUNCTIONS

COMMENTARY

Objectives

In order to understand and predict the behaviour of organisations, it is necessary to be clear about their objectives. Complications arise when objectives vary at different levels, and this is certainly true of trade unions. However, bearing this qualification in mind, some guidance may be derived from statements made in legislation, in union rules, and in pronouncements by the T.U.C. and other organisations.

The classic statement of the objectives of trade unions is incorporated in a definition produced by Sidney and Beatrice Webb (1.1); although wider aims must be assumed in modern conditions, the essence is there. A statutory definition of a trade union, contained in the Trade Union Act 1913, took account of broader purposes, but was still restricted (2.1).[1] Statements in union rule books tend to be of a wider nature. The emphasis placed on different objectives varies considerably, according as to whether the union represents manual, white-collar or professional employees (3.1) (3.2) (3.3). Although a basic pattern is followed by most unions, there are many variations. Some unions specify policy aims at considerable length (3.4). The purposes of others are obviously influenced by special problems of their industries, e.g., those of the miners (3.5) and of the post office engineers (3.6). Many unions reveal their particular views on questions of optimum structure, desirable forms of industrial and economic organisation, etc. Thus the miners, already mentioned, are concerned to promote industrial unionism and the growth of the international trade union movement; they also advocate the public ownership of industries. The largest of the railwaymen's unions is likewise concerned with industrial unionism and public ownership (3.7). The Union of Post Office Workers also favours industrial unionism, and, until comparatively recently, sought a radical change in the extent of worker participation in the control of the industry (3.8).

Besides formal statements in their rules, unions generally present their objectives in more popular—and less idealistic—terms in their information booklets and organising literature; the services offered to members are

[1] For a definition proposed in section 59 of the Industrial Relations Bill 1970, see Document 88.2.

generally emphasised. The tone of such publications, and their points of emphasis, vary considerably (3.9) (3.10).

Federations of unions also publish objectives which, in scope and variety, parallel those of individual unions (64.1) (64.2) (65.1) (66.1).

The T.U.C., in its capacity as the central forum for British trade unionism, has frequently provided statements of the aims of the movement as a whole, these showing a considerable widening of scope over time (4.1) (4.2).

Functions

As the T.U.C. has pointed out (4.2), there can be no absolute distinction between the objectives and functions of trade unions. However, for purposes of exposition, separation of the two is justified.

COLLECTIVE BARGAINING[1]

Perhaps the most important function undertaken by trade unions is that of engaging in 'collective bargaining' (5.1). The principle of collective bargaining has been strongly supported by the International Labour Organisation, and Conventions, ratified by the United Kingdom, proclaim the right to organise and bargain collectively (6.1) (6.2). There are, in addition, certain statutes which demonstrate the desire of Parliament to support collective bargaining in, for example, nationalised industries (74.1). In 1969, in pursuance of this policy, the Labour Government announced its intention of providing means to facilitate the recognition of trade unions by employers for bargaining purposes (6.3).

In the United Kingdom collective agreements between unions and employers' associations have traditionally not been treated as legally binding contracts (7.1), and the merits of this position have frequently been endorsed (7.2) (7.3) (35.2). Collective bargaining, nonetheless, has operated within a powerful framework of conventions. For example, it has been declared invidious for one party to demand concessions of another as a prior condition of bargaining (8.1), or for pressure to be put upon individual members of a negotiating team, in their capacities as employers or workers, in order to win concessions (8.2).

The inter-war years brought a general development of collective bargaining at industry level. Considerable impetus was given by the reports of the Committee on Relations between Employers and Employed, under the chairmanship of the Rt. Hon. J. H. Whitley, which were published in 1917 and 1918. The name 'Whitley Councils' or 'Joint Industrial Councils' has been given to the industry-level bodies organised along lines suggested by the Committee (9.1). These have, as one of their basic principles, joint control of the mechanism of collective bargaining by the parties in the industry. Bargaining at industry level, however, has increasingly been supplemented by local bargaining, which is frequently autonomous, fragmented and informal (9.2).

A distinction may be drawn in collective bargaining between procedural and substantive content. The former relates to the processes to be followed

[1] In the Industrial Relations Bill 1970, various changes were proposed relating to the pre-conditions of collective bargaining and to the legal scope and status of collective agreements. See Document 88.1, in particular Parts II and III.

in the conduct of bargaining and the settlement of disputes, whilst the latter deals with actual terms and conditions of employment. While frequently a single bargain encompasses both elements, in some major industries separate agreements are struck. Many procedural agreements define an important role for a Joint Industrial Council. An example is to be found in the chemical industry (10.1). Other industries rely much more on *ad hoc* procedures, the practice adopted in the engineering industry being a celebrated case in point (10.2) (10.3). Procedure agreements are sometimes intended to deal with specific problems, for example, the resolution of demarcation disputes (10.4). An example of a substantive agreement shows the detailed regulation of wage rates, hours of work, and holidays, etc. which is customary (11.1).

The content of collective agreements has widened, especially since the Second World War. The emergence of productivity agreements, of which those at Fawley (12.1) are considered archetypes, has been of particular significance, with widespread ramifications for workers and unions (12.2). The basis upon which such bargains should be concluded in particular circumstances has been examined in a number of industries, for example, in chemicals (12.3). Productivity agreements have often been associated with a further development, namely, that of the agreement designed to last a specified period of time, for example, three years (12.4). Needless to say, the implications of this innovation have been carefully scrutinised by trade unions (12.5). Settlements containing provisions whereby workers receive compensation in the event of redundancy (12.6) (12.7) have increased in number. 'Fringe benefits', covering such matters as payment in the event of sickness (12.8), have also increasingly found their way into agreements. Another tendency has been the spread of 'check off' arrangements, whereby deductions of worker's trade union contributions are made by the employer at source (12.9).

There has thus evolved a system of collective bargaining which possesses considerable sophistication. However, its operation has been subject to criticism. Instances have been cited in which industry-level agreements appear to be of limited efficacy (13.1) (13.2), although it is clear that in considerable sections of British industry they are regarded as of considerable importance (13.3). The Royal Commission confirmed the widespread development of local bargaining, often informal, in many industries (7.2), and concluded that this, and the system of industry-level negotiations, were in conflict (14.1). The Commission called for reform of collective bargaining based on the formalisation and regularisation of industrial relations at local level (15.1). The industry-level agreement was by no means condemned, but it was suggested that it should be confined to those matters which it could effectively regulate. The Labour Government in its subsequent appraisal of industrial relations followed this advice.

SAFEGUARDING AND INCREASING EMPLOYMENT OPPORTUNITIES[1]

The control of entry into jobs, and the regulation of the manner in which they

[1] In the Industrial Relations Bill 1970, various changes were proposed affecting traditional methods. See Document 88.1, in particular Part II.

are undertaken, constitute two of the most important means whereby organised labour pursues its objectives. The resultant rules may be written or unwritten. Sometimes they are the result of agreements reached by the officials of a union and employers, or they may be imposed, with or without the support of employers and official union leadership, by groups of workers.

A powerful weapon to control the supply of labour to a job has been the device of the closed shop, two types of which may be distinguished, the 'pre-entry' and the 'post-entry' (16.1). Sometimes a closed shop is the subject of a written agreement between employers and employed; an example, relating to the post-entry closed shop, is found in the Scottish baking industry (16.2). Less formal undertakings, however, are more common (54.6). The closed shop can confer certain benefits, but it has been argued that it can diminish the freedom of individuals within or without the union, and that it has deleterious economic effects. Nonetheless, after considering its advantages and disadvantages, the Royal Commission refrained from recommending any fundamental interference with the practice. Certain safeguards for the individual were, however, proposed (16.3) (60.4). The view of the Labour Government, made clear in 1969, accorded with this line of reasoning (16.4). The T.U.C. encouraged its affiliates to adapt their rules if necessary (54.11).

Another method adopted to control job entry has lain in the fixing of the proportions of different types of workers to be employed on the job. Such a policy has been applied, for instance, to apprentices (16.5). Elaborate regulations may sometimes be found concerning the terms on which women can enter certain sections of industry, these not necessarily being expressed in terms of ratios but, for example, by reference to the wages required to be paid to women (16.6).

Within the confines of the job, many regulations can be enforced, designed to prevent available work being performed by fewer workers. There may, for example, be agreements governing the conditions under which payment by results systems may be introduced and operated (17.1). Again, overtime and shiftwork may be controlled, a guaranteed weekly wage negotiated (and therefore, in effect, a minimum working week ensured), and rules laid down as to the circumstances under a which worker may be transferred from one job to another (11.1). Agreements relating to redundancy (12.6) (12.7) are partly designed to discourage employers from a casual approach to the laying-off of labour. In certain industries, insistence on demarcation and other restraints on the utilisation of labour are long-established (17.2).

It has not been found easy to define 'restrictive practices', or to distinguish them from accepted areas of job regulation (17.3). Their existence, however, has been alleged in shipbuilding (17.2), printing (17.4) and the docks (17.5).

Restrictive practices can have complex origins and their removal is a formidable undertaking in which, it has been argued, Government and the parties concerned must all play a part (17.6). However a member of the Royal Commission, in a *Note of Reservation*, suggested the creation of a procedure whereby, in certain cases, monetary penalties could be imposed on either side of industry in the event of a failure to bargain effectively on the removal of restrictive practices (17.7). This view did not commend itself to the majority of the Royal Commission, who held that the proposed reform of collective bargaining would provide a preferable approach towards a more rational use of manpower (17.8).

THE USE OF THE STRIKE[1]

Sometimes the pursuit of trade union objectives entails the use of the strike. The terms 'trade dispute' and 'strike' have been given separate statutory definition (18.1) (86.7) (18.2) (18.3), although in common usage they have often been treated as coterminous. Attempts of a less formal nature have been made to classify strikes according as to whether they are official, unofficial or unconstitutional (18.4). The European Social Charter, which includes support for the principle of the right to strike, has been ratified by the United Kingdom (19.1).

Strike action is seldom entered upon lightly by a trade union, and rule books often stress, implicitly or explicitly, the desirability of finding a peaceful and honourable settlement with employers when differences arise (20.1). Provision is often made for a vote by the membership concerned upon the desirability of strike action, and for the control of such action to be placed in the hands of an elected body of the union (20.2) (55.5) (55.7). Regulations bearing on the conduct of strikes are also to be found in the rules of some federations, national (64.1) (64.2) (64.3) (66.1) and international (46.2), and in the Constitution of the T.U.C. (67.1).

A number of statutory restraints have been placed upon the use of the strike. A general restraint, intended to secure the safety of persons and property, was provided by the Conspiracy, and Protection of Property Act 1875 (21.1), whereby in certain circumstances a strike could be held to constitute a criminal offence. Another general restraint was embodied in the Emergency Powers Act 1920, as amended by the Emergency Powers Act 1964, (21.2) which, although not expressly restricting the right to strike, nonetheless could be made the source of regulations designed to diminish the effectiveness of a strike. Further general restraints followed the General Strike of 1926. The Trade Disputes and Trade Unions Act 1927 (21.3) was designed to make illegal such sympathetic action as had been demonstrated in the Strike. This Act was totally repealed in 1946. Under the terms of the Prices and Incomes Act 1966 (86.7), further general restrictions were made available, in this case to support the incomes policy adopted by the Government.

Specific restraints, applying to certain categories of workers, are also to be found. By the Conspiracy, and Protection of Property Act 1875, strikes by workers in gas and water undertakings could constitute criminal offences (21.4); similar restraints were later extended to workers in electricity (21.5). The employees of local or other public authorities were made subject to analogous restraints under the Trade Disputes and Trade Unions Act 1927 (21.6). The freedom of seamen in respect of strike action has also been circumscribed (21.7), and penalties have been introduced in respect of actions

[1] For some developments relating to the use of the strike after 1969, see Appendix, pp. 567, 569–70. In the Industrial Relations Bill 1970, various changes were proposed affecting strike action. Some existing legislation would be repealed, although much of its content would be re-enacted, and certain new restraints would be introduced. See Appendix, p. 571 and Document 88.1, in particular Parts V, VII and VIII.

37

designed to cause members of the police force to strike (21.8). A further instance of a specific restraint appeared in the Aliens Restriction (Amendment) Act 1919 (21.9), under which aliens in certain circumstances could be subject to penalties for promoting industrial unrest.

Further restraints have been imposed upon the tactics which may be used in industrial action. Checks were embodied in the Conspiracy, and Protection of Property Act 1875 (21.10), whilst, during the currency of the Trade Disputes and Trade Unions Act 1927, the law relating to the conduct of trade disputes was given a more rigorous application (21.11).

A number of legal safeguards for unions engaging in strike action were provided by the Conspiracy, and Protection of Property Act 1875 (22.1), and by the Trade Disputes Act 1906 (22.2). In 1965, the Trade Disputes Act (22.3) was passed to resolve an ambiguity regarding the protection afforded to unions.

The attitude of the State, in its capacity as a provider of social security, is one of neutrality. Thus, no person on strike by reason of a trade dispute is prejudiced in his use of employment exchange facilities (23.1). On the other hand, the provision of unemployment benefit to strikers is restricted, although in 'urgent cases' payment can be made (23.2). Under the Contracts of Employment Act 1963, a worker's right to receive a minimum period of notice could be jeopardised by his taking part in a strike in breach of contract (72.1); this disability was removed by the Redundancy Payments Act 1965. Nonetheless, the State has an obvious interest in preventing or settling disputes, and has at different times provided a variety of means to that end (75.1) (75.2) (75.3).

The problem of industrial disputes has long been the subject of scrutiny and debate. Shortly after the First World War, at a time of considerable industrial unrest, the Government convened an Industrial Conference. The Conference advocated the creation of a National Industrial Council, drawn from both sides of industry, to advise the Government on industrial questions. The prime causes of industrial unrest were felt to lie in such matters as unemployment, hours of work, and wages (24.1). However, a Memorandum submitted by trade union representatives suggested that the roots of discontent went far deeper (24.2). A few years later, in 1926, industrial unrest culminated in a General Strike which the Government maintained was directed against the constitution (24.3), a charge which the T.U.C. denied (24.4) (24.5). After the Strike the idea of a National Industrial Council was again mooted, this time in the course of a series of conferences held by the T.U.C. and representatives of certain employers; the conferences, generally called the 'Mond–Turner Conversations', discussed many other matters, such as unemployment, housing, and international economic policy (24.6).

At the time of the setting up of the Royal Commission of 1965–68, the problem of industrial unrest, and in particular the rising incidence of unofficial and unconstitutional strikes, had become the subject of renewed anxiety. The Commission's analysis of strikes was particularly devoted to the problem of the unofficial strike (25.1). The evidence of one major organisation, the Transport and General Workers' Union, stressed that strikers were not invariably irresponsible, nor employers always blameless (25.2), and the Commission in its Report confirmed the complexity of the factors underlying strikes in particular industries (25.3). The solution proposed was the reform of the system of collective bargaining; the use of legal sanctions was envisaged only as an emergency and *ad hoc* device (25.4).

The Labour Government's proposals were published in 1969. A considerable extension of legal intervention was contemplated. A mandatory 'conciliation pause', in which unconstitutional strikers would return to work and endeavours would be made to settle disputes, was proposed, as was a procedure whereby unions could be required to hold a ballot of their members before embarking on major official strikes. Collective agreements were to be made legally binding, but only by the wish of the parties concerned and by express permission in such agreements (25.5). Both the conciliation pause and the plan for ballots were subsequently dropped, largely due to trade union pressure. The T.U.C., however, agreed to initiate a scheme designed to reduce the incidence of unconstitutional strikes (25.6); the Constitution now incorporates these provisions (67.1).

BENEFIT AND WELFARE PROVISION

Practically all unions are concerned to raise and disburse money on benefit and welfare activities. The distinction may be said to lie between financial claims which are related to a member's subscription, and those which are not so related. The former category can include dispute benefit, unemployment benefit, sickness and accident benefit, and death benefit; examples of welfare activities are legal aid and educational services. The more prosperous unions of skilled workers have generally added superannuation, compensation for loss or damage to tools, and other items.

Although the development of the Welfare State has considerably reduced the need for certain of these services, many unions still attach great importance to them, especially in so far as they provide security for the worker (26.1). The content of benefit and welfare provision varies according as to whether the union caters for manual or white-collar workers (3.9) (26.2).

Conditions governing provision of benefits are stated with great care and at great length in most rule books, different grades of membership being entitled to pay different contributions and receive different treatment (27.1) (27.2). While a certain basic pattern is followed by most unions, many variants may be found. Thus the Transport and General Workers' Union provides convalescent-home benefit and 'distress' pay (28.1), and, until the rules revision of 1968, paid benefit for eviction from tied cottages (28.2); the Draughtsmen's and Allied Technicians' Association extended payment of dispute benefit to cases of 'victimisation' (28.3); the National Union of Boot and Shoe Operatives in 1967 still provided 'travelling assistance' (28.4); the National Union of Public Employees makes special provision for accidents involving loss of sight or limb (28.5); Division 1 of the Society of Graphical and Allied Trades, previously the National Society of Operative Printers and Assistants, provides for surgical appliances and medical consultancy and also gives 'marriage dowry' and special 'Christmas grants' (28.6); and the National Union of Railwaymen provides for orphans of deceased members (28.7).

On the welfare side, certain unions give particular attention to education

39

for union members and, sometimes, their families (29.1) (29.2) (29.3), and to legal services (29.4). Emphasis is frequently placed on the importance of publications (29.5). The T.U.C. is also extremely concerned with the advancement of trade union education (67.2), and spends considerable sums in promotional effort (67.3).

Some of the largest unions collect and spend very considerable sums in connection with benefit and welfare activities; a case in point is the Transport and General Workers' Union (30.1). However, on average, income and expenditure on a *per capita* basis are modest (30.2).

SHARING IN CONTROL OF INDUSTRY

Unions have attempted, in various ways, to increase the degree of worker participation in the control of industry. This aim is clearly stated in the rule books of a number of unions (3.1) (3.4), and in those of some federations (64.1) (64.2). The T.U.C. has frequently listed increased participation as an objective of the trade union movement (4.1) (4.2) (67.1), and has presented an argued case (31.1).

Different methods whereby "workers' control" might be obtained have been canvassed. One approach was that of syndicalism, fashionable around the time of the First World War, which, in the British context, implied that workers in particular industries should take over and administer the means of production. This theory was associated with notions of industrial unionism (49.1) and with 'direct action' (the strike) as a means of overthrowing the existing system (32.1). Another viewpoint was represented by Guild Socialism which, whilst being similar to syndicalism in respect of worker control of industry (3.8), nonetheless placed stress upon democratic and orderly change (32.2); it also sought to retain the State as owner of the means of production and defender of consumer interests. Neither of these radical forms of "workers' control" made much headway. However, modest success has attended other schemes which are less explicitly revolutionary in their aims, such as producers' co-operatives (33.1), co-partnership and profit-sharing (33.2). The demand for nationalisation was in part the reflection of a desire by workers to achieve a measure of control over their industries (34.1) (34.2); the massive programme implemented between 1945 and 1951 gave a good deal of experience of, and rapidly diminishing enthusiasm for, this expedient.

By the late 1950s, unions' demands for "workers' control" generally meant little more than insistence on the right to be consulted on appropriate matters (35.1). Joint consultation itself has had a considerable history. Deriving from the reports of the Committee on Relations between Employers and Employed, the 'Whitley Committee' (35.2), (9.1) which placed particular emphasis on the desirability of joint consultation at workshop level (35.3), it has taken many different forms (35.4). Joint Production Committees established during the Second World War, although more specifically concerned with productivity matters, were in the same tradition (80.1). In various nationalisation acts of the years 1946–51 the Government gave further encouragement to developments in the public sector (74.1); a particularly impressive response was obtained from the coal mining industry (35.5).

40

Of recent years, the T.U.C. and the Labour Party have shown a marked revival of interest in a more active form of worker participation, even arguing for worker-directors on boards of enterprises (36.1) (36.2). An interesting experiment in this direction was introduced upon the re-nationalisation of the iron and steel industry in 1967 (36.3). Much less enthusiasm for worker participation, as an important constituent of any ideal system of industrial relations, has been shown by employers in the private sector (37.1). The Labour Government of the late 1960s, while favouring experiments in appointing worker representatives to the boards of undertakings, placed decidedly more emphasis on improved collective bargaining in promoting worker participation (37.2).

POLITICAL ACTIVITIES

Trade unions have long realised the importance of political activity, local and national, and most unions, in their rules or general literature, state political objectives in broad terms (3.2) (3.5) (3.7) (3.9). The T.U.C. has expressed similar aims (4.2) (67.1), and has made more specific statements on purpose, methods and expected benefits (38.1).

The right to engage in political activities, on certain conditions, was clearly laid down in the Trade Union Act 1913 (39.1). The conditions were changed, in such a way as to make the financing of political activity more difficult, by the Trade Disputes and Trade Unions Act 1927; by the same measure, restrictions were placed on the political activities of certain classes of worker (39.2). The pre-1927 position was restored by the Trade Disputes and Trade Unions Act 1946. The Chief Registrar of Friendly Societies[1] issued a set of model rules, suggesting how the legal conditions governing the raising and disbursing of political funds should be stated, and most unions adopted the prescribed form (39.3).

Information on income raised and payments made for political purposes is available from annual returns made by trade unions under the Trade Union Act 1913 (40.1). The larger unions raise substantial sums, and indulge in considerable political activity, including the direct sponsoring of Members of Parliament (41.1) (41.2).

The trade union movement's links with the Labour Party, in respect of constitutional power (42.1), membership (42.2), and finance (42.3), are strong. The T.U.C. provides one-third of the representatives on the National Council of Labour, a body designed to co-ordinate the political activities of Congress, the Labour Party, and the Co-operative Union. The relationship with the Labour Party, though secure, is not without its stresses, potential and actual (42.4) (42.5). The T.U.C. has frequently voted in support of resolutions opposed to Party policy, even on issues as important as nuclear disarmament and the extension of public ownership (42.6).

SERVING AS AGENCIES FOR COMMENTARY ON CONTEMPORARY ISSUES

Trade unions have always been concerned to promote working class interests

[1] A new office of Chief Registrar of Trade Unions and Employers' Associations was proposed in Part IV of the Industrial Relations Bill 1970. See Document 88.1.

in political, economic and social matters by public commentary. Although statements are frequently made by individual unions in their journals and other literature (43.1) (43.2), a more authoritative platform is provided through resolutions submitted to the annual Trades Union Congress (42.6). The T.U.C. itself, however, is the main, and most influential, source of commentary (44.1) (44.2) (44.3) (44.4).

INTERNATIONAL ACTIVITIES

British trade unionism has made important contributions to the international working class movement. International activity is sometimes included among the objectives of individual unions (3.5), although specific statements of aims have usually been left to the T.U.C. (45.1) (67.1). Some unions have maintained overseas sections (46.1), and most of the larger unions are members of International Trade Secretariats (46.2). The T.U.C. supplies British trade unionism's representation on the International Confederation of Free Trade Unions (47.1). The Confederation's formal arrangements with the International Trade Secretariats (47.1) (47.2) provide opportunities for indirect participation in its affairs by individual British unions. The T.U.C. also provides representation of the British movement on the International Labour Organisation (47.3), the current aims and purposes of which are set out in detail in the celebrated 'Declaration of Philadelphia' (47.4). Congress exercises a watching brief on trade union developments overseas, and devotes a substantial proportion of its revenues to promoting trade unionism in developing countries (47.5) (67.2) (67.3).

DOCUMENTS

Objectives

1 The traditional view

1.1 Webb, S. J. and Webb, B., *The History of Trade Unionism* Revised edition (London, Longmans, 1920), p. 1

A Trade Union, as we understand the term, is a continuous association of wage-earners for the purpose of maintaining or improving the conditions of their working lives.[1]

[1] In the 1894 edition of *The History of Trade Unionism* the definition had 'employment' in place of 'working lives'; this was changed in the 1920 edition, because of the implication that trade unions contemplated a perpetual continuance of the capitalist or wage system; but the intention of the 1894 edition was that of the 1920 wording.

2 The legal view

2.1 Trade Union Act 1913[1]

1. (1) The fact that a combination has under its constitution objects or powers other than statutory objects within the meaning of this Act shall not prevent the combination being a trade union . . . so long as the combination is a trade union as defined by this Act, and, subject to the provisions of this Act as to the furtherance of political objects, any such trade union shall have power to apply the funds of the union for any lawful objects or purposes for the time being authorised under its constitution.

(2) For the purposes of this Act, the expression "statutory objects" means . . . the regulation of the relations between workmen and masters, or between workmen and workmen, or between masters and masters, or the imposing of restrictive conditions on the conduct of any trade or business, and also the provision of benefits to members.

2. (1) The expression "trade union" . . . means any combination, whether temporary or permanent, the principal objects of which are under its constitution statutory objects: Provided that any combination which is for the time being registered[2] as a trade union shall be deemed to be a trade union as defined by this Act so long as it continues to be so registered.

3 Statements by individual unions

3.1 Amalgamated Society of Woodworkers, *Rules* 1964 (as amended to 1965)

PREFACE

. . . . . .

THE Amalgamated Society of Woodworkers has for its primary object the

---

[1] For changes proposed in the Industrial Relations Bill 1970, see Appendix, p. 571.

[2] By the Trade Union Act 1871 a union, 'registered' with the Registrar of Friendly Societies, acquired certain minor privileges. 'The advantages of registration under the Act are not of great importance and no serious detriment is suffered by non-registration. The chief advantage, perhaps, is that a registered trade union is entitled in certain circumstances to exemption from income tax in respect of interest and dividends applicable and applied solely for the purpose of provident benefits. For the rest, the advantages are largely administrative. For example, on a change of trustees the land and other property of the union which is vested in them (other than stock in the public funds) automatically vest in the new trustees without the necessity for a conveyance or transfer. There are summary remedies available to a registered union for the recovery of its property and effects from treasurers and other officers and from any person obtaining possession of union funds, books or other effects by fraud. A registered union may sue and be sued in its own name.' [Royal Commission on Trade Unions and Employers' Associations 1965–1968, *Report* (Cmnd. 3623) 1968, para. 789.] For changes in registration procedure proposed in Part IV of the Industrial Relations Bill 1970, see Document 88.1.

raising of the status of the artisans engaged in these trades, and generally to improve the social conditions under which they labour.

Trade unions are acknowledged now, by most writers on Industrial History and the general public, as important and essential factors in the life of a community. The experience of the past has proved that the best security which can be furnished for the rule of reason in trade negotiations, and the due observance of covenants entered into for regulating conditions of employment, is a well-conducted union of operatives, strong in numbers.

The growth of science and mechanical invention, together with ever-increasing specialised processes, and the changes arising from the continual introduction of new and substitute materials, with the growing fluctuations in employment, demands that labour should solidly unite for its mutual protection and support. Every operative in a given occupation has an interest in common with those similarly engaged in forming regulations by which that particular industry should be governed. It is necessary, moreover, in order to continue progress and provide against contingencies that may arise in times of trade depression, that there should be a connecting link between all members of a trade, and this can only be efficiently obtained through a trade union.

In many other directions membership in a trade union is beneficial. Principles of independence and self-reliance are thereby inculcated. We are taught the prudence of self-denial to-day in order that we may secure to ourselves and others greater advantages to-morrow. The provision of funds available for the support of unemployed, sick, disabled, infirm and superannuated members, and affording aid to families bereaved by death, must appeal to all. It will further be admitted that those who, by foresight and self-denial, make such provision for themselves and families in times of distress, or old age, contribute to their social comfort and intellectual advancement. An active interest also in the affairs of a trade union, calling for adherence to rule and discipline, tends to a knowledge of business principles which qualify members desirous of obtaining positions of responsibility and trust.

. . . .

RULE 1
NAME, OBJECTS, AND CONSTITUTION

. . . . . .

2. The principal objects of the society are to promote the social and economic advancement of the members and of workers generally, and industrially the regulation of relations between workpeople and employers and between workers and workers, and also the provision of benefits to members as may be provided in these rules.

The organisation into membership of joiners, carpenters, cabinet makers and other operatives engaged in woodworking and allied processes, and such workers as may be deemed eligible by the Executive Council in accordance with the following rules, and the obtaining and maintaining of just and proper hours of work, rates of wages, and working conditions in whatever industry they are employed.

The settling and negotiating of differences and disputes between the mem-

44

bers of the society and employers, and other trade unions and persons by collective bargaining or agreement, withdrawal of labour, or otherwise.

The provision of benefits to members as follows:

(i) Assistance to members, or particular classes of members, (1) when out of employment or in distressed circumstances; (2) in cases of sickness, accident and disablement; (3) in old age; (4) in trade disputes; (5) for funeral expenses; (6) such other forms of assistance as may from time to time be decided by the society or the Executive Council.

(ii) Legal advice and legal assistance to the society or its members . . .

(iii) The provision of educational facilities, including scholarships to members and the making of grants and endowments to the colleges or institutions having among their objects the education of trade unionists.

The furtherance of political objects.

The furtherance of, or participation, financial or otherwise, directly or indirectly, in the work or purpose of any association or federal body having for its objects the furthering of the interests of labour, trade unionism, or trade unionists, including the securing of a real measure of control in industry and participation by the workers in the management, in the interests of labour and the general community.

The furthering of any other action or purpose, or the participation, financial or otherwise, directly or indirectly, in any other purpose, so far as may be lawful, which is calculated, in the opinion of the society or the Executive Council, to further the interests of labour, trade unionism, or trade unionists.

In order to achieve the above objects the society shall have the power, in addition to any other powers given them by law or by these rules, to impose such restraints upon the labour of its members, or generally to interfere, whether such interference is in restraint of trade or not, but so far only as may otherwise be lawful, with the trade or conduct of such industries, businesses, and occupations as may be deemed expedient.

3.2 National and Local Government Officers' Association, *Constitution and Rules* 1967

3. The objects for which the Association is established are:

(a) To organize the whole of the officers in all departments of each and every service.

(b) To improve the conditions and protect the interests of the Association's members by collective bargaining, agreement, withdrawal of labour, or otherwise.

(c) To regulate the relations between such members and between them and their employers.

(d) To do all such things as may from time to time be considered necessary or advisable to promote, safeguard, maintain or improve the interests and status of officers and each and every service.

(e) To give active support to any member in any cause or matter affecting the rights and interests of officers.

(f) To give to the legislature, government departments and others, facilities for conferring with, and ascertaining the views of, persons engaged or interested in each and every service, and to confer or co-operate with government departments and employing authorities in regard to each and every service and officers.

(g) To consider all Bills presented to, and all questions raised in, Parliament affecting the interests of officers.

(h) To introduce such parliamentary or other measures, from time to time as may be deemed advisable for promoting and securing the interest of officers and each and every service.

(j)[1] To diffuse information upon any matters affecting each and every service and officers in such ways as may be thought desirable.

(k) To establish and support schemes of an economic character, whereby provision may be made for financial assistance to members and their dependants in the event of sickness or death and to encourage thrift, life assurance, and schemes of a similar nature . . .

(l) To assist necessitous members or their dependants, and the widows and children or other dependants of deceased members, in such ways as may be thought desirable.

(m) To provide and maintain educational facilities, to hold examinations, and to grant diplomas.

(n) To promote, maintain and support schemes for the physical and social welfare of members, by the organization of sports or such other means as may from time to time be thought desirable.

(o) To do all such things as may from time to time be considered necessary or advisable to promote, safeguard, maintain or improve the status or influence of the Association, its district councils and branches.

(p) To make contributions to non-political bodies or public charities.

(q) To do all such other lawful things as are incidental or conducive to the attainment of the above objects, or any of them.

3.3 Association of Scientific Workers,[2] *Rules* 1967

3. The objects of the Association shall be:—

A1. To develop a professional organisation of qualified men and women.

A2. To watch over, promote, and protect the common and individual interests of its members, and to regulate the relations between members and employers, and between individual members, or with regard to the classification of members, and for that purpose to impose all such professional conditions as may be considered expedient.

A3. To provide legal protection for members . . .

A4. To secure to members the benefits which may be allowed by the rules for the time being in force.

A5. To set up an employment bureau.

A6. To set up a register of places of employment . . .

B1. To promote the development of Science in all its aspects and to maintain the honour and interests of the scientific profession.

[1] The Association does not use the letter (i) in its Rules.

[2] In 1968 the A.Sc.W. joined with the Association of Supervisory Staffs, Executives and Technicians to form the Association of Scientific, Technical and Managerial Staffs.

46

B2. To secure that the practice of science for remuneration shall be restricted by law to persons possessing adequate qualifications; and to co-operate with those bodies legally empowered to grant certificates of qualification in order that high standards of professional competence may be established and maintained.

B3. To secure representation upon such public and other bodies as may affect by their policy the interest of science and its profession.

B4. To further, or participate in, financially, or otherwise directly or indirectly, the work or purpose of any association or federal body having for its objects the furthering of the interests of science and its profession.

B5. To secure the wider application of science and the scientific method for the welfare of society.

B6. To secure in the interests of national efficiency that all groups of scientific and technical workers in the public service, in industry, and in the academic world, shall normally be under the immediate supervision of persons of adequate scientific and technical attainments.

B7. To extend and improve scientific and technical education and the professional training of those seeking to become fully qualified scientific or technical workers.

B8. To promote and encourage scientific research in all its branches.

B9. To obtain adequate endowment for research, and to advise as to the administration of such endowment.

B10. To provide financial assistance to members who have withdrawn their labour with the authority of the Executive Committee, or who are locked out as a result of a dispute with their employer, or who are able to prove to the satisfaction of the Executive Committee that they have lost their employment through action taken in the interests of the Association, the Executive Committee deciding what allowances shall be paid in such cases.

B11. To pursue the furtherance of political objects . . .

3.4 National Union of Boot and Shoe Operatives, *Rules* 1967

3. The objects of the Union shall be to secure the complete organisation of all workers . . . to regulate the relations between employee and employer and between employee and employee, and to use all legitimate means for the moral, social, educational, economic and political advancement of its members.

4. The objects of the Union shall further include:—

   (*a*) The establishment of branches and districts throughout Great Britain and Northern Ireland, together with the appointment of full-time branch officers wherever practicable.

   (*b*) The establishment of Boards of Conciliation and Arbitration in all Centres.

   (*c*) The establishment of healthy and proper workshops above ground level: the employer to find room, grindery, fixtures, heat, light and tools, free of charge, and the abolition of all home employment by parliamentary effort or otherwise.

   (*d*) The establishment of a minimum wage rate throughout the Union . . . to apply to all employed in the industry, regardless of sex.

47

(e) The establishment of a guaranteed working week of 35 hours, and the minimum condition of a week's notice on either side in all employment contracts, subject to the provisions of the Contracts of Employment Act, 1963, together with the total abolition of overtime and of all minute notice contracts.

(f) The establishment of 24 days holiday per year with pay for all operatives. . . .

(g) The establishment of a Central Fund for the industrial protection of members and advancement of wages; to raise such other funds as may be necessary for the mutual support of members in times of unemployment, sickness, and for the burial of deceased members and their wives, and to assist members who may be compelled to travel in search of employment.

(h) The establishment and adoption, as far as possible, as a permanent policy of the Union, of the system of piecework quantity statements, supplementary wages or payment by results, and to seek to embody these principles in all districts, and in present and future agreements, awards or decisions.

(i) To control the number of apprentices, and to fix for them a standard rate of wages . . . and do our utmost to ensure adequate training facilities by the employers.

(j) To secure legal enforcement of all National Conference[1] Agreements.

(k) To federate or amalgamate with other trade unions in Great Britain and Northern Ireland having similar objects and to establish a system of intercommunication with boot and shoe operatives of other countries.

(l) To persuade members to refuse to work with non-unionists, when all reasonable argument has failed, and to advocate unfettered recognition by the Employers' Federation that the only safe guarantee of peace in the industry is membership of the Union.

(m) To advocate that all raw materials and component parts used in the manufacture of boots and shoes must be produced under conditions no worse than those governing the industry. . .

(n) To issue a list of manufacturers whom the Union can recommend to buyers, and a list of retailers who deal in goods we can recommend to the general public as being produced under fair and proper conditions.

(o) To advocate the use of a trade union stamp by manufacturers and repairers to indicate that all goods bearing such stamp are made by trade unionists under fair conditions of labour.

(p) To make provision for the Union being represented in Parliament by members, who shall pledge themselves to work for the realisation of the Union's objects, and carry out the decisions of the Trades Union Congress and the Labour Party. . .

(q) To advocate the socialisation of the means of production, to be controlled by a democratic State in the interests of the entire community,

[1] Meetings of representatives of the employers' federation and the Union to settle terms and conditions of employment.

and the complete emancipation of labour from the domination of capitalism and landlordism, with the establishment of a social and economic equality between the sexes.

(*r*) To use all legitimate means and funds to further the extension of Old Age Pensions by the State, by reducing the age limit and increasing the allowance, and to advocate free Secular and Further Education, at the cost of the State, from the Primary School to the University.

(*s*) To seek to establish a Superannuation Scheme covering all work-people in the industry.

(*t*) The establishment of adequate compensation to workers declared redundant.

(*u*) To seek the establishment of a transferable non-contributory Sickness Payments Scheme for the Industry.

3.5 National Union of Mineworkers, *Rules* 1962 (as amended to 1969)

3. The objects of the Union shall be:—

(*a*) To secure the complete organisation in the Union of all workers employed in or connected with the Coal Mining Industry of Great Britain, and membership of the organisation shall be a condition of employment in the industry.

. . . .

(*e*) To promote legislation in the interests of members and the Coal Mining Industry.

. . . .

(*g*) To employ and organise the appointment of persons on the work-men's behalf to make inspection under the provisions of the Coal Mines Act, 1911 (and any other enactments which may be for the time being in force) or in pursuance of any agreement or arrangement with mineowners or association of mineowners of any coal mines.

(*h*) To represent members of the Union and the interests of the Coal Mining Industry before and present evidence and information to Government, Parliamentary, Municipal, Local Government, Official and other Commissions, Committees and bodies of Enquiry or Investigation or authorities.

(*i*) To assist members or their dependants in obtaining compensation for accidents under the Workmen's Compensation Acts which are now or may hereafter be in operation, or at Common Law, and to contest any legal question affecting the interest of members or their dependants or the Coal Mining Industry.

. . . .

(*o*) To contribute from the funds of the Union to any International Trade Union Movement.

. . . .

(*r*) To seek the establishment of Public ownership and Control of the mining industry.

49

(s) To promote and secure the passing of legislation for improving the condition of the members and ensuring them a guaranteed week's wage with protective clauses for the miners even when they cease work, when cessation is due to causes beyond the immediate control of the members, and to join in with other organisations for the purpose of and with the view to the complete abolition of Capitalism.

3.6 Post Office Engineering Union, *Rules* 1964

RULE 3

1. The objects for which the Union is established are:—

. . . .

(vii) To give such (if any) assistance as the Executive Council in its absolute discretion thinks fit to fully paid-up members of the Union in prosecutions for offences under the Road Traffic Act, 1930, or under any Regulations made thereunder or under any Statute amending the same, providing that such member at the time of the alleged offence was driving a Post Office vehicle and was so driving it while in the course of his employment on Post Office duty and was in no way deviating from that course.

(viii) To give such assistance as the Executive Council in its absolute discretion thinks fit to the representative or representatives of fully paid-up members of the Union in the conduct of proceedings at Coroners' Inquests, appropriate assistance to be given also to the representative or representatives of members in Scotland.

(ix) To give such (if any) assistance as the Executive Council in its absolute discretion thinks fit to fully paid-up members of the Union, or their representative or representatives, in cases arising directly or indirectly from their employment, and in cases arising while travelling to their places of employment from their normal places of residence, and while travelling from their places of employment to their normal places of residence.

3.7 National Union of Railwaymen, *Rules* 1965 (as amended to 1968)

RULE 1

4. (a) The objects of the Union shall be to secure the complete organisation of all workers employed by any Board, Company or Authority in connection with railways and other transport and ancillary undertakings thereto . . . To work for the supersession of the capitalist system by a Socialistic order of society. . . . To amalgamate and pay the expenses of amalgamation with any other union whose objects are similar to or of a kindred nature with the objects of this Union . . .

3.8 Union of Post Office Workers, *Programme, Rules and Standing Orders* 1953

2. The objects of the Union shall be:—

. . . .

(c) To encourage the amalgamation into one Union of all Post Office Associations with objects similar to those of the Union of Post Office Workers.

(d) The organisation of Post Office workers into a comprehensive industrial Union with a view to the service being ultimately conducted and managed as a Guild.[1]

3.9 Transport and General Workers' Union, *Members Handbook* 1966, pp. 41–46, 49–50

THE UNION AT WORK

The first . . . important task of our Union is to organise the workers in the trades and occupations which it covers. . . . There is, however, much more in organising than merely enrolling members. . . . It means building up an efficient organisation in which all members have the opportunity of helping to achieve the Union's objects.

One of the most obvious things which the Union does to assist its members is to provide cash benefits in times of dispute, victimisation, sickness and accident, funeral benefit, and so on. It is true that the need for dispute and victimisation benefit is less marked than it was in the days of the pioneers, and that there are State schemes in operation in the field of sickness and accident. Even the best State schemes can usefully be supplemented, however, and it is as well to remember that the trade unions were the first, not only to stress the necessity for such provisions, but also to show by practical example what could be done.

Another great service provided by the Union for its members is what is loosely called "legal aid." Assistance is given to members in connection with matters arising out of their employment. For instance, many of the occupations in which our members are engaged are highly dangerous, though every effort is made by the Union to introduce safety measures. Wherever there is evidence that the employer or some other party has been negligent, the Union does not hesitate to press a claim for an injured member. . . . Where necessary, cases are taken from the High Court to the Court of Appeal, and even to the House of Lords. A large number of cases reaching the department are concerned with accidents at work, but others arise out of claims to unemployment or other National Insurance Benefits, disputes about payment for work done, or wages in lieu of notice, claims arising from alleged wrongful dismissal, claims arising out of road transport law, etc. . . .

. . . .

[1] For an example of a form of guild, see Document 32.2.

The Legal Department is also concerned to watch the incidence of Industrial Diseases and the development of safety measures in Industry generally. . . .

. . . .

Our Union provides a variety of educational facilities to assist active lay members. Of primary importance is the Union's own home study course, describing the history, structure and functions of the Union. Correspondence courses in subjects like industrial relations, economics and statistics for trade unionists organised by the Trades Union Congress are also available. A Basic Training Programme of one-day and week-end schools is run by our Regions. . . . In conjunction with the W.E.A.[1] our Regions have embarked on a new enterprise of Diploma Classes in Labour Statistics and Industrial Relations. One-week residential branch officers' training courses are held by the Union each summer for branch chairmen, secretaries, shop stewards and other active lay members. Selected students from these courses are then sent to the T.U.C. Training College for a one- or two-week "follow-on" course. A few full-time scholarships are awarded for one-year courses at Ruskin College, the London School of Economics, Fircroft College, Hillcroft College and Coleg Harlech. All the Union's educational facilities are available free of charge to the student, and suitable allowances are given where applicable. Every member can take advantage of the courses, provided he is keen to learn and possesses the requisite membership qualifications. . . .

Of very great help to a large number of members is the convalescent home service of the Union. Members in need of rest and recuperation after illness receive a fortnight's treatment free of all cost and have their rail fares paid. . . .

No account of the work of the Union, however brief, can ignore the vital importance of political action. Our Union pays affiliation fees to the Labour Party, locally and nationally, and gives financial assistance to selected Members of Parliament and prospective candidates and their constituencies. These Members of Parliament perform their ordinary parliamentary duties as Labour Members and, in addition, assist the Union on matters which come before Parliament . . . Many members of the Union also engage in political activities as members of local authorities and of the Labour Party. . . .

. . . .

We now come to perhaps the most important job of all those which our Union does. This is the maintaining and improving of the conditions of our members' working lives, by means of collective bargaining. Trade unions have had a hard fight for the right to do this, and the struggle is not yet over. Employers do not easily surrender the power to lay down whatever conditions they choose, secure in the knowledge that if they make separate agreements with individual workers it will be on a "take it or leave it" basis. . . .

. . . .

The officers and staff of the Union have a very heavy responsibility in connection with the proper discharge of the various functions described above. Unless these officers and members of the staff are sufficient in number, highly trained and of great skill and energy, the Union will certainly not be able to give the best possible service to its members.

[1] Workers' Educational Association.

But the services described do not depend for their effectiveness on the work of the officers and staff alone. On the contrary, every member has a right to these services, and it follows, therefore, that each has the duty of sharing in the work necessary to provide and maintain them. . . .

3.10 Association of Scientific, Technical and Managerial Staffs, Advertisement in *The Times* November 27th 1968

"THE BOARD AND I HAVE DECIDED WE DON'T LIKE THE COLOUR OF YOUR EYES."

It's not usually as brutal as that.

Usually, there's a polite phrase about a 'clash of personalities'.

But the end result is the same. A man gets the push because his face doesn't fit.

It could only happen at one level in British industry—the top.

Managers and executives in Britain today are working under conditions the workers wouldn't tolerate.

Most of them don't have any kind of service agreement.

They work long hours without overtime. Their pension schemes restrict their movement from job to job.

Taxation blunts their initiative. Mergers can leave them in middle-age out of a job. With a past, but no future.

Thrombosis claims more of them than it does of any other working sector.

. . . .

You may not know it, but the Prices and Incomes Board[1] is shortly going to review executive and managerial salaries.

Your salary. Your future.

When it's done, it'll pass its recommendations on to the Government for action.

Before that happens, we think somebody ought to speak on your behalf. And that somebody is going to be us.

The Association of Scientific, Technical and Managerial Staffs will be presenting evidence to the Board, arguing for a revaluation of your status and salary.

Amongst our 100,000 members, we have more than 8,000 managers in British industry.

But we know we'll be speaking for a lot more people than that.

Some of the problems we want to discuss will be sickeningly familiar to you.

Salaries. Should you get increases on a regular basis? Should there be a minimum amount? Or must how well *you* do always depend on how well your firm does?

Extra duties. Should you get extra money? Extra leave? Is there a difference between the odd occasion and systematic overtime, like weekend work?

[1] National Board for Prices and Incomes.

Holidays. Considering the responsibilities of your job, do you get enough time away from it?

Contracts. Is an agreement necessary? Need it be in writing?

Inventions. Do they belong to you or the company?

Publications. Should companies stop you publishing the results of original work?

Dismissal. What's fair compensation for loss of your job? If 'misconduct' is alleged, who should judge whether it's true or not?

Restrictive covenants. Should an executive leaving a job be prevented from working for a competitor?

Until these, and many more questions are answered, we can't see how anyone can make a fair assessment of your position.

And it's vital that the assessment is fair.

· · · · · · · ·

We think it important that we speak up for *all* executives and managers. Not just our members.

Because if we don't, who will?

4 Statements by the Trades Union Congress

4.1 General Council of the Trades Union Congress, *Interim Report on Post-War Reconstruction*[1] 1944

THE OBJECTIVES OF THE TRADE UNION MOVEMENT

20. We think it necessary at the outset of our report to set out at least the main objectives of the Trade Union Movement which bear on the formulation of its economic policy.

21. The first of these is unquestionably that of maintaining and improving wages, hours and conditions of labour. This in itself relates to more than rates of wages or earnings measured in monetary terms or other payments and conditions settled by collective bargaining. We are also concerned with what wages can buy—with the cost of living and the general level of prices. We are in fact concerned with increasing the size of the real national income and with the share of it which should accrue to workpeople in terms of goods and services, conditions of work and leisure, as well as opportunities for individual and social development.

22. Secondly, the Trade Union Movement is concerned with the opportunities which exist for the worker to obtain work. "Full employment" is an aim which the Trade Unions have always pursued. It must be emphasised, however, that the "right to work" which the Trade Unions have sought to establish, is not merely a claim for a job of any kind. We are concerned to

[1] Published as Appendix D of the *Trades Union Congress Report* 1944 (London, Trades Union Congress, 1944).

54

ensure that every worker shall be able, within limits determined only by the need to safeguard the reasonable freedom of others, to choose freely work which he prefers and for which he is trained at rates of wages and in conditions commensurate with his skill and the nature of the work.

23. Thirdly, the Trade Union Movement exists to extend the influence of workpeople over the policies and purposes of industry and to arrange for their participation in its management.

. . . .

25. The General Council wish to re-emphasise the view which has been expressed in previous statements of policy issued by the T.U.C. that it is only within a system of public control that much of what is implied in the above objectives can be fulfilled.

4.2 Trades Union Congress, *Trade Unionism*[1] 2nd edition (London, Trades Union Congress, 1967)

TRADE UNION OBJECTIVES

93 Because they are adaptable to changing external circumstances, trade union objectives are always changing, yet in another sense they always remain the same. There are in fact many different senses in which the phrase "trade union objectives" can be used. There are objectives which are capable of achievement once and for all, those which can be met but which are immediately replaced by new ones, and there are those which are of such a nature that they can be termed permanent objectives, though their precise connotation will alter as the years go by. . . .

94 Several kinds of continuing objectives can be distinguished. These are to some extent complementary and there is always a choice to be made as to which broad objective is to be given the greatest emphasis at any given time. This problem of priorities is inseparable from one of the most important facets of trade union function, that of providing a means whereby working people can discuss and decide which objective corresponds to the greatest degree of common interest among them at a given time.

95 The trade union Movement, comprising a whole spectrum of occupations from musicians to doctors, miners to shopworkers, obviously cannot formulate even a general list of objectives which are equally relevant to the competence of all its constituent unions or to the needs of all their members.

96 To attempt to set out the objectives of trade unions as a whole is to describe these objectives in a way which no individual union and no individual trade unionist might find entirely adequate or satisfactory. It is perhaps for this reason that the Webbs, when writing the definitive work of their time, did not describe trade union objectives at all explicitly but stated simply that a trade union was "a continuous association of wage earners for the purpose

[1] The evidence of the Trades Union Congress to the Royal Commission on Trade Unions and Employers' Associations.

55

of improving the condition of their working lives."[1] This remains a valid statement of trade unions' central purpose. . .

97 These objectives can be distinguished as follows:
- (i) improved terms of employment
- (ii) improved physical environment at work
- (iii) full employment and national prosperity
- (iv) security of employment and income
- (v) improved social security
- (vi) fair shares in national income and wealth
- (vii) industrial democracy
- (viii) a voice in government
- (ix) improved public and social services
- (x) public control and planning of industry.

98 It will be seen that these objectives are of many different kinds. Some do not concern employment as such but are nevertheless common objectives of employed persons. Again, some may be termed substantive in nature and others more concerned with the way in which things are done. There can be no absolute distinction however between methods and objectives. All these objectives are seen as the means to the good life, which is the ultimate objective in all of them.

Functions

COLLECTIVE BARGAINING

5 Definition[2]

5.1 Ministry of Labour, *Industrial Relations Handbook* Revised edition (London, H.M.S.O., 1961), p. 18

The term 'collective bargaining' is applied to those arrangements under which wages and conditions of employment are settled by a bargain, in the form of an agreement made between employers or associations of employers and workers' organisations.

[1] This is a paraphrase of the quotation contained in Document 1.1.

[2] For a definition proposed in section 158 (1) of the Industrial Relations Bill 1970, see Document 88.2.

6 Bargaining rights

6.1 International Labour Conference, *Convention (No. 87) Concerning Freedom of Association and Protection of the Right to Organise*[1] (Cmd. 7638) 1949

PART I. FREEDOM OF ASSOCIATION

ARTICLE 1

Each Member of the International Labour Organisation for which this Convention is in force undertakes to give effect to the following provisions.

ARTICLE 2

Workers and employers, without distinction whatsoever, shall have the right to establish and, subject only to the rules of the organisation concerned, to join organisations of their own choosing without previous authorisation.

ARTICLE 3

1. Workers' and employers' organisations shall have the right to draw up their constitutions and rules, to elect their representatives in full freedom, to organise their administration and activities and to formulate their programmes.
2. The public authorities shall refrain from any interference which would restrict this right or impede the lawful exercise thereof.

ARTICLE 4

Workers' and employers' organisations shall not be liable to be dissolved or suspended by administrative authority.

ARTICLE 5

Workers' and employers' organisations shall have the right to establish and join federations and confederations and any such organisation, federation or confederation shall have the right to affiliate with international organisations of workers and employers.

ARTICLE 6

The provisions of Articles 2, 3 and 4 hereof apply to federations and confederations of workers' and employers' organisations.

ARTICLE 7

The acquisition of legal personality by workers' and employers' organisations, federations and confederations shall not be made subject to conditions of such a character as to restrict the application of the provisions of Articles 2, 3 and 4 hereof.

[1] Ratified by the United Kingdom in 1949. Such Conventions are not part of the law of the United Kingdom unless embodied in legislation.

ARTICLE 8

1. In exercising the rights provided for in this Convention workers and employers and their respective organisations, like other persons or organised collectivities, shall respect the law of the land.

2. The law of the land shall not be such as to impair, nor shall it be so applied as to impair, the guarantees provided for in this Convention.

ARTICLE 9

1. The extent to which the guarantees provided for in this Convention shall apply to the armed forces and the police shall be determined by national laws or regulations.

2. In accordance with the principle set forth in paragraph 8 of Article 19 of the Constitution of the International Labour Organisation[1] the ratification of this Convention by any Member shall not be deemed to affect any existing law, award, custom or agreement in virtue of which members of the armed forces or the police enjoy any right guaranteed by this Convention.

ARTICLE 10

In this Convention the term "organisation" means any organisation of workers or of employers for furthering and defending the interests of workers or of employers.

PART II. PROTECTION OF THE RIGHT TO ORGANISE

ARTICLE 11

Each Member of the International Labour Organisation for which this Convention is in force undertakes to take all necessary and appropriate measures to ensure that workers and employers may exercise freely the right to organise.

6.2 International Labour Conference, *Convention (No. 98) Concerning the Application of the Principles of the Right to Organise and to Bargain Collectively*[2] (Cmd. 7852) 1949

ARTICLE 1

1. Workers shall enjoy adequate protection against acts of anti-union discrimination in respect of their employment.

2. Such protection shall apply more particularly in respect of acts calculated to—

[1] See Document 47.3.

[2] Ratified by the United Kingdom in 1950. Also see footnote to Document 6.1.

(*a*) make the employment of a worker subject to the condition that he shall not join a union or shall relinquish trade union membership;

(*b*) cause the dismissal of or otherwise prejudice a worker by reason of union membership or because of participation in union activities outside working hours or, with the consent of the employer, within working hours.

ARTICLE 2

1. Workers' and employers' organisations shall enjoy adequate protection against any acts of interference by each other or each other's agents or members in their establishment, functioning or administration.

2. In particular, acts which are designed to promote the establishment of workers' organisations under the domination of employers or employers' organisations, or to support workers' organisations by financial or other means, with the object of placing such organisations under the control of employers or employers' organisations, shall be deemed to constitute acts of interference within the meaning of this Article.

ARTICLE 3

Machinery appropriate to national conditions shall be established, where necessary, for the purpose of ensuring respect for the right to organise as defined in the preceding articles.

ARTICLE 4

Measures appropriate to national conditions shall be taken, where necessary, to encourage and promote the full development and utilisation of machinery for voluntary negotiation between employers or employers' organisations and workers' organisations, with a view to the regulation of terms and conditions of employment by means of collective agreements.

ARTICLE 5

1. The extent to which the guarantees provided for in this Convention shall apply to the armed forces and the police shall be determined by national laws or regulations.

2. In accordance with the principle set forth in paragraph 8 of Article 19 of the Constitution of the International Labour Organisation[1] the ratification of this Convention by any Member shall not be deemed to affect any existing law, award, custom or agreement in virtue of which members of the armed forces or the police enjoy any right guaranteed by this Convention.

ARTICLE 6

This Convention does not deal with the position of public servants engaged in the administration of the State, nor shall it be construed as prejudicing their rights or status in any way.

[1] See Document 47.3.

6.3 *In Place of Strife: A Policy for Industrial Relations* (Cmnd. 3888) 1969

TRADE UNION MEMBERSHIP

55. The Industrial Relations Bill[1] will lay down the principle that no employer has the right to prevent or obstruct an employee from belonging to a trade union. This principle will become a part of all contracts of employment, and the Bill will provide that any stipulation contrary to it should be void in law. The Bill will further provide that no Friendly Society should have a rule debarring trade unionists from membership. Employees will also be given a remedy if they are dismissed on account of trade union membership. Article 1 of the International Labour Convention on the Right to Organise and on Collective Bargaining 1949 (No. 98),[2] which the United Kingdom has ratified, requires adequate protection for workers against acts of anti-union discrimination, and the measures to be proposed in the Bill will give this statutory support.

RECOGNITION OF TRADE UNIONS BY EMPLOYERS

56. Recognition disputes are of two kinds:
   (a) where an employer refuses to recognise any unions, and
   (b) where he bargains with some unions but excludes others.

Disputes may also arise where an employer recognises but will not negotiate with a union. In all these cases the Government will empower the C.I.R.[3] to investigate and report on such disputes referred by the Secretary of State. It will be able to take evidence from management and unions, and to look into the facts of the situation, such as the degree of support for the union or unions involved. It will be empowered to hold a secret ballot if this is thought to be desirable.

57. In the first type of case the Government will expect the C.I.R. normally to favour recognition, if the union is appropriate and can establish that it has reasonable support. A ballot is one way of showing this, but the question cannot be settled by ballot in every case, for a union can often find little immediate support where there has hitherto been little hope of recognition and perhaps little opportunity for recruitment; increased support and membership follow, not precede, recognition.

58. The Government expects that in such cases most employers will agree to accept an independent and unbiased recommendation by the C.I.R. It proposes, however, to provide in the Industrial Relations Bill that where,

---

[1] A measure proposed in this White Paper to implement reform in industrial relations, chiefly in the light of the *Report* of the Royal Commission. A Bill was duly introduced in April 1970, but lapsed at the General Election of June 1970.

[2] See Document 6.2.

[3] Commission on Industrial Relations. A body proposed in this White Paper, and set up in the form of a Royal Commission in 1969, having as its primary concern the reform of collective bargaining. It is analogous to the Industrial Relations Commission (see Document 15.1) which was proposed by the Royal Commission.

despite a C.I.R. recommendation in favour of recognition, an employer continues to refuse recognition, the Secretary of State should be able to take action. One possible course would be for the Secretary of State to order the employer to bargain in good faith, subject to a penalty if he does not. But this would be an inadequate way of resolving the position, since it would often be very difficult for the courts to decide whether the employer was refusing to bargain in good faith or simply taking a tough bargaining position. Instead, therefore, the Government proposes that where the C.I.R. recommends in the first type of case that a union or unions should be recognised, the Secretary of State should be empowered to require the employer by Order to recognise and negotiate with the union. If he does not, the union will be able unilaterally to take him to arbitration before the Industrial Court, whose award will be legally binding.

59. The Donovan Report[1] also points out that there may be other circumstances in which the employer already recognises a union but refuses to bargain genuinely with it. For example, this may take the form of exploiting the weak organisation of his employees or their reluctance to strike. This refusal of genuine bargaining may extend over the whole field of industrial relations in the undertaking, or it may be only in respect of certain matters. In either event, where, because of the employer's refusal to negotiate, the unions are unable to get substantive claims properly considered, the Industrial Relations Bill will further propose that, in these circumstances too, the Secretary of State should be able to make an Order by which the union could unilaterally take the employer to legally binding arbitration before the Industrial Court.

60. Questions of conflict for recognition between rival unions present greater difficulties. As the Donovan Report pointed out, multi-unionism can be a potent source of industrial disputes and the Government looks to the T.U.C. to take positive initiatives and to strengthen its procedures for dealing with it. . . . Disputes over recognition between powerful unions can cause widespread disruption and, unless peaceful methods of finding a solution can be evolved, such disputes will be settled on the basis of which union or group of unions can do, or threaten to do, the greatest damage to the economy. The Government believes that this is intolerable in a modern society and is confident that the T.U.C. shares its view that peaceful solutions must be found. The C.I.R. can play a useful role in bringing persuasion to bear on the unions involved and in reinforcing the efforts of the T.U.C. If, despite these efforts, a dispute is threatened, the Government will ask the T.U.C. to try to resolve the conflict between its constituent unions. If, however, the T.U.C. cannot persuade the parties within a reasonable time to accept a settlement, the Secretary of State will refer the dispute to the C.I.R. In some cases the C.I.R. may only be able to produce a durable solution by recommending the exclusion of one or more unions from recognition. In such a situation the Government will look to all the parties involved to accept the recommendations of the C.I.R. If they do not, the Industrial Relations Bill will propose a power for the Secretary of State where necessary to give effect

[1] The *Report* of the Royal Commission. The Chairman of the Royal Commission was the Rt. Hon. Lord Donovan.

by Order to the C.I.R's recommendations. The employer would then be liable to a financial penalty if he refused to recognise the union or unions which the C.I.R. recommended should be recognised, or recognised one against which it had recommended. A union which used coercive action to obstruct the implementation of the C.I.R's recommendations would also be liable to a financial penalty.

7 Legal status

7.1 Trade Union Act 1871[1]

4. Nothing in this Act shall enable any court to entertain any legal proceeding instituted with the object of directly enforcing or recovering damages for the breach of any of the following agreements, namely,

1. Any agreement between members of a trade union as such, concerning the conditions on which any members for the time being of such trade union shall or shall not sell their goods, transact business, employ, or be employed:

2. Any agreement for the payment by any person of any subscription or penalty to a trade union:

3. Any agreement for the application of the funds of a trade union,—
   (a.) To provide benefits to members; or
   (b.) To furnish contributions to any employer or workman not a member of such trade union, in consideration of such employer or workman acting in conformity with the rules or resolutions of such trade union; or
   (c.) To discharge any fine imposed upon any person by sentence of a court of justice; or,

4. Any agreement made between one trade union[2] and another; or,

5. Any bond to secure the performance of any of the above-mentioned agreements.

But nothing in this section shall be deemed to constitute any of the above-mentioned agreements unlawful.

7.2 Royal Commission on Trade Unions and Employers' Associations 1965–1968, *Report* (Cmnd. 3623) 1968

COLLECTIVE AGREEMENTS AND THE LAW

. . . .

471. This lack of intention to make legally binding collective agreements,

[1] The repeal of this Act was proposed in the Industrial Relations Bill 1970. See Appendix, p. 571.

[2] The definition of a trade union, given in the Trade Union Act 1913, embraced associations of employers as well as those of workers. See Document 2.1.

or, better perhaps, this intention and policy that collective bargaining and collective agreements should remain outside the law, is one of the characteristic features of our system of industrial relations which distinguishes it from other comparable systems. It is deeply rooted in its structure. . . . collective bargaining is not in this country a series of easily distinguishable transactions comparable to the making of a number of contracts by two commercial firms. It is in fact a continuous process in which differences concerning the interpretation of an agreement merge imperceptibly into differences concerning claims to change its effect. Moreover, even at industry level, a great deal of collective bargaining takes place through standing bodies, such as joint industrial councils and national or regional negotiating boards, and the agreement appears as a "resolution" or "decision" of that body, variable at its will, and variable in particular in the light of such difficulties of interpretation as may arise. Such "bargaining" does not fit into the categories of the law of contract.

472. . . . collective bargaining takes place at a number of levels simultaneously, and, in so far as it takes place at workshop or plant level, it is fragmented and it is informal. That it is fragmented means, from the legal point of view, that it is difficult and perhaps often impossible to identify the "party" who made it on the workers' side, and that it is informal means that it would sometimes and probably very often be impossible for a court to receive evidence enabling it to ascertain the content of the "agreement" in a way required for its legal enforcement. In fact most of these "agreements" would probably, in the legal sense, be "void for uncertainty". Industry-wide bargaining and workshop or plant bargaining are however closely intertwined. To enforce one without the other would be to distort the effect of our collective bargaining system. That system is today a patchwork of formal agreements, informal agreements and "custom and practice". No court, asked to "enforce" a collective agreement, could disentangle the "agreement" from the inarticulate practices which are its background.

473. It may be alleged that none of these considerations applies to procedure agreements. Nevertheless it is a generally admitted fact that even procedure agreements are not contracts, and this again for the reason that the parties to them do not intend to create legal obligations. This lack of intent is manifest from the style in which the agreements are expressed. . . .

7.3 Industrial Council, *Report on Enquiry into Industrial Agreements* (Cd. 6952) 1913

SUMMARY

. . . .

61. . . . among the various suggestions that we have had under consideration with respect to the first part of our reference, *i.e.*, as to the best method of securing the due fulfilment of industrial agreements, are the following:—

(1.) Organisation (*i.e.* complete and effective organisation on the part of both employers and workpeople).

(2.) Moral obligation.

(3.) Monetary penalties and prohibition of assistance to persons in breach.

(4.) Monetary Guarantees.

The whole organisation of collective bargaining, of which we have expressed our approval, is based upon the principle of consent. We have found that such collective agreements have been as a rule kept, and we are loth either to interfere with the internal organisation of the Associations on both sides by putting upon them the legal necessity of exercising compulsion upon their members, or to introduce a new principle which might have far-reaching and unexpected effects upon the natural growth of such Associations or upon the spirit with which as a rule they have been carried on. We have therefore . . . come to the conclusion that the establishment of a system of monetary penalties is not desirable, and that such penalties as prohibition of assistance to persons in breach should not be made legally obligatory. We have stated, however, and we wish to give our opinion the maximum degree of emphasis, that where a breach of an agreement has been committed no assistance, financial or otherwise, should be given to the persons in breach by any of the other members of the Associations connected with the agreement. The language of our Report is intended to express as strongly as possible our adherence to the view that moral influence should in every feasible way be brought to bear in favour of the strict carrying out of agreements, and that, in cases where . . . a breach is found to have been committed, Associations should . . . exercise to the full the disciplinary powers of their organisation, assisted, as would no doubt be the case, by the force of public opinion.

8 Conventions

8.1 Court of Inquiry into a Dispute between the British Transport Commission and the National Union of Railwaymen, *Final Report* (Cmd. 9372) 1955

COMMENTARY ON NEGOTIATIONS

· · · · · · ·

51. A further point which requires condemnation is the N.U.R.'s insistence that the Commission should, before negotiations even began, give a guarantee that a substantial part of the claim would be conceded. We consider such a requirement to be wholly improper as tending to reduce all industrial negotiation to a farce; and Mr. Campbell[1] on behalf of the Union admitted that acceptance of it would be "foreign to his experience".

[1] The then General Secretary of the National Union of Railwaymen.

8.2 Court of Inquiry into a Dispute between the National Federated Electrical Association and the Electrical Trades Union, *Report* (Cmd. 8968) 1953

CONCLUSIONS

. . . .

84. Further, we can only condemn as striking at the root of organised industrial negotiations the action of the Executive Council of the Union ... when they decided to call strikes at the sites where contracts were being carried out by members of the employers' side who had been present at the abortive meeting of the N.J.I.C.[1] on the same date. It is fundamental that those who are called upon to represent and negotiate on behalf of the two sides in industry shall do so in the knowledge that their personal position will not be prejudiced by the course they take in what they honestly believe to be the legitimate interests of their constituents. . . .

9 Industry-wide and workplace

9.1 *Model Constitution and Functions of a Joint Industrial Council* [Ministry of Labour, *Industrial Relations Handbook* Revised edition (London, H.M.S.O., 1961), Appendix 1]

(A) FUNCTIONS OF A JOINT INDUSTRIAL COUNCIL

1. To secure the largest possible measure of joint action between employers and workpeople for the development of the industry as a part of national life and for the improvement of the conditions of all engaged in that industry.

It will be open to the Council to take any action that falls within the scope of this general definition. Among its more specific objects will be the following:

NOTE. *No hard and fast policy is suggested as to what should constitute the functions of an Industrial Council. This is a question which the employers and workpeople in each industry must settle for themselves.*

2. Regular consideration of wages, hours and working conditions in the industry as a whole.

3. The consideration of measures for regularising production and employment.

4. The consideration of the existing machinery for the settlement of differences between different parties and sections in the industry, and the establishment of machinery for this purpose where it does not already exist, with the object of securing the speedy settlement of difficulties.

[1] The National Joint Industrial Council for the Electrical Contracting Industry had met on August 31st to discuss a wage claim. The results were inconclusive. On the same day, strikes were called at sites where contracts were being carried out by members of the employers' side who had been present at the meeting.

5. The collection of statistics and information on matters appertaining to the industry.

6. The encouragement of the study of processes and design and of research, with a view to perfecting the products of the industry.

7. The provision of facilities for the full consideration and utilisation of inventions and any improvement in machinery or method, and for the adequate safeguarding of the rights of the designers of such improvements, and to secure that such improvement in method or invention shall give to each party an equitable share of the benefits financially or otherwise arising therefrom.

8. Inquiries into special problems of the industry, including the comparative study of the organisation and methods of the industry in this and other countries, and where desirable the publication of reports.

9. The improvement of the health conditions obtaining in the industry, and the provision of special treatment where necessary for workers in the industry.

10. The supervision of entry into and training for the industry, and co-operation with the educational authorities in arranging education in all its branches for the industry.

11. The issue to the Press of authoritative statements upon matters affecting the industry of general interest to the community.

12. Representation of the needs and opinions of the industry to the Government, Government Departments and other authorities.

13. The consideration of any other matters that may be referred to it by the Government or any Government Department.

14. The consideration of the proposals for District Councils and Works Committees put forward in the Whitley Report,[1] having regard in each case to any such organisations as may already be in existence.

NOTE. *The following have also been included among the functions in some of the provisional constitutions which have been brought to the notice of the Ministry of Labour:*

(i) The consideration of measures for securing the inclusion of all employers and workpeople in their respective associations.

(ii) The arrangement of lectures and the holding of conferences on subjects of general interest to the industry.

(iii) Co-operation with the Joint Industrial Councils for other industries to deal with problems of common interest.

(B) THE CONSTITUTION OF A JOINT INDUSTRIAL COUNCIL

1. MEMBERSHIP

The Council shall consist of   members, appointed as to one half by Associations of Employers and as to the other half by Trade Unions.

. . . .

A generic term relating to the five reports produced by the Committee on Relations between Employers and Employed, under the Chairmanship of the Rt. Hon. J. H. Whitley, in 1917 and 1918.

2. REAPPOINTMENT

The representatives of the said Associations and Unions shall retire annually, and shall be eligible for reappointment by their respective Associations and Unions. Casual vacancies should be filled by the Association concerned, which shall appoint a member to sit until the end of the current year.

3. COMMITTEES

The Council may delegate special powers to any Committee it appoints.

The Council shall appoint an Executive Committee and may appoint such other Standing or Sectional Committee as may be necessary. It shall also have the power to appoint other Committees for special purposes. The Reports of all Committees shall be submitted to the Council for confirmation, except where special powers have been delegated to a Committee.

4. CO-OPTED MEMBERS

The Council shall have the power of appointing on Committees or allowing Committees to co-opt such persons of special knowledge not being members of the Council as may serve the special purposes of the Council, provided that so far as the Executive Committee is concerned:

(*a*) the two sides of the Council shall be equally represented, and

(*b*) any appointed or co-opted members shall serve only in a consultative capacity.

N.B. It is desirable to take power to appoint representatives of scientific, technical and commercial Associations upon Committees and Sub-Committees of the Council, and the above clause would give this power.

5. OFFICERS

The officers shall consist of a Chairman or Chairmen, a Vice-Chairman, a Treasurer and a Secretary or Secretaries.

(1) *The Chairmen.*

N.B. The Whitley Report suggests that the appointment of a Chairman or Chairmen should be left to the Council, who may decide that there should be—

(*i*) *a Chairman for each side of the Council,*

(*ii*) *a Chairman and Vice-Chairman selected from the members of the Council (one from each side of the Council),*

(*iii*) *a Chairman chosen by the Council from independent persons outside the industry, or*

(*iv*) *a Chairman nominated by such persons or authority as the Council may determine, or failing agreement, by the Government.*

(2) *Secretary.*

The Council *shall be* empowered to maintain a Secretary or Secretaries and such clerical staff as it may think fit.

All honorary officers shall be elected by the Council for a term of one year.

6. MEETINGS OF THE COUNCIL

The ordinary meetings of the Council shall be held as often as necessary and not less than once a quarter. The meeting in the month of shall be the annual meeting. A special meeting of the Council shall be called within   days of the receipt of a requisition from any of the constituent Associations or from the Executive Committee. The matters to be discussed at such meetings shall be stated upon the notice summoning the meeting.

7. VOTING

The voting both in Council and in Committees shall be by show of hands or otherwise as the Council may determine. No resolution shall be regarded as carried unless it has been approved by a majority of the members present on each side of the Council.

8. QUORUM

The quorum shall be   members on each side of the Council.

9. FINANCE

The expenses of the Council shall be met by the Associations and Trade Unions represented.

9.2 Royal Commission on Trade Unions and Employers' Associations 1965–1968, *Report* (Cmnd. 3623) 1968

66. Workplace bargaining is largely autonomous because, however the external collective bargaining procedures respond to its growth, their control has continued to diminish, and with it the control of trade unions and employers' associations.

67. Workplace bargaining is fragmented because "it is conducted in such a way that different groups in the works get different concessions at different times".[1] The consequence is competitive sectional wage adjustments and disorderly pay structures. . . .

68. Workplace bargaining is informal because of the predominance of unwritten understandings and of custom and practice. Informality applies not only to arrangements concerning pay and conditions of work at the factory, but also to the procedure under which these arrangements are reached. Most industry-wide agreements give only sketchy guidance about the procedure to be followed within the factory. There is, for example, rarely any provision for compensating shop stewards for any loss of earnings due to their work as stewards. Usually nothing is said about stewards holding meetings with their constituents on the employers' premises, inside or outside working hours. Our investigations show that in factories with several shop stewards there is usually a "senior steward" or "convenor of stewards", but no provision is made for this in engineering or in many other procedures. Joint committees of stewards and managers to discuss and settle problems are also normal, but if they are mentioned in industry-wide pro-

---

[1] A quotation from written evidence submitted by Mr A. Flanders. See Royal Commission on Trade Unions and Employers' Associations, *Selected Written Evidence Submitted to the Royal Commission* (London, H.M.S.O., 1968), p. 553.

cedure agreements there may be little guidance on their powers and conduct of business. Some managements draw up their own procedures in agreement with their shop stewards or district union officers, but it is more common to rely on precedent. Even where written procedures are established they often come to be "short-circuited" in the interests of speedy settlements.

10 Procedural

10.1 Chemical and Allied Industries Joint Industrial Council, *Constitution* 1967

TITLES

1. The title of the Joint Industrial Council shall be the Chemical and Allied Industries Joint Industrial Council, hereinafter referred to as the Main Council. . . .

There shall also be Group Joint Industrial Councils hereinafter referred to as Group Councils. The present Group Councils are the Heavy Chemical Joint Industrial Council, the Fertiliser Joint Industrial Council, and the Plastics Joint Industrial Council.

. . . .

FUNCTIONS OF MAIN COUNCIL

3. It shall be the function of the Main Council to negotiate and settle the basic rates of wages, hours and general conditions of work commonly applicable to member firms in the several Groups forming the Chemical Industries Association.

FUNCTIONS OF A GROUP COUNCIL

4. It shall be the function of a Group Council to negotiate and settle the non-basic rates of wages, hours and conditions of work commonly applicable to all the member firms of the Group.

. . . .

DISPUTES PROCEDURE

17. (a) In the event of any dispute arising between an employer and his employees it shall be dealt with in the first place by the employees or the Trade Union shop representative on their behalf and by the appropriate representative of the management.

(b) Failing a settlement within the works, the dispute shall be discussed by the Trade Union officer and by the appropriate representative of the management who may avail themselves of the services of the Chemical Industries Association.

(c) In the event of local agreement not being reached, the dispute shall be referred for settlement to the appropriate Trade Union headquarters and to the Chemical Industries Association.

(d) In cases where the Trade Union headquarters and the Chemical Industries Association fail to arrive at a settlement, the dispute shall be reported forthwith to the Joint Secretaries of the Joint Industrial Council. Upon a dispute being reported, the Joint Secretaries shall arrange for the dispute to be referred to the Main or a Group Joint Industrial Council, or to such committee thereof as may have power to deal with the same.

REFERENCE FOR DISPUTES

18. Disputes relating to matters within the jurisdiction of the Main Council shall be referred to the Main Council, and disputes relating to matters within the jurisdiction of a Group Council shall be referred to a Group Council.

Where a matter within the jurisdiction of the Main Council and a matter within the jurisdiction of a Group Council are together in dispute or where there is doubt about the appropriate reference, the dispute shall be referred to the Main Council.

RESTRICTIONS ON STRIKES AND LOCK-OUTS

19. If the Main Council or Group Council is in dispute or fails to settle a dispute, before any party to the dispute gives notice of a cessation of work the question of voluntary submission of the dispute to arbitration shall be discussed between the parties at a further meeting.

Neither a strike nor a lock-out shall take place at any factory or works in the absence of a dispute at that factory or works.

10.2 Engineering and Allied Employers' National Federation and the Trade Unions, *Agreement: Procedure—Manual Workers* 1922 (amended to 1955)

I. GENERAL PRINCIPLES

(a) The Employers have the right to manage their establishments and the Trade Unions have the right to exercise their functions.

(b) In the process of evolution, provision for changes in shop conditions is necessary, but it is not the intention to create any specially favoured class of workpeople.

(c) The Employers and the Trade Unions, without departing in any way from the principles embodied in Clause (a) above, emphasise the value of consultation, not only in the successful operation of the Procedure set out in Section II but in the initial avoidance of disputes.

II. PROCEDURE FOR DEALING WITH QUESTIONS ARISING

(1) GENERAL

(*a*) The procedure of the Provisions for Avoiding Disputes so far as appropriate, applies to:—

(i) General alterations in wages;

(ii) Alterations in working conditions which are the subject of agreements officially entered into;

(iii) Alterations in the general working week;

but such alterations shall not be given effect to until the appropriate procedure between the Federation and the Trade Union or Unions concerned has been exhausted.

(*b*) When the Management contemplates alterations in recognised working conditions which do not involve a change in material, means or method, and would result in work currently done by one class of workpeople in future being done by another class of workpeople in the establishment, the Management shall give the workpeople directly concerned or their representatives in the shop intimation of their intention, and afford an opportunity for discussion with a deputation of the workpeople concerned and/or their representatives in the shop. In the event of no settlement being reached, the Procedure outlined in Section (2)—Provisions for Avoiding Disputes—shall be operated. The alterations concerned shall not be implemented until settlement has been reached or until the Procedure has been exhausted.

Where a contemplated alteration involves a change in the material, means or method and may result in one class of workpeople being replaced by another in the establishment, the Management shall as soon as possible notify their proposals to the workpeople directly concerned and/or their representatives in the shop in order that there may be consultation between the parties concerned with a view to reaching agreement. If agreement is not achieved the workers concerned may give notice of an apprehended dispute, in which case the Management will not operate the proposed change for seven working days. The matter may be dealt with in accordance with the Provisions for Avoiding Disputes, the change being without prejudice to either party in any discussions which may take place.

(*c*) Where any class of workpeople is displaced by reason of any act of the Management, consideration shall be given to the case of workpeople so displaced with a view, if practicable, of affording them in the establishment work suitable to their qualifications.

(*d*) Questions arising which do not result in one class of workpeople being replaced by another in the establishment and on which discussion is desired, shall be dealt with in accordance with the Provisions for Avoiding Disputes and work shall proceed meantime under the conditions following the act of the Management.

(*e*) Where a change is made by the Management involving questions of money payments and, as a result of negotiations in accordance with the recognised procedure, it is agreed that the claim of the workpeople is established, the decision so arrived at may be made retrospective on the particular claim to a date to be mutually agreed upon, but not beyond the date upon which the question was raised.

(*f*) Where any local agreement conflicts with the terms of this Agreement, the provisions of this Agreement shall apply.

(*g*) Nothing in the foregoing shall affect the usual practice in connection with the termination of employment of individual workpeople.

(2) *PROVISIONS FOR AVOIDING DISPUTES*

(*a*) When a question arises, an endeavour shall be made by the Management and the workman directly concerned to settle the same in the works or at the place where the question has arisen. Failing settlement deputations of workmen who may be accompanied by their Organiser (in which event a representative of the Employers' Association shall also be present) shall be received by the Employers by appointment without unreasonable delay for the mutual discussion of any question in the settlement of which both parties are directly concerned. In the event of no settlement being arrived at, it shall be competent for either party to bring the question before a Local Conference[1] to be held between the Local Association[2] and the local representatives of the Society.[3]

(*b*) In the event of either party desiring to raise any question a Local Conference for this purpose may be arranged by application to the Secretary of the Local Association or to the local representative of the Society.

(*c*) Local Conferences shall be held within seven working days, unless otherwise mutually agreed upon, from the receipt of the application by the Secretary of the Local Association or the local representative of the Society.

(*d*) Failing settlement at a Local Conference of any question brought before it, it shall be competent for either party to refer the matter to a Central Conference[4] which, if thought desirable, may make a joint recommendation to the constituent bodies.

(*e*) Central Conference shall be held on the second Friday of each month at which questions referred to Central Conference prior to fourteen days of that date shall be taken.

(*f*) Until the procedure provided above has been carried through, there shall be no stoppage of work either of a partial or a general character.

(3) *SHOP STEWARDS AND WORKS COMMITTEE[5] AGREEMENT*

.   .   .   .

(*c*) *Functions and Procedure*

(7) The functions of Shop Stewards and Works Committee, so far as they

---

[1] The first stage of negotiation outside the workplace.

[2] Of engineering employers.

[3] The trade union concerned.

[4] Held monthly at York; the ultimate stage in the avoidance of disputes under this procedure.

[5] A committee specifically set up under the terms of this procedure, by voluntary agreement, with the object of settling disputes on a domestic basis.

are concerned with the avoidance of disputes, shall be exercised in accordance with the following procedure:—

(*a*) A worker or workers desiring to raise any question in which they are directly concerned shall, in the first instance, discuss the same with their foreman.

(*b*) Failing settlement, the question shall be taken up with the Shop Manager and/or Head Shop Foreman by the appropriate Shop Steward and one of the workers directly concerned.

(*c*) If no settlement is arrived at the question may, at the request of either party, be further considered at a meeting of the Works Committee. At this meeting the O.D.D.[1] may be present, in which event a representative of the Employers' Association shall also be present.

(*d*) Any question arising which affects more than one branch of trade or more than one department of the Works may be referred to the Works Committee.

(*e*) The question may thereafter be referred for further consideration in terms of the "Provisions for Avoiding Disputes".

(*f*) No stoppage of work shall take place until the question has been fully dealt with in accordance with this Agreement and with the "Provisions for Avoiding Disputes".

(*d*) General

(8) Shop Stewards shall be subject to the control of the Trade Unions and shall act in accordance with the Rules and Regulations of the Trade Unions and agreements with Employers so far as these affect the relation between employers and workpeople.

(9) In connection with this Agreement, Shop Stewards shall be afforded facilities to deal with questions raised in the shop or portion of a shop in which they are employed. Shop Stewards elected to the Works Committee shall be afforded similar facilities in connection with their duties, and in the course of dealing with these questions they may, with the previous consent of the Management (such consent not to be unreasonably withheld), visit any shop or portion of a shop in the establishment. In all other respects, Shop Stewards shall conform to the same working conditions as their fellow workers.

(10) Negotiations under this Agreement may be instituted either by the Management or by the workers concerned.

(11) Employers and Shop Stewards and Works Committee shall not be entitled to enter into any agreement inconsistent with agreements between the Federation or Local Association and the Trade Unions.

(12) For the purpose of this Agreement the expression "establishment" shall mean the whole establishment or sections thereof according to whether the Management is unified or sub-divided.

(13) Any question which may arise out of the operation of this Agreement shall be brought before the Executive of the Trade Union concerned or the Federation as the case may be.

---

[1] Organising District Delegate.

10.3 Marsh, A. I., *Disputes Procedures in British Industry* [Royal Commission on Trade Unions and Employers' Associations, *Research Papers* 2(1) (London, H.M.S.O 1966)]

THE PATTERN OF PROCEDURES

. . . .

53. Engineering has ... provided, arising from its original concept of the opposing nature of "managerial" and "trade union" functions, the logical basis for one side of the distinction between "*ad hoc*" and "joint standing" procedural machinery which exists in Britain. Those industries which have followed the engineering convention tend to suggest that, though trade unions have functions in procedure, these should not be allowed to impinge upon the right of management to manage. If this is so, there are limits beyond which it is wrong to suppose that trade unions and managements can make *joint* decisions in procedure, and equally illogical to suppose that, in referring matters through procedure, a union is doing anything more than referring its complaints to engineering employers to have grievances redressed. In the engineering pattern, therefore, *employers' panels* rather than joint committees must always decide whether a procedural claim is justified or not, and all meetings must be *ad hoc*, because if this were not so, they would take on a joint standing character which would compromise managerial rights. Where such a practice exists, employers are clearly acting, when they adjudicate upon a claim, both as representatives of the managerial interest and, if they are to settle the issue, in part as conciliators. The engineering form may therefore with some accuracy be regarded as "employer conciliation".

54. While the engineering pattern has been adopted in some industry procedures, it has been more usual to make no clear distinction between managerial and trade union rights, and to allow for machinery, outside the immediate factory situation, allowing, at each stage, for *joint* settlement, normally by standing joint committees. This structure was derived from the nineteenth century device of joint conciliation boards, and recommended by the Whitley Committee[1] in the form of Joint Industrial Councils, a panel of both employers and trade union officials making decisions at each stage on a joint basis, often with the chairman of the panel alternating between the employer and the union side.

[1] See *supra*, p. 5, footnote 5.

10.4 Shipbuilders and Repairers National Association and Trade Unions Affiliated to the Confederation of Shipbuilding and Engineering Unions, *Memorandum of Agreement: Procedure for Dealing with Demarcation Disputes* 1969

PREAMBLE

The Parties to this Agreement acknowledge that past demarcation disputes have had a detrimental effect upon industrial relations in shipbuilding and shiprepairing, upon the efficient use of productive resources, and upon the Industry's reputation and competitive ability. In recognition of these factors, they accept the need for the introduction of a new procedure for resolving any demarcation issues which may arise in the future. . . .

INTERPRETATION

1.

. . . .

(b) In the context of this Agreement, the expressions 'demarcation dispute' and 'dispute' shall include any dispute or disagreement between two or more classes of workpeople regarding the right to carry out any job, undertake any process, use any tool, machine or other equipment, or work with any substance or material.

. . . .

(e) If any differences or difficulties arise as to the interpretation of this Agreement, or as to related matters not covered by its terms, they shall be dealt with by the Director or a Joint Secretary of the National Association and the Presidents or General Secretaries of the Trade Unions concerned.

FIRST STAGE OF PROCEDURE—DISCUSSIONS BETWEEN REPRESENTATIVES OF CLASSES INVOLVED

2. In the event of a demarcation dispute arising, it shall be the duty of the shop stewards of the claimant class to report the matter immediately to their foreman. The foreman will report the situation to the management who will immediately make arrangements for a meeting between the shop stewards of the claimant class and the shop stewards of any other classes involved, or likely to be involved, in the dispute. . . .
3. If the shop stewards do not achieve a mutually satisfactory solution (which is also acceptable to the management) within forty-eight hours of the inception of the dispute, the issue shall be reported by the management to the District Officials of the Unions whose members are involved in the dispute.

4. (a) The District Officials will investigate the issue with their members directly involved in the dispute, and discussions will take place between the District Officials of the classes concerned with a view to devising a solution acceptable to all parties.

. . . . . .

FINAL STAGE OF PROCEDURE—INDEPENDENT ARBITRATION

5. If no solution acceptable to the management has been achieved within forty-eight hours of the time at which the dispute was reported to the District Officials (or their duly nominated substitutes), the issue will immediately be referred to independent arbitration.

. . . . . .

8. An outline of the work in dispute and of their grounds for claiming it shall be submitted in writing to the arbiter by the District Officials of the Unions involved. These particulars shall be furnished within forty-eight hours of the time at which the appointment of the arbiter is made known to the District Officials, but the arbitration proceedings shall not be delayed because of the failure of any of the parties to lodge their grounds of claim within this time-limit.
9. The arbitration hearing shall take place within seventy-two hours of the time of appointment of the arbiter.

. . . . . .

11. The question referred to arbitration will be dealt with in relation to the particular shipyard or shiprepairing establishment concerned, and references to practices in other firms and districts will not be introduced by any of the parties in the presentation of their case.
12. The decision of the arbiter, which shall be given as soon as possible after the conclusion of the hearing, will be final and binding upon all parties, including the management.

. . . . . .

GENERAL

. . . . .

15. .... If there is a failure to take the prescribed action within any of the stipulated time-limits, the case will automatically pass on to the next stage in procedure.
16. Demarcation disputes shall not give rise to any stoppage of work of either a partial or a general nature or to any other form of industrial action.
17. If a demarcation dispute arises which could delay the launch, trials, delivery, docking, undocking or sailing of a ship on a pre-arranged date, the management shall be entitled to make a temporary decision to ensure that the work is completed on time. Notwithstanding any such interim allocation of the work in dispute, the issue shall be progressed through the procedure prescribed by this Agreement, on the understanding that the management's temporary decision will be without prejudice to the final outcome of the case or to any further questions of a similar nature.

11 Substantive

11.1 Chemical and Allied Industries Joint Industrial Council, *Schedule of Wage Rates and Working Conditions* 1967

1. JURISDICTION:

Wage rates and conditions . . . shall be applicable to factories in the United Kingdom and shall represent the minimum basis of employment for all workers on the process, in the services, in the yard and assisting on construction and maintenance.

2. BETTER CONDITIONS PREVAILING:

Where any class of operatives at any individual works is in receipt of a higher rate of wages and/or where better conditions of employment prevail, the operatives concerned shall not suffer any reduction or be in any way prejudiced by the operation of the terms and conditions hereinafter formulated.

3. HOURS OF WORK:

The hours of work for a normal working week shall be:—
>**Day workers:**   40 hours a week.
>**Shift workers:**   40 hours a week.

Whether the working week shall be one of 5 or $5\frac{1}{2}$ days shall be decided by the individual management after consultation with the workers.

4. CONDITIONS OF ROTA WORKING:

Rotas for shift and day working or for alternating periods of shift and day working adapted to the hours fixed by the J.I.C shall be decided by the individual management after consultation with the workers, provided that the average weekly hours in the cycle do not exceed 40.

The weekly hours worked by day workers or by shift workers may be unequal, provided that the average weekly hours in the cycle do not exceed 40.

In the case of a rota for day or for shift workers requiring the working of unequal weekly hours overtime payments shall become due after the hours fixed for each day or shift in the rota have been worked.

A shift of 8 hours worked continuously may only be exceeded by local agreement and permission of the J.I.C.

5. TRANSFER TO OTHER JOBS:

Where a worker who has performed a particular job or jobs for a minimum

77

of four consecutive weeks, unless employed as a relief worker, is asked by the management to transfer to another job, he shall, wherever possible, be given at least one week's notice of the change. Where this is done, he shall be paid the rate for the job from the time of transfer except in the case of a shift worker transferred to day work who will be paid the day rate from the beginning of the following day.

If a worker is not given one week's notice of transfer, the following shall apply:—

(a) Where a shift worker is transferred to day work because there is no longer any shift work for him or because of any re-arrangement of duties on his plant or job, he shall be paid his existing hourly shift rate for the hours worked for one week from the time of transfer. If he continues on day work at the expiration of the period he shall be paid the appropriate day rate.

(b) Where a day or shift worker is transferred from a higher to a lower paid job, he shall be paid the rate of pay prior to transfer for the hours worked for one week from the time of transfer, after which he shall be paid the rate for the job.

(c) Where a day or shift worker is transferred from a lower to a higher paid job, he shall be paid the prevailing rate for the new job whilst so engaged as from the time of transfer.

(d) Where a day worker is asked by the management to take on the work of a shift worker either at the conclusion of his normal work for the day or when sent home to resume work later the same day as a shift man during ordinary shift hours, he shall be paid on the basis of the prevailing shift rate for the particular job and all hours in excess of his normal day's work shall rank for overtime.

(e) The prevailing rate under (c) and (d) covers any learner's rate where this applies.

Where a worker who has performed a particular job for less than four consecutive weeks or who is employed as a relief worker is asked by the management to transfer to another job, he shall be paid the rate for the job from the time of transfer except in the case of a shift worker transferred to day work who will be paid the day rate from the beginning of the following day.

6. OVERTIME RATES:

Overtime work shall be paid for as follows:—

Day workers: Time-and-a-half—Monday to Saturday. Sunday work, from midnight to midnight, to be paid for at the rate of double time.

For the purposes of calculating overtime each day or shift shall stand by itself.

In the case of day workers called in to work on a free Saturday whether free by reason of a 5-day week, or under a rota, standard overtime rates shall be paid.

When a day worker who has worked overtime continuously since the previous day is sent home after midnight he shall be paid in addition to overtime for the hours worked plain time for the time between being sent home and 6 a.m. This additional payment shall not apply to the worker called in.

Shift workers: Extra time necessitated by the rotational change-over of shifts shall be paid for at the plain time rate or at the plain time rate plus any appropriate week-end payment.

When overtime is worked by shift men at the request of the management, such extra time shall be paid for at the rate of time-and-a-half, except from 6 a.m. Saturday to 6 a.m. Monday when the appropriate shift rate shall be paid.

Where a 48-hour shift week is regularly worked, overtime shall be calculated as if the pay week ended on a plain time shift, thereby ensuring that the shift workers shall be paid on a uniform basis. Local arrangements already existing to produce the same results shall remain valid.

Overtime for Pieceworkers: Pieceworkers employed on overtime shall receive a time plus rate equivalent to that in operation for a corresponding time worker.

Rest Period: Where a day man or shift man has worked continuously to within 8 hours of his next normal starting time he shall be guaranteed a rest period of 8 hours from his stopping time. Any normal working hours thereby lost shall be treated for all purposes as though he had worked during those normal working hours.

7. SHIFT WORKERS—EXTRA PAYMENT FOR WEEK-END WORK:

Normal week-end work in the case of shift workers shall be paid for as follows:—

Double time for the three Sunday shifts, and time-and-a-half for the remainder of the hours between 6 a.m. Saturday and 6 a.m. Monday, except where other mutual arrangements have already been made.

Where the 10 p.m. Saturday to 6 a.m. Sunday shift is worked as individual overtime, double time shall be paid.

When a shift man is required to work on a rest day, he shall be paid at the rate of time-and-a-half except in the case of a shift subject to a week-end payment, when the appropriate week-end payment should be made.

8. CALLING-IN PAYMENT:

In the case of a worker who has left the factory for the day being summoned from home to return to work, he shall be paid, in addition to his overtime rate in respect of the hours so worked, the sum of 15/- in respect of a call between midnight and 4 a.m., or the sum of 10/- for a call at other times. A minimum of 4 hours' pay at the appropriate overtime rate shall be paid for each call. "Call money" will also be payable to a worker who is summoned from home on a Sunday or other rest day or on a declared holiday to work on that day.

It is recommended that where a day worker has been called in, works a long period of overtime during the night and is not able to get an adequate period of rest, he should in the interest of safety, efficiency and welfare be sent home for the whole or an appropriate part of the following day. Any normal hours thereby lost shall be treated for all purposes as though he had worked during those normal working hours.

9. WAGES:

The standard minimum rates of wages for able-bodied adult male workers at present in operation are set out in Appendix A.

The London rate for adult male workers is 2¼d. per hour above the national rate and is payable within a radius of 15 miles of Charing Cross.

Plus rates are additions to the basic day or shift rate payable to individual workmen or classes of workmen on account of skill, responsibility, arduousness, etc., and may be fixed by the management in agreement with the men concerned, who may avail themselves of the services of their Trade Union official.

Pieceworkers: Piecework rates shall be fixed so as to enable a worker of average ability to earn at least 27 per cent. more than a time worker employed during the same period on the same job.

10. NON-ROTATING SHIFT WORK:

An extra payment of 2d. per hour shall be made to an employee for continual working of the morning shift, where this begins 1½ hours or more earlier than the normal day-work starting time; 7½d. per hour shall be paid for continual working of the 2.00 p.m.-10.00 p.m. or equivalent evening shift.

11. RATES OF PAY OF WOMEN AND GIRLS:

The standard minimum rates of wages for women and girls and for women on two 8-hour shift systems at present in operation are set out in Appendix A.

The London Rate for women is 1¾d. per hour and for girls is 1½d. per hour above the national rate and is payable within a radius of 15 miles of Charing Cross.

.   .   .   .

12. RATES OF PAY FOR YOUTHS ON SHIFT WORK:

The shift differential for youths and girls on two shifts at all ages is 3¾d. per hour, and for youths on three shifts, 5d. per hour from the age of 18.

The London rate for youths is 1½d. per hour above the national rate and is payable within a radius of 15 miles of Charing Cross.

13. RATES OF PAY FOR YOUTHS ON MEN'S WORK:

Youths of 18 and upwards not under training, who are doing men's work effectively without additional supervision or assistance, shall receive the men's rate.

14. ANNUAL HOLIDAY:

Two weeks' annual holiday with pay shall be given in accordance with the regulations fixed and agreed upon from time to time by the Chemical and Allied Industries Joint Industrial Council.

. . . .

Additional days of holiday shall be given in accordance with the Agreement at Appendix C.

15. STATUTORY HOLIDAYS:

The Public and Statutory Holidays in England and Wales recognised by the Joint Industrial Council are Good Friday, Easter Monday, Spring Bank Holiday, Summer Bank Holiday, Christmas Day and Boxing Day, and Holidays proclaimed by the Queen, or any day in lieu thereof.

In Scotland six holidays shall be given. These shall be the customary holidays in the locality, and in case of doubt they shall be agreed upon in advance between the management and the workers or their Trade Unions.

. . . .

APPENDIX A

CHEMICAL AND ALLIED INDUSTRIES JOINT INDUSTRIAL COUNCIL

The following are the minimum wage rates to operate with effect from the beginning of the first full pay week commencing on or after 20th May, 1966.

	Heavy Chemical, Plastics Fertiliser Class I.	Fertiliser Class II.	London
Adult Male Day Workers ...	5/5	5/4¼	5/7¼
3-shift Workers ... ... (differential 7¾d. per hour)	6/0¾	6/0	6/3
2-shift Workers ... ... (differential 5½d. per hour)	5/10½	5/9¾	6/0¾
Night Workers ... ... (differential 1/2d. per hour)	6/7	6/6¼	6/9¼
Non-Rotating Shift Workers (Morning shift differential 2d. per hour)	5/7	5/6¼	5/9¼
Non-Rotating Shift Workers (Evening shift differential 7½d. per hour)	6/0½	5/11¾	6/2¾
Women on Women's Work	3/11½	3/11	4/1¼
Women on 2-shift Work ... (differential 4½d. per hour)	4/4	4/3½	4/5¾
Women on Men's Work ... (1st Month)	3/11½	3/11	4/1¼
Women on Men's Work ... (2nd month and thereafter[1] ...)	4/1½	4/1	4/3¼

[1] Subject to the provisions of Appendix G Clause 3 (not here reproduced). By this Clause, a woman at the end of the seventh month of her employment could receive the full adult male rate, if it was agreed that she was in all respects performing the same work as a man, without assistance or supervision.

		Heavy Chemical, Plastics Fertiliser Class I.	Fertiliser Class II.	London
Boys and Youths	Age 15	2/4½	2/4⅛	2/6
	16	2/10¾	2/10⅜	3/0¼
	17	3/6¾	3/6⅜	3/8¼
	18	4/1¾	4/1⅜	4/3¼
	19	4/10¾	4/10⅜	5/0¼
	20	5/2¼	5/1⅞	5/3¾
Girls	Age 15	2/1	2/0⅝	2/2½
	16	2/6	2/5⅝	2/7½
	17	2/11¼	2/10⅞	3/0¾
	18	3/6½	3/6⅛	3/8
	19	3/9	3/8⅝	3/10½
	20	3/9¾	3/9⅜	3/11¼

The London Rate is payable within a radius of 15 miles of
Charing Cross

. . . . . .

APPENDIX C

AGREEMENT ON EXTENSION OF ANNUAL HOLIDAYS

1. An extra day's holiday with pay shall be given in 1963/64 to all workers who have worked continuously throughout a firm's qualifying year for annual holidays. The extra day's holiday shall be given before 31st March, 1964.
2. Extra days of holiday with pay shall be given on the same basis as follows:—

2 days in 1964/5
3 ,, ,, 1965/6
4 ,, ,, 1966/7
5 ,, ,, 1967/8

. . . . . .

4. Payment for the separate days of holiday shall be such that the normal weeks' earnings, exclusive of overtime, shall not be affected by the incidence of the holidays.

. . . . . .

7. The additional J.I.C. holidays shall be substituted for extra holidays where given by individual companies. It is not the intention that any worker shall lose any additional days of holiday given by the individual firm but an additional holiday shall not be given except in cases where the number of

additional days of holiday for the particular year are less than in this agreement.

8. Member firms are not entitled to give nor trade unions to apply locally for additions to holidays.

9. It is agreed that this 5-year agreement will not be changed during its currency.

. . . .

APPENDIX E

. . . . . .

<small>PAYMENT OF A GUARANTEED WAGE</small> is agreed upon the following terms:—

(1) Workers whose wage rates are regulated by the Chemical and Allied Industries J.I.C. and who have been in the employment of their firm for not less than four consecutive weeks shall be guaranteed in each pay week a wage equivalent to their plain time rate for their normal working hours in the case of time workers or at a plain time rate equivalent to that in operation for corresponding time workers in the case of workers employed wholly or partly on any system of payment by results. PROVIDED that, during the hours constituting their normal week, they are, and remain, capable of, available for and willing to perform satisfactorily the work associated with their usual occupation, or reasonable alternative work if their usual work is not available.

. . . .

(3) The guarantee shall be reduced in respect of any week to the extent that a worker fails in that week to be capable of, available for and willing to perform satisfactorily the work associated with his usual occupation or reasonable alternative work if his usual work is not available.

(4) The guarantee shall be similarly reduced in respect of any pay week in the course of which a worker has been suspended for disciplinary reasons to the extent of the suspension occurring in that pay week.

(5) In the case of a holiday recognised by agreement, custom or practice, the guarantee shall be reduced in respect of the pay week in which the holiday takes place in the same proportion as the normal working hours for the time being have been reduced in that pay week.

(6) A firm shall not be liable to make any payment of guaranteed wages under this Agreement if it is prevented from providing work by dislocation of production caused directly or indirectly by strike action within any of its works, or by shortage of raw materials, fuel, power or transport facilities, occasioned by circumstances outside the employer's control.

(7) This Agreement shall come into force in the pay week beginning on or immediately after 1st March, 1947.

(8) This Agreement may be terminated or varied by not less than three months' notice given in writing by either of the parties thereto.

12 Widening of scope and content

PRODUCTIVITY BARGAINING

12.1 Transport and General Workers' Union and Esso Petroleum Co. Ltd, *Memorandum of Agreement: Refinery, Fawley* 1960

It is agreed that the implementation of the proposals which are described in this document will make possible . . . payment of . . . various wage increases . . .

SECTION A. M. & C.[1] DEPARTMENT

1. THE CARRYING-OUT OF SLINGING WORK BY CRAFTSMEN

In keeping with the general desire to eliminate avoidable delays, it is recognised that the amount of slinging work currently performed by craftsmen can usefully be increased.

It is accordingly agreed that where straightforward lifts are involved, craftsmen will, when built-in facilities are provided, lift loads up to approximately 30 cwts, and elsewhere with runners, davits, shear legs or 'A' frame assistance will lift to a limit of approximately 10 cwts. Where lifts are clearly of a complex nature but are within the limits specified above, Rigger assistance will be provided.

It is also agreed that initially, the Rigger group will be maintained at its present strength, until, by a process of attrition, it becomes possible to stabilise the size of the group at a smaller figure.

2. INCREASE OF FLEXIBILITY BETWEEN BRICKLAYERS AND INSULATOR/CLEANER LABOURERS

Due to the relatively small amount of bricklaying work in the Refinery it is possible to employ regularly only a small force of Bricklayers whose workload varies considerably. At times there is more work than Bricklayers can adequately cope with, while on other occasions they cannot be fully and usefully employed solely on bricklaying work.

In order to overcome this situation it is agreed that:-
1) When necessary, Cleaner/Labourers will assist Bricklayers in the finishing of concrete and refractory work with a float.
2) Insulators will, when necessary, assist and/or supplement Bricklayers on such jobs as:-
    a. Trowelling up behind guniters.
    b. Work on castable refractory walls.
    c. Insulation of furnace roofs.

[1] Maintenance and Construction. This agreement extended to other departments, e.g. Technical Department, Process Department.

3) Bricklayers, when not fully employed on their own craft will work as Insulators (i.e. carry out their own mixing, etc.).

3. CONSOLIDATION OF GRADES AND ABOLITION OF THE POINTS RATING SCHEME

It is recognised that a need exists to increase versatility at the Refinery in order to improve efficiency and provide people with more satisfying work. It is in keeping with this need to abolish the existing Points Rating Scheme and consolidate the existing job and pay grades.

It is accordingly agreed that the existing 25 job grades and 18 pay grades within M. & C. Department should be consolidated to 16 job grades and 4 pay grades . . .

. . . .

4. MATES

It is recognised that many of the functions currently carried out by mates can, by their nature, be performed more effectively in other ways. It is accordingly agreed that the job of mate will be abolished.

The mates concerned (with the exception of some in the Electrical Section who may be afforded the opportunity to train for craft status) will all be redeployed to other non-craft work. Training for this alternative work will be carried out as soon as is practicable, but up to 24 months may elapse before the last mate is assigned and ready to take up his new job.

5. INTRODUCTION OF 40 HOUR WEEK AND WITHDRAWAL OF CERTAIN TIME ALLOWANCES

(a) Day Forces

It is recognised that the attainment of a 40 hour week is a desirable objective in the progress towards a better standard of living. In order to achieve this objective immediately without suffering a loss of productive work, the following changes are agreed:-
1. All existing changing and washing time allowances will cease with the exception of a limited number of jobs for which washing is a statutory requirement.
2. a) Fixed tea breaks will cease and the distribution of tea and food by the Canteen will be discontinued.
   b) Each day man will be provided with a free thermos flask initially, and thereafter, one free flask per year.
   c) Tea will in future only be taken during a natural break in the work sequence.

. . . .

(b) Shift Forces

In order to achieve an average 40 hour week for shiftworkers, it is agreed that the present shift rota will be modified to allow an additional 13 days off per year. These will be taken at Management's discretion. In order that these 13 days off shall be paid when taken, every normal working week will be treated as a five shift week for pay purposes, whether 5 or 6 shifts are worked. So far as overtime is concerned, the rota will be the basis of calculation.

. . . .

6. PROGRESSIVE REDUCTION OF OVERTIME

It is mutually agreed that the working of overtime at its present level is an undesirable feature of Refinery activity. While the complete elimination of overtime is not possible, it is agreed that a reduction from the existing 18% M. & C. average to a 2% M. & C. average can be achieved over a period of two years.

The progressive increase of basic rates of pay . . . has been tied to the antici- pated reduction of overtime. The 24 month period will be divided into four sub-periods of 6 months. During the four sub-periods the anticipated average overtime level will be reduced as shown below:-

Present average overtime level	18%
Immediate initial overtime level	14%
After 6 months	11%
After 12 months	8%
After 18 months	5%
After 24 months	2%

As overtime is reduced and the overtime element in pay packets is lessened, it is recognised that greater flexibility in the administration of overtime will be required. It will be necessary to extend the period of equalisation, immediately to a quarterly, and eventually to a yearly, basis.

7. THE TRAINING OF PROCESS WORKERS TO DO CERTAIN MINOR MAINTENANCE WORK NOW DONE BY M. & C. FORCES

It is recognised that there is a need to improve the progression of minor routine plant maintenance. This would enable the plants to operate more efficiently, and would free M. & C. forces for the more important major maintenance jobs. It is accordingly agreed that Process workers should be trained to do a specified list of minor maintenance jobs, and that they should be free to carry out this work whenever circumstances permit.

. . . .

8. RE-ORGANISATION OF THE PERMANENT M. & C. SHIFT FORCE

It is recognised that if overtime is to be reduced to an average of 2%, the permanent shift force must be employed on important Refinery-wide main- tenance and construction jobs, and not mainly on minor maintenance work as has been the case to date. To achieve this objective, it is necessary to create a mobile, versatile and well-equipped group.

It is accordingly agreed that on a volunteer basis, the scope of the perma- nent shift force will be widened to include rigging and other skills.

The hours of work will continue as at present, but overtime will only be worked to cover unexpected absences and then only on the decision of the

Shift Maintenance Supervisor. If coverage for holidays and planned absences is required, or circumstances call for a supplemented force to cope (for example) with long start-up periods, day-workers will be transferred to shift-work on a temporary and voluntary basis, and will be paid the shift differential. In the case of holiday coverage, shift-workers' and day-workers' holidays will need to be geared together so that sufficient day-workers will in fact be available for coverage purposes.

9. THE INTRODUCTION OF ADDITIONAL PERMANENT AND TEMPORARY SHIFT SYSTEMS

a) A permanent five-day three-shift system for chauffeurs

Because the times during which chauffeur driver transport is required invariably extends beyond normal day hours and in order, therefore, to avoid the regular need to work overtime, it is agreed that a permanent overlapping five day (Monday to Friday) three-shift system be introduced.

. . . .

b) A permanent five-day two-shift system in the workshops

Because the workshops are unaffected by weather conditions, daylight hours and Process plant conditions, and in order to minimise the need to work overtime to meet field requirements, it is agreed that a permanent five-day two-shift system for the workshops should be introduced.

. . . .

c) A temporary two-shift or three-shift system from Mondays to Fridays

In order to reduce the Refinery overtime average, as agreed, it is envisaged that work commitments in the field and shops may from time to time necessitate working a second shift, or second and third shift for a limited period.

. . . .

10. THE ADMINISTRATIVE SUPERVISION OF ALL CRAFT AND NON-CRAFT PERSONNEL BY AREA SUPERVISORS

Whilst the Company would normally, as a matter of policy, require Area Supervisors to work through first line supervision, it is agreed that occasions will arise where it is expedient for the Area Supervisor to direct a man himself.

11. LINE SUPERVISORS

It is agreed that the Union affiliation of Line Supervisors will not be allowed to become a source of embarrassment to them in their position as Supervisors.

12. LEADING HANDS

It is agreed that the position of Leading Hand be eliminated when six months have elapsed and that the people currently holding this position should have their Leading Hand differential absorbed in the pay increases.

13. ELIMINATION OF SPECIAL PAYMENTS

It is agreed that the rates of pay now agreed take care of all conditions likely to be experienced on an oil refinery. The practice of agreeing special payments for 'exceptional' conditions will accordingly cease.

Height money, however, will continue to be paid as at present. For flare stacks and chimney stacks, except where these are fully scaffolded, payment will be based on distance above the ground. In the case of the Hydroformer and Cat.[1] Plant stacks, payment will only be made for work carried out above the 11th and 9th platforms respectively based upon the distance above these platforms.

All payments will be made in accordance with the agreed rates.

12.2 *Productivity Bargaining* [Royal Commission on Trade Unions and Employers' Associations, *Research Papers* 4(1) (London, H.M.S.O., 1967)]

WHAT IS PRODUCTIVITY BARGAINING?

4. National negotiations at industry level have traditionally concentrated on wage rates and have said little about the work which is to be performed in return for wages. However, various kinds of collective bargaining do take the performance of work into account (such as for example negotiation about piece-rates). Collective bargaining which does this may be termed "wage-work bargaining".

5. Productivity bargaining may be described as a type of wage-work bargaining. The term "productivity bargain" lacks precision, but broadly it may be described as an agreement in which advantages of one kind or another, such as higher wages or increased leisure, are given to workers in return for agreement on their part to accept changes in working practice or in methods or in organisation of work which will lead to more efficient working. . . .

6. The concessions on the workers' part must, if the agreement is to be a "productivity agreement" in the generally accepted sense, be in concrete terms. Thus agreements which contain general remarks about the need for efficiency do not on that account become productivity agreements, and indeed experience has shown that they frequently contribute very little to efficiency in real terms. . . .

7. A distinction may be made between a productivity agreement and an agreement to introduce a new system of payment by results the purpose of which is to give higher wages in return for higher production. The latter type of agreement does not necessarily involve any change in working practice or in conditions, but concentrates essentially on stimulating greater effort. Such "effort-bargains" may of course certainly be successful in raising productivity, and illustrate a point that needs emphasising—that productivity agreements provide by no means the only method of raising labour productivity . . .

. . . .

[1] Catalytic.

WHAT GAINS HAVE WORKERS MADE THROUGH PRODUCTIVITY BARGAINING?

95. *Pay.* The first and most obvious benefit to workers has been higher wages. Some increases have been large, and without doubt a good deal larger than would have been forthcoming if the workers concerned had relied on conventional bargaining for pay increases. . . .

. . . .

99. . . . The *security* of workers' pay has also been greatly increased. When pay is largely dependent on overtime there is an inevitable uncertainty as to how long a pay packet enlarged by overtime pay is going to stay large. While managements are powerless to reduce overtime in boom conditions they may be brought to do so if a recession begins to bite. Moreover even if the average amount of overtime remains high the groups who benefit from it may change, and overtime may come in rushes (e.g. when there are plant overhauls) so that the pay packet may fluctuate very considerably from one week to the next.

100. Thus, in all the undertakings which have linked reduced overtime with increased pay one of the results has been to improve security in pay for the workers affected. . . .

101. Improved basic rates of pay also reflect themselves in other advantages to workers. It means that holiday pay is also improved, and may also mean improvements in other payments if they are linked with basic rates— e.g. pay during sick absences. . . .

. . . .

103. *Hours of Work.* . . . a very considerable reduction in hours of work has been secured or is planned in many productivity agreements. . . .

. . . .

106. *Fringe benefits.*[1] Many productivity agreements provide fringe benefits of one kind or another. . . .

. . . .

109. *Promotion.* Some agreements improve the prospects of advancement for some categories of worker. First, there are those mates who are fortunate enough to have received the opportunity of being accepted as craftsmen. . . .

110. Secondly, where pay structures are simplified and mobility improved it may mean better opportunities for advancement for some workers. . . .

111. It may also be presumed that relaxation of customs under which for example a foreman must be skilled in the craft of the craftsmen he supervises provides wider promotion opportunities. . . .

112. *Security against redundancy.* Since the object of productivity agreements is to get labour better used it is natural that the possibility of redundancy should be of great importance. One factor which helps to make it particularly important is that the attitudes of work groups are so deeply involved. Work groups would be extremely reluctant to agree to changes which would benefit some of their number while resulting in others being sacked. A

---

[1] Returns from employment other than straight payments for work done, e.g. retirement pensions, sick pay, provision of recreational facilities.

guarantee against redundancy is therefore often regarded as in practice an indispensable pre-requisite for any serious negotiations.

113. Hence, many productivity agreements provide workers with an explicit assurance of security against dismissal which they did not previously possess, and to that extent they have greater job security. . . .

·   ·   ·   ·   ·   ·

116. *Other benefits.* The advantages so far listed are the more tangible ones. However there are other intangible benefits which it is claimed workers gain. It is said that morale is raised. Workers whose jobs are enlarged have more interest in their work. The cutting out of time-wasting makes workers feel that their work is both valuable and valued. It is impossible to quantify gains of this kind. That they may exist and be felt to be of great importance is hardly deniable.

·   ·   ·   ·   ·   ·

WHAT DISADVANTAGES HAVE WORKERS SUFFERED AS A RESULT OF PRODUCTIVITY BARGAINING?

118. The most immediate threat to workers from any drive to improve the use of labour is redundancy. In general however it has been accepted that workers must be given security against this threat if their co-operation in a bargain is to be gained.

119. Secondly, some workers' earnings tend to suffer as a result of productivity bargains. A bargain may result in raising earnings on average, but some workers—those for example who have been working particularly large amounts of overtime before its elimination or reduction—will find that their earnings have been reduced. . . .

120. Thirdly, it is frequently a part of an agreement that workers will accept hours of work which are economically of advantage but which from the workers' point of view are inconvenient and disturbing. Shift work may be extended at the expense of day work.

121. Fourthly, the status of workers may be threatened. Thus craftsmen may feel that their skills are devalued if mates are eliminated. Particular groups may feel threatened if the demarcations which protect their particular jobs are reduced.

122. More generally, productivity agreements involve change, and change is disturbing. While change is going on workers may feel anxiety about their jobs . . . Valued social groups may be broken up. Most people dislike change, and it is this dislike which accounts for a good deal of the initial resistance to productivity bargains. By the same token, once changes have been introduced they seem on the whole to be accepted surprisingly quickly.

·   ·   ·   ·   ·   ·

WHAT ADVANTAGES AND DISADVANTAGES ARE THERE TO UNIONS AS SUCH IN PRODUCTIVITY BARGAINS?

124. It is useful to consider what advantages and disadvantages there are in productivity bargaining for unions as institutions. The interests of unions

do not of course necessarily coincide with those of their members individually; to take an obvious example, the single-manning agreement with British Rail will lead eventually to the employment of 9,000 less footplatemen and this will have a considerable effect on the membership of the principal union concerned, the Associated Society of Locomotive Engineers and Firemen.

125. To look at the credit side first, if productivity bargains produce substantial benefits for trade union members then it is reasonable that the trade unions which negotiate them should gain in prestige thereby both with the members who directly benefit and more generally because they enable the unions to appear in a progressive light. More than this, the improvement of its members' conditions is the basic diet of any union, and success in securing this improvement is vital to its well-being. Productivity bargaining offers an attractive way of making progress since it means by definition bargaining with an employer who is ready to give; and what he gives may then perhaps be sought elsewhere too.

126. Secondly, productivity bargains tend to be explicit about matters which were previously not explicit, but where formally management could exercise its prerogative but in practice a good deal of control was exercised by work groups. The result of the formality of a written agreement is to emphasise the union's share in control.

127. Thirdly, agreements have not invariably resulted in loss of membership. . . . No doubt . . . to the extent that productivity agreements are successful and the concerns that conclude them flourish there is a likelihood in the long term that they will expand, and with it trade union membership will also expand.

128. Finally, productivity bargains may result in understandings with management under which union membership becomes compulsory. . . .

129. The foremost possible disadvantage of a productivity agreement to a union has already been mentioned in paragraph 124—that it may result in reduced membership. . . .

130. Secondly, agreements may result in a loss in the amount of control a union exercises over a job. Thus if demarcations between craftsmen and craftsmen or between craftsmen and process workers are relaxed a decrease in the control exercised by craft unions is involved. To an extent the workers are exchanging the security provided by the union for security provided by the firm, and the consequence is some loss of union power.

131. Again, a productivity agreement may involve a union in accepting responsibility which it did not previously have to accept. Thus unions will have to deal with the discontented minorities who have done least well out of agreements.

132. Finally, productivity bargaining tends to commit unions heavily in terms of the time and effort of its officials. . . . In so far as productivity bargains at the level of plants or undertakings become more common the greater the strain this will put on trade union resources. This is a most important point. There is no doubt that if productivity bargaining is to become more general it will be essential for trade unions to increase the numbers of their officials.

12.3 Chemical Industries Association Limited and Associated Trade Unions, *Joint Agreement on Principles and Procedures of Productivity Bargaining* 1968

INTRODUCTION

1. This joint agreement outlines the bases upon which productivity bargaining should be developed. . . .

. . . .

CONDITIONS NEEDED

15. For successful productivity bargaining certain conditions are needed. The main conditions relate to:—
   (*a*) objectives
   (*b*) measurement
   (*c*) planning
   (*d*) communications
   (*e*) industrial relations
   (*f*) negotiating procedures
   (*g*) training.

16. Objectives.—Such bargaining cannot occur without the objectives being clear to management in relation to labour utilisation changes and to Trade Unions in relation to wages structure changes, with an early development of an appreciation by each of the other's objectives.

17. Measurement.—For the determination of objectives and the establishment of an agreement, the effect of the changes proposed must be capable of measurement and the costing related to possible savings must be known and made available if needed to the participants in the negotiations.

It follows from this that management must be able to assess the savings to be made, and to have available some form of work measurement to this end. This and other management techniques will be needed for these purposes and in order to maintain control of the situation after the agreement. If these management skills are not available they must be developed as a prerequisite to a productivity agreement, either by the recruitment of suitably qualified staff or through the services of a consultant.

18. Planning.—Both sides should take into account the extent to which the negotiation of a productivity agreement is likely to make susbstantial demands upon their available time and manpower. The parties should plan the operation with a clear idea of the time involved. Rewards should be given coincidentally with the changes made.

19. Communications.—The essence of productivity bargaining is the involvement in the process of change, to produce higher efficiency, of those proposing change—managements—and those subject to it—the workers and their representatives. The objectives sought, the methods to be used and the areas to be examined should be known to the management, supervision, workpeople's representatives and the workers. It is essential that effective two-way communication is established.

20. Industrial Relations.—The creation of good Union/management relations is essential as resistance to change is likely to occur where there is absence of trust and good relations and where shop stewards have not been used to consultation and negotiation with local management.

21. Negotiating Procedures.—Productivity agreements of the nature described usually involve more than one Union. It will, therefore, be necessary for Unions, or Groups of Unions, to hold discussions and negotiate jointly.

22. Training.—As training, or re-training, will be required by many of the employees, the appropriate facilities will need to be created in anticipation of the introduction of the agreement.

23. All employees, particularly those taking part in the negotiations, should have a knowledge of training plans and management techniques involved and such other knowledge as will allow judgment on the proposals to be discussed.

RELATIONSHIP TO NATIONAL AGREEMENTS

24. Productivity bargaining should be conducted within the framework of established national agreements and it demands a situation at factory or Company level where all the Trade Unions concerned bargain jointly.

25. For the purpose of encouraging and guiding productivity bargaining, a Joint Standing Committee has been established at national level between representatives of the Craft and General Worker Unions and representatives of C.I.A. Its . . . functions are set out below.

26. The following points are agreed to establish the relationship between nationally agreed wages and conditions and variations in the wages and conditions agreed locally through Productivity Agreements.

(a) The wage rates in the national agreements are minima.

(b) Each productivity agreement shall include a clause determining the manner in which future national wage increases shall be applied.

(c) Nationally agreed hours of work and duration of annual holidays and number of statutory holidays shall remain standard conditions, not subject to local variation.

(d) Other nationally agreed conditions will remain standard but may be varied in the context of productivity agreements provided that any such variations are notified to and approved by the appropriate national negotiating bodies through the Joint Standing Committee.

(e) Sick pay schemes and pension schemes remain local matters.

FUNCTIONS OF JOINT STANDING COMMITTEE

27. The prime purpose of the Joint Standing Committee is to guide and encourage the process of productivity bargaining and to give general oversight. In addition it will sanction local variations from nationally agreed conditions in accordance with paragraph 26.

12.4 Engineering Employers' Federation and Confederation of Shipbuilding and Engineering Unions, *Memorandum of Agreement: 40-hour Week and Related Matters* 1964

PREAMBLE

1. The parties, recognising the vital contribution of the Engineering Industry to the well-being and prosperity of the country, reaffirm their support for measures intended to modernise and improve the productive efficiency of the Industry. They recognise that the provisions of this Agreement, particularly the reduction in normal weekly hours to 40, reinforce the need for the maximum utilisation of all production resources and the most effective deployment and use of manpower. They agree that restrictions on the economic utilisation and transfer of labour which are not based on considerations of skill or ability to do the job are contrary to the well-being of the Industry and should be eliminated. Both parties undertake to give their full support to efforts made to remove any impediments of this kind to which their attention may be directed.

2. The parties re-state their acceptance of the principle that it is in the best interests of all concerned that any questions which arise should be settled in accordance with the Provisions for Avoiding Disputes, contained in the National Procedure Agreement[1] without prior stoppage of work or departure from normal working. The Employers welcome the greater use now made of the Procedure as the medium for settling disputes; the Unions re-affirm their intention of ensuring that this practice is maintained.

3. The parties having in mind that this is the first long-term National Agreement covering the Engineering Industry pledge themselves and their constituent members to work together to make its operation successful.

I. HOLIDAYS

1. The National Holidays Agreement between the parties, dated 18th January, 1961, shall be amended to provide:—
   (i) one additional day of paid holiday from 1965, and a further additional day of paid holiday from 1966;
   (ii) an improvement in the minimum rate of holiday payment from consolidated time rate plus one-sixth to consolidated time rate plus one-third.

2. In order to overcome the well-known difficulty arising from the incidence in the calendar of the Christmas and New Year holidays, although this does not occur every year, if Employers wish to use one of these additional days of holiday for the purpose of overcoming this difficulty, they shall have the

[1] See Document 10.2.

right to do so. The other additional day shall be fixed by mutual consent. On those occasions when the incidence of the Christmas or New Year holiday does not provide a problem both additional days shall be fixed by mutual consent.

II. ESTABLISHMENT OF NEW MINIMUM EARNINGS LEVELS AND RATES OF PAY

1. The principle underlying this part of the Agreement is that over the next three years new minimum earnings levels higher than the current agreed minimum national or district rates shall be established in the Industry. At the end of the three-year period new minimum time rates will be established by the substitution of the minimum earnings levels for the existing minimum time rates.

2. Minimum earnings levels shall be progressively achieved by the introduction at 6-monthly intervals of special increments . . .

In those districts where the minimum rates for fitters and labourers are higher than the current national minimum rates the increments shall be proportionately smaller.

It is agreed in principle that national craft differentials, where they exist, should be negotiated as uniform rates instead of existing widely varying amounts. This will necessarily be a long-term operation to be achieved through discussions between representatives of the Federation and of the Union, or Unions, concerned with the craft under discussion.

3. Workpeople whose remuneration, however made up, is not less than the appropriate earnings levels for a normal week are not entitled to any increase in such remuneration. In those cases where such remuneration is less than the appropriate level, additional payments will be necessary in order to meet the standard for the week, or weeks, in question.

4. At the end of the three-year period, viz., on Monday, 1st January, 1968, the minimum earnings levels established on 3rd July, 1967, shall be converted into new minimum time rates, this to be achieved by the substitution of the minimum earnings levels for the existing minimum time rates. . . .

. . . .

V. THE WORKING WEEK

1. The standard hours of the normal working week shall be 40. In all cases normal hours shall be reduced from their current level to 40 but in the event of current normal hours amounting to 40 or less per week there shall not be any reduction of such hours as a result of this Agreement.

. . . . . .

4. In consideration of the reduction in the hours of the normal working week provided for in this Section of the Agreement the Unions agree as follows:
   (a) That they will take steps to emphasise to their members that the Agreement provides for a normal week of 40 hours' work.
   (b) That they support the full utilisation of working hours with particular reference to starting and finishing times.

(c) That Managements and their workpeople are free to reach Agreements for the revision or elimination of paid breaks.

(d) That in order to secure the maximum utilisation of plant and equipment which is all the more vital if working hours are to be reduced, it is recognised that the introduction or extension of nightshift, double day-shift and/or three-shift systems, may become necessary.

5. Consequent upon the introduction of the 40-hour week the following amendments to existing National Agreements shall be made:

(i) The Guarantee of Employment Agreement dated 15th February, 1957, shall be amended to the following:

All hourly rated manual workers who have been continuously employed by a federated firm for not less than four weeks shall be guaranteed employment for five days in each normal pay week. In the event of work not being available for the whole or part of the five days, employees covered by the guarantee will be assured earnings equivalent to their consolidated time rate for 40 hours.

This guarantee is subject to the following conditions:

(a) That the employees are capable of, available for, and willing to perform satisfactorily, during the period of the guarantee, the work associated with their usual occupation, or reasonable alternative work where their usual work is not available.

(b) Where approved short time is worked as an alternative to redundancy, or in the case of a holiday recognised by agreement, custom or practice, the guarantee shall be reduced proportionately.

(c) In the event of dislocation of production in a federated establishment as a result of an industrial dispute in that or any other federated establishment, the operation of the period of the guarantee shall be automatically suspended.

(d) In computing the assured earnings referred to above, premium payments due for overtime worked on weekdays, and premium payments for work done on Sundays and holidays, shall be ignored.

(ii) Each of the Bank or other holidays provided for ... shall be paid for on the basis of a uniform working day of eight hours for all workers.

6. The position of workpeople employed on the double dayshift and/or three shift system shall be the subject of a separate agreement.

VI. GENERAL

1. The parties to this Agreement, having in mind that earnings normally increase with increases in productivity, agree that the benefits provided in this Agreement represent the limit of the concessions which employers shall be required to make up to 1st January, 1968.

It is therefore agreed that until that date there shall not be any national or local claims relating to wages or working conditions which are:

(i) of a general character covering all manual workers.

(ii) of a sectional character covering all manual workers employed in a specific section or sections of the Industry, and

(iii) of an occupation character covering manual workers of a specified occupation or occupations, the concession of which would involve increases in costs.

(iv) As regards domestic claims there shall not be any of a general character covering all or substantially all of the manual workers in an establishment. Claims on behalf of individuals or groups of workpeople within an establishment shall be permitted provided they are based on alleged anomalies or inequities. Those responsible for presenting such claims would be required not only to substantiate their merits but also to give suitable assurances that any settlement would not be contrary to the spirit and intention of this Agreement.

2. It is the spirit and intention of this Agreement that improvements in wages and working conditions during the period of its operation shall be related to the growth which the Industry is expected to achieve and should be confined to those which normally take place arising from increased productivity in the Industry, coupled with those expressly provided for in the Agreement itself. The object, to which both parties subscribe, of attempting to assist in forward planning and stabilisation of costs by matching improvements with anticipated growth rates will not be achieved if, in addition to the improvements referred to above, there are widespread changes resulting in increased costs, whether they are either conceded or domestically volunteered.

3. The various provisions of this Agreement are interdependent and it is accepted that violation of any part of the Agreement may justify reconsideration of the whole.

4. If there is an increase of 5 points or more in the Index of Retail Prices during the period of twelve months from 4th January, 1965, and this increase is maintained for three consecutive months within such twelve months' period or if such an increase takes place and is similarly maintained in either of the succeeding twelve months' periods, the Unions shall be released from the restriction imposed by virtue of Clause 1 (i) of this Section. If, during the period of this Agreement, legislation relating to industrial employment adds seriously to costs, the Federation shall have the right to call for a revision of the Agreement.

5. The Unions shall be at liberty at any time within the last four calendar months of the period of operation of this Agreement to seek a meeting with the Federation for the purpose of discussing future arrangements.

12.5 Association of Supervisory Staffs, Executives and Technicians, *Are Long-Term Contracts Good? A National Executive View* (London, A.S.S.E.T., 1964)

At the 1963 ADC[1] the following resolution was carried:

That this ADC directs the NEC to investigate the possibility of entering into long-term group contracts with employers where groups of ASSET members are organised so that such a contract could operate advantageously. . . .

. . . .

[1] Annual Delegate Conference.

There are obvious difficulties, from the procedural point of view at least, to negotiating any such contract in the engineering industry—on an industry-wide basis. In any case this seems to be most undesirable because of the diverse nature of that industry.

If such contracts are to be considered at all, they will need to be negotiated either with individual companies or groups of companies or compact well-defined industries.

When such contracts are discussed the main question is obviously salary increases; from the employers' viewpoint the achievement of such arrangements on fixed terms suitable to them would seem to be to their advantage. Wage and salary rates are set for two or three years ahead and the relative stability this tends to give in fixing prices is something most firms would welcome. What worries them, of course, are the cash terms of the final settlement. From the worker's viewpoint he is guaranteed wage or salary increases over the period—but is this sufficient? If the employer is to have relative price stability as part of the bargain, should not the worker at least be guaranteed employment for the duration?

In the settlement of any agreement of this kind certain estimates have to be made, i.e. the profitability of the company, increases in productivity and rises in the cost of living. So far as productivity claims are concerned there are severe problems. . . . If the productivity of an enterprise increases, everybody is entitled to share in it. Some changes in productivity arise as a direct result of the efforts of development engineers, designers and supervisors. Should their share of the increase be greater? Any negotiations must be carried out on behalf of supervisory and technical grades by their own organisations and not as part and parcel of claims on behalf of everybody employed within the industry. One of the first requirements of any negotiations on this broad issue is to establish the correct rate for the various grades involved. Any settlement for the future, which has as its basis existing differentials can only be to the employer's advantage. Supervisors and technicians are entitled to a new deal in return for any long-term contract.

So far as productivity and cost-of-living forward estimates are concerned, these are capable of being proved wrong by events. Both could rise more steeply than anticipated and any contract must have safeguards built into it. An index should be set which measures a maxima for productivity and cost-of-living increases beyond which fresh salary increases can be negotiated within the term of the contract.

Guarantees of employment are just as vital as guarantees of salary increases and it must be emphasised that the aim should be to achieve contracts of employment and not just salary contracts. This part of the agreement would guarantee in all reasonable circumstances continuity of employment for the period of the contract, and if for any reason this promise cannot be met, proper compensation should be provided.

One of the side effects of the reaching of such agreements is the dulling of trade union activity, giving rise to apathy. This need not automatically happen because there are plenty of other things for trade unions to be tackling once some stability has been obtained on the salary front for a year or two. However, it seems to be absolutely vital that one condition of such contracts should be the requirement of an employee to belong to his appropriate trade union.

It is quite obvious that a contract in the terms mentioned above will not easily be obtained and frankly, as unsatisfactory as the present method of wage and salary bargaining may be, it would be quite wrong as a general principle to embark on the new policy of long-term contracts without obtaining these guarantees.

The NEC is therefore recommending to the Annual Delegate Conference that long-term contracts can be negotiated where appropriate with individual firms or small groups of firms aiming at employment guarantees, new improved minimum supervisors' and technicians' salaries, a requirement for trade union membership—followed by guaranteed annual increases over a two- or three-year period. Built into any such contract must be provisions for increases additional to those provided for, should productivity or consumer prices rise more steeply than anticipated.

The NEC advises that this matter be approached with extreme caution, with each case dealt with on its merits.

REDUNDANCY PROVISION

12.6 Gas Council, *Scheme with regard to compensation in the event of redundancy among employees coming within the purview of the National Joint Council for Gas Staffs*[1] 1963

GENERAL

1. This Scheme . . . is intended to provide . . . for compensation of staff employees under the age of 65 and under 60 years of age in the case of women (or such lower ages as may be prescribed for normal retirement under the provisions of certain pension schemes) who are made redundant by an Area Board as a result of re-organisation.

2. An Area Board shall, in the first instance, decide in each case whether the circumstances under which a staff employee is made redundant are such that the Scheme should operate, and whether the provisions . . . should be applicable to him. In that event, the Area Board shall indicate to the employee in writing, that he is redundant, and shall give him an appropriate period of notice.

3. A staff employee who is made redundant will be eligible for consideration under this Scheme provided he has completed a period of 5 years' continuous service in the Gas Industry. . . . If the services of a staff employee with an Area Board have terminated, and he is later re-employed in the Gas Industry, service prior to re-employment will not count as qualifying service in the event of his becoming redundant.

[1] That is, administrative, professional, technical and clerical staffs.

4. There will be no entitlement to consideration if an individual—
   (a) is over the age limits in Clause 1;
   (b) refuses suitable alternative employment within the Industry not involving additional travelling and/or change of residence; or
   (c) unreasonably refuses a transfer within the Industry which does involve additional travelling and/or change of residence; or
   (d) leaves without the consent of the Area Board before the expiry of the period of notice required by his contract of service or conditions of employment.

COMPENSATION FOR LOSS OF EMPLOYMENT

5. The compensation payable to a redundant staff employee under this Scheme will be a sum of money calculated on the basis of one-sixth of his monthly salary at the date of loss for each completed year of continuous service, subject to a maximum payment of an amount equivalent to six months' salary.

6. In addition, a redundant staff employee who is over 45 years of age and has a minimum of 8 years' continuous service, shall be granted—
   (a) a further sum equivalent to one-sixth of his monthly salary for each completed year of continuous service between the attainment of the age of 45 and the attainment of the age of 55 (50 years of age in the case of women). The compensation in this sub-paragraph shall not be extended to those over 55 years of age (50 years in the case of women).
   (b) a period of notice equal to one month for each completed year of continuous service between the attainment of the age of 45 and the attainment of the age of 55 (50 years of age in the case of women) subject to a maximum of 6 months' notice. Notice under this Clause will be additional to the normal period of notice agreed between the Area Board and the staff employee under the staff employee's contract of service. The period of notice set in this sub-paragraph shall not be extended to those over 55 years of age (50 years of age in the case of women).

(Note: For purposes of payment under Clauses 5 and 6 above, monthly salary means one-twelfth of annual salary.)

·   ·   ·   ·   ·   ·

DIFFERENCES

9. Any points of difference or dispute arising from the operation of this Scheme, will be dealt with through the appropriate conciliation machinery.

REVIEW OF TERMINATION OF SCHEME

10. The Scheme will be subject to review from time to time and may be terminated by 3 months' notice in writing by either Side of the National Joint Council for Gas Staffs.

(Note: For purposes of this Scheme "Area Board" includes "Gas Council".)

NOTE CONCERNING PENSION PROVISIONS
SUPPORTING THE STAFF COMPENSATION
SCHEME

This document is not part of the Scheme for the compensation of staff in the event of redundancy, but merely sets out . . . certain supporting pension provisions which will be available in conjunction with the Scheme to employees, to whom that Scheme applies.

A MEMBER OF A GAS STAFF PENSION SCHEME who at the date when made redundant is:-

(a) Age 30 or over but under age 45 and has 10 years' continuous service *may* if he so requests and the Gas Council or Area Board concerned having regard to special circumstances so determines, be granted a deferred pension . . . in lieu of a return of his own contributions.

(b) Age 45 or over and has 10 years' continuous service *will as a right* be granted if he so requests a deferred pension . . . in lieu of a return of his own contributions.

(c) Age 50 to 55 (45 to 50 women) and has 10 years' continuous service and chooses a deferred pension . . . in lieu of a return of his own contributions, may elect to commence to receive a pension at any time from age 55 (50 women) onwards, in which case the amount of the original deferred pension payable at normal pension age would be reduced . . .

(d) Age 55 and over (50 women) will receive an immediate pension if so qualified under the provisions . . . of the Scheme.

Where an employee to whom the Staff Compensation Scheme applies is a member of a pension scheme other than a Gas Staff Pension Scheme, he may become a Transferred Member of a Gas Staff Pension Scheme . . . if this would enable him to qualify for the benefits outlined above.

12.7 Chemical and Allied Industries Joint Industrial Council, *Schedule of Wage Rates and Working Conditions* 1967

APPENDIX K

RECOMMENDATION UPON DEALING WITH CASES OF REDUNDANCY

(*as amended on 14th October, 1958*)

It is recommended that in dealing with cases of redundancy employers should have regard to the following practices:—

1. When redundancy is foreseen the earliest possible consultation with the local Trade Union officials concerned.

2. The planning of recruitment well ahead to take account of changes in labour requirements.

3. A stop to the recruitment of workers when a prospect of any redundancy arises.

4. An order of discharge beginning with the workers with least service, other things being equal.
5. Consultation with the local Trade Union officials on the management's lists of redundant workers.
6. Not less than four weeks prior warning to workers who are likely to become redundant, which will include the J.I.C. one week's notice of termination of employment.
7. Co-operation between firms locally in the placing of redundant workers.
8. Advance consultation with the local office of the Ministry of Labour.
9. The question of any payment in respect of redundancy to be a matter for consultation between the firm and the local Trade Union officials.
10. These recommendations would not apply to redundancy arising from industrial disputes.

FRINGE BENEFITS

12.8 National Joint Industrial Council for the Electricity Supply Industry, *Agreement relating to the terms and conditions of employment of Industrial Staff in the service of Electricity Boards* 1968

DEFINITION

151. In this part the following word has the meaning hereby assigned to it: *Illness* is deemed to include injury and other disability but unless a Board decides otherwise it shall not include any injury or other disability due to active participation in sport as a profession nor in respect of which negligence by the employee is proved.

SCALE OF ALLOWANCES

152. Subject to the provisions of clauses 153 and 154,[1] an employee who is absent from duty owing to his illness shall be entitled to receive, during his illness, a sick allowance in accordance with the following scale:

[1] Not here reproduced. Clause 153 related to the calculation of allowances, which would depend *inter alia* on previous periods of sickness, and benefits received under statutory schemes. Clause 154 set out conditions of allowances, e.g. submission of medical evidence relating to illness.

Period of continuous service	Period of sick allowance in months at full salary	Period of sick allowance in months at half salary
Not exceeding 4 months	1	–
Over 4 months up to 1 year	1	2
Over 1 year up to 2 years	2	2
Over 2 years up to 3 years	3	3
Over 3 years up to 4 years	4	4
Over 4 years up to 5 years	5	5
Over 5 years	6	6

For the purpose of calculating the period of sick allowance, a month shall be deemed to be 26 days, excluding Sundays.

.   .   .   .

MATERNITY LEAVE

158. (a) Subject to the provisions of sub-clauses (c) to (f) below, a woman employee shall be allowed 18 weeks' maternity leave with pay on the following basis:
For the first 4 weeks of absence: Full salary less the amount of benefits (excluding Maternity Grant) payable under the National Insurance Act, 1965, as amended from time to time.
For the remaining 14 weeks of absence: Half salary without deduction of National Insurance benefits unless the said benefits payable when added to half salary exceed the amount of full salary; in such a case, the amount in excess of full salary shall be deducted.

(b) Leave without pay in excess of this period may be allowed at the discretion of the Board, but absence on account of illness, due or attributable to the pregnancy, which occurs outside the period of 18 weeks shall be treated as absence on sick leave within the provisions of the sick pay scheme.

(c) The maternity leave will be reckoned against her normal sick leave entitlement under the sick pay scheme.

(d) The employee shall have completed at least 12 months' continuous service at the date of application for maternity leave, which application shall be made as soon as practicable and in any case not later than 3 months before the expected week of confinement.

(e) The employee shall commence her maternity leave at least 11 weeks before the expected week of confinement and shall remain absent for a period of 18 weeks, or, if the child does not live, until 1 month after the confinement. She shall not in any case return to duty before she is certified medically fit to do so.

103

(f) Payments by the Board during the period of maternity leave shall be made on the understanding that the employee will return to duty. If she does not return, she shall refund the moneys so paid, or such part thereof, if any, as the Board at their discretion may decide.

CHECK-OFF ARRANGEMENTS

12.9 Electricity Supply Industry, *Scheme for the Deduction of Trade Union Contributions from the Salaries of Members Employed* 1967

The Electricity Council and the Electricity Boards in Great Britain (referred to as the Boards) are prepared to deduct union contributions from the salaries of members employed in the industry, subject to individual unions agreeing to the following conditions . . .

. . . . . .

2. That the administrative costs incurred by Boards shall be offset by the retention by them of $2\frac{1}{2}\%$ of the contributions which they collect.
3. That the . . . standard form shall be used by union members to authorise the deduction from their salaries. . . .

. . . . . .

5. That Boards shall transfer union contributions to . . . such offices as are agreed between individual boards and unions, these transfers to take place at intervals to be locally agreed but in any case not more frequently than monthly.
6. That transfers of contributions to each union shall be by cheque or credit transfer. Initially, and annually thereafter, the transfer shall be accompanied by a statement giving the name of the member (and other information needed for purposes of identification) and the amount currently being deducted for him. . . .
7. That the practice whereby union contributions (of whatever nature) are collected by stewards or other union officers during working hours shall cease. Boards recognise, however, that some unions will be faced with practical difficulties in fulfilling this condition immediately and, subject to unions taking all reasonable steps towards achieving this end, no time limit is placed on its fulfilment. Each Board will, at the end of six months from the date on which the service is introduced for an individual union, review progress made. Each Board reserves the right to withdraw the service should it, at any time thereafter, consider that such progress has been unsatisfactory.
8. That any board or union shall be free to withdraw from this service, subject to three months' notice being given of its intention to do so.

13 The efficacy of industry-wide agreements

13.1 National Board for Prices and Incomes, *Report No. 49: Pay and Conditions of Service of Engineering Workers* (*First Report*) (Cmnd. 3495) 1967

OUR SHORT-TERM RECOMMENDATIONS
· · · · · ·

104. The main lesson to be drawn from the results of the 1964 agreement for manual workers[1] relates to the purpose of national agreements and the relationship between national agreements and settlements in the individual company or plant. We see no virtue in incorporating in a national agreement general wage increases, for a number of reasons. First, uniform wage increases are inappropriate in an industry which contains such a diversity of earnings levels and opportunities. Secondly, there is no justification for general wage awards to workers who receive adequate earnings increases through plant wage determination. Thirdly, general increases confirm existing anomalies and inequities, and indeed render their removal more difficult, for less money will be available for adjusting the differentials between, say, the skilled low-paid time workers and the better paid less skilled piece-workers. Moreover, general wage increases cannot be meaningfully related to the productivity of plants. They therefore militate against a satisfactory productivity-earnings relationship and will be abortive as an instrument for securing changes in working practices. Furthermore, we have found no evidence that the size of general wage increases has any significant effect on the size of increase in earnings at plant level.

13.2 National Board for Prices and Incomes, *Report No. 65: Payment by Results Systems* (Cmnd. 3627) 1968

THE ROLE OF NATIONAL AGREEMENTS

201. The significance of industry-level negotiations in relation to individual enterprises varies between industries. We may broadly distinguish between three groups. First, there are industries where a national agreement completely regulates both payment systems and levels of pay because the rates of pay in the agreement are standard throughout the industry. Electrical contracting is a case in point. Such agreements rarely include PBR, and do not therefore come within our purview.

202. Secondly, there are a number of industries where PBR is operated, but where the national agreements may lay down the major payment systems, perhaps together with associated piece-rates, or limit the choice available to individual enterprises, or seek to control a key element in the system. We have studied factories in two industries, footwear and cotton spinning, where

[1] See Document 12.4.

a national agreement and national machinery seek to determine and control PBR systems. . . . These arrangements generally work well, although some wage drift[1] does occur. Our case studies, for example, show that plant management does not always accept the national agreements as given, and modifies or manipulates them in a number of ways. Recently both industries have concluded agreements to promote greater standardisation and control.

203. In a third group of industries, however, the link between industry and plant agreements has been effectively "fractured". This situation is often associated with the prevalance of PBR systems determined exclusively by workplace, plant or company arrangements. The "fractured" situation is most notable in the engineering industries. . . . but our impression is that it has been spreading rapidly in other industries. For instance, it is now widespread in building and printing, as well as in several industries where district piece-rates have been traditional.

204. We have considered whether industry-wide agreements could be held to have any future role at all in what we call the "fractured" situation. . . .

205. We consider, however, that there are many respects in which industry-wide negotiating and conciliation systems can serve a valuable purpose. In particular, apart from providing a desirable common framework of standard conditions in such matters as working hours and holiday arrangements, they can be developed so as to provide external support and guidance for the reform of payment systems at the enterprise.

206. If industry-wide agreements in the "fractured" situation are to fulfil this role of helping to reform the system of payment at the enterprise, it seems to us that they must cease to concern themselves primarily with the negotiation of general "across the board" pay increases. They should, we think, rather aim to meet four main functions. First, to promote the conclusion of plant or company agreements by, for instance, negotiating standard procedures for bargaining at the enterprise level. Secondly, to lay down general guidelines for plant payment systems, allowing for variations in local or sectional conditions as far as possible. Thirdly, to provide a means of correcting faults in such systems as they arise. And fourthly, to correct adverse consequences of plant wage-determination by *selective* wage increases to groups such as the low-paid or others whose pay needs to be changed in relation to the rest of the industry. If, for example, increases in earnings at the plant level can be kept below the average rate of increase in national productivity, scope is left for doing something for the low-paid through a national agreement without incurring inflation.

13.3 National Federation of Building Trades Employers, *Statement of Evidence to the National Board for Prices and Incomes* (London, N.F.B.T.E., 1968)

2. N.F.B.T.E. ATTITUDE TO WAGE FIXING

2.1 The N.F.B.T.E. has recently reviewed its policy on national negotiat-

[1] See Document 85.8.

ing, but has decided that the policy of national determination of wage rates and conditions of employment continues to be right for the building industry. Firm opposition has been expressed to the negotiation of wage rates at company or site level . . .

2.2 The general support of federated firms for the continuance of national negotiations on both rates of wages and conditions of employment is based . . . on the following special conditions under which building work is carried out:—

2.2.1 On a large part of building work there is a divorce between the responsibilities for design and for construction. The contractor builds according to the design and the instructions of the architect. Failures by architects to produce drawings, information and instructions in time to meet the planning requirements of the contractor are frequent. Changes in designs and in instructions during the progress of the job also are too common. This situation has a direct bearing on the ability of the contractor to ensure a smooth flow of work on every job. He must have the flexibility afforded by incentive schemes which permit on the spot target fixing.

2.2.2 The work-places are always temporary and their number is very large. On the other hand the number of operatives employed by a single contractor on any one job is usually small: there are few sites where one contractor employs more than 200 men.

2.2.3 The labour force for each job is assembled ad hoc, whether it is composed of men in the company's regular employment, of men specially recruited, or of a combination of the two. Its size and composition by trades vary from time to time according to the requirements of the work.

2.2.4 To have to negotiate rates of wages job by job would place on management a considerable and an unnecessary load of additional work.

2.2.5 It would be undesirable to have site negotiations without the assistance of the full-time officers of the trade unions. The building trade unions simply do not have the resources to supervise site negotiations.

2.2.6 The wide variations in type of work and the differences in conditions from place to place make it equally undesirable to have company agreements on wage rates. The companies which might be large enough to negotiate their own agreements operate over wide areas—in many cases throughout the country—and they have to have the flexibility afforded by incentive schemes to meet the (often unknown) problems that arise site by site.

2.2.7 The system of competitive tendering makes it desirable to have as high a degree of uniformity and stability as possible in basic labour costs. In particular subcontractors employing building trade labour need to know that their tenders are based on the

107

same collective agreement as is the tender of the main contractor, who is likely to be employing the same class or classes of labour.

2.3 The N.F.B.T.E. view is that because of these special conditions the best way to remunerate building trade labour is through standard wage rates plus incentive schemes under which targets are fixed on the job and earnings in excess of the standard rate are related to production. The N.F.B.T.E. believes that in the post-war period the national negotiations have in fact had the effect of controlling the rate of growth in earnings, and that if national wage fixing were abandoned competition for labour would lead to accelerated wage inflation.

14 The 'two systems' of industrial relations

14.1 Royal Commission on Trade Unions and Employers' Associations 1965–1968, *Report* (Cmnd. 3623) 1968

THE TWO SYSTEMS

143. We can now compare the two systems of industrial relations. The formal system assumes industry-wide organisations capable of imposing their decisions on their members. The informal system rests on the wide autonomy of managers in individual companies and factories, and the power of industrial work groups.

144. The formal system assumes that most if not all matters appropriate to collective bargaining can be covered in industry-wide agreements. In the informal system bargaining in the factory is of equal or greater importance.

145. The formal system restricts collective bargaining to a narrow range of issues. The range in the informal system is far wider, including discipline, recruitment, redundancy and work practices.

146. The formal system assumes that pay is determined by industry-wide agreements. In the informal system many important decisions governing pay are taken within the factory.

147. The formal system assumes that collective bargaining is a matter of reaching written agreements. The informal system consists largely in tacit arrangements and understandings, and in custom and practice.

148. For the formal system the business of industrial relations in the factory is joint consultation and the interpretation of collective agreements. In the informal system the difference between joint consultation and collective bargaining is blurred, as is the distinction between disputes over interpretation and disputes over new concessions; and the business of industrial relations in the factory is as much a matter of collective bargaining as it is at industry level.

149. The formal and informal systems are in conflict. The informal system

undermines the regulative effect of industry-wide agreements. The gap between industry-wide agreed rates and actual earnings continues to grow. Procedure agreements fail to cope adequately with disputes arising within factories. Nevertheless, the assumptions of the formal system still exert a powerful influence over men's minds and prevent the informal system from developing into an effective and orderly method of regulation. The assumption that industry-wide agreements control industrial relations leads many companies to neglect their responsibility for their own personnel policies. Factory bargaining remains informal and fragmented, with many issues left to custom and practice. The unreality of industry-wide pay agreements leads to the use of incentive schemes and overtime payments for purposes quite different from those they were designed to serve.

150. Any suggestion that conflict between the two systems can be resolved by forcing the informal system to comply with the assumptions of the formal system should be set aside. Reality cannot be forced to comply with pretences.

15 Reconciliation of the 'two systems'

15.1 Royal Commission on Trade Unions and Employers' Associations 1965–1968, *Report* (Cmnd. 3623) 1968

THE REFORM OF COLLECTIVE BARGAINING

. . . .

182. In order to promote the orderly and effective regulation of industrial relations within companies and factories we recommend that the boards of companies review industrial relations within their undertakings. In doing so, they should have the following objectives in mind:

(1) to develop, together with trade unions representative of their employees, comprehensive and authoritative collective bargaining machinery to deal at company and/or factory level with the terms and conditions of employment which are settled at these levels:

(2) to develop, together with unions representative of their employees, joint procedures for the rapid and equitable settlement of grievances in a manner consistent with the relevant collective agreements;

(3) to conclude with unions representative of their employees agreements regulating the position of shop stewards in matters such as: facilities for holding elections; numbers and constituencies; recognition of credentials; facilities to consult and report back to their members; facilities to meet with other stewards; the responsibilities of the chief shop steward (if any); pay while functioning as steward in working hours; day release with pay for training;

(4) to conclude agreements covering the handling of redundancy;

(5) to adopt effective rules and procedures governing disciplinary matters, including dismissal, with provision for appeals;

(6) to ensure regular joint discussion of measures to promote safety at work.

· · · · · · ·

191. . . . a statute, which might be called the Industrial Relations Act, should lay an obligation on companies of a certain size to register collective agreements with the Department of Employment and Productivity. Initially the limit should be set high, say at 5,000 employees, in order to keep the administrative burden within bounds. The objective would be two-fold; to impress upon the boards of companies, and upon the public, that the primary responsibility for the conduct of industrial relations within a concern, and for the framework of collective agreements within which those relations are conducted, lies with the board; and, secondly, to draw attention to the aspects of industrial relations such as those set out in paragraph 182 which the public interest requires should be covered wherever possible by clear and firm company and factory agreements.

· · · · · · ·

194. . . . companies may prefer to register separate agreements for each of their factories. There is no reason why factory agreements should not deal satisfactorily with all the items on the list. The obligation upon the company to register them, however, will emphasise the final responsibility of the board for the conduct of industrial relations throughout the undertaking.

195. A company may be unable to register an agreement on a particular matter because, despite its efforts to negotiate, the union or unions are unwilling to settle, perhaps because of inter-union disagreements. If so the facts should be reported. Similarly a company may report different agreements with two or more groups of unions, when it would prefer to negotiate comprehensive agreements covering all its manual workers, or both manual and white-collar employees.

196. If a company does not recognise trade unions, it will have no agreements to register, and this will have to be reported to the Department of Employment and Productivity with reasons. In this event the company will be failing in its public duty unless it can show that its employees are unwilling to join trade unions and to be represented by them.

197. The Act should apply to nationalised industries and to public services other than the civil service. The obligation to register agreements will rest upon the employing authority. In fact its requirements could be met by most public authorities and boards with less changes than in private industry.

198. In addition to the obligations it places upon companies and employing authorities, the Act should establish an Industrial Relations Commission, with a full-time chairman and other full-time and part-time members, who should include persons with practical experience in industrial relations, and power to appoint its own administrative and research staff. Among its duties the Commission will be expected, on a reference from the Secretary of State for Employment and Productivity, to investigate and report upon cases and problems arising out of the registration of agreements. . . .

199. Agreements will be registered with the Department of Employment and Productivity, not the Commission, and the Department's industrial relations

service will handle queries and problems up to the point at which a reference to the Commission is thought advisable. . . .

200. Our recommendations and the operation of the Act should lead to an early review by smaller companies of their industrial relations. In any case it will not be possible to prevent difficulties and disputes arising in such companies about issues which fall within the scope of the Commission's responsibility, which is the proper functioning of the machinery of collective bargaining. It must therefore be possible for the Secretary of State to refer such difficulties and disputes, if they are urgent, to the Commission. . . . Disputes concerning substantive agreements and their interpretation are referable to arbitration; disputes concerning procedural agreements, including disputes about whether such agreements should be concluded and with whom, will fall within the province of the Commission.

201. This does not mean that the Industrial Relations Commission's investigation should be confined to procedural agreements. In practice procedural and substantive agreements are closely intermeshed in the working of industrial relations. The effectiveness of a pay structure depends in large measure on the method of reviewing claims for pay adjustments; the method of fixing piecework prices is crucial to the successful operation of a system of piecework payment. The Industrial Relations Commission should be the body to carry out inquiries into the general state of industrial relations in a factory or an industry . . . But if it was required to arbitrate on particular disputes about terms and conditions of employment its attention would be diverted from the proper functioning of the machinery of collective bargaining to finding acceptable settlements, and from long-term objectives to short-term compromises.

202. We have considered whether industry-wide agreements as such should be registered with the Department of Employment and Productivity. . . . so long as an industry-wide agreement is applied within any company which is required to register, that agreement itself will be registered. To place the obligation on the company emphasises that the primary responsibility for the conduct of industrial relations within the company rests on the board, and that industry-wide agreements are to be judged first of all by their effect on relationships within companies and factories.

203. It would be wrong to attempt to lay down a detailed set of rules to which the Commission will be expected to work. It will be entrusted with a novel task and will therefore have to develop its own rules and methods in the course of its work. Equally, however, it will be important that the principles which guide the Commission's work should be known and understood. We suggest that they might be these:

    (1) that collective bargaining is the best method of conducting industrial relations. There is therefore wide scope in Britain for extending both the subject matter of collective bargaining and the number of workers covered by collective agreements;

    (2) that, since collective bargaining depends upon the existence, strength and recognition of trade unions, the test in dealing with any dispute over recognition—other than a dispute between unions over recognition—should be whether the union or unions in question can

reasonably be expected to develop and sustain adequate representation for the purpose of collective bargaining among workers in the company or factory concerned, or among a distinct section of those workers. A ballot may be useful in applying the test, but could rarely determine the issue by itself;

(3) that a system of industrial relations must be judged principally by its effects in the company, the factory and the workshop. Industry-wide procedures and agreements should be confined to those issues which they can effectively regulate;

(4) that wherever possible, collective agreements should be written and precise;

(5) that pay agreements should provide intelligible and coherent pay structures;

(6) that it is desirable for agreements whenever it is possible to link improvements in terms and conditions of employment with improvements in methods of operation;

(7) that procedure agreements should be comprehensive in scope and should provide for the rapid and equitable settlement of disputes, whether they refer to the interpretation of existing or the making of new agreements;

(8) that it is desirable for each company or factory to be covered by a single set of comprehensive agreements applying to all the unions representing its employees; if this is unattainable, that separate sets of agreements covering distinct groups of employees should be accepted by all the unions representing workers within each group. This principle should guide the solution to any dispute between unions concerning recognition.

204. Failure on the part of a company to register its agreements, or to report that it has no agreements and why, will render it liable to a monetary penalty. . . .

SAFEGUARDING AND INCREASING EMPLOYMENT OPPORTUNITIES

16 Restrictions upon entry into employment

16.1 McCarthy, W. E. J., *The Closed Shop in Britain* (Oxford, Basil Blackwell, 1964), pp. 3, 16

. . . the 'closed shop'—defined as a situation in which employees come to realize that a particular job is only to be obtained and retained if they become and remain members of one of a specified number of trade unions.

. . . .

The important distinction to be made . . . concerns whether or not the

112

individual worker has to join the union, or be accepted by it, *before* he can be engaged by the employer. If this is necessary we may speak of the existence of a *pre-entry* closed shop. If, on the other hand, the employer is free to engage a non-unionist, so long as he agrees to join the union immediately or shortly after engagement, then the practice may be described as a *post-entry* closed shop.[1]

16.2 National Joint Committee for the Scottish Baking Industry, *National Working Agreement* Revised edition 1966

CLAUSE I. CONDITIONS OF ENGAGEMENT

. . . .

(b) As from 1st August, 1946, all workers falling into the categories defined by the Agreement who may be engaged by an employer shall be required to be members of the Union, provided that it shall be open to the employer or the worker to seek permission of the National Joint Reference Committee, as established by the National Conciliation Agreement, for exemption from the terms of this paragraph, stating the grounds on which such exemption is sought.

16.3 Royal Commission on Trade Unions and Employers' Associations 1965–1968, *Report* (Cmnd. 3623) 1968

THE CASE FOR THE CLOSED SHOP

592. The two most convincing arguments for the closed shop . . . depend upon the close link between effective collective bargaining and strong trade unions. The first is that in some industries it is impossible or difficult for a union to establish effective and stable organisation without the help of the closed shop; the second is that even where membership can be recruited and retained without its assistance there are instances where it is needed to deploy the workers' bargaining strength to the full.

593. There are, however, other arguments which can apply even where these two lack force. London Transport told us that they saw advantage in the closed shop,[2] since, as they put it, it ensured that in dealings with the union they were meeting an organisation "which does represent all your people". A similar argument is that the closed shop helps to secure the observance of agreements, since it adds to the power of the union to discipline those who ignore them.

594. It must not be supposed, however, that good industrial relations are the

[1] The concepts of 'agency shops' and 'approved closed shops' were introduced in sections 10 and 16 of the Industrial Relations Bill 1970. See Document 88.1, Part II, and Document 88.2.

[2] For the form operated, see Document 54.6.

invariable accompaniment of the closed shop. On the contrary the closed shop is widespread in motor manufacturing, shipbuilding, coal-mining and the docks, the four industries in which strikes in breach of agreement have been most common in recent years.

THE CASE AGAINST THE CLOSED SHOP

595. Against the closed shop, it is argued that it reduces the individual's freedom in a number of ways. If he is to obtain or retain employment where there is a closed shop, he has no choice but to join the trade union and to pay a subscription. The trade union may refuse to accept him as a member, and is answerable to nobody for its decision. Once a member of the union, the individual has to comply with any relevant decisions it may make; if he does not he may be disciplined, and if things go too far he may eventually be expelled and lose his job in consequence. So far as he is concerned, therefore, the trade union is no longer a "voluntary" organisation, at least in the normal sense, and he cannot register his disagreement with the union in the normal way open to members of voluntary organisations—by resignation—unless he is prepared also to face losing his job.

596. The importance of the loss of individual freedom is reinforced by the extent to which . . . power in trade unions rests with work groups. Where matters are left to work groups to settle, they may need to support their decisions with some authority. Unions' disciplinary procedures designed with the needs of the branch in mind sometimes appear irrelevant to the work group when shop floor questions are at issue. As a result informal disciplinary measures, such as ostracism, may be used. Occasionally, trade union authority is wholly usurped . . .

597. The second principal objection advanced against the closed shop concerns its economic effects. Essentially, what is at issue here is entry to the skilled trades. It is argued that the craft unions use the closed shop to restrict to their own members, or certain classes of their own members, the right to do skilled work; and because they limit the number of entrants they will allow to be trained in the requisite skills, or refuse to recognise as eligible to do skilled work members who have not served apprenticeships, they cause shortages of skilled labour which are economically damaging.

SHOULD THE CLOSED SHOP BE PROHIBITED?

598. In our view the closed shop as it operates at present is not always in the best interests either of workers or of the community as a whole. It is liable from time to time to cause substantial injustice to individuals from which they have no effective means of redress. It also contributes to the maintenance of a system of training which is out of date and inadequate to the country's needs.

599. It might be argued on these grounds that the closed shop should be prohibited. As part of the argument for prohibition it might be said that since we suggest elsewhere[1] that any condition in a contract of employment

[1] Para. 245, not here reproduced.

114

that the employee shall not join a union is to be void in law, it would be right to treat in the same way a condition that a worker *shall* join a union. However, the two are not truly comparable. The former condition is designed to frustrate the development of collective bargaining, which it is public policy to promote, whereas no such objection applies to the latter.

600. In any case, however, a prohibition could not be made effective. Express stipulations in written agreements for the imposition or maintenance of a closed shop would no doubt disappear in the face of a legal prohibition but this would affect less than a fifth of the workers covered by the closed shop. Since moreover some employers as well as trade unionists support the closed shop, there could be no guarantee that formal agreements would not be replaced by informal and tacit understandings of the kind which are much more commonly found. The law would presumably declare such things to be void, but this of itself would not necessarily deprive them of practical effect.

601. Some difficult problems could then arise. For example, if all the employees in a particular plant or enterprise at present subject to the closed shop agreed informally among themselves that they would try to maintain it, would this itself be an offence? If so, what punishment would be imposed, assuming the offence could be proved? The matter would no doubt come into the open when some employee refused to join the union, or resigned and refused to rejoin. If the remaining employees then threatened to withdraw their labour unless the non-unionist was dismissed, how would the law meet this situation? By prosecution of the strikers for conspiracy or for some other offence? If for conspiracy, much of the present law ousting such a charge in the circumstances of a trade dispute, or alternatively the present legal definition of a trade dispute, would have to be re-written. By yielding to the threat of a strike, and dismissing the non-unionist, would the employer be regarded as aiding and abetting the strikers? As regards the dismissed employee himself, what rights or remedies would be given to him? Compulsory reinstatement in his job where he would have to work alongside his hostile fellows would hardly be practicable. The alternative would presumably be damages for the loss of his job to be paid either by the union or by the strikers, with perhaps some contribution by the employer according to the degree of responsibility which each bore. But this would mean that the closed shop remained, and that the law had been defeated, albeit at a price. It is no doubt because of such difficulties as these that no reasoned case has been put to us in evidence for prohibiting the closed shop, even by those who strongly object to it.

· · · · · · ·

SAFEGUARDS FOR THE INDIVIDUAL: OUR PROPOSALS

609. As things are, nobody applying for trade union membership has any right to become a member, whether or not his prospects of employment depend upon membership. Acceptance of his application is entirely at the union's discretion: and in those cases where admissions are dealt with by union branches, entirely at the discretion of a branch, acting through a branch committee.

610. There is little evidence that applications for membership are dealt with

unfairly, or that membership is capriciously refused. . . . trade unions must retain ultimate discretion in decisions about whom to admit and whom not to admit . . . we think that an unsuccessful applicant for admission to a trade union, or to the skilled section of a trade union, should be able to lodge a complaint that that discretion has been arbitrarily exercised.

611. The complaint should in the first instance lie to the executive committee of the trade union concerned. . . .

612. . . . we think that a rejected applicant who still considers that his application has been arbitrarily rejected, and who considers also that the rejection is causing him substantial injustice, for example by unduly handicapping him in earning his living, should have a further right of complaint to a new and independent review body. He should be entitled to ask that body for a declaration that, upon his undertaking to abide by the rules of the union affecting existing members, he should, notwithstanding any absolute discretion vested in the union or in any committee of the union, become and remain a member. It would be open to the union to defend its decision by establishing that in refusing the application it was not dealing with the matter in an arbitrary fashion, but was acting impartially and fairly and in furtherance of the legitimate interests of the union. If the union's evidence satisfied the review body that this was so, no order would be made. Otherwise it should grant the declaration requested by the rejected applicant.

. . . .

613. If despite the terms of such a declaration the union sought to withhold any of the rights of membership from such an individual he would be in the same position under the general law as any other member as regards redress, and would therefore be able to bring an action as for breach of contract against the union. If the union took some other retaliatory action against him designed to secure that he would be unable to continue in any employment dependent upon continued membership of the union, and such action succeeded, then the individual should have the right to receive compensation from the union. . . This would not involve the discontinuance of the particular closed shop. It would in effect mean that the union regarded full control over it as worth preserving at the cost involved.

614. At the time at which a trade union secures a closed shop, some non-members may decline to join and lose their jobs in consequence. Alternatively a non-member may be dismissed as a result of shop-floor pressure. In either case an employee may have conscientious or other reasonable grounds for refusing to join the union in these circumstances, and a majority of us take the view that he should have a right of complaint[1] to the labour tribunal[2] on the grounds of unfair dismissal. . . .

[1] Against the employer.
[2] See Document 76.2.

16.4 *In Place of Strife: A Policy for Industrial Relations* (Cmnd. 3888) 1969

COMPLAINTS AGAINST TRADE UNIONS

. . . .

115. Complaints against trade unions by individuals who have no access to, or have exhausted, the union's own appeals procedure will be considered in the first instance by the Registrar,[1] who will have the duty of advising the complainants and trying to promote an amicable settlement. In some cases where this cannot be achieved there is already a legal remedy in the ordinary courts, but in others there is no remedy at present. The Industrial Relations Bill will provide that complaints by individuals of unfair or arbitrary action by trade unions resulting in substantial injustice may be referred to the Industrial Board[2] . . .

116. In cases heard by the Board, every opportunity will be given to the trade unions concerned to prepare their own answers to complaints. The object will be to ensure fair play and justice, rather than to put obstacles in the way of unions. If complaints are found to be justified, the Board will have power to award damages, or admission or re-instatement in a union. In these cases the Board will consist of a legal chairman from the Industrial Court and two members of the employees' panel of the Court.

. . . .

118. Before agreeing to a closed shop, employers should seek to obtain suitable protection for people who refuse to join trade unions on conscientious grounds. Many unions are prepared to accept such people in a closed shop, if they in their turn are prepared to show good faith, for example by contributing to charity instead of paying a union subscription. When such employees are dismissed from employment because they will not join a union, the Government proposes that they should have a right of complaint to an Industrial Tribunal as a case of alleged unfair dismissal. The Government agrees with the majority of the Royal Commission that the Tribunal should have power to award compensation to be paid by the employer, since it is his responsibility in concluding a closed shop agreement to bear in mind the interests of existing employees who are not in the union, and to ensure that they are adequately safeguarded. The Tribunal should also have power to award compensation to be paid by the employer if the closed shop is not a formal one established by agreement with a union, but an informal one resulting from the unwillingness of employees to work with a non-unionist. The Tribunal will have to consider whether the employer should in any way be liable for acquiescence in the development of such a closed shop, and the extent to which the em-

[1] The Registrar of Trade Unions and Employers' Associations. This was a new post, proposed in this White Paper, and intended at least initially to be combined with that of the Registrar of Friendly Societies. The Registrar would supervise the registration of the rules of trade unions, in the light of certain criteria relating to admission, discipline etc., set out in paras 107–113, not here reproduced.

[2] See *supra*, p. 24.

117

ployer should compensate an employee whom he has dismissed because he considered it to the advantage of his business to do so in the circumstances.

16.5 British Furniture Trade Joint Industrial Council, *National Labour Agreement* 1946, amended to 1968

18. CONDITIONS OF EMPLOYMENT FOR APPRENTICES LEARNERS AND JUNIOR PRODUCTIVE WORKERS

(i) Every male worker under 21 years of age and every female worker under 20 years of age who is not solely employed exclusively on work recognised by the Furniture Manufacturing Trade as incidental to production (e.g. drawing-off from machines or carrying material or other portering or labouring work, or packing) shall undergo a period of apprenticeship or learnership commencing between the ages of 16 and 17 years, unless an earlier or later commencement is authorised in a particular case by the appropriate Joint Industrial Council Local Learnership Committee.

(ii) A junior productive worker is a male worker under 21 years of age or a female worker under 20 years of age, for the period of such worker's employment before or after the apprenticeship or learnership period and who is not solely employed exclusively on work recognised by the Furniture Manufacturing Trade as incidental to production (e.g. drawing-off from machines or carrying material or other portering or labouring work, or packing).

. . . .

(iv) The proportion in any factory at any time of apprentices, learners or junior productive workers to journeymen or journeywomen shall be not more than one apprentice or learner or junior productive worker to three and not fewer than three journeymen or journeywomen in the craft in which the apprentice or learner or junior productive worker is to be engaged, except that one apprentice or learner or junior productive worker may be employed where either one or two journeymen or journeywomen are employed on the specific craft.

(v) For the purpose of the last foregoing rule
   (a) The ratio of apprentices, learners or junior productive workers to journeymen and journeywomen shall be established separately for males and females and be based on the average number of journeymen or journeywomen employed over a period of six months.
   (b) Casual absence of journeymen or journeywomen or a casual vacancy for a short period in the number of journeymen or journeywomen employed shall not affect compliance with condition (iv).
   (c) Where an employer works as a journeyman he shall be treated as a journeyman for the purpose hereof.
   (d) The Standing Committee of the Joint Industrial Council may authorise in writing the employment of an additional number of

apprentices or learners or junior productive workers in a particular factory for a specified period in excess of the proportion stated in sub-clause (iv) above provided always that the said Committee is satisfied that the type of production being carried out in such factory ensures that facilities are available for the effective instruction of apprentices or learners in their selected crafts.

16.6 Engineering and Allied Employers' National Federation and the Amalgamated Engineering Union, *Memorandum of Agreement: To Provide for the Temporary Relaxation of Existing Customs* 1940 (as amended to 1956)

Additional women may be drafted into the industry for the purpose of manufacturing engineering products, with special regard for increasing output and to meet war-time emergencies.

1. Women drafted into the industry under the provisions of this Agreement shall be regarded as temporarily employed.

2. An agreed record shall be kept of all changes made under this Agreement.

3. (*a*) The provisions of this Agreement will not affect the employment of women workers engaged on work commonly performed by women in the industry.

(*b*) There shall be no objection to the extension of employment of women in establishments where women have not hitherto been employed on work commonly performed by women in the industry, subject to the general undertaking contained in Clauses 1 and 2.

4. Women workers may be employed in suitable work hitherto performed by boys and youths under 21 years of age.

5. In the case of the extension of employment under Clause 3 (*b*) and 4 the national agreed scale of wages of women workers shall apply or the boys' and youths' schedule of wages shall be applied whichever is the greater.

6. Women workers may be employed on work of a suitable character hitherto performed by adult male labour subject to the following conditions:—

(*a*) Such women workers shall serve a trial period of 8 weeks at the female worker's national schedule rates.

(*b*) Thereafter

(i) Women who are unable to carry out their work without additional supervision or assistance shall receive a negotiated rate—lying between the female worker's national schedule rate and the rate appropriate to the adult male labour replaced—according to the nature of the work and the ability displayed.

(ii) Women who are able to carry out the work of the men they replace without additional supervision or assistance shall receive the rate appropriate to the adult male labour replaced.

(*c*) On payment by results the base rate and supplement paid shall be in accordance with sub-sections (*a*) and (*b*) of this Clause. When the work is carried out without additional supervision or assistance the male worker's piecework price shall be given. When additional supervision or assistance is provided the piece prices shall be negotiable under the principles of sub-section (*b*) (i).

7. Notwithstanding anything herein provided, women who might enter employment fully qualified to perform, without further training and without additional supervision or assistance, work heretofore recognised as work done by male labour, shall be paid the rate ... appropriate to the male labour they replace.

17 Control of the use of labour

17.1 British Furniture Trade Joint Industrial Council, *National Labour Agreement* 1946, amended to 1968

15. PAYMENT BY RESULTS

GENERAL PROVISIONS

(i) A scheme of Payment by Results, approved by the appropriate Union, may apply to individual workers or to a group of workers or to a department of a factory or to a whole factory.

(ii) Every scheme shall be subject to the following provisions:

(a) No worker shall receive less than the wages to which he or she would be entitled as consolidated rate under this Agreement for those not working under an approved scheme of payment by results.

. . . .

(c) The scheme shall provide for the appropriate consolidated rate being paid for time lost in the factory caused by lack of materials, faulty materials, alteration of design or other causes beyond the control of the worker.

(d) The scheme shall provide for enabling the workers affected, or the representatives of these workers at the request of these workers, to be satisfied of the correctness of the payments made.

TIMES ON INDIVIDUAL JOBS

(iii) Jobs shall be assessed in terms of agreed times allowed for the job, and not in terms of price.

(iv) (a) Such allowed times shall be set by a system of timing agreed between the employer and the workers affected, or the shop representatives of these workers, and no variation of times shall be made except in the same way.

The Parties to this Agreement accept the need for factual information as the basis of assessment of times allowed for jobs and acknowledging the need and importance of work study techniques including effort rating they will use their best endeavours to reach factory agreement on systems of timing embodying such techniques.

(b) A log book of times so arranged or varied shall be kept available to both sides for reference.

(c) Allowed times shall be such as may reasonably be expected to enable the average productive worker by appropriate effort to earn at least $12\frac{1}{2}\%$ more than the appropriate consolidated rate.

COLLECTIVE PRODUCTION BONUS

(v) Every scheme of collective bonus shall be subject to the following provisions in addition to the above General Provisions:

(a) The basis of the bonus shall be such as may be reasonably expected to enable the group of workers co-operating in the earning of it to receive among them as a whole at least $7\frac{1}{2}\%$ more than the wages which they would be entitled to receive among them as a whole at the appropriate consolidated rates.

(b) Each scheme under which the bonus payable for any week or other period is dependent upon the output of work during a previous week or other period shall provide that for the first or introductory week or other period an individual bonus of $7\frac{1}{2}\%$ will be paid to each co-operating worker.

17.2 Royal Commission on Trade Unions and Employers' Associations, *Minutes of Evidence 48, Witness: The Shipbuilding Employers' Federation* (London, H.M.S.O., 1967), Appendix E

RESTRICTIVE PRACTICES

(A comprehensive list of such practices would be of unacceptable length. Only a very small selection is given to illustrate what is happening in a general way. The practices listed are not necessarily applied in every yard or in every district. Those marked with an asterisk are of general application.)

1. LACK OF FLEXIBILITY

No man who has not served a craft apprenticeship of five years is allowed to do any work "belonging to" that craft. This involves that many jobs incidental to a man's work and which are within his competence cannot be done by him, but require to be carried out by a member of another trade. Hundreds of examples could be given, but the following illustrate the position:—

A plater, a burner and a tack-welder are required to carry out fairing work, although one man could effectively complete all these operations.

In one yard shipwrights insist that they should stand by while other tradesmen are burning and chipping open butts, although this is quite unnecessary.

Although at some yards blacksmiths carry out their own welding, at others boilermaker-welders have to be called in to the blacksmiths' shop for electric welding.

Plumbers weld pipe work, but supports for this work on the ship must be welded by boilermakers. At some yards boilermakers insist on welding all pipe work on ship.

* Drilling holes in steel work can only be done by a driller, although this is within the competence of many other trades.

2. LACK OF INTERCHANGEABILITY

* There are five separate trades covered by the Boilermakers' section of the Amalgamated Society of Boilermakers, Blacksmiths, Shipwrights and Structural Workers, but no interchangeability is permitted between these trades except for some slight relaxation in the case of caulkers and burners.

* Most yards require to employ riveters but find it difficult to keep them fully occupied. When there is no riveting work available, these men could readily do tack welding or jobbing plater work, but although they are both sections of the Boilermakers' Society they are not permitted to do this. Even in yards where some degree of interchangeability is allowed, any riveter doing plating work must be paid off if there is even one unemployed plater in the district.

When sheet ironworkers are scarce, yards are not allowed to recruit sheet metal-workers (who do exactly the same work) because they belong to a different union.

3. OVERMANNING OF MACHINES

*Twin fillet welding machines must be manned by a welder and an apprentice, although the apprentice is unnecessary.

Drillers at many yards insist that all portable machines be manned by two time-served craftsmen.

In double bottoms, the welders insist on three men manning two arcs.

Flame cutting machines must be manned by two craftsmen (a burner and a plater).

4. GENERAL RESTRICTIONS

A caulker if he starts using a burning cutter one day, will not on the same day operate a caulking machine or engage in water testing. In the event of his working overtime, he must be employed on the same equipment as he has operated in normal hours.

A welding apprentice is not allowed to operate Fuse-arc and submerged arc machines, except as an assistant to a journeyman.

No trade other than welders is allowed to carry out tack welding.

Platers in the shop insist on slinging their own plates although this could easily be done by a labourer.

Because the small Profile Burning Machine is operated by a caulker, platers will not allow it to be used for the burning of small brackets.

*All boilermaking trades (and some others) impose restrictions on the recruitment of apprentices, related to the number of journeymen in employment even when this number falls short of the normal complement.

In some yards welders insist upon examining applicants for employment, and will not work with them if their membership has been obtained by transfer from another boilermaking trade.

In one yard welders will not allow the firm to employ any welder trained in another district.

*Only men who have been apprentices to their craft can be employed, e.g. men retrained in Government Training Centres cannot be employed.

Burners are not allowed to lift plates on or off their burning tables. A plater must be summoned to do this work.

Cranemen refuse to move from one crane to another within a half-shift.

*Many jobs are no longer skilled by reason of the introduction of new machines or techniques. The craft unions will not allow such jobs to be done by anyone other than a craftsman although they could readily be done by a semi-skilled man.

*Most craftsmen insist on having a helper although in many cases this is quite unnecessary.

5. RESTRICTIONS ON OUTPUT

Caulkers refuse to use the arc-air gouging machines. (This is because of the high working speed of these machines.)

Shipwrights using wood deck caulking machines place a limitation on output.

*Many pieceworkers (in particular, welders) place a "ceiling" on earnings. This is generally related to payment per hour, and when a pieceworker is near his limit on any given day he restricts his output for the rest of the day. Men found earning money in excess of the "ceiling" are regularly "branched" and fined by the District Committee.

6. EMBARGOES ON OVERTIME

A number of trades refuse to work overtime unless the whole department or section are offered overtime. This is known as the "all or none" embargo and applies even if only two men may be required.

Many trades refuse to work evening overtime if weekend overtime is not available.

*Many demands for increases in wages are accompanied by threats of bans on overtime or blacking of particular work unless the claim is conceded at once. These threats are frequently carried out.

*Craftsmen put an embargo on overtime if there is even one man of that craft unemployed in the district.

7. TIMEKEEPING

*In the nature of shipbuilding, many men have to work at some distance from the Time Office. Although clocking in at the right time, such men regularly are very dilatory in proceeding to their place of work, and leave their place of work well before finishing time so that they are ready to go off a ship or to leave a yard immediately the hooter goes. Attempts to control these habits are met with strike action.

8. PAYMENT OF ALLOWANCES

In common with other industries, the Shipbuilding Industry has agreements providing for payment of outworking allowances, travelling time etc. to men employed on work away from their yard. These are local agreements which vary according to the circumstances in the locality. In some cases where yards have amalgamated men have refused to move from one yard to another within a group unless outworking allowances etc. are paid, even although the other yard may be nearer their homes.

17.3 *Restrictive Labour Practices* [Royal Commission on Trade Unions and Employers' Associations, Research Papers 4(2) (London, H.M.S.O., 1967)]

HOW CAN RESTRICTIVE LABOUR PRACTICES BE DEFINED?

1. It is not useful to define a restrictive labour practice simply as any practice which restricts the use of labour. . . . there are many restrictions on the use of labour which virtually everyone accepts as desirable, for example the fixing of normal hours of work by collective agreement and regulations made in the interests of safety, health and welfare under the Factories Act.[1]

2. There are two broad grounds on which a restriction on the use of labour is generally accepted as justified. First, there are economic grounds: it may for example be more efficient to prevent excessive hours of work, since people when they are tired may do bad work and do it slowly. Secondly, there are social grounds: a normal working week of even 60 hours might not in some cases be excessive in terms of efficiency, but it would certainly be agreed that it was unacceptable on social grounds. . . .

3. Whether "practice" is an apt word is debatable. In this context it might be taken to imply something over which workers alone have full control. But . . . restrictions on the use of labour may be laid down by employers and trade unions collectively or by statute. . . .

4. The term "restrictive labour practice" may thus be defined as "an arrangement under which labour is not used efficiently and which is not justifiable on social grounds".

5. It may be said that this is not a very useful definition because it does not provide a measure by which one can tell readily whether any particular practice is a restrictive labour practice. But it is of the essence of the problem that this should be so. Flagrant restrictive practices do exist and can easily be seen to be such, but this is because the economic and social judgements involved are easy to make. Perhaps much more often these judgments are not so easy to make, and cases have to be judged on their merits and in the light of particular circumstances. Overmanning provides an example. As a general proposition overmanning may appear indefensible at a time of full employ-

[1] 1961.

ment. However the retention of labour during a temporary recession may make economic (as well as social) sense, if it prevents the dispersal of a trained and experienced work-force. And of course when there is heavy unemployment, the employer who retains unneeded labour on his books may be a public benefactor.

. . . .

CIRCUMSTANCES OF RESTRICTIVE LABOUR PRACTICES

14. *Security*. It is a commonplace that a desire by workers for security is a very important motive for imposing restrictions on the use of labour. . . . Obviously workers feel the need for this most where the security provided by employers is least. It is not perhaps surprising therefore that restrictive labour practices are often most remarked in industries where there is little security of employment (especially if there has been a history of high unemployment): in shipbuilding, for example, and in the docks. It is also noteworthy that practices adopted in defence against insecurity may themselves help to perpetuate that insecurity: thus the more elaborate demarcation becomes and the narrower the range of skills a worker is allowed to exercise, the more difficult it is for an employer to provide a permanent job for that worker.

15. *Bargaining strength*. A further motive for imposing restrictions on the use of labour is to maintain or improve bargaining strength. . . .

16. *Management weakness*. It appears also that restrictive labour practices can often be put down in large measure to management weakness. The growth of unnecessary overtime results initially from insufficient control by management. Again the docks provide an example where casual management has permitted the growth of bad working habits such as poor timekeeping. The newspaper industry also provides an example. It is an industry perhaps particularly favourable to the growth of strong unions, being well-defined and with a highly skilled workforce. The newspaper employers on the other hand appear to have got into a weak position because their product is . . . highly perishable . . . and competition between employers is great and they have not proved able to muster a very high degree of unity in the face of union pressure. To this must be added a lack (on the whole) of foreign competition, so that inefficiency has not led to the industry as a whole being subjected to external pressure. In its report which concerned general printing and provincial newspapers the National Board for Prices and Incomes said that the printing employers seemed to display a "fatalistic acceptance"[1] of restrictive labour practices.

17. *Tradition*. The importance of tradition and convention in producing inefficient use of manpower needs to be noted. . . .

. . . .

19. *Work groups*. The influence of the work group has already been referred to, and it needs to be strongly emphasised. In any given situation groups of workers will have shared interests which they will wish to preserve. . . . In this it must be understood that work groups' motives are not negative—they

[1] See Document 17.4.

do not set out to prevent management succeeding; rather their objective is the quite rational and positive one of promoting their own interests. . . .

17.4 National Board for Prices and Incomes, *Report No. 2: Wages, Costs and Prices in the Printing Industry* (Cmnd. 2750) 1965

THE STATE OF THE INDUSTRY

. . . .

44. As for the unions, possibly the greatest complaint voiced by the employers is with regard to the restriction on the intake of young trainees and apprentices. Entry into the industry is restricted by traditional quota agreements with the craft unions. The arrangements prescribe a smaller proportion of apprentices in big firms than in small; even so there is some evidence that big firms do not take up their full quota. Inevitably therefore there is much poaching of trained labour from the smaller concerns.

45. The restrictions on entry certainly constitute a serious problem. More serious, however, in our view is the inefficient use of manpower that occurs within the industry. If this were put right, the complaints about a shortage of manpower would lose much of their justification. The problem is bound up in large part with the problem of demarcation; this is found both within and between unions, craft unions and non-craft unions. Printing is a long-established industry, and the printing craftsman has jealously defended his craft status. The original aim was legitimate and justifiable, but what started as a protective measure has in the modern context become restrictive, and a check to higher productivity. For technical change implies changing jobs; and rigid preservation of craft status implies resistance to changing jobs. In particular the technical developments of recent years have tended to blur the old distinctions between unions and to throw all categories of workers into a closer relationship. Parts of the industry continue, therefore, to be plagued by the question of who shall do what, and this has markedly impeded the efficient introduction of new processes and techniques which make demands that cut across the established manning arrangements.

46. We have been given many examples of practices which have the effect of limiting productivity, the arrangements very often being in defiance of the spirit of current national agreements. They included the following:—

   (a) Demarcation, particularly between craft and non-craft unions. Thus a union may insist that messages must be carried and floors swept by a craftsman; paper being transferred from one department to another may change hands at a line drawn on the floor; a machine minder may decline to carry out certain tasks, such as cleaning, on a machine in his care, and in other cases he may not be allowed to— for instance, a non-craft union has the traditional right to push buttons on a craft-controlled machine. Even within some individual unions there are strict limits between different categories of work,

126

another.

(b) Restrictions on upgrading. It is difficult, and sometimes impossible, for machine assistants to graduate to become machine minders even though they may be sufficiently skilled. In one union there is an annual quota for probationers to be accepted for upgrading over a period of three years.

(c) Overmanning. Where there are batteries of printing machines, or batteries of printing units in one machine, it would often be possible to reduce the manning. Thus, where one assistant may be needed on one machine, only six may be needed on twelve machines, but in fact twelve are employed.

(d) Pegged outputs. Outputs on various machines and other operations such as packing parcels are controlled to fixed, maximum limits well below the reasonable potential. In other cases fixed times are taken for such duties as oiling and cleaning machines, irrespective of the varying circumstances.

(e) Other restrictions include the imposition of rotas for overtime which result in people being paid for work they have not done; the traditional working day starting later and finishing earlier than the official times; and the control by one union of the transfer of men from one company to another.

.   .   .   .

48. It is only fair to say, however, that there is another side to the picture. The unions have demonstrated their willingness to negotiate progressive agreements with progressive employers. . . .

49. Employers frequently express themselves forcibly about the restrictions imposed and yet in practice seem to display a fatalistic acceptance of them as part of the very character of the printing industry. The belief, however, that they all spring from sheer perversity on the part of the worker is, in our view, unfounded. We consider that the employer must carry his share of the responsibility for failing to remove the sense of insecurity which accounts in large measure for the workers' attitude. . . .

17.5 Committee of Inquiry under the Rt. Hon. Lord Devlin into certain matters concerning the Port Transport Industry, *Final Report* (Cmnd. 2734) 1965

TIME-WASTING PRACTICES

.   .   .   .

CONTINUITY RULE

29. As a casual labourer a man is engaged only for the turn.[1] So at the end of the half day (if the continuity rule does not apply) the employer can put the

[1] The half day.

man off and look for another to take his place; or the man, if he chooses, can go back to the pool and try for another job. Where the rule applies, a man is entitled and is required to complete the job which he has begun; and it may well be a job that lasts for several days.

The rule has obvious advantages. If, as is usual, the job is paid for at a piecework rate, it prevents a gang from picking the best of the work and then going off and doing the same thing on another job. Inevitably, there are some jobs that are wholly disagreeable where, but for the rule, the employer might have to get in a new gang at every turn; alternatively, in another job he might want to substitute a blue-eyed[1] for a casual. If a man was under no obligation to take the rough with the smooth, it might easily lead to quarrels and dissensions. Up to this point the rule is acceptable to both sides of the industry.

30. But it has under a casual system an inevitable corollary; and that is that when the job finishes, whether or not it finishes at the end of a turn, the man is entitled to look for another one. He is not obliged to transfer immediately to a second job that the employer may have available for him. If he were so obliged, he would lose his freedom of choice. The employer would have an option, either to keep him or to let him go. Naturally the employer would keep on a good gang and get rid of a bad one and the consequence would be that the good gangs would be in constant employment and the men left in the pool would not get a look-in. If there were no continuity rule, it is probable that some other method of work-sharing . . . would have to be evolved in order to keep the labour force as a whole contented. When the men who have finished the first job return to the pool, the other men there have in theory at least an equal chance of being chosen for the second job. But from the employer's point of view, if the job ends, say, in the middle of the morning, the rest of the morning is wasted until he can get a gang again at the afternoon call; and then as likely as not he will be able to pick the gang he had in the morning. Although in theory the rule should apply only to casual workers who can exercise a right to return to the pool, in practice it applies also to perms.[2] As most gangs are composed partly of perms and partly of casuals, the absence of the casuals would in any event prevent the gang as a whole being transferred to a second job. But in any event, no doubt because of the suspicion with which the perm is viewed, the rule is always insisted upon in his case also.

. . . .

32. The rule, especially as it is enforced in the enclosed docks in London—most of the complaints about it came from there—is wasteful in terms of money, time and efficiency. . . .

Waste of money—in the sense of payment for no work—is perhaps the least important of the three consequences. . . .

33. . . . But the loss of an hour or two can be very exasperating to a ship which is anxious for a quick turn round. If a ship has four or five holds, the

[1] The favourites of a particular foreman whom he will always select when they are available.
[2] Workers in permanent employment, usually employed by the week, also sometimes referred to as 'weekly workers'.

loading or discharging of them will not always finish simultaneously. But for the rule, a gang that has finished early could conveniently be transferred to "double bank" with the gang on another hatch. There is no lack of incentive here, for the former gang could increase its piecework earnings. But the rule forbids it until the beginning of the next turn. In the same way, if through labour shortage there are not enough gangs to discharge each hold simultaneously, the gang that finishes on one hatch in the middle of the morning will refuse to start on the unworked hatch until the afternoon. . . .

34. By loss of efficiency we mean principally that the need to observe the continuity rule hampers the efficient organisation of a job. . . .

17.6 *Restrictive Labour Practices* [Royal Commission on Trade Unions and Employers' Associations, *Research Papers* 4 (2) (London, H.M.S.O., 1967)]

REMOVAL OF RESTRICTIVE LABOUR PRACTICES

33. It does not of course at all follow that because the removal of restrictive labour practices is primarily a matter for industry itself there is no room for action by the Government based on the national interest. There is, first, indirect action of various kinds with the object (among other things) of creating conditions where restrictive labour practices are less likely to exist. For example the statutory provision of redundancy pay is calculated to reduce both the adverse consequences which change is liable to have for workers and the fears which go with it. A more powerful influence even than this is full employment, especially in so far as there is confidence that full employment is likely to continue. There are many other aspects of Government activity which have a bearing on the problem of restrictive practices—for example housing policy and the provision of training facilities for people who are obliged to change their jobs.

35. Secondly, and less indirectly, there is action whose aim is to improve management's handling of labour relations. . . . There is much that might be done here by way of education and training and by the improvement of the advisory services upon which employers can call. There are a number of possible sources from which help might come: for example, the Ministry of Labour itself; employers' associations; management consultants; and voluntary bodies. . .

36. Thirdly, the modernisation of the structure of the trade unions may have an important effect. . . .

37. Finally, there is direct intervention. This does of course already take place from time to time. A situation may deteriorate to a point where the Government act in the national interest, for example by setting up a committee of inquiry. . . .

17.7 Royal Commission on Trade Unions and Employers' Associations 1965–1968 *Report* (*Note of Reservation by Mr Andrew Shonfield*) (Cmnd. 3623) 1968

CONTROL OF RESTRICTIVE PRACTICES

23. One . . . matter where the need for a new set of rules is apparent now is collective bargaining on restrictive practices that have been shown to cause a significant loss of production. . . .

24. . . . One of the departments of the IRC[1] would specialise in the problem of work practices, using where necessary the advice of industrial consultants to make international and inter-firm comparisons. . . .

25. Where investigation indicated that restrictive work practices were in use. the case would go to the IRC Tribunal,[2] which after hearing the evidence would decide whether to issue an order to the trade union and the employer to negotiate about the elimination of the restrictive practice. The Tribunal would not lay down the terms of any new arrangement; its power would be limited to an order to the parties to bargain in good faith about a particular set of work practices. After a reasonable interval, the Tribunal would expect a report on progress, and if this was unsatisfactory, the two sides would be called upon to state the reasons why they had failed to advance. If the Tribunal found there was no adequate justification for their inactivity, it would, in the last resort, have the power to impose a monetary penalty on a recalcitrant trade union or employer.

26. It is argued in the main Report that trade union negotiators would be able "to parry almost indefinitely" any accusation that they were deliberately avoiding serious negotiation.[3] . . . The judgment in such a case must clearly depend in the end on whether the Tribunal is able to say that the demands of either party are so unrealistic as to imply an unwillingness to engage in serious bargaining on the subject. There will undoubtedly be occasions when it will be impossible to make a judgment of this sort—either because the two parties have in fact negotiated in good faith and honestly failed to reach agreement or because it is impossible to demonstrate that the bargaining position of either side, although very tough, amounts to a deliberate attempt to sabotage the negotiation. But there will be other cases where the Tribunal will be able to say, on the basis of what is being demanded, that one or the other party has no serious intention of making a bargain on the subject in question. . . .

27. . . . The sole purpose of the present proposal is to compel the trade union and the employer to acknowledge their responsibility for *trying* to achieve certain improvements. If they were able to demonstrate that their authority was insufficient to ensure that a negotiated agreement on the elimination of a restrictive practice would be carried out, this would absolve them from any penalty. It would then be the duty of the IRC to explore other possibilities of

[1] Industrial Relations Commission. See Document 15.1.

[2] A special section of the I.R.C., proposed in this *Note of Reservation* in paras 17–18, not here reproduced.

[3] See Document 17.8.

negotiation between the employer and the workers responsible for the maintenance of restrictive practices in defiance of the wishes of their trade union. 28. The effect of the proposed reform would therefore be limited. Its intention is to use the law in the same spirit as it has been used, for example, to persuade people to change their practices of burning fuel which are also often hallowed by long-standing custom, in a smoke-controlled zone. The law helps first of all by setting a clear timetable for change, which will usually be faster than the pace that is likely to be achieved by relying exclusively on the spontaneous response to reasoned argument. Secondly, the existence of legal authority makes it much easier to identify and investigate any persistent obstacles to change. Thirdly, because a social rule is set out in the form of a law from which there are no exceptions, the main body of those who wish to abide by the rule in any case will not be deterred from doing so, or be tempted to indulge the occasional impulse to disobey, by the sense that someone else who is not motivated in the same way is ignoring the rule and getting away with it. 29. It may be said that this measure would not touch those who are chiefly responsible for restrictive labour practices in British industry—the unofficial groups of trade unionists who organise themselves at plant level . . . There are two points which are worth making about this aspect of the problem. First, although it is true that many restrictive practices have been established as a result of unofficial action, this does not mean that unions do not take the initiative sometimes in negotiating the terms on which they are to be eliminated. . . . It is to be expected that unions will take such initiatives more frequently in the future if, as a result of the reforms proposed in the main Report, they re-establish their authority over what happens at the workplace . . . Secondly, while it is true that trade unions do not, for the most part, officially support restrictive practices—though there are important exceptions to this rule . . .—there is plenty of evidence that the action of workshop leaders who force the wasteful use of manpower on employers by insisting on inefficient methods of work is condoned by trade unions. . . . The pressure, under the proposed reform, will take the form of demanding of the trade union leadership that it defines its position in relation to restrictive practices. It is, of course, assumed that it will be doing this in the context of the measures proposed in the main Report for the reform of the whole process of collective bargaining. . . .

17.8 Royal Commission on Trade Unions and Employers' Associations 1965–1968, *Report* (Cmnd. 3623) 1968

A RESTRICTIVE LABOUR PRACTICES TRIBUNAL?

312. It has been suggested to us[1] that it may be desirable to deal with restrictive labour practices by means of a tribunal, and we now consider this. . . . 313. The Restrictive Trade Practices Act 1956 is sometimes quoted as a

[1] By the Engineering Employers' Federation.

parallel. This Act lays down that certain trading practices are *prima facie* against the public interest, and the Restrictive Practices Court's task is to judge whether particular practices satisfy conditions justifying the making of an exception. It would however be out of the question to list all restrictions on the use of labour and say that these were to be assumed to be against the public interest, unless the contrary were proved. Only those which "unduly hinder" the efficient use of manpower could be included. But it would be impracticable to list them, since the same practice may be efficient in one set of circumstances while inefficient in another. It is in any case mistaken to think that it is possible to deal with practices which are part of a worker's way of life in the same way as specific and clearly identifiable trading practices.

314. It might still be argued that a tribunal could deal with specific complaints that particular restrictive practices were being unilaterally imposed; it might be said that it would be easy to show that these were unreasonable and restrictive, and that a tribunal should be able to order union officials supporting them to desist. The matter is not however so simple. One is often dealing with what is essentially a bargaining situation. The real question at issue may be the rates to be paid for new jobs or the proper safeguards or compensation to accompany change. Often the difficulty runs deeper. Craftsmen may be firmly convinced that it is their duty to guard and uphold the "rights" of their craft. This is essentially a situation in which only educative processes and reasoning can lead people to revise their attitudes, and become willing to bargain.

315. In situations of these kinds it would not be useful or desirable to have a procedure under which a tribunal could order those insisting on or indulging in a restrictive practice to desist from doing so. Nor would it conduce to good industrial relations to enforce such an order by committing to prison for contempt of court those who refused to obey it. As regards the workers themselves such enforcement would be impracticable. Enforcement of the tribunal's order by punishment of their trade union officials (as envisaged by the Federation) would also be unlikely to promote efficiency, quite apart from considerations of justice. If employers are seeking increased co-operation from their employees, resort to legal sanctions is not likely to produce it.

316. It could be argued alternatively that what is needed is not a tribunal which will order people to desist from restrictive labour practices, but one which will promote collective bargaining by hearing complaints of failure to negotiate in good faith. Where it found that trade union officials were not negotiating in good faith because they were not making a reasonable attempt to reach a settlement providing for improved working practices, then the tribunal might order them to do so; and if they did not do so, a monetary penalty might in the last resort be inflicted on the union.

317. . . . . Trade union negotiators have the skill to parry almost indefinitely allegations that they are not acting in good faith. In any case the major difficulty is not a lack of good faith but disagreement as to what would constitute a reasonable bargain. The tribunal would in effect be asked to define an area marking out the limits of reasonable negotiation; and the danger is that the area so marked out would either be so large that the tribunal's judgment would have little or no effect on the situation or so narrow that it

would amount to an attempt to impose an arbitration decision. The former would be valueless, the latter impracticable.

. . . . . .

329. Our proposals for the reform of the collective bargaining system are . . . fundamental to the improved use of manpower. They will get rid of assumptions and attitudes to collective bargaining which have allowed restrictive labour practices to grow and efficiency to languish. . . .

USE OF THE STRIKE

18 Definitions of 'trade dispute' and 'strike'[1]

18.1 Trade Disputes Act 1906[2]

5. (3) In this Act and in the Conspiracy, and Protection of Property Act, 1875, the expression "trade dispute" means any dispute between employers and workmen, or between workmen and workmen, which is connected with the employment or non-employment, or the terms of the employment, or with the conditions of labour, of any person, and the expression "workmen" means all persons employed in trade or industry, whether or not in the employment of the employer with whom a trade dispute arises. . . .

18.2 Trade Disputes and Trade Unions Act 1927

8. (2) For the purposes of this Act—
(a) the expression "strike" means the cessation of work by a body of persons employed in any trade or industry acting in combination, or a concerted refusal, or a refusal under a common understanding of any number of persons who are, or have been so employed, to continue to work or to accept employment . . .

18.3 Contracts of Employment Act 1963

SCHEDULE 1

. . . . . .

INTERPRETATION

11. (1) In this Schedule, unless the context otherwise requires,—

. . . . . .

[1] For a definition of 'strike' proposed in section 158 (1) of the Industrial Relations Bill 1970, see Document 88.2.
[2] The Repeal of this Act was proposed in the Industrial Relations Bill 1970. See Appendix, p. 571.

"strike" means the cessation of work by a body of persons employed acting in combination, or a concerted refusal or a refusal under a common understanding of any number of persons employed to continue to work for an employer in consequence of a dispute, done as a means of compelling their employer or any person or body of persons employed, or to aid other employees in compelling their employer or any person or body of persons employed, to accept or not to accept terms or conditions of or affecting employment . . .

18.4 Royal Commission on Trade Unions and Employers' Associations 1965–1968, *Report* (Cmnd. 3623) 1968

INCIDENCE OF STRIKES AND OTHER INDUSTRIAL ACTION

· · · · · · ·

367. . . . We mean by an official strike one which has been sanctioned or ratified by the union or unions whose members are on strike, all others being unofficial. Unofficial strikes are also in practice usually, though not always, "unconstitutional" in the sense that they take place in disregard of an existing agreement laying down a procedure for the attempted settlement of a dispute before strike action is taken. . . .

19 The right to strike

19.1 *European Social Charter 1961*[1] (Cmnd. 1667) 1962

ARTICLE 6
THE RIGHT TO BARGAIN COLLECTIVELY

With a view to ensuring the effective exercise of the right to bargain collectively, the Contracting Parties undertake:
(1) to promote joint consultation between workers and employers;
(2) to promote, where necessary and appropriate, machinery for voluntary negotiations between employers or employers' organisations and workers' organisations, with a view to the regulation of terms and conditions of employment by means of collective agreements;
(3) to promote the establishment and use of appropriate machinery for conciliation and voluntary arbitration for the settlement of labour disputes;
and recognise:
(4) the right of workers and employers to collective action in cases of conflicts of interest, including the right to strike, subject to obligations that might arise out of collective agreements previously entered into.

· · · · · · ·

[1] Ratified by the United Kingdom in 1962.

ARTICLE 31
RESTRICTIONS

1. The rights and principles . . . when effectively realised, and their effective exercise . . . shall not be subject to any restrictions or limitations not specified . . . except such as are prescribed by law and are necessary in a democratic society for the protection of the rights and freedoms of others or for the protection of public interest, national security, public health, or morals.

20 Union strike procedures

20.1 Society of Graphical and Allied Trades, Division A,[1] *General Rules* 1966 (as amended to 1968)

RULE 16
DISPUTES AND GRIEVANCES

1. Every means shall be adopted by the Branch Committee to prevent disputes with employers, they being hereby declared to be generally injurious to our trade, and . . . all parties shall strive as much as possible (consistent with honour) to prevent the same, and endeavour as speedily as possible to bring matters to a good understanding between employers and employed.

20.2 National Union of General and Municipal Workers, *Rules* 1965 (as amended to 1968)

RULE 27.—DISPUTES

1. Should any dispute arise the members concerned shall make the same known to their Branch Secretary, who shall immediately report the same to the District Secretary for submission to the District Committee, but in no case shall a cessation of work be threatened or take place without the sanction of the District Committee or National Executive Committee as required by rule. A District Committee shall have power to sanction a strike where not more than 300 members are involved.

· · · · · · ·

3. No cessation of work shall take place unless two-thirds of the members belonging to the Branch or body immediately concerned shall have voted in favour of the adoption of such course, and then only with the express sanction of the National Executive Committee, and after legal notice to terminate contracts of service has been given. Every member affected shall have an opportunity of recording his vote at a special meeting, for and against

---

[1] Formerly the National Union of Printing, Bookbinding and Paper Workers

handing in notice to cease work. In no case shall members be entitled to strike benefit if they enter upon a strike without the sanction of the National Executive Committee. The National Executive Committee shall have power to refer a dispute to arbitration. . . .

. . . .

5. In the event of a strike or lock-out, a committee not exceeding nine may be elected from and by the members implicated. This committee shall be subject to the authority of the District Committee or officials of the District. When a dispute occurs in an industry over an area, and covering more than one town, and affects a number of Branches, the District Committee shall have power to appoint such Strike Committees as are deemed necessary.

. . . .

RULE 28.—STRIKE BENEFIT

1. Where labour is withdrawn unconstitutionally, no benefit of any description can be paid without the approval of the National Executive Committee. . . .

21 Statutory restraints on strike action

GENERAL

21.1 Conspiracy, and Protection of Property Act 1875

5. Where any person wilfully and maliciously breaks a contract of service or of hiring, knowing or having reasonable cause to believe that the probable consequences of his so doing, either alone or in combination with others, will be to endanger human life, or cause serious bodily injury, or to expose valuable property whether real or personal to destruction or serious injury, he shall on conviction thereof by a court of summary jurisdiction, or on indictment as herein-after mentioned, be liable either to pay a penalty not exceeding twenty pounds, or to be imprisoned for a term not exceeding three months, with or without hard labour.

21.2 Emergency Powers Act 1920

1. (1) If at any time it appears to His Majesty that [there have occurred, or are about to occur, events of such a nature][1] as to be calculated, by interfering with the supply and distribution of food, water, fuel, or light, or with the

[1] The words in square brackets are an amendment introduced by the Emergency Powers Act 1964 s.1.

means of locomotion, to deprive the community, or any substantial portion of the community, of the essentials of life, His Majesty may, by proclamation (hereinafter referred to as a proclamation of emergency), declare that a state of emergency exists.

No such proclamation shall be in force for more than one month, without prejudice to the issue of another proclamation at or before the end of that period.

(2) Where a proclamation of emergency has been made the occasion thereof shall forthwith be communicated to Parliament . . .

2. (1) Where a proclamation of emergency has been made, and so long as the proclamation is in force, it shall be lawful for His Majesty in Council, by Order, to make regulations for securing the essentials of life to the community, and those regulations may confer or impose on a Secretary of State or other Government department, or any other persons in His Majesty's service or acting on His Majesty's behalf, such powers and duties as His Majesty may deem necessary for the preservation of the peace, for securing and regulating the supply and distribution of food, water, fuel, light, and other necessities, for maintaining the means of transit or locomotion, and for any other purposes essential to the public safety and the life of the community, and may make such provisions incidental to the powers aforesaid as may appear to His Majesty to be required for making the exercise of those powers effective:

Provided that nothing in this Act shall be construed to authorise the making of any regulations imposing any form of compulsory military service or industrial conscription:

Provided also that no such regulation shall make it an offence for any person or persons to take part in a strike, or peacefully to persuade any other person or persons to take part in a strike.

(2) Any regulations so made shall be laid before Parliament as soon as may be after they are made, and shall not continue in force after the expiration of seven days from the time when they are so laid unless a resolution is passed by both Houses providing for the continuance thereof.

(3) The regulations may provide for the trial, by courts of summary jurisdiction, of persons guilty of offences against the regulations; so, however, that the maximum penalty which may be inflicted for any offence against any such regulations shall be imprisonment with or without hard labour for a term of three months, or a fine of one hundred pounds, or both such imprisonment and fine, together with the forfeiture of any goods or money in respect of which the offence has been committed: Provided that no such regulations shall alter any existing procedure in criminal cases, or confer any right to punish by fine or imprisonment without trial.

. . . .

(5) The expiry or revocation of any regulations so made shall not be deemed to have affected the previous operation thereof, or the validity of any action taken thereunder, or any penalty or punishment incurred in respect of any contravention or failure to comply therewith, or any proceeding or remedy in respect of any such punishment or penalty.

21.3 Trade Disputes and Trade Unions Act 1927

1. (1) It is hereby declared—

(*a*) that any strike is illegal if it—

(i) has any object other than or in addition to the furtherance of a trade dispute within the trade or industry in which the strikers are engaged; and

(ii) is a strike designed or calculated to coerce the Government either directly or by inflicting hardship upon the community . . .

. . . .

and it is further declared that it is illegal to commence, or continue, or to apply any sums in furtherance or support of, any such illegal strike . . .

For the purposes of the foregoing provisions—

(*a*) a trade dispute shall not be deemed to be within a trade or industry unless it is a dispute between employers and workmen, or between workmen and workmen, in that trade or industry, which is connected with the employment or non-employment or the terms of the employment, or with the conditions of labour, of persons in that trade or industry; and

(*b*) without prejudice to the generality of the expression "trade or industry" workmen shall be deemed to be within the same trade or industry if their wages or conditions of employment are determined in accordance with the conclusions of the same joint industrial council, conciliation board or other similar body, or in accordance with agreements made with the same employer or group of employers.

(2) If any person declares, instigates, incites others to take part in or otherwise acts in furtherance of a strike . . . declared by this Act to be illegal, he shall be liable on summary conviction to a fine not exceeding ten pounds or to imprisonment for a term not exceeding three months, or on conviction on indictment to imprisonment for a term not exceeding two years:

Provided that no person shall be deemed to have committed an offence under this section or at common law by reason only of his having ceased work or refused to continue to work or to accept employment.

(3) Where any person is charged before any court with an offence under this section, no further proceedings in respect thereof shall be taken against him without the consent of the Attorney-General except such as the court may think necessary by remand (whether in custody or on bail) or otherwise to secure the safe custody of the person charged, but this subsection shall not apply . . . to any prosecution instituted by or on behalf of the Director of Public Prosecutions.

(4) The provisions of the Trade Disputes Act, 1906, shall not, nor shall the second proviso to subsection (1) of section two of the Emergency Powers Act, 1920, apply to any act done in contemplation or furtherance of a strike . . . which is by this Act declared to be illegal, and any such act shall not be deemed for the purposes of any enactment to be done in contemplation or furtherance of a trade dispute:

Provided that no person shall be deemed to have committed an offence under any regulations made under the Emergency Powers Act, 1920, by reason only of his having ceased work or having refused to continue to work or to accept employment.

2. (1) No person refusing to take part or to continue to take part in any strike . . . which is by this Act declared to be illegal, shall be, by reason of such refusal or by reason of any action taken by him under this section, subject to expulsion from any trade union or society, or to any fine or penalty, or to deprivation of any right or benefit to which he or his legal personal representatives would otherwise be entitled, or liable to be placed in any respect either directly or indirectly under any disability or at any disadvantage as compared with other members of the union or society, anything to the contrary in the rules of a trade union or society notwithstanding.

· · · · · · ·

7. Without prejudice to the right of any person having a sufficient interest in the relief sought to sue or apply for an injunction to restrain any application of the funds of a trade union in contravention of the provisions of this Act, an injunction restraining any application of the funds of a trade union in contravention of the provisions of section one of this Act may be granted at the suit or upon the application of the Attorney-General.

· · · · · · ·

8. (2) (c) a strike . . . shall not be deemed to be calculated to coerce the Government unless such coercion ought reasonably to be expected as a consequence thereof.

CLASSES OF INDUSTRY AND PERSONS

21.4 Conspiracy, and Protection of Property Act 1875[1]

4. Where a person employed by a municipal authority or by any company or contractor upon whom is imposed by Act of Parliament the duty, or who have otherwise assumed the duty of supplying any city, borough, town, or place, or any part thereof, with gas or water, wilfully and maliciously breaks a contract of service with that authority or company or contractor, knowing or having reasonable cause to believe that the probable consequences of his so doing, either alone or in combination with others, will be to deprive the inhabitants of that city, borough, town, place, or part, wholly or to a great extent of their supply of gas or water, he shall on conviction thereof by a court of summary jurisdiction, or on indictment as herein-after mentioned, be liable either to pay a penalty not exceeding twenty pounds or to be imprisoned for a term not exceeding three months, with or without hard labour.

[1] The repeal of the section here quoted was proposed in the Industrial Relations Bill 1970. See Appendix, p. 571.

21.5 Electricity Supply Act 1919[1]

31. Section four of the Conspiracy, and Protection of Property Act, 1875 (which relates to breaches of contract by persons employed in the supply of gas or water), shall extend to persons employed by a joint electricity authority or by any authorised undertakers in like manner as it applies to persons mentioned in that section, with the substitution of references to electricity for the references to gas or water.

21.6 Trade Disputes and Trade Unions Act 1927

6. (4) There shall be added to section five of the Conspiracy, and Protection of Property Act, 1875, the following provision, that is to say:—

"If any person employed by a local or other public authority wilfully breaks a contract of service with that authority, knowing or having reasonable cause to believe that the probable consequence of his so doing, either alone or in combination with others, will be to cause injury or danger or grave inconvenience to the community, he shall be liable, on summary conviction, to a fine not exceeding ten pounds or to imprisonment for a term not exceeding three months."

21.7 Merchant Shipping Act 1894[2]

221. If a seaman lawfully engaged, or an apprentice to the sea service, commits any of the following offences he shall be liable to be punished summarily as follows:—

(*a*) If he deserts from his ship he shall be guilty of the offence of desertion and be liable to forfeit all or any part of the effects he leaves on board, and of the wages which he has then earned, and also, if the desertion takes place abroad, of the wages he may earn in any other ship in which he may be employed until his next return to the United Kingdom, and to satisfy any excess of wages paid by the master or owner of the ship to any substitute engaged in his place at a higher rate of wages than the rate stipulated to be paid to him; and also, except in the United Kingdom, he shall be liable to imprisonment for any period not exceeding twelve weeks with or without hard labour;

(*b*) If he neglects or refuses without reasonable cause, to join his ship, or to proceed to sea in his ship, or is absent without leave at any time within twenty-four hours of the ship's sailing from a port, either at the commencement or during the progress of a voyage, or is absent at any time without leave and without sufficient reason from his ship or from his duty, he shall, if the offence does not amount to desertion, or is not treated as such by the master, be guilty of the offence of absence without

[1] The repeal of the section here quoted was proposed in the Industrial Relations Bill 1970. See Appendix, p. 571.

[2] Changes were introduced under the Merchant Shipping Act 1970. See Appendix p. 570, and Document 87.1.

leave, and be liable to forfeit out of his wages a sum not exceeding two days pay, and in addition for every twenty-four hours of absence, either a sum not exceeding six days pay, or any expenses properly incurred in hiring a substitute; and also, except in the United Kingdom, he shall be liable to imprisonment for any period not exceeding ten weeks with or without hard labour.

. . . .

225. (1) If a seaman lawfully engaged or an apprentice to the sea service commits any of the following offences, in this Act referred to as offences against discipline, he shall be liable to be punished summarily as follows; (that is to say,)

(a) If he quits the ship without leave after her arrival at her port of delivery, and before she is placed in security, he shall be liable to forfeit out of his wages a sum not exceeding one month's pay:

(b) If he is guilty of wilful disobedience to any lawful command, he shall be liable to imprisonment for a period not exceeding four weeks, and also, at the discretion of the court, to forfeit out of his wages a sum not exceeding two days pay:

(c) If he is guilty of continued wilful disobedience to lawful commands or continued wilful neglect of duty, he shall be liable to imprisonment for a period not exceeding twelve weeks, and also, at the discretion of the court, to forfeit for every twenty-four hours continuance of disobedience or neglect, either a sum not exceeding six days pay, or any expenses properly incurred in hiring a substitute:

. . . .

(e) If he combines with any of the crew to disobey lawful commands, or to neglect duty, or to impede the navigation of the ship or the progress of the voyage, he shall be liable to imprisonment for a period not exceeding twelve weeks:

. . . .

236. (1) If a person by any means whatever persuades or attempts to persuade a seaman or apprentice to neglect or refuse to join or proceed to sea in or to desert from his ship, or otherwise to absent himself from his duty, he shall for each offence in respect of each seaman or apprentice be liable to a fine not exceeding ten pounds.

(2) If a person wilfully harbours or secretes a seaman or apprentice who has wilfully neglected or refused to join, or has deserted, from his ship, knowing or having reason to believe the seaman or apprentice to have so done, he shall for every seaman or apprentice so harboured or secreted be liable to a fine not exceeding twenty pounds.

21.8 Police Act 1964[1]

53. (1) Any person who causes, or attempts to cause, or does any act calculated to cause, disaffection amongst the members of any police force, or

[1] This section supersedes analogous provisions in the Police Act 1919.

induces or attempts to induce, or does any act calculated to induce, any member of a police force to withhold his services or to commit breaches of discipline, shall be guilty of an offence and liable—

    (*a*) on summary conviction, to imprisonment for a term not exceeding six months or to a fine not exceeding £100, or to both;

    (*b*) on conviction on indictment, to imprisonment for a term not exceeding two years or to a fine or to both.

(2) This section applies to special constables appointed for a police area as it applies to members of a police force.

21.9 Aliens Restriction (Amendment) Act 1919

3. (2) If any alien promotes or attempts to promote industrial unrest in any industry in which he has not been bona fide engaged for at least two years immediately preceding in the United Kingdom, he shall be liable on summary conviction to imprisonment for a term not exceeding three months.

METHODS EMPLOYED

21.10 Conspiracy, and Protection of Property Act 1875

7. Every person who, with a view to compel any other person to abstain from doing or to do any act which such other person has a legal right to do or abstain from doing, wrongfully and without legal authority,—

1. Uses violence to or intimidates such other person or his wife or children, or injures his property; or,
2. Persistently follows such other person about from place to place; or,
3. Hides any tools, clothes, or other property owned or used by such other person, or deprives him of or hinders him in the use thereof; or,
4. Watches or besets the house or other place where such other person resides, or works, or carries on business, or happens to be, or the approach to such house or place; or,
5. Follows such other person with two or more other persons in a disorderly manner in or through any street or road,

shall, on conviction thereof by a court of summary jurisdiction, or on indictment as herein-after mentioned, be liable either to pay a penalty not exceeding twenty pounds, or to be imprisoned for a term not exceeding three months, with or without hard labour.

21.11 Trade Disputes and Trade Unions Act 1927

3. (1) It is hereby declared that it is unlawful for one or more persons (whether acting on their own behalf or on behalf of a trade union or of an individual employer or firm, and notwithstanding that they may be acting in contemplation or furtherance of a trade dispute) to attend at or near a house or place where a person resides or works or carries on business or happens to be, for the purpose of obtaining or communicating information or of persuading or inducing any person to work or to abstain from working, if they so attend in such numbers or otherwise in such manner as to be calculated to intimidate any person in that house or place, or to obstruct the approach thereto or egress therefrom, or to lead to a breach of the peace; and attending at or near any house or place in such numbers or in such manner as is by this subsection declared to be unlawful shall be deemed to be a watching or besetting of that house or place within the meaning of section seven of the Conspiracy, and Protection of Property Act, 1875.

(2) In this section the expression "to intimidate" means to cause in the mind of a person a reasonable apprehension of injury to him or to any member of his family or to any of his dependants or of violence or damage to any person or property, and the expression "injury" includes injury to a person in respect of his business, occupation, employment or other source of income, and includes any actionable wrong.

(3) In section seven of the Conspiracy, and Protection of Property Act, 1875, the expression "intimidate" shall be construed as having the same meaning as in this section.

(4) Notwithstanding anything in any Act, it shall not be lawful for one or more persons, for the purpose of inducing any person to work or to abstain from working, to watch or beset a house or place where a person resides or the approach to such a house or place, and any person who acts in contravention of this subsection shall be liable on summary conviction to a fine not exceeding twenty pounds or to imprisonment for a term not exceeding three months.

22 Statutory safeguards for trade unions

22.1 Conspiracy, and Protection of Property Act 1875[1]

3. An agreement or combination by two or more persons to do or procure to be done any act in contemplation or furtherance of a trade dispute ... shall not be indictable as a conspiracy if such act committed by one person would not be punishable as a crime.

Nothing in this section shall exempt from punishment any persons guilty of a conspiracy for which a punishment is awarded by any Act of Parliament.

Nothing in this section shall affect the law relating to riot, unlawful assembly, breach of the peace, or sedition, or any offence against the State or the Sovereign.

A crime for the purposes of this section means an offence punishable on indictment, or an offence which is punishable on summary conviction, and

---

[1] Section 3 of this Act was amended by the Trade Disputes Act 1906. See Document 22.2. The repeal of this amendment was proposed in the Industrial Relations Bill 1970. See Appendix, p. 571. That part of section 7 here quoted was repealed by the Trade Disputes Act 1906. See Document 22.2.

for the commission of which the offender is liable under the statute making the offence punishable to be imprisoned either absolutely or at the discretion of the court as an alternative for some other punishment.

Where a person is convicted of any such agreement or combination as aforesaid to do or procure to be done an act which is punishable only on summary conviction, and is sentenced to imprisonment, the imprisonment shall not exceed three months, or such longer time, if any, as may have been prescribed by the statute for the punishment of the said act when committed by one person.

.   .   .   .

7. . . . Attending at or near the house or place where a person resides, or works, or carries on business, or happens to be, or the approach to such house or place, in order merely to obtain or communicate information, shall not be deemed a watching or besetting within the meaning of this section.[1]

22.2 Trade Disputes Act 1906[2]

1. The following paragraph shall be added as a new paragraph after the first paragraph of section three of the Conspiracy, and Protection of Property Act, 1875:—

"An act done in pursuance of an agreement or combination by two or more persons shall, if done in contemplation or furtherance of a trade dispute, not be actionable unless the act, if done without any such agreement or combination, would be actionable."

2. (1) It shall be lawful for one or more persons, acting on their own behalf or on behalf of a trade union or of an individual employer or firm in contemplation or furtherance of a trade dispute, to attend at or near a house or place where a person resides or works or carries on business or happens to be, if they so attend merely for the purpose of peacefully obtaining or communicating information, or of peacefully persuading any person to work or abstain from working.

(2) Section seven of the Conspiracy, and Protection of Property Act, 1875, is hereby repealed from "attending at or near" to the end of the section.

3. An act done by a person in contemplation or furtherance of a trade dispute shall not be actionable on the ground only that it induces some other person to break a contract of employment or that it is an interference with the trade, business, or employment of some other person, or with the right of some other person to dispose of his capital or his labour as he wills.

4. (1) An action against a trade union, whether of workmen or masters, or against any members or officials thereof on behalf of themselves and all other members of the trade union in respect of any tortious act alleged to have been committed by or on behalf of the trade union, shall not be entertained by any court.

[1] For the remainder of this section, see Document 21.10.
[2] The repeal of this Act was proposed in the Industrial Relations Bill 1970. See Appendix, p. 571.

22.3 Trade Disputes Act 1965[1]

1. (1) An act done after the passing of this Act by a person in contempla-tion or furtherance of a trade dispute (within the meaning of the Trade Disputes Act 1906) shall not be actionable in tort on the ground only that it consists in his threatening—

(*a*) that a contract of employment (whether one to which he is a party or not) will be broken, or

(*b*) that he will induce another to break a contract of employment to which that other is a party;

or be capable of giving rise to an action of reparation on the ground only that it so consists.

23 Social security and strike action

23.1 Employment and Training Act 1948

2. (5) No person shall be disqualified or otherwise prejudiced in respect of facilities provided at any employment exchange . . . on account of his refusal to accept employment found for him through such an exchange if the ground of his refusal is that a trade dispute which affects his trade exists, or that the wages offered are lower than those current in the trade in the district where the employment is found.

23.2 Ministry of Social Security Act 1966

10. (1) Subject to subsection (2) of this section, where by reason of a stoppage of work due to a trade dispute at his place of employment a person is without employment for any period during which the stoppage continues and he has not during that stoppage become bona fide employed elsewhere in the occupation which he usually follows or become regularly engaged in some other occupation, his requirements for that period shall be disregarded for the purposes of benefit except so far as they include the requirement to provide for any other person.

(2) Subsection (1) of this section does not apply in the case of a person who proves—

(*a*) that he is not participating in or financing or directly interested in the trade dispute which caused the stoppage of work; and

(*b*) that he does not belong to a grade or class of workers of which, immediately before the commencement of the stoppage, there were members employed at his place of employment any of whom are participating in or financing or directly interested in the dispute.

. . . .

[1] The repeal of this Act was proposed in the Industrial Relations Bill 1970. See Appendix, p. 571.

13. (1) Nothing in ... this Act ... shall prevent the payment of benefit in an urgent case ...

(2) Where by virtue only of this section any sums are paid to a person engaged in remunerative full-time work the Commission[1] may determine that the whole or part thereof shall be recoverable from him by the Minister,[2] if they are satisfied that the circumstances are such that the recovery would be equitable.

24 The 'strike problem': the inter-war years

24.1 Provisional Joint Committee, *Report to Industrial Conference 1919* (Cmd. 501) 1920, pp. 3, 12–15

At the Industrial Conference called by the Government and held at the Central Hall, Westminster, on 27th February last, it was resolved:
"That this Conference, being of the opinion that any preventable dislocation of industry is always to be deplored, and, in the present critical period of reconstruction, might be disastrous to the interests of the Nation, and thinking that every effort should be made to remove legitimate grievances, and promote harmony and goodwill, resolves to appoint a Joint Committee, consisting of equal numbers of employers and workers, men and women, together with a Chairman appointed by the Government, to consider and report to a further meeting of this Conference on the causes of the present unrest and the steps necessary to safeguard and promote the best interests of employers, workpeople and the State, and especially to consider:—

"1. Questions relating to Hours, Wages and General Conditions of Employment;

"2. Unemployment and its prevention;

"3. The best methods of promoting co-operation between Capital and Labour."

. . . . . .

NATIONAL INDUSTRIAL COUNCIL

... the Committee are impressed with the importance of establishing without delay some form of permanent representative National Industrial Council. The considered views of the Committee are as follows:—

PREAMBLE

A National Industrial Council should not supersede any of the existing agencies for dealing with industrial questions. Its object would be to supplement and co-ordinate the existing sectional machinery by bringing together the knowledge and experience of all sections and focussing them upon the prob-

---

[1] The Supplementary Benefits Commission.
[2] Of Social Security.

lems that affect industrial relations as a whole. Its functions, therefore, would be advisory.

. . . .

In order that the Council may have the necessary independent status and authority if it is to promote industrial peace, the Government should recognise it as the official consultative authority to the Government upon industrial relations, and should make it the normal channel through which the opinion and experience of industry will be sought on all questions with which industry as a whole is concerned.

In addition to advising the Government the Council should, when it thought fit, issue statements on industrial questions or disputes for the guidance of public opinion.

OBJECTS

To secure the largest possible measure of joint action between the representative organisations of employers and workpeople, and to be the normal channel through which the opinion and experience of industry will be sought by the Government on all questions affecting industry as a whole.

It will be open to the Council to take any action that falls within the scope of its general definition. Among its more specific objects will be:—

(a) The consideration of general questions affecting industrial relations.
(b) The consideration of measures for joint or several action to anticipate and avoid threatened disputes.
(c) The consideration of actual disputes involving general questions.
(d) The consideration of legislative proposals affecting industrial relations.
(e) To advise the Government on industrial questions and on the general industrial situation.
(f) To issue statements for the guidance of public opinion on industrial issues.

CONSTITUTION

I. The Council

1. The Council shall consist of four hundred members fully representative of and duly accredited by the Employers' organisations and the Trade Unions, to be elected as to one half by the Employers' organisations and as to one half by the Trade Unions.

. . . .

4. The Council shall meet at least twice a year, and in addition as often as the Standing Committee hereafter referred to deem to be necessary.

5. The Minister of Labour for the time being shall be President of the Council and shall, when possible, preside at its meetings. There shall be three Vice-Presidents, one appointed by the Government to be Chairman of the Standing Committee hereafter referred to, one elected by and from the Employers' representatives on the Council, one elected by and from the Trade Unions' representatives. In the absence of the President, the Chairman of the Standing Committee shall preside, in his absence one of the other Vice-Presidents.

M
147

The Chairman of the Committee shall be a whole-time officer, and shall have associated with him two secretaries, one appointed by the Employers' representatives on the Council, one appointed by the Trade Unions' representatives.

· · · · · · ·

7. Finance.—The expenses of the Council, subject to sanction by the Treasury, shall be borne by the Government.

· · · · · · ·

II. The Standing Committee

1. There shall be a Standing Committee of the Council, consisting of 25 members elected by and from the employers' representatives of the Council, and 25 members elected by and from the trade union representatives.

· · · · · · ·

3. The Standing Committee shall be empowered to take such action as it deems to be necessary to carry out the objects of the Council. It shall consider any questions referred to it by the Council or the Government, and shall report to the Council its decisions.

· · · · · · ·

6. The Standing Committee shall meet as often as may be necessary, and at least once a month.

· · · · · · ·

SUMMARY

The views of the Committee on the questions with which they have been able to deal in the time at their disposal, may be summarised as follows:—

HOURS

(a) The establishment by legal enactment of the principle of a maximum normal working week of 48 hours, subject to—

(b) Provision for varying the normal hours in proper cases, with adequate safeguards.

(c) Hours agreements between employers and trade unions to be capable of application to the trade concerned.

(d) Systematic overtime to be discouraged, and unavoidable overtime to be paid for at special rates.

WAGES

(a) The establishment by legal enactment of minimum time-rates of wages, to be of universal applicability.

(b) A Commission to report within three months as to what these minimum rates should be.

(c) Extension of the establishment of Trade Boards for less organised trades.

(d) Minimum time-rates agreements between employers and trade unions to be capable of application to all employers engaged in the trade falling within the scope of the agreement.

· · · · · · ·

(*f*) Trade Conferences to be held to consider how war advances and bonuses should be dealt with, and, in particular, whether they should be added to the time-rates or piece-work prices or should be treated separately as advances given on account of the conditions due to the war.

RECOGNITION OF, AND NEGOTIATIONS BETWEEN, ORGANISATIONS OF EMPLOYERS AND WORKPEOPLE

(*a*) Basis of negotiation between employers and workpeople should be full and frank acceptance of employers' organisations and trade unions as the recognised organisations to speak and act on behalf of their members.

(*b*) Members should accept the jurisdiction of their respective organisations.

(*c*) Employers' organisations and trade unions should enter into negotiations for the establishment of machinery, or the revision of existing machinery, for the avoidance of disputes, with provision for a representative method of negotiation in questions in which the same class of employers or workpeople are represented by more than one organisation respectively, and for the protection of employers' interests where members of Trade Unions of workpeople are engaged in positions of trust or confidentiality, provided the right of such employees to join or remain members of any Trade Union is not thereby affected.

UNEMPLOYMENT

(*1*) *Prevention of Unemployment*

(*a*) Organised short time has considerable value in periods of depression. The joint representative bodies in each trade afford convenient machinery for controlling and regulating short time.

(*b*) Government orders should be regulated with a view to stabilising employment.

(*c*) Government housing schemes should be pressed forward without delay.

(*d*) Demand for labour could be increased by State development of new industries.

(*2*) *Maintenance of Unemployed Workpeople*

(*e*) Normal provision for maintenance during unemployment should be more adequate and of wider application, and should be extended to under-employment.

(*f*) Unemployed persons, and particularly young persons, should have free opportunities of continuing their education.

(*g*) The employment of married women and widows who have young children should be subject of a special enquiry.

(*h*) The age at which a child should enter employment should be raised beyond the present limit.

(*i*) Sickness and Infirmity Benefits, and Old Age Pensions require immediate investigation with a view to more generous provisions being made.

24.2 Joint Committee, Trade Union Representatives, *Memorandum to Industrial Conference 1919: Causes of and the Remedies for Industrial Unrest* (Cmd. 501) 1920, Appendix I, pp. xi–xii

The fundamental causes of Labour unrest are to be found rather in the growing determination of Labour to challenge the whole existing structure of capitalist industry than in any of the more special and smaller grievances which come to the surface at any particular time.

These root causes are twofold—the breakdown of the existing capitalist system of industrial organisation, in the sense that the mass of the working class is now firmly convinced that production for private profit is not an equitable basis on which to build, and that a vast extension of public ownership and democratic control of industry is urgently necessary. It is no longer possible for organised Labour to be controlled by force or compulsion of any kind. It has grown too strong to remain within the bounds of the old industrial system and its unsatisfied demand for the re-organisation of industry on democratic lines is not only the most important, but also a constantly growing cause of unrest.

The second primary cause is closely linked with the first. It is that, desiring the creation of a new industrial system which shall gradually but speedily replace the old, the workers can see no indication that either the Government or the employers have realised the necessity for any fundamental change, or that they are prepared even to make a beginning of industrial re-organisation on more democratic principles. The absence of any constructive policy on the side of the Government or the employers, taken in conjunction with the fact that Labour, through the Trades Union Congress and the Labour Party and through the various Trade Union Organisations, has put forward a comprehensive economic and industrial programme, has presented the workers with a sharp contrast from which they naturally draw their own deductions.

It is clear that unless and until the Government is prepared to realise the need for comprehensive reconstruction on a democratic basis, and to formulate a constructive policy leading towards economic democracy, there can be at most no more than a temporary diminution of industrial unrest to be followed inevitably by further waves of constantly growing magnitude.

The changes involved in this reconstruction must, of course, be gradual, but if unrest is to be prevented from assuming dangerous forms an adequate assurance must be given immediately to the workers that the whole problem is being taken courageously in hand. It is not enough merely to tinker with particular grievances or to endeavour to reconstruct the old system by slight adjustments to meet the new demands of Labour. It is essential to question the whole basis on which our industry has been conducted in the past and to endeavour to find, in substitution for the motive of private gain, some other motive which will serve better as the foundation of a democratic system. This motive can be no other than the motive of public service, which at present is seldom invoked save when the workers threaten to stop the process of production by a strike. The motive of public service should be the dominant motive throughout the whole industrial system, and the problem in industry at the present day is that of bringing home to every person engaged in industry the feeling that he is the servant, not of any particular class or person, but of the community as a whole. This cannot be done so long as industry continues to be conducted for private profit, and the widest possible extension of public ownership and democratic control of industry is therefore the first necessary condition of the removal of industrial unrest.

24.3 *Message from the Prime Minister*[1] (*The British Gazette*, No. 2 May 6 1926)

Constitutional Government is being attacked. Let all good citizens whose livelihood and labour have thus been put in peril bear with fortitude and patience the hardships with which they have been so suddenly confronted. Stand behind the Government, who are doing their part, confident that you will co-operate in the measures they have undertaken to preserve the liberties and privileges of the people of these islands. The laws of England are the people's birthright. The laws are in your keeping. You have made Parliament their guardian. The General Strike is a challenge to Parliament and is the road to anarchy and ruin.

24.4 *Message to all Workers* (*The British Worker*, Wednesday evening, May 5 1926)

The General Council of the Trades Union Congress wishes to emphasise the fact that this is an industrial dispute. It expects every member taking part to be exemplary in his conduct and not to give any opportunity for police interference. The outbreak of any disturbances would be very damaging to the prospects of a successful termination to the dispute.

The Council asks pickets especially to avoid obstruction and to confine themselves strictly to their legitimate duties.

24.5 Trades Union Congress, *Official Bulletin No. 5*, 8 May 1926

CONSTITUTION NOT CHALLENGED

The General Council does not challenge the Constitution.
It is not seeking to substitute unconstitutional government.
Nor is it desirous of undermining our Parliamentary institutions.

AN INDUSTRIAL DISPUTE

The sole aim of the Council is to secure for the miners a decent standard of life.

[1] The Rt. Hon. Stanley Baldwin.

151

The Council is engaged in an Industrial dispute.
THERE IS NO CONSTITUTIONAL CRISIS.

THE ONLY ISSUE

In any settlement, the only issue to be decided will be an industrial issue, not political, not constitutional.

24.6 Conference on Industrial Reorganisation and Industrial Relations, *Interim Joint Report* (adopted by the Full Joint Conference on 4th July, 1928)

STATEMENT AND AGENDA

The object of the Conference to discuss the entire field of industrial reorganisation and industrial relations is to assist in the solution of the greatest problem confronting the country at the present time, namely, the restoration of industrial prosperity and with it the progressive improvement in the standard of living of the population. . . .

It is realised that industrial reconstruction can best be undertaken in conjunction with, and with the co-operation of, those entitled and empowered to speak for organised Labour. Every effort will, therefore, be made to further the co-operation of all those who participate in production and to secure the objective that all those who participate in production should also participate in the prosperity of industry. It is agreed that the most effective co-operation in industry can be obtained by deliberation and negotiation with the accredited representatives of affiliated Trade Unions.

The topics which arise for detailed discussion and investigation might be conveniently arranged under the following eight main heads. . . .

I. THE ORGANISATION OF INDUSTRIAL RELATIONS

(*a*) Trade Union Recognition.

(*b*) Collective Bargaining.

(*c*) SECURITY AND STATUS.—The formulation of means for increasing security of employment and for raising the status of the industrial worker . . .

(*d*) Victimisation of Employees or Employers.

(*e*) Legal regulation of hours of Labour.

(*f*) Management and labour.

(*g*) Works Councils.

(*h*) INFORMATION. The provision of information on the facts of industry to all those concerned in industry.

(*i*) PRELIMINARY INVESTIGATION. The application of preliminary investigation into potential causes of industrial disputes before their actual declaration.

(*j*) The extension of the function of Industrial Courts.

(*k*) Factory legislation.

(*l*) Health and Unemployment Insurance (National and Industrial).

(*m*) Provision of machinery for suggestion and constructive criticism.

(*n*) Maintenance of personal relationship.

II. *UNEMPLOYMENT*

III. *THE DISTRIBUTION OF THE PROCEEDS OF COMMODITIES AND SERVICES*

(*a*) High Wages Policy.

(*b*) The consideration of plans for the participation by all concerned in industry in the prosperity of their industry and in the benefits of increased production, including share holding, profit and cost sharing.

(*c*) Payment by results.

(*d*) Minimum Wage Principles.

IV. *THE ORGANISATION, TECHNIQUE, AND CONTROL OF INDUSTRY*

(*a*) RATIONALISATION. The advantages to be gained by the scientific organisation of industries in production, administration, processes, plant, standardisation of product, simplification, scientific costing, elimination of waste in raw materials, power, etc., the greatest possible use of machinery and mechanical power, scientific layout of works. The tendency towards the grouping of industries in large units; the desirability of the development of this tendency towards the promotion of industrial efficiency. The effects upon Labour temporarily and finally of rationalisation, and how those effects could be satisfactorily adjusted by mutual arrangement. Interchangeability or flexibility, elasticity and testing of experimental conditions, demarcation, displacement of labour, compensation, and pensions.

(*b*) The effect of unnecessary internal competition.

(*c*) Sheltered and unsheltered industries.

(*d*) Distribution.

V. *FINANCE*

(*a*) Monetary technique. Banking and credit systems and policy.

(*b*) Industrial Finance.

(*c*) Taxation and Local Rates.

VI. *CONSTITUTIONAL*

(*a*) National Industrial Council. The creation of some permanent Standing Committee to meet for regular consultation on matters affecting industry.

(*b*) The co-ordination of the present and if necessary the provision of further machinery for continuous investigation into industrial conditions.

VII. INTERNATIONAL

(a) Competition of countries with lower labour standards.
(b) International Agreements and Conventions.
(c) International Economic Conference.

VIII. GENERAL

(a) Housing.
(b) Health problems.
(c) Education. To see how far the educational methods in vogue to-day can be best adapted to the modern needs of industry.
(d) Technical education (including apprenticeship).
(e) Research.

.   .   .   .

NATIONAL INDUSTRIAL COUNCIL

It is agreed that it is desirable for the continuous improvement of industrial reorganisation and industrial relations that a National Industrial Council should be formed, and it is recommended that the necessary steps for its formation should be taken immediately.

It is recommended that the composition of the National Industrial Council should be as follows:—

A. The representatives of the workers should be the members of the General Council of the Trades Union Congress.

B. An equal number of representatives of the employers should be nominated by the Federation of British Industries and the National Confederation of Employers' Organisations.

It is agreed that the three main functions of the National Industrial Council should be:—

1. To hold regular meetings once a quarter for general consultation on the widest questions concerning industry and industrial progress.

2. To establish a Standing Joint Committee for the appointment of Joint Conciliation Boards . . .

3. To establish and direct machinery for continuous investigation into industrial problems.

25 The 'strike problem': the post-war period

SIGNIFICANCE

25.1 Royal Commission on Trade Unions and Employers' Associations 1965–1968, *Report* (Cmnd. 3623) 1968

THE IMPORTANCE OF STRIKES

409. It is now possible to make some estimate of the importance of strikes

and other industrial action in economic terms. Official strikes tend to be much more serious individually in terms of working days lost, and individual official strikes may have particularly serious economic effects. . . . Nevertheless official strikes are relatively infrequent and their number shows no consistent tendency to grow. Since the end of the war there have been only three years when major official strikes have resulted in raising the number of working days lost above the 4 million mark; these were 1957, 1959 and 1962 when the numbers lost were 8·4m., 5·3m. and 5·8m. respectively.

410. So far as unofficial strikes are concerned, the immediate effect in terms of working days lost might seem to indicate that in economic terms no very serious problem is involved. . . .

411. That tally gives a very imperfect measure of the economic consequences of a strike. It records days lost at the place of work, whether by the strikers or by other workers laid off in consequence of the strike. Days lost at other establishments because of the indirect effects of a stoppage are not included in the statistics, though they may nevertheless be substantial, especially in any industry where a strike by a handful of workers may make idle hundreds or even thousands of workers at other establishments . . . Similarly a railway or a bus strike may prevent other workers from getting to work. On the other hand it is possible for some of the loss of working days to be made good after a strike, either by overtime or by greater effort under incentive schemes.

412. It is also necessary to take account of the effects on management of fear of the possibility of strikes even if they do not take place. If an employer forestalls a strike by making concessions in the face of threats which it might have been better to resist, or by refraining from introducing changes which he believes to be necessary in the interests of efficiency, then the economic consequences of his doing so may be more serious than those to which a strike would have given rise. Naturally, however, it is impossible to measure such consequences statistically.

413. It is in fact only when the impact on managements of unofficial strikes and other forms of unofficial action is taken into account that their gravity becomes apparent. Such action may face a manager with a sudden and acute dilemma. He may be under severe pressure from customers to produce goods or materials by a particular deadline, and in a competitive market such pressure is not easy to resist. No doubt it should be resisted if the alternative is to surrender to blackmail exerted by unofficial strikers. But it is not surprising if managers sometimes make unwise concessions which secure peace for the time being at the cost of storing up trouble for the future.

414. Moreover it is characteristic of unofficial action that it is unpredictable. . . . The upshot is that some managements lack confidence that the plans they make and the decisions they reach can be implemented rapidly and effectively or, in extreme cases, at all.

415. This situation is found in its most acute form in the small number of establishments where there is what might be termed an "endemic" strike situation. In 1965 thirty-one establishments experienced five or more officially-recorded strikes, and in 1966 the number was twenty-seven, several of them appearing in both lists. In many of them the number of unrecorded strikes was probably much higher. In these establishments managers and supervisors

are in a constant state of anxiety lest they do something which might inadvertently lead to a strike. . . . The economic implications are obvious and serious; the country can ill afford the crippling effect which such managerial attitudes are liable to have on the pace of innovation and technological advance in industry. We have no hesitation therefore in saying that the prevalance of unofficial strikes, and their tendency (outside coalmining) to increase, have such serious economic implications that measures to deal with them are urgently necessary.

CAUSES

25.2 Royal Commission on Trade Unions and Employers' Associations, *Minutes of Evidence 30, Witness: Transport and General Workers' Union* (London H.M.S.O., 1966)

STRIKES

.   .   .   .

153. Workers who go on strike sacrifice a great deal. Benefits payable from union funds are less than a quarter of the average earnings of adult male workers, and although there may be some local supplementation, this is not considerable or widespread. Workers who are on strike in circumstances not recognised by the union receive no strike pay at all.

154. It seems worthwhile to stress this point because it is often assumed that employers are the greater losers by strike action. In fact the loss to an employer in money or in orders or production by a short-term strike may easily be over-estimated, especially if it takes place when stocks are high and markets low. Nor should it be accepted without question that people who go on strike are always acting "irresponsibly" or that they are primarily the people to blame for the dispute. A worker sells his labour and unless his ability to bargain puts him in a position of equal strength with the employer, his only means of registering dissatisfaction with a given situation is to refuse to sell at the price the employer is willing to pay. We cannot advocate or agree to legal sanctions against workers who withdraw their labour, since the right to do this is an essential freedom, which cannot and ought not to be impaired. A man's labour cannot be separated from his whole personality and cannot therefore be the subject of the same sort of bargain or contract as can his money or his possessions. Men are not slaves and can neither sell themselves nor be sold. The direction and control of labour, and the making of strikes illegal in wartime, was accepted as a desperate necessity. No one pretends that it was anything but a grave invasion of liberty, wholly unacceptable in other circumstances.

155. We do not find the distinction normally made between official and unofficial strikes a practical way of examining their causes or of suggesting methods of avoiding them. Still less do we consider the word "wildcat" as

156

being useful except as a term of abuse. We think the only really sensible method is to look at the circumstances in which disputes occur.

156. The union may give notice of strike action when negotiations have taken place and there is failure to agree. Such notice is a last resort, and could be avoided by an effective system of arbitration.

157. Notice of withdrawal of union labour may also be given if an employer has refused to meet the union, or to recognise its right to negotiate on behalf of its members; again, an effective system of arbitration would overcome this difficulty.

158. Many strikes are caused or prolonged by employers refusing to operate agreed procedure; by incompetence, ill temper, or failure in communications on the part of management and by the absence of speedy and genuine consultation at the workplace. Strikes caused by anger at what is believed to be the unfair treatment of an individual or the victimisation of a union official or active union member; or by a change (actual or anticipated) in wages, piece-rates, earnings or working conditions, all come under this heading, as do strikes which occur when negotiations at workplace level are too slow in starting or get bogged down, because those who undertake them lack essential information or the authority to settle. Some occur because of rumours which may be unfounded, or exaggerated.

159. In these cases, there is no possibility of notice of a strike being given, since the withdrawal of labour is a spontaneous revulsion, consequent upon management blunders, ineffective consultation or negotiation (sometimes all three). Most of these strikes are unofficial in the first place; but often the union, on investigating the facts, concludes that the members have got a case, and are entitled to receive union support.

25.3 Royal Commission on Trade Unions and Employers' Associations 1965–1968, *Report* (Cmnd. 3623) 1968

CAUSES

. . . .

379. So far as official strikes are concerned, no elaborate analysis of cause is necessary. Most major strikes, though not all, are official and result from a breakdown of negotiations at industry level about a claim tabled by the trade union or unions concerned for improved terms and conditions of employment....

. . . . . .

382. In order better to understand the causes of strikes, and their nature generally, we decided to investigate more fully the causes of unofficial strikes in the motor vehicle manufacturing industry....

. . . . . .

389. ... In our view the failure to devise adequate wage structures, and to agree upon them in comprehensive negotiations with representatives of all the

workers concerned, is responsible to a large extent for the industry's industrial relations difficulties.

390. Most of the unofficial strikes which are not over wages in the motor industry arise from disputes over "working arrangements, rules and discipline" or "redundancy, dismissal, suspension, etc." Disputes from such causes reflect in part the insecurity of the industry. They also reflect the increased power and readiness of workers, in conditions of full employment, to resist unwelcome disciplinary or other managerial decisions by their employers. There is no standard by which to measure whether the decisions taken by management are or are not justified in such cases, nor whether it is reasonable or not of the workers concerned to reject or resist them. A number of points are however clear. First, these are workplace issues, not issues regulated at industry level. Secondly, one is concerned here with an area in which it is for the most part nominally within management's prerogative to reach decisions unilaterally, but in which workers can and do dispute the decisions so arrived at. Thirdly, in modern circumstances—the most significant of which is full employment—workers are more ready to insist on what they regard as fair and reasonable treatment. Management is less able to wield its traditional disciplinary sanction—the sack—than in the past and workers' organisation at the workplace is now highly developed. Workers expect their interests, and such rights as they have acquired by custom, to be increasingly respected by management. Finally, in matters of this kind the disputes procedure cannot always work satisfactorily because it does not offer an effective means of redressing grievances about decisions which, once implemented, can no longer be effectively challenged. Altogether the number of unofficial disputes which arise over "working arrangements, rules and discipline" and "redundancy, dismissal, suspension, etc." in the motor industry ... indicates that there is considerable confusion as to what management does and does not have the right to do; or, where it is conceded to have the right, whether it is or is not making reasonable use of it.

· · · · · · ·

393. The engineering industry's disputes procedure[1] must bear a large share of the responsibility for the failure of federated undertakings to devise adequate wage structures and for their inability to solve disputes over other issues in a constitutional manner. The procedure functions slowly. It hampers the development of well-designed pay structures by allowing sectional claims to be pursued right through to "central conference" regardless of their implications for other workers in the same factory. It discourages effective company personnel policies because companies have no place in the agreed procedure, unresolved disputes in individual factories being referred to local conference and not to the company. It provides no general guidance on dealing with issues of discipline, redundancy and work practices and it is not well equipped to handle individual disputes on these topics, which, it implies, fall within the prerogative of employers "to manage their own establishments", despite the obvious impossibility of fixing clear and immutable limits for such a prerogative. Those companies which are not "federated" have been obliged

[1] See Documents 10.2 and 10.3.

to devise procedures suitable to their own circumstances, a situation which, so far as we are aware, has brought no disadvantages in its train.

394. The charge can justly be made against trade unions that they have failed to respond adequately to the challenge inherent in the growth of workplace bargaining. Their leaders have remained pre-occupied with collective bargaining at industry level, while shop stewards have been left largely on their own to set the pace in negotiations at plant level. The disputes procedure in the engineering industry indeed offers no formal part to full-time trade union officials at an earlier stage than a "works conference"; that is until all the stages of negotiation within the plant have been observed without success. Union leaders however have made no sustained efforts to improve the procedure. Communications between the rank-and-file and the leadership have been left in a very poor state. The defect is made good only to a very limited extent by meetings between union officials and shop stewards at district committee and other meetings. The multiplicity of unions operating within plants has hindered the development of an organic link between negotiators at plant level and those higher up in the hierarchies of trade unions.

395. The shop steward system has developed its strength in an informal and piecemeal way. Thus it is that, despite the great importance of shop stewards to the maintenance of good industrial relations in the industry, they still do not have the facilities or the status which are desirable. . . .

396. To summarise, it is apparent that the causes of unofficial strikes in the motor manufacturing industry are complex, and that employers and unions both bear a considerable responsibility for them. Insofar as fluctuations in demand have been caused by fiscal measures which fall with particular force on the motor industry, Governments too must take some responsibility, since these fluctuations have led to insecurity of employment and of earnings. Employers have failed to develop adequate management policies, and in particular have not tackled effectively the problem of devising rational wage structures. Trade unions have been handicapped by their multiplicity and consequent rivalry, and have failed to bring an effective influence to bear at workplace level.

.   .   .   .

398. The further we have pursued our inquiries, the stronger has become our belief that the motor industry's difficulties over strikes arise in the main not so much from special factors peculiar to the industry as from factors which are present in many other industries, although to a less marked degree. The analysis . . . of the shortcomings of the industrial relations system emphasises how important and how general a failure there has been to devise institutions in keeping with changing needs. Unofficial strikes and other types of unofficial action are above all a symptom of this failure.

25.4 Royal Commission on Trade Unions and Employers' Associations 1965–1968, *Report* (Cmnd. 3623) 1968

OUR CONCLUSIONS

500. It is imperative that the number of unofficial and especially of unconstitutional strikes should be reduced and should be reduced speedily. This is not only a serious, it is also an urgent problem, and our recommendations are designed to deal with it. Such differences of opinion as exist among us refer not to the end to be achieved, but to the means of achieving it.

501. . . . The first and the most important step to be taken in order to get rid of unconstitutional strikes is the reform of our collective bargaining system. This is our central recommendation. We cannot recommend anything that may jeopardise its success.

502. We are not in principle opposed to the use of legal sanctions for the enforcement of agreed procedures. No such sanctions can however be enforced without the active participation of the employer. . . . It follows that sanctions will remain unworkable until a fundamental change in our system of industrial relations has led to a situation in which employers may be able and willing to use such rights as the law gives them. At the present time legislation making procedure agreements legally enforceable would not in fact be enforced, and like all legislation that is not enforced would bring the law into disrepute.

503. It would, moreover, be unjust to ask men to abide by procedures which, as everyone knows, cannot deal with some of the most important grievances, and which more often than not yield no result at all. It would be futile to expect men to be deterred from using the strike weapon if they know that its speedy use is the only means at their disposal to get speedy redress for their grievances.

504. Those resorting to unconstitutional action should not be threatened with any disadvantages imposed by law until new procedures have been put into operation, procedures which are clear where the present procedures are vague, comprehensive where the present procedures are fragmentary, speedy where the present procedures are protracted, and effective where the present procedures are fruitless.

·   ·   ·   ·   ·   ·

506. We thus reject the proposal to make collective agreements—whether substantive or procedural—enforceable at the present time. We do so, not because we think that the law could not in any circumstances assist in the reduction of the number of unofficial strikes. It cannot do so in this country today—this is the point. To take steps in this direction today would be not only useless but harmful, and they would undo a great deal of the good we hope to see done through the reform of the collective bargaining system which we recommend.

·   ·   ·   ·   ·   ·

511. If legal sanctions have to be applied this will have to be done *ad hoc*. Our attitude to the use of legal sanctions for the enforcement of procedure agreements is identical with that which we have adopted towards the problem of the recognition of trade unions by employers. In both cases we hope and expect that the work of the Industrial Relations Commission[1] will make the use of legal sanctions unnecessary, that is, that the persuasive influence of the Industrial Relations Commission will suffice to produce the necessary improvements. In both cases we envisage the use of legal enforcement machinery only as an emergency device, to be used from case to case and in exceptional situations in which it is inescapable, and that it should remain operative only for a limited period. This "case by case" or *ad hoc* approach would also be analogous to that adopted in the Terms and Conditions of Employment Act 1959, section 8.[2] Under that provision the substantive terms of collective agreements can be given legally binding force only for such enterprises in which a need for doing so has arisen and has been proved. In the same way procedure agreements would be given legal effect only in concerns or factories where the strike situation makes it necessary.

512. We are of the opinion that it should be for the Secretary of State for Employment and Productivity to initiate the proceedings for making a procedure agreement legally binding in an enterprise or establishment. The decision to institute these proceedings should be in the discretion of the Secretary of State, who should be responsible to Parliament for its exercise. It should however be for an independent body to make the order giving legal force to an agreement. This jurisdiction should therefore be vested in the Industrial Court.

513. Before applying to the Industrial Court for an order the Secretary of State would have to consult both sides of the industry concerned and the Industrial Relations Commission.

514. To proceed further, the Secretary of State would, on the basis of this consultation, have to be satisfied:

(*a*) that the disputes procedure has been agreed between the employer and the union or unions concerned;

(*b*) that it complies with the standards we have set out in paragraph 182(2)[3] . . .

(*c*) that in the enterprise or establishment unconstitutional strikes continue to be a serious problem;

(*d*) that the employer considers the situation sufficiently serious to be willing to enforce such sanctions as may be put at his disposal; and

(*e*) that the threat or the enforcement of legal sanctions can be expected to lead to a reduction in the number or in the magnitude of unconstitutional stoppages in the enterprise or establishment.

515. The Industrial Court would have to hear the two sides of industry, the employer and the shop stewards or other representatives of those employed in the enterprise or establishment. If it found that the conditions listed in the previous paragraph were fulfilled, it would, by order, declare the procedure agreement to be legally binding on the employer and on all those employed by him in the enterprise or establishment to which the order applies. The order

[1] See Document 15.1.   [2] See Document 74.9.   [3] See Document 15.1.

161

would be in force for a limited period of, say, one year, but it could be extended by the Industrial Court for further periods if the Court, on application by the Secretary of State and after hearing those concerned, was satisfied that this step was necessary.

516. Only the parties themselves could enforce an agreement which has been declared binding. . . . The only way to enforce an agreement is through civil actions for damages. . . . the loss suffered by the plaintiff would be the measure of the damages payable by the defendant. They would not, as are damages for breach of the contract of employment, be restricted to the amount of the wages payable for the period of notice.

25.5 *In Place of Strife: A Policy for Industrial Relations* (Cmnd. 3888) 1969

COLLECTIVE AGREEMENTS AND THE LAW

. . . . . .

46. The Government think it right to ensure . . . that there is no legal impediment to the observance of collective agreements negotiated between employers or employers' associations and trade unions by any method freely decided upon by the two parties. For this reason it will propose in the Industrial Relations Bill[1] the modification of section 4 (4) of the Trade Union Act 1871, so that agreements between trade unions and employers' associations will be put in the same position as those between trade unions and individual employers. The Bill will further propose that agreements could be made legally binding only by an express written provision in the agreement. It would thus have no effect on the legal status of existing agreements, or of future agreements, if the parties did not expressly decide in writing to make them legally binding.

. . . . . .

A CONCILIATION PAUSE

93. . . . the Government will seek to reinforce, through the Industrial Relations Bill, the machinery of conciliation which already exists. The method proposed would be to give the Secretary of State a discretionary reserve power to secure a "conciliation pause" in unconstitutional strikes and in strikes where, because there is no agreed procedure or for other reasons, adequate joint discussions have not taken place. The power would only be used when, if the strike (or lock-out) continued, the effects were likely to be serious.

94. It would only be used, moreover, where the Department of Employment and Productivity's normal conciliation methods had first been tried. In many strikes the employer is at fault, for example in cases of victimisation, or when the employer has introduced a change in working methods without adequate notice and discussion. An essential part, therefore, of the efforts

[1] See footnote to Document 6.3.

to get the strikers to return to work would be to require management to withdraw the offending action till adequate discussion had taken place. In many other cases it would be desirable to preserve the status quo in order not to prejudice negotiations or an inquiry. If, despite these steps and despite the setting up by the D.E.P. of an inquiry or other appropriate machinery, the strike went ahead, the Secretary of State would, after warning the two sides, be able to issue an Order requiring those involved to return to work and to desist from industrial action for a period of twenty-eight days, and at the same time requiring the employer to observe specified conditions or terms during the pause, the conditions normally being those that existed before the dispute. If either side failed to comply with this Order the Industrial Board[1] at its discretion could impose financial penalties. Before doing so, it would take into account the circumstances of each particular case.

95. This "conciliation pause" would enable every opportunity for negotiation to be explored. In particular, it would allow time for any suitable disputes procedure to be used. Under a good procedure, it should be possible for an urgent matter normally to be fully considered within twenty-eight days. Unless the Secretary of State was satisfied that adequate machinery for reaching a settlement existed and would be used, a suitable inquiry would be held. After the end of the pause there would be no power to delay or restrict a strike or lock-out arising from the dispute in question.

STRIKE BALLOTS

98. It is . . . a matter for concern that at present it is possible for a major official strike to be called when the support of those involved may be in doubt. A number of unions already have provisions in their rules making a ballot of their members obligatory before a strike. In other cases the holding of a ballot is discretionary; in others there are no provisions about ballots in the rules. Where a major official strike is threatened the Secretary of State will discuss with the unions concerned the desirability of holding a strike ballot and will seek to persuade them to consult their members unless there are valid reasons why they should not. Where no agreement is reached, the Industrial Relations Bill will give the Secretary of State discretionary power to require the union or unions involved to hold a ballot on the question of strike action. The power will be used where the Secretary of State believes that the proposed strike would involve a serious threat to the economy or public interest, and there is doubt whether it commands the support of those concerned. The object will not be to place a prohibition on such strikes, but to help to ensure that before strikes of this importance take place the union members themselves are convinced that they are right to go on strike. The ballot will be conducted by the union, in accordance with its own rules as approved by the proposed Registrar of Trade Unions and Employers' Associations[2] . . . which should of course provide for the fair and efficient conduct of a poll. Apart from giving approval to the form of the question to be put to the vote, the Secretary of

[1] See *supra*, p. 24.
[2] See footnote to Document 16.4.

State will not intervene in the conduct of the ballot. If members raise any questions of procedure, including entitlement to vote, these will be resolved in the same way as similar disputes in relation to a ballot called by the union itself. Similarly, in all other respects the powers of unions under their rules to decide whether or not to strike, or to end a strike, will remain unaltered.

25.6 General Council of the Trades Union Congress, *Announcement of June 18, 1969*[1]

The General Council have agreed unanimously to a solemn and binding undertaking the text of which is set out in the annex to this statement. The General Council have further agreed that this undertaking will forthwith govern the operation by the General Council of Congress Rule 11[2] . . . This undertaking unanimously given by the General Council will have the same binding force as the T.U.C. Bridlington Principles[3] and Regulations.

THE TEXT OF THE ANNEX . . .

The General Council have unanimously agreed that in operating Congress Rule 11 . . .

(a) where a dispute has led or is likely to lead to an unconstitutional stoppage of work which involves directly or indirectly large bodies of workers or which, if protracted, may have serious consequences, the General Council shall ascertain and assess all the facts . . .

(b) In cases where they consider it unreasonable to order an unconditional return to work, they will tender the organisation or organisations concerned their considered opinion and advice with a view to promoting a settlement.

(c) Where, however, they find there should be no stoppage of work before procedure is exhausted, they will place an obligation on the organisation or organisations concerned to take energetic steps to obtain an immediate resumption of work, including action within their rules if necessary, so that negotiations can proceed.

(d) Should an affiliated organisation not comply with an obligation placed on it under (c) above, the General Council shall duly report to Congress or deal with the organisation under Clauses (b), (c), (d) and (h) of Rule 13.[4]

[1] Published in *Industrial Relations, Programme for Action* [*Report* of a Special Trades Union Congress, June 5 1969 (London, Trades Union Congress, 1969)].
[2] See Document 67.1.   [3] See Document 67.4.   [4] See Document 67.1.

26 Importance in union functions

26.1 Trades Union Congress, *Trade Unionism*[1] 2nd edition (London, Trades Union Congress, 1967)

SERVICES FOR MEMBERS

144 Autonomous action by trade unions is not limited to, and it could be argued does not find its main expression in, autonomous job regulation. Trade unions have always provided, and continue to provide, a wide range of services for their members which do not involve employers or any outside agency. Trade unions' role as friendly societies administering schemes for mutual insurance represents the characteristic method by which working people themselves seek to insure against interruption of earnings and unforeseen financial commitments. The progress which has been achieved in the field of social insurance, to a considerable extent through policies advocated by trade unions, has had the effect of reducing the relative importance of traditional benefits in union expenditure and has led to a modification in the range of services provided.

145 The two main factors responsible for this change have been the growth of alternative provision for interrupted earnings and the post-war establishment of full employment with a great measure of economic stability. . . .

146 There is no one pattern of services provided by a selected trade union which can be said to be typical. To some extent differences may be explained by tradition or by differences in individual and collective preferences. There are also differences which can be explained by reference to the circumstances of the trade. Thus, the importance of legal services is far greater in some unions than in others. Trade unions are spending increasing sums on educational services, where the emphasis is increasingly on matters directly affecting trade union interests. In recruiting new members trade unions obviously depend on the quality of all their services and it would be a mistake to imagine that the mere listing of various services could show the value of trade union membership. Some two thirds of total trade union expenditure comprises "working expenses," a term which is hardly illuminating. There are a thousand and one ways in which trade unions look after the interests of their members, inquiring into the circumstances of thousands of individual cases where the trade union is the natural source of advice and assistance for the individual member. To trade unionists, this goes without saying, though perhaps to a wider audience it needs to be said.

[1] See footnote to Document 4.2.

26.2 National and Local Government Officers' Association, *About Nalgo* 1968

Whenever its members need help, in their work, in their play, and in their domestic life, NALGO comes to their aid . . .

NALGO's legal department—staffed by a team of expert lawyers—is ready to help you. It spends thousands of pounds every year representing members in the courts. It wins thousands of pounds for them every year in compensation for loss of office, for injury, for libel and slander, and other difficulties. Every year, too, it helps hundreds of members to solve individual problems arising out of pensions (including pensions increase matters), national health and unemployment insurance and industrial injury benefits. In fact, it covers everything connected with your work, other than criminal proceedings (with certain exceptions).

Employees of services subject to the control of Parliament are especially liable to be affected by legislation, which may change their jobs or their conditions of work. NALGO's legal department protects you. It scrutinizes every Bill, Order or Regulation presented to Parliament or decided by a Minister, and takes action whenever the conditions of members are threatened.

NALGO believes that education and training are the keys to a successful career, and that an informed membership is the key to trade union strength. Hence it provides vocational and trade union education services.

Correspondence and residential course tuition is provided for professional examinations and residential courses on background, departmental and management studies. There is a students' library and a careers advisory service.

Trade union education is important at branch and district, as well as national level, and is being developed through schools of varying length, the award of scholarships to T.U.C., W.E.A.[1] and University extra-mural courses, and by providing reading material and visual aids.

NALGO has been a pioneer in the development of public relations in the public services.

Recognising that the salary, working conditions and status of the public servant must largely depend on popular appreciation of the value of his work, it has striven for years to increase that appreciation. Through its Public Relations Department at Headquarters, and the efforts of its hundreds of voluntary district and branch public relations officers, it has developed an intensive and continuous programme of activities—exhibitions, press articles, broadcasts, books, leaflets and a wide variety of public events such as brains trusts and film shows—to show people what is being done in the services employing its members.

.   .   .   .

MONEY TO INVEST? Or needed to buy a house? Either way the Nalgo Building Society, now merged with Leek & Westbourne Building Society, is waiting to serve you—at advantageous terms for NALGO borrowers. They form Britain's sixth biggest Society (assets over £200 million, reserves of over £9 million).

[1] Workers' Educational Association.

NALGO has its own insurance society—LOGOMIA. It will give you maximum protection at minimum cost on almost every class of insurance, including life, endowment, family income, decreasing mortgage cover, fire, householders' comprehensive, and motor.

COMPLETE REST and every attention are assured, for you or your dependants, when warding off or recuperating from illness, at NALGO's convalescent homes at Bournemouth or Lytham St. Annes.

THE ASSOCIATION arranges holidays by air abroad for members and their friends. NALGO has its own Holiday Centres . . .

BUYING A CAR, or running one, NALGO can help you. Finance is available at moderate terms from its insurance society, LOGOMIA, for various models, not more than five years old. And when ownership becomes a fact, the NALGO Motoring Association is open to you. *The annual subscription which includes full associate membership of the R.A.C. is £1 15s. 0d. plus 10/- joining fee.*

NALGO can help you to cut the cost of living. It runs a Thrift Scheme, through which discounts can be obtained on a wide range of goods, from carpets to cameras, sewing-machines to shirts.

FOR MANY MEMBERS and their families, one of NALGO's greatest services is its Benevolent and Orphan Fund. This Fund, run by members for members, spends over £82,000 a year in giving help to those who suffer financial distress through illness, death of the "bread winner", or other cause. The Fund also has places in the Crossways Trust Homes for aged and infirm people.

27 Conditions governing payments

27.1 Amalgamated Society of Woodworkers, *Contributions and Benefits* (*The Woodworkers' Journal*, No. 4, October 1969)

NO. 1 SECTION: CONTRIBUTIONS 4s. 4d. PER WEEK

NOTE: No person shall be admitted into this Section after 31st March, 1958.

Unemployment Benefit:
15 weeks at 12s. per week.

Accident Benefit:
£200.

Tool Benefit:
£25.
Tool Box, 10s.; Tool Bass,[1] 10s.
No claim allowed less than 5s.

Sickness Benefit:
15 weeks at 17s. 6d. per week.
52 weeks at 7s. 6d. per week.
35 years' membership:
6s. per week for remainder of sickness.

Funeral Benefit:
£20.
On death of wife, £10.
Balance on death of member, £10

Superannuation:
65 years of age and 35 years' membership, 10s. per week.
65 years of age and 40 years' membership, 11s. per week.

Trade Privileges:[2]
£5 per week.

Legal Assistance.

[1] Tool bag.   [2] Dispute benefit.

167

NO. 2 SECTION: CONTRIBUTIONS 3s. 1d. PER WEEK

19 years and over: Entrance, 5s.; Readmission, 10s. minimum.

Unemployment Benefit:
12 months' membership:
15 weeks at 8s. per week.

Sickness Benefit:
12 months' membership:
24 weeks at 10s. per week in any period of 12 months.

Trade Privileges:
3 months' membership, £2 10s. per week.
6 months' membership, £5 per week.

Tool Benefit:
3 months' membership, £10.
12 months' membership, £25.
Tool Box, 10s.; Tool Bass, 10s.
No claim allowed less than 5s.

Accident Benefit:
2 years' membership, £100.
5 years' membership, £200.
If under 50 years of age at date of entrance into Society.

Funeral Benefit:
£20.
On death of wife, £10.
Balance on death of member, £10.
If under 60 years of age at date of entrance and completed 5 years' continuous Society membership.

Legal Assistance.

NO. 3 SECTION: CONTRIBUTIONS 1s. 8d. PER WEEK

Commencement of employment to 19 or 21 years: No Entrance Fee until transferred to No. 2 Section. When transferred, Entrance Fee 2s. 6d.

Sickness Benefit:
12 months' membership:
15 weeks at 5s. per week.
15 weeks at 2s. 6d. per week

Tool Benefit:
12 months' membership:
Claims from 5s. up to £10.

Funeral Benefit:
12 months' membership, £10.

Legal Assistance.

NO. 4 SECTION (SPECIAL TRAINEE SECTION): CONTRIBUTIONS 1s. 5d. PER WEEK

Entrance Fee, 2s. 6d.; Readmission, 7s. 6d. minimum.

Trade Privileges: 3 months' membership, £2 10s. per week. 6 months' membership, £5 per week.

Legal Assistance.

NO. 5 SECTION (WOMEN SECTION): CONTRIBUTIONS 1s. 5d. PER WEEK

Entrance Fee, 1s.; Readmission, 1s. minimum, 10s. maximum.

Trade Privileges: 3 months' membership, £2 10s. per week. 6 months' membership, £5 per week.

Legal Assistance.

Members in Nos. 1, 2, and 3 Sections are exempt from payment of contributions for each week or weeks that they are in receipt of Society unemployment, sickness, or superannuation benefits, or trade privileges, from Monday to Saturday inclusive.

27.2 Transport and General Workers' Union, *Rules* 1968

SCHEDULE II—CONTRIBUTIONS, BENEFITS AND PENALTIES

(A) CONTRIBUTIONS AND BENEFITS. (NOTE: DISTRESS BENEFIT (OPTIONAL) 3d. PER WEEK EXTRA ON BOTH SCALES)

Scale 1

. . . .

Contribution: 1s. 9d. per week (including Quarterage and Political Contribution).

Benefits: Dispute, Lock-out and Victimisation Benefit, £4 per week.

Legal Assistance and Advice.

Funeral Benefit, £5 to £20.

Convalescent Home Benefit.

Accident Benefit, £2 per week for 10 weeks.

Fatal Accident (at work) Benefit, £250.

Females and Youths: Females who are not in receipt of men's rates of wages and youths under 18 years of age may pay 1s. per week and receive half financial benefits.

Scale 2

. . . .

Contribution: 2s. 6d. per week (including Quarterage and Political Contribution).

Benefits: Dispute, Lock-out and Victimisation Benefit, £4 per week.

Legal Assistance and Advice.

Funeral Benefit, £5 to £30.

Convalescent Home Benefit.

Incapacity (Sickness or Accident) Benefit, £2 5s. per week for 10 weeks.

Fatal Accident (at work) Benefit, £500.

169

Qualifications:
      (i) Open to male members under 50 years of age and female members under 35 years of age. Males 50 years of age and over and females 35 years of age and over are not eligible to contribute to this scale, excepting members who, as at December 25, 1965, were contributing for Sickness Benefit, and elected to contribute to this Scale prior to February 5, 1966.

      (ii) Females under 35 years of age who are not in receipt of men's rates of wages and youths under 18 years of age, may pay 1s. 6d. per week and receive half financial benefits.

. . . .

QUARTERAGE.—6d. per member per quarter in the case of members paying full scale contributions and 3d. per member per quarter in the case of members contributing for half-scale benefits shall be returned to regions for local purposes including the payment of affiliation fees to Trades Councils, and shall be disposed of for the benefit of members in such manner as the regional committee may direct, subject to a minimum of 1d. per member per quarter being retained under the jurisdiction of the regional committee for benevolent purposes. . . .

. . . .

(N) BENEFITS UNDER AMALGAMATING UNIONS

1. A member who was a member of one of the unions which amalgamated together in October 1921, who elected within the prescribed period to continue paying his or her old rate of contribution (being not less than the minimum set forth in Schedule II (a)) may:—

(a) continue to pay the old rate of contribution and retain the benefits for same, and no future conference shall have the power to reduce such benefits except by consent of the members concerned; or

(b) transfer to a scale of contributions and benefits under Schedule II (a).

2. No member of the Union may pay less than the minimum set forth in Schedule II (with such exceptions as may be provided in these rules and schedules), subject to rules . . . in regard to the political fund contributions.

In selecting scales, members shall be entitled to the whole of only one scale.

(O) SCALE TRANSFERENCE

A member may transfer to an alternative scale, subject to age and other necessary qualifications provided in these rules and after serving the qualifying period from the day of transference shall be entitled to the benefits under the scale to which he or she is transferred.

(P) GENERAL CLAUSE

Subject to the qualifications contained within these rules, new members may choose one of the scales set out in Schedule II (a), and pay contributions and receive benefits accordingly.

170

28 Variants in benefit provision

28.1 Transport and General Workers' Union, *Rules* 1968

SCHEDULE II—CONTRIBUTIONS, BENEFITS AND PENALTIES

. . . .

(*J*) *DISTRESS PAY*

Any member having three months' membership, having made 13 weekly payments to date of alleged offence, and being in compliance,[1] who has been ordered to pay any sum of money by a court of justice in circumstances arising out of the member following his occupation, shall, if so decided by the General Executive Council having regard to the circumstances associated with the case, be granted assistance, the extent of such assistance to be at the absolute discretion of the General Executive Council.

. . . .

(*L*) *CONVALESCENT HOME BENEFIT*

Subject to the qualifications contained within these rules a member with nine months' membership, having made 39 weekly contributions according to the Scale to which he or she is contributing and being in compliance ... shall be entitled to convalescent home benefit (covering railway fare to the convalescent home and two weeks' free maintenance at the home), subject to the following conditions:—

An applicant for convalescent home benefit must have been ill for a period of not less than two weeks prior to date of application and produce a doctor's certificate to the effect that he or she is in need of convalescent treatment.

Applications for convalescent home benefit must be made on the prescribed form which must be completed with all the requisite particulars and signed by the branch chairman and branch secretary, or regional secretary.

28.2 Transport and General Workers' Union, *Rules* 1962

SCHEDULE III.—OTHER CONTRIBUTIONS AND BENEFITS

. . . .

(*H*) *EVICTION BENEFIT*

Eviction benefit shall be granted to members contributing to the Agricultural Workers Scale ... who are unjustifiably dismissed and evicted from a tied cottage by their employers.

The amount of benefit shall be determined by the General Executive Council.

[1] Not six or more weeks in arrears with contributions.

28.3 Draughtsmen's and Allied Technicians' Association, *Rules* 1965 (as amended to 1968)

VICTIMISATION

12. Any member victimised by dismissal or otherwise, solely or mainly on account of his/her membership of, or work for the Association, or on account of refusal to undertake duties of other employees involved in a dispute, should report the fact to the Branch Secretary and the Divisional Organiser immediately. He/she may claim assistance from the Executive Committee, which, if satisfied as to the facts of the case, shall take action on the member's behalf.

(*a*) Any member claiming immediate benefit under this rule must notify the firm in writing after his/her claim has been approved by the Executive Committee that he/she considers himself/herself victimised, and that the matter has been reported to the Association. The General Secretary or other official if instructed by the Executive Committee, will then approach the firm demanding reinstatement of the member.

(*b*) Any member victimised by dismissal, and whose claim has been approved by the Executive Committee, shall receive benefit at a rate not less than two-thirds of his/her salary. The Executive Committee may, if deemed advisable, pay the equivalent of full salary.

28.4 National Union of Boot and Shoe Operatives, *Rules* 1967

TRAVELLING ASSISTANCE

115. (*a*) . . . any member unable to find employment in the district in which his Branch is situated may, if obtaining employment outside the district, apply to the Branch Secretary for the necessary travelling expenses.

(*b*) The Branch Secretary must ascertain from the Secretary of the Branch to which the member desires to travel that Union conditions prevail at the firm where employment is available.

(*c*) (i) On production of evidence that employment is available at the place to which he desires to travel, the member shall be entitled to travelling expenses not exceeding a total of £2 10s.

(ii) However, no member shall receive a total of more than £5 in any twelve consecutive months.

28.5 National Union of Public Employees, *Rules* 1967

10. BENEFITS

. . . . . .

(*H*) *TOTAL LOSS OF SIGHT*

Financial members[1] sustaining an accident whilst following their occupa-

[1] Members not disqualified from benefit rights because of arrears of contributions.

tion at their usual place of employment, which accident results in the total and irrecoverable loss of sight of both eyes, shall be entitled to the following:—

£200 after 1 year's continuous membership.

(I) LOSS OF LIMB OR SIGHT OF EYE

Financial members sustaining an accident whilst following their occupation at their usual place of employment shall be entitled to the following, if such accident results in the loss of a limb or the sight of one eye:—

£50 after 5 years' continuous membership;
£100 after 10 years' continuous membership;
£150 after 15 years' continuous membership.

The Executive Council shall be the judge as to whether any member is entitled to these benefits or not, and their decision shall be final.

Members claiming benefits under these Rules must, if required by the Executive Council, submit themselves for medical examination by any medical practitioner appointed by the Executive Council, whose decision shall be binding and final.

28.6 Society of Graphical and Allied Trades, Division 1,[1] *Rules* 1966 (as amended to 1968)

RULE 33
BENEFITS

. . . .

(M.) SURGICAL AND MEDICAL APPLIANCE BENEFIT

Surgical and Medical Appliance Benefit to be provided for members of such a character and to the extent as may be decided by and under such conditions as may be set out by the Executive Council.

(N.) CONSULTANT BENEFIT

Surgical and Medical Consultant Services to be provided for members where recommended by the member's doctor under such conditions as may be set out by the Executive Council.

(O.) MARRIAGE DOWRY

1. The marriage dowry provided for female members shall be paid in accordance with such conditions and upon such forms as the E.C. may from time to time determine, provided always (a) that benefit be paid only to members actually leaving work at the date of marriage, and (b) subject to the same being claimed within one month (i.e., 28 days) of the marriage.

2. Any member receiving the marriage dowry returning to the trade within twelve months of marriage shall pay a re-entrance fee equal at least to the amount of such dowry and the minimum re-entrance fee of the Branch combined; but notwithstanding the foregoing the Branch Committees may impose

[1] Previously the National Society of Operative Printers and Assistants.

lower fees in cases where return to the trade is due to the death, unemployment, or infirmity of the husband.

(P.) *CHRISTMAS GRANTS*

CHRISTMAS GRANTS FOR MEMBERS UNEMPLOYED AND MEMBERS IN RECEIPT OF DISTRESS BENEFIT.[1]—These grants shall be a sum not less than one week's ordinary benefit to all members actually unemployed or in receipt of Distress Benefit for the full week preceding the week in which Christmas Day falls. All such payments to be considered as benefits directly payable from the General Fund and the amount expended in any Branch to be treated as remittances by the Branch to the General Fund. Members still remaining sick and having exhausted Distress Benefit shall be entitled to the Christmas Grant, even when not actually in receipt of Benefit.

28.7 National Union of Railwaymen, *Rules* 1965 (as amended to 1968)

RULE 15
ORPHAN FUND

1. This Fund shall be set up on 1st January, 1965, by an initial transfer from the Union's funds of a sum calculated to represent residual donations in the past to the Death and Orphan Fund and shall be supported by subsequent annual transfers from the General Fund on the basis of 1d. per week per member. The Fund shall be further supported by donations, subscriptions, entertainments, collections, etc., and such other revenue as in the opinion of the Executive Committee may be necessary.

2. The Executive Committee and each branch of the Union are empowered to appoint collectors to solicit aid from the public. . . .

3. In the event of any member who has been a member of the Union for 12 calendar months and been credited with not less than 52 weeks' contributions thereto, and whose contributions are not 13 weeks or more in arrears, dying and leaving a child, children, stepchildren, or adopted children under 15 years of age (or under 18 years of age if still receiving full-time education), the branch of which he or she was a member shall claim from the Executive Committee for his or her child, or children, the following benefits of the fund; for the first child 15s. per week, and for each additional child 8s. per week. Benefits in respect of each child shall continue until the child ceases full-time education or reaches 18 years of age, whichever is the sooner.

In cases of mentally defective and other physical disabilities where the child is unable to follow any employment or normal educational vocation, benefit may, subject to the Executive Committee being satisfied with the merits of the case, be extended to 18 years of age.

·   ·   ·   ·   ·   ·   ·

[1] Benefit payable to certain classes of members who can produce evidence of absence from work through personal sickness or accident for 26 weeks during the 30 weeks immediately preceding the application.

4. As each child in a family ceases to qualify for benefit as provided for in Clause 3 of this Rule, a deduction from the weekly benefit shall be made to the extent of the lowest amount being paid for any one child. On the youngest child of a family ceasing to so qualify, payment of benefit shall cease.

.   .   .   .

6. It shall be the duty of the Secretary, or other officer appointed by the branch, to ascertain the conditions of the orphans aided from the fund, and from time to time to report to the branch or to the Executive Committee as to their cleanliness, clothing, schooling, and general treatment.

7. Should it be found that from any cause the orphans are neglected, and the moneys not applied to their benefit by their guardians, the Executive Committee reserve to itself the right to withhold the moneys from the guardian, and to authorise the branch officers to expend the allowances in food and clothing for the children.

8. Should any orphan or orphans entitled to the benefit of the fund be or become bereft of both parents, and have no relative or friend willing to take charge of them, the branch shall use its best efforts to prevail on kind friends in the locality to adopt the children. The Executive Committee shall have the power in such cases to increase the allowance by 2s. per week per child ... The Executive Committee and the local branch shall have the authority to raise a special fund in addition to the allowance from the Orphan Fund, or to take other means of securing the entrance of parentless or guardianless orphans to any home for orphans in which they will be properly cared for.

9. Should the mother or father of any orphan or family of orphans re-marry, the children shall cease to be entitled to the benefit. Should the mother or father again become a widow or widower, the children shall be re-admitted to the benefits of the fund. Should the mother or father of a family receiving the benefit of the fund be guilty of immorality, the Executive Committee shall have power, on the representation of the branch, to withhold payment of the benefit while the children remain with the mother or father, or to apply it for the benefit of the children if separated from the mother or father.

29 Variants in welfare provision

29.1 Royal Commission on Trade Unions and Employers' Associations, *Minutes of Evidence 57, Witness: Electrical Trades Union* (London, H.M.S.O., 1967)

THE ETU EDUCATIONAL PROGRAMME

127. The ETU is proud of the fact that it had led trade unions of this country in the field of education. It is, of course, affiliated to various workers' educational organisations. In addition to this, however, it has had its own college at Esher Place since 1952.

128. The education carried on at the college is primarily straight trade union training and about 800 ETU members attend one-week or two-week residential courses annually. Courses cover the following subjects: Shop stewards and their duties; Branch secretaries' and chairmen's courses; ordinary members' courses in which the principles and policies of the Union are explained; courses related to specific agreements in the electricity supply industry, the electrical contracting industry, the engineering industry and all the other industries in which the ETU members work. In addition full time officials attend special courses for the professional officer. These are designed to help keep them abreast of new techniques in productivity bargaining, costing, industrial and trade union law and special subjects that require time for study and a refreshing of knowledge.

129. The ETU has long been teaching the principles of work study and of modern productivity techniques. These studies have now been deepened to the point at which the teaching of principles has been joined to the actual productivity process in which the members work. Management and outside specialists are brought in together with full time trade union officers as tutors and discussion group leaders. The results so far have been most rewarding and productive.

130. The character of the courses and the problems dealt with vary greatly. Some have been straightforward work study courses related directly to the problems in the plant or industry. Some have been on the subject of existing agreements that have run into snags. Others have been on agreements newly signed and the problems of their implementation. It is the aim of the ETU increasingly to direct these courses for the solution of a specific problem. This will involve joint training with a firm or industry concerned.

131. The first of these joint training courses was held with ICI.[1] The company had just signed a new agreement with the trade unions and was having some difficulty in implementing it at plant level. The agreement was designed to get away from personal incentives and create the conditions for staff status expressed in terms of an annual salary to be paid weekly. Eight salary levels were to be established reflecting the company's concept of the differing job values. A detailed assessment method was laid out on the basis of placing the job within the salary structure.

. . . .

134. The agreement was examined stage by stage in great detail. The objects of the new agreement were studied. Its aims and how it would affect different groups of workers in separate trades and workers in the same trade were given careful consideration. Information was eagerly sought and eagerly given. By this method concrete problems of conflict and mutual interest were brought out, debated and, in many instances, resolved.

135. The course for ETU shop stewards employed by the Greater London Council . . . was a straightforward work study course including an examination of how work study could be employed in the GLC.

136. As examples of good industrial communications these were most

[1] Imperial Chemical Industries Limited.

rewarding exercises. So it was with British Railways main workshops, with BEA,[1] with BOAC[2] and with several others.

137. Probably the most exciting and rewarding courses were those run in conjunction with the new management of Fairfields Shipyard. Management, in this case, brought down to the college all their shop stewards and deputies, boilermakers, engineers, electricians, carpenters, painters—all 13 unions with the shop stewards in the plant were brought to the college in three courses. Top managements, including most members of the Board, technical management at key levels, PA (Management Consultants), trade union officials, all applied themselves to looking at the problems facing the new company. They determined how work study and critical path analysis could help to solve the production problems of their enterprise and how, if successfully applied, they could guarantee all their employees . . . a high level of earnings.

· · · · · · ·

139. Trade union education must reflect the changing pattern of industrial relations. New skills will be needed by the trade union educationist. It seems, for example, reasonably certain that job evaluation will play an increasingly important part in wage agreements of the future. A trade union official must, therefore, be as expert in the principles of job evaluation as those who are applying them for management and many of the questions to be dealt with will differ from those that have had to be dealt with in the past, and different educational skills will be required. A special course for all ETU officials was held in 1964.

140. In the field of joint union/management courses great benefits are waiting to be reaped. An increasing number of firms are now realising that the training of their work-people in the application of work study, for instance, should be viewed with as great an importance as the training of technical skills. New bridges require to be built; they are indeed being built, but too slowly.

141. At boardroom level the tendency is to ask what the catch is. At trade union local level there is still the fear of the past and of being brain-washed for the future. But the need is a real one and it must be satisfied.

142. The ETU is eager and able to satisfy that need. What it requires is co-operation from a much wider range of employers than has yet been willing to give co-operation. Also, since the benefits, to be gained from such courses, will accrue not only to the members of the ETU but also to the firm it would seem not unreasonable if they were to bear some of the costs. In the cases so far cited the firms concerned have been co-operative in this respect as in so many others.

[1] British European Airways.
[2] British Overseas Airways Corporation.

29.2 Transport and General Workers' Union, *Report and Balance Sheet for the year ended December 1966* (London, T. & G.W.U., 1967), pp. 217–220

EDUCATION

During the past two years the Union's educational work has been developed in conjunction with the work of the T.U.C.'s Education Department ...

THE UNION'S HOME STUDY COURSE

. . . . . .

The first stage of the course consists of six question papers taken one a month, in which the student has merely to answer "Yes" or "No" to some 50 questions based upon an issued booklet. Students who achieve a satisfactory standard on Stage 1 may, if they wish, compete for a certificate awarded by the Education Committee of the General Executive Council. This second stage is an essay-writing exercise set by the Education Department.

The third stage for which a certificate with distinction is awarded demands a high level of achievement. The few students who are successful in this stage receive, in addition to their certificate, a book of their own choice for their future studies.

The table sets out statistical details of the course.

The Union's Home Study Course
(Comparative Analysis)

	1965/66		1963/64		1961/62
Number enrolling	4,031	..	4,475	..	3,803
Number completing.........	1,996	..	2,484	..	2,050

. . . . . .

CORRESPONDENCE COURSES PROVIDED BY THE T.U.C.

In the two years 1965/66 the T.U.C.'s system of operating their correspondence courses has become firmly established. ...

Participation of T.G.W.U. members was proportionately slightly less than we were due in terms of our membership. But of course correspondence courses with the T.U.C. form merely a supplement to the much more substantial enrolments in our own Home Study Course. ...

The Union's method of preventing applicants from taking a further course until they have completed any previous course has led to a much lower rate of discontinuance on the part of our members. The T.U.C's Education Committee has drawn attention to the extremely low level of failures amongst our members.

T.G.W.U. and T.U.C. Correspondence Course enrolments

	1965/66		1963/64
Union's Home Study Course	4,031	..	4,475
T.U.C. Courses	2,507	..	1,863
	6,538	..	6,338

DAY AND WEEKEND SCHOOLS

The Union's Day and Weekend School Courses show a fairly substantial drop as compared with 1963/64. This drop has occurred in spite of the fact that the Head Office allocation for this type of school was raised from £7,000 to £8,000 at the beginning of 1965. The decline in activity is a result of the increase in accommodation and other costs. Statistics however materially underestimate the total activity. Several regions drew substantially from their funds during the period and these courses are not shown in the returns. The Union continues to send students to One-Day and Weekend Schools organised by the T.U.C. and the Irish Congress of Trade Unions.

Students at Courses Lasting One, Two or Three Days

	1965/66	1963/64	1961/62	1959/60
Union-sponsored schools	4,062	4,695	4,274	3,636

BRANCH OFFICERS' ONE-WEEK TRAINING COURSES

The Union continued to run its one-week Branch Officers' Training Courses at the Royal Agricultural College, Cirencester, for five weeks during the summer. Each course lasted one week and was arranged for Branch Chairmen, Secretaries, Shop Stewards and members with responsibilities for organising. There was, in addition, a special course for women members. Members needed to have two years' continuous financial membership[1] and to have completed, or be working through, the Union's Home Study Course in order to be eligible to attend.

... Training was given to all groups in communications—speech making; letter writing; report drafting and motion framing. In addition, each of the groups dealt with problems arising from its own branch responsibilities. The chairmen practised, amongst other subjects, meeting procedure and control of debate; the secretaries, minute writing and the planning of meetings; the shop stewards, grievances and accident procedure; the organisers, leaflet drafting and open-air speech-making; while the women's group examined the propaganda available and practised methods of putting the case for women workers to join the Union. The emphasis throughout this training was to give the students as much practice as possible in carrying out their various jobs within the branch.

The W.E.A.[2] continued to provide the tutors for the school. In the academic sessions, they worked with small groups of students and discussed the place of this Union within the wider Trade Union and Labour Movement. Once again, the emphasis in this part of the course was on student participation. Each student was given an assignment to prepare his or her own statement from sources of information provided at the school.

In 1965/66 a special course for Shop Stewards in Work Study and Incentive Systems of Payments was continued and developed.

[1] A financial member is a member with not less than 26 weeks' membership who has made 26 weekly payments and is less than six weeks in arrears.
[2] Workers' Educational Association.

FOLLOW-ON TRAINING

A proportion of the students at the Branch Officers' Training Courses were recommended for follow-on training. The majority of these were enrolled for the T.U.C.'s Training College where they took courses in industrial relations; industrial welfare and social security; trade union aspects of management techniques and general training. A small number of students received a place at follow-on courses held at the same time as the Union's Branch Officers' Training Courses at the Royal Agricultural College at Cirencester. In 1965/66 the subject of these courses was trade union and industrial law.

Two legally qualified tutors were provided by the W.E.A. to run these Follow-On Courses.

Students at Courses Lasting One or Two Weeks

	1965/66	1963/64	1961/62
T.U.C.	249 ..	244 ..	226
Union Training Courses......	1,026 ..	974 ..	916
	1,275 ..	1,218 ..	1,142

FULL-TIME SCHOLARSHIPS

There was some falling off in the number of full-time scholarship awards as compared with the previous two year period.

Up to twelve full-time scholarships may be awarded each year and distributed between Ruskin College, Coleg Harlech, Fircroft College (men only), Hillcroft College (women only), and the London School of Economics Trade Union Study Course. Scholarships cover board, lodging and tuition, allowances for dependants, pocket money, fares and books.

The conditions with which applicants must comply are two years' continuous financial membership and an age-limit of over 20 to under 46 years of age. Candidates have to submit essays of a very high standard after receiving recommendation from their Regions. Those who are short-listed are called to an interview before the Education Committee of the General Executive Council.

Full-time students are kept in touch with the Union through the Secretary of the Education Department.

Students at Full-Time Courses

	1965/66	1963/64	1961/62
Wholly maintained by the Union..	7 ..	10 ..	7
Assisted by the Union	2 ..	2 ..	2
	9 ..	12 ..	9

EVENING CLASSES

The Union continued to promote the Labour Statistics and Industrial Relations Course based on 24 evening classes in conjunction with the W.E.A. During the two year period under review the courses were held in Regions 5, 7, 10 and 1.[1]

A classroom was made available in "Transport House"[2] to house the Labour Statistics course run for members of Region No. 1 coming from within travelling distance of Central Office. The Union provided slide rules and demonstration equipment for members taking these courses, which were widely utilised. The W.E.A. provided the tutors, but the Union recruited the students through the Regions. At the end of the course, an examination for a diploma was held. Students who gained the highest marks received a diploma and a book of their choice.

THE T.U.C.'S EDUCATIONAL SCHEME

The Union continued to take a close interest in the development of the T.U.C.'s educational scheme. We submitted an amendment to an educational motion at the 1965 T.U.C. recommending the establishment of an Advisory Committee to the T.U.C.'s Education Department. This amendment was withdrawn on the understanding that the T.U.C.'s Education Committee were already sympathetically considering such a proposal. In 1966 a Consultative Group was set up. Two T. & G.W.U. representatives served on it.

The Union is keeping a close watch to ensure that our members get their fair share of the facilities available. The available statistics indicate that a problem may be developing and that new methods of recruitment might be called for.

29.3 National Union of General and Municipal Workers, *Rules* 1965 (as amended to 1968)

RULE 35
UNIVERSITY BURSARIES FOR SONS AND DAUGHTERS OF MEMBERS

Subject to such conditions as the National Executive Committee may from time to time determine, a bursary of not more than £50 a year for a maximum period of two years will be paid to a member to assist in the maintenance of a son or daughter attending a full-time course of study at a recognised college leading to the award of a degree by a British university, provided such member, at the time of having cause to claim the bursary, has been a member of the Union for at least five years, and is not more than six weeks in arrears with his contributions. In no case shall the amount of the bursary be such as

---

[1] Midlands, Scotland, East Coast, and London and Home Counties.
[2] The London headquarters of the Union.

to cause reduction in any other grant receivable by the member or the member's son or daughter from the State or any other source.

29.4 Transport and General Workers' Union, *Report and Balance Sheet for the year ended December 1966* (London, T. & G.W.U., 1967), pp. 199–203, 205, 214–215

LEGAL DEPARTMENT

This is a summary of the legal aid work in its various phases during 1965 and 1966, which work also embraces activities concerned with the health, safety and welfare of the membership.

DAMAGES AND COMPENSATION

The Union's legal aid work has continued to good purpose during the two years under review. Cases continue to be handled at first instance by the Regional Legal Claims Departments, the administration for this work having been intensified and ... the whole field of this case work co-ordinated through the Central Legal Department.

. . . .

We have continued to speed-up the handling of cases, and there is earlier reference to the Central Legal Department of complex and serious injury cases as well as most of the cases involving fatalities. For the normal case it is for the Regional Legal Claims Department to decide in first instance whether a prima facie case exists. There is always a proportion of cases brought to the Union by our members which do not involve a claim beyond the Industrial Injuries Act[1] as no negligence has been indicated or can be proved.

Every case, however, is carefully considered and every effort made to ensure that a member is properly advised. Cases brought to the Union and dealt with at Regional level in the first instance have as already indicated increased, and they run into many thousands.

Cases referred to the Central Legal Department totalled 5,649, an increase of 1,172. 2,747 cases were settled compared with 2,376 for the previous biennial period.

The total amount of damages and compensation recovered through the Central Legal Department (which also includes the work of the Union's solicitors) totalled £2,164,181 11s. 1d. which is again a record sum. The comparable amount for the previous biennial period was £1,951,827 13s. 4d.

To this has to be added the results achieved by the Regional Legal Claims Departments through which 9,767 cases were concluded resulting in the sum of £2,044,892 11s. 6d., these being easily the highest figures so far recorded. The comparable figures for 1963–64 were 8,467 cases and £1,823,270 17s. 11d.

[1] National Insurance (Industrial Injuries) Act 1965.

being recovered. The overall result is, therefore, the grand total of £4,209,074 2s. 7d. an increase of £433,975 11s. 4d. over the previous biennial period which up to then was an all-time record. The current figures are in respect of 12,514 cases—an increase of 1,671.

.   .   .   .

The Union's policy in this field is designed to encourage settlement of cases by reasonable negotiation wherever possible, and a very substantial proportion of cases have been disposed of in this way both at Regional and Central Legal Department level. In fact, by the concluding quarter of 1966 the figure of cases concluded by negotiation at all Union levels and without recourse to solicitors had risen to 90 per cent, this demonstrating that cases can be handled both efficiently and expeditiously by trade union personnel specifically trained for this essential work.

On the other hand, we never hesitate to instruct solicitors wherever the circumstances of cases call for this and to authorise legal proceedings where it is proper to do so. . . .

The Central Legal Department continues to have the responsibility for watching cases closely where solicitors are instructed, thus ensuring that the interests of an injured member are fully protected throughout. Even where our solicitors have to intervene no opportunity is lost to effect a settlement if this is at all possible, and of the cases where legal proceedings have to be started many come to be settled at some stage of the proceedings or even at the door of the Court. . . .

With the results of this two years' work the total sum of damages and compensation recovered for Union members since the Union's inception has now reached £34,839,319 18s. 10d., and it is significant that nearly one-eighth of that sum has been recovered during the last two years.

The figure in the last paragraph does not take into account weekly payments of compensation made under the old Workmen's Compensation Acts except where such cases are finally concluded. Outside the Republic of Ireland the Workmen's Compensation Acts no longer operate. We still have a number of old compensation cases remaining under our scrutiny, though this number is progressively diminishing. . . .

.   .   .   .

INDUSTRIAL INJURIES ACT

In addition to pressing claims for damages in cases where the facts justify this course, the Union service is also designed to ensure that in all industrial accidents members receive their proper benefit entitlements under the Industrial Injuries Act. This service continues to be given mainly through the medium of District Officers who provide the necessary representation at Local Tribunals and Medical Appeal Tribunals, the latter appeals, of course, arising out of decisions of Medical Boards. Thousands of members are assisted in this way every year and the advice leaflet "Industrial Injuries Act—What you Have to Do" continues to circulate to good purpose and in an improved form. The Advice Folder issued for the assistance of Officers and which has been kept up to date maintains handy advice for this purpose.

Cases requiring the consideration of the Industrial Injuries Commissioner by way of appeal continue to be handled through the Central Legal Department.

. . . .

TO AND FROM WORK

The extension of our Legal Aid Rule (which is limited to deal with cases of personal injury sustained by members proceeding directly to and from work), continues to operate with beneficial results to many members and families concerned.

FATAL ACCIDENTS

Both in the industrial field and in connection with road accidents, including those referred to in the preceding paragraph, we become involved in many tragic cases. There is no diminution in the number of fatal cases handled each year, this being again a grim reminder of the hazards to which many members are daily exposed. There may not be a basis for a successful claim in every case but each case is given the closest possible attention, and in this way every endeavour made to ease the anxiety of families and to provide material assistance wherever possible at a time when their need is greatest.

WAGES IN LIEU AND WRONGFUL DISMISSAL

A number of cases have to be dealt with concerning claims for wages in lieu and wrongful dismissal, and also in respect of claims for wages outstanding, wrongful deductions outstanding, holiday pay, etc. At all times we endeavour to see that justice is done, and where the facts make this possible the Union endeavours to apply the necessary corrective. We do not hesitate to take legal proceedings where this is justified, and in a number of cases either the threat or the serving of a County Court Summons has had the desired effect. We have a fair measure of success in this direction and a number of our members have benefited as a result.

ASSAULTS ON PASSENGER TRANSPORT PERSONNEL

There continues to be anxiety concerning the number of assaults perpetrated by the public on our members in this vital public transport service. . . . So far as compensation is concerned, such cases have always been difficult but the position has been materially eased by the establishment of the Criminal Injuries Compensation Board[1] to which reference was made in the last Report. This scheme has continued to work satisfactorily, and valuable assistance has been given to our members in this field particularly at District Officer level.

. . . .

[1] The body charged with administering the scheme for compensating victims of crimes of violence which was announced in both Houses of Parliament on June 24th, 1964, and came into operation on August 1st, 1964.

184

We continue to operate this adjunct to the legal aid service ... which originally developed out of wartime conditions. This service is designed to assist members with advice on personal problems and through it advice is given on a wide range of questions. As in the past, it operates through District Officers with the Central Legal Department continuing to assist where more specialised advice is called for. An important aspect of this service continues to be in respect of War Pensions cases, and whilst these will naturally diminish with the passage of time we can again report there has been valuable intervention in a number of cases in some of which direct representations before tribunals have been made ...

$\cdot \quad \cdot \quad \cdot \quad \cdot \quad \cdot \quad \cdot \quad \cdot$

DEFENCE OF MEMBERS

Legal defence continues pursuant to rule, where this appears to be necessary for members who are confronted with charges arising out of their employment on the roads. . . . the main charges usually arise under ... the Road Traffic Act, 1960, though, on occasion, it is necessary to defend on a lesser charge. . . .

When the facts justify that course, the member is, as is customary, defended and the standard of representation has, as in the past, led to many acquittals. In this way, penalties have, in many cases, been kept within reasonable proportions, but there is a clear pattern of increasing penalties. . . . It is certain that without this kind of service many members, who would be unable to obtain proper legal defence, would be very handicapped in obtaining justice.

$\cdot \quad \cdot \quad \cdot \quad \cdot \quad \cdot \quad \cdot \quad \cdot$

CONCLUSION

This Report will convey something of the range of the work of the Legal Department, involved as it is in many directions with matters not simply related to legal issues but having a bearing on the social well-being of the membership. The scope of this work is ever-widening and has become an integral part of the everyday activity of the Union. Indeed, the modern trade union can hardly be doing its job unless this were so. This Union has a proud record of service in this field, second to none, and we shall at all times endeavour to ensure that this standard of service is maintained.

29.5 Post Office Engineering Union, *Rules* 1964

RULE 13
UNION JOURNAL

1. A Journal containing information on matters relative to the Union, and news and comments on such matters, and all other matters as may be deemed to be of interest to members as such, or as employees of the Post Office, shall

be issued under the title of "THE POST OFFICE ENGINEERING UNION JOURNAL," at such intervals as the Executive shall from time to time direct.

2. It shall be published by the Executive at the Head Office of the Union, and all matters in reference to staffing, policy, contents, and style of editing and supply thereof, as well as any expenditure incurred or to be incurred in connection with it, shall be solely and entirely under the control of the Executive.

3. Every effective member of the Union shall be entitled to one free copy of each ordinary issue of *The Journal*, and any person shall be entitled to a copy of such issue, if there are sufficient in stock, at a price, excluding postage, to be determined from time to time by the National Executive Council.

30 Levels of expenditure

30.1 Transport and General Workers' Union, *Report and Balance Sheet for the year ended December 1966* (London, T. & G.W.U., 1967), p. 24

GENERAL FUND EXPENDITURE ACCOUNT

1965			1966	
£	£		£	£
		BENEFITS—		
	74429	Dispute and Victimisation	108859	
	—	Incapacity	958470	
	152074	Accident.................................	222797	
	118874	Sick......................................	4792	
	—	Convalescent Home	44313	
	18299	Superannuation	18163	
	8864	Medical Reports	10032	
	51247	Distress	56842	
	—	Fatality	35000	
	108746	Funeral	117326	
	30689	Funeral—Free Card	30170	
	144	Wives' and Children's Insurance ..	76	
	64288	Legal and Medical Costs in Compensation Cases	60036	
	36336	Legal Defence of Members	46070	
	216	Retiring Allowances and Marriage Dowry	335	
	29163	Education Grants	36510	
	57	Education Benefit.....................	2	
693490	*64*	Shipwreck	—	1749793
27018		GRANTS, ETC..............................		25189
720508		TOTAL BENEFITS, ETC.		1774982

30.2 Chief Registrar of Friendly Societies, *Report for the year 1968, Part 4: Trade Unions* (London, H.M.S.O., 1969), p. 9

AVERAGE INCOME AND EXPENDITURE PER MEMBER

Industrial Group	Average contribution per member for all purposes	Average expenditure per member (a) — Provident etc. Benefits						Working Expenses	Other Outgoings [2]	For all purposes
		Unemployment Benefit	Dispute Benefit	Sick and Accident Benefits	Death Benefit	Superannuation Benefit	Miscellaneous Benefits [1]			
	s. d.	s. d.	s. d.	s. d.	s. d.	s. d.	s. d.	s. d.	s. d.	s. d.
1. General Labour Organizations	74 3	(b)	2 6	16 3	3 0	0 3	3 7	47 9	4 3	77 6
2. Agriculture, Forestry, Fishing	56 5	(b)	(b)	2 2	3 6	—	4 8	52 7	3 11	66 5
3. Coal Mining	97 5	0 9	3 9	2 0	2 11	16 10	0 1	59 11	20 5	117 7
4. All Other Mining and Quarrying	32 8	1 1	—	0 6	2 1	0 1	0 2	41 11	4 5	57 9
5. Food, Drink and Tobacco	76 0	—	—	11 6	1 0	0 1	1 5	57 7	4 2	78 5
6. Chemicals and Allied Industries	24 9	—	—	1 4	—	—	—	20 6	2 7	26 3
7. Metal, Engineering, Shipbuilding, Vehicles, etc.	92 9	2 4	5 5	8 3	1 10	14 6	5 1	57 0	16 6	111 8
8. Cotton, Flax, Man-made Fibres	46 11	3 2	0 2	4 5	1 11	4 5	11 8	49 11	14 11	90 8
9. All Other Textile Industries	52 7	1 6	(b)	5 2	0 10	2 1	0 3	39 1	10 6	60 7
10. Leather, Leather Goods, Fur	48 5	0 5	(b)	5 7	1 2	—	4 3	41 7	3 6	54 1
11. Clothing other than Footwear	58 8	0 2	—	12 0	0 11	(b)	1 7	46 10	8 11	70 10
12. Footwear	78 0	3 0	—	23 4	0 11	—	1 3	73 4	4 3	108 9
13. Bricks, Pottery, Glass, Cement, etc.	45 2	0 10	2 0	0 4	2 3	—	4 8	35 9	3 4	56 4
14. Timber, Furniture, etc.	94 2	4 7	5 0	5 3	4 7	8 8	3 8	62 0	8 2	97 1
15. Paper, Printing, Publishing	127 8	3 8	—	3 9	1 5	14 1	10 4	92 10	15 11	141 2
16. Other Manufacturing Industries	67 11	0 9	1 1	9 2	2 8	—	1 4	46 11	6 4	83 9
17. Construction	103 11	1 4	—	0 10	7 5	10 5	5 8	70 3	12 7	107 1
18. Gas, Electricity, Water	112 8	0 4	0 5	0 2	1 6	—	1 0	97 9	5 0	112 9
19. Railways	125 6	—	0 5	4 9	1 2	—	21 9	87 0	5 4	146 9
20. Other Transport and Communication	107 5	1 3	—	17 11	2 6	5 0	7 6	91 9	3 0	117 9
21. Distributive Trades	87 2	—	—	(b)	—	4 1	6 6	66 11	5 0	94 11
22. Insurance, Banking and Finance	38 7	—	—	(b)	—	—	0 9	35 11	3 2	39 5
23. Educational Services	55 6	—	—	—	0 3	—	0 5	59 1	—	66 11
24. All Other Professional and Scientific Services	60 4	(b)	6 10	0 1	2 8	0 6	1 3	56 9	5 11	71 7
25. Cinemas, Theatres, Radio, Sport	121 5	—	8 7	0 2	1 8	—	7 3	105 0	13 8	137 10
26. All Other Miscellaneous Services	77 1	0 8	—	0 1	1 1	—	6 11	84 3	2 11	95 4
27. National Government Services	67 2	—	—	5 0	1 4	—	2 2	55 2	5 6	53 10
28. Local Government Services	56 0	—	0 2	—	—	—	2 2	39 8	—	55 7
All Unions of Employees 1968	87 3	1 1	2 9	9 5	3 1	6 6	5 5	59 9	5 11	98 0
1967	85 9	1 2	1 1	9 5	3 0	6 6	5 2	55 9	9 5	90 2
1963	71 4	1 0	1 1	4 11	2 4	6 10	3 3	42 2	6 11	68 10
1958	55 3	0 9	1 3	3 6	2 0	5 11	3 3	32 1	4 11	55 7

(a) *The amounts given are based on the total membership. In some unions not all members contribute for every benefit, e.g. provident etc. benefits.* (b) *An insignificant amount.*

[1] E.g. legal aid, distress and educational grants, convalescent benefits and grants to dependants of members.

[2] Including political expenditures, for which see Document 40.1

31 Objectives

31.1 Trades Union Congress, *Trade Unionism*[1] 2nd edition (London, Trades Union Congress, 1967)

INDUSTRIAL DEMOCRACY

106 Workpeople form trade unions to assert their right to have a say in matters which are of close concern to them. . . . even the most limited definition of what constitutes the terms of employment covers the content of the job as well as the wages to be paid for doing it. However, workpeople do not just have views on this limited, though important, subject. They have a continuing interest and experience in all matters affecting their employment and together have potentially the competence to make an essential contribution to decisions affecting the enterprise in which they work. The extent of this contribution has hitherto been limited by the nature of the master and servant relationship. Workpeople, through their trade unions, can play no responsible role in such circumstances as there is nothing that they can be responsible for. If all decisions affecting the running of an enterprise are made unilaterally by the employer there can be no basis of mutual respect. Workpeople seek to enhance their status in industry and to make a real contribution to the advancement of their own interests which over a wide range of matters are the common interest of all those concerned with the enterprise in which they work. There are many unsolved problems associated with the objective of furthering industrial democracy. Not least, there are problems of trade union function and trade union organisation. There exists, however, within the trade union Movement a growing determination to tackle these problems.

·   ·   ·   ·   ·   ·   ·

JOINT CONSULTATION

137 Joint consultation is the term which has hitherto been used in Britian to describe a degree of workers' participation in deciding questions of concern to them but which are nevertheless not the subject of bargaining. It concerns questions where it is the responsibility of management to give a lead (though they often do not) whereas trade unionists normally take the lead in bargaining. Not all matters are issues between the two sides of industry and not all matters can be settled by collective bargaining. Moreover it would complicate bargaining unnecessarily to bring within its scope every single matter which affects the interests of workpeople. To exclude a whole range of matters from collective bargaining ought not, however, to deny workpeople the right to a say in decisions on these questions. Workpeople have a very large stake

[1] See footnote to Document 4.2.

188

in the enterprise in which they work and the success of an enterprise requires their active co-operation.

. . . .

139 Joint consultation, or workers' participation, takes a multiplicity of forms. It operates at plant level, in works committees, works councils and joint production committees, at industry level through joint consultative committees in nationalised and other industries, and through Economic Development Committees[1] which work under the aegis of the National Economic Development Council, where trade union representatives participate in national economic planning. Consultation with Government itself takes many forms . . . Consultation is largely a matter of communications and the many levels at which consultation takes place create the need for communication between these different levels within the two sides of industry as well as between them. The work of the Economic Development Committees, for example, has created the need for procedures for reporting back and in fact for two-way communications within the trade union movement on detailed questions of industrial planning. This process has itself shown how bilateral committees are needed at the level of the individual firm to discuss how national targets and other recommendations can be put into practice. It is at the level of the individual firm that changes have to take place if the work of the EDCs is to make a real contribution to economic growth by generating the innovations for which there is certainly the potential.

140 It is clear that the development of consultation and trade union participation in economic planning has manifold implications for both sides of industry. The management side will have to take workers' participation much more seriously and be much less secretive about the firm's trading position. Trade unions will have to give further consideration to the relationship between workplace representatives and branch and other local officials, a problem which affects bargaining machinery as well as consultative machinery. In general terms, managements show little enthusiasm for changing the status quo and they have to be persuaded that the affairs of their company are not their exclusive concern. . . .

. . . .

NATIONALISED INDUSTRY AND PRIVATE INDUSTRY

263 . . . these two sectors of the economy have a great deal in common; in particular, the structure of management control in the nationalised industries runs along the same lines as that in comparably large enterprises in the private sector. In both cases the existence of various levels of management reflects similar problems of administration . . . Nationalised industries are however in the position, and should be encouraged to grasp the opportunity, to take the lead in new ideas on management practice . . .

264 Considerations which affect the proper role of workers' participation in private industry are different from those which obtain in nationalised industry only in the sense that the Government has in the former case obviously not

[1] See *supra*, p. 16.

189

the same authority to take the lead in shaping the structure, and in the final analysis in deciding what that shape should be. . . .

· · · · · · ·

THE WIDER CASE FOR INDUSTRIAL DEMOCRACY

283 The case for industrial democracy in whatever form is therefore to some extent an empirical one. In other words, it is a question of recognising the existing extent of workers' participation in the control of the job. There are, however, wider reasons why these developments should not just be grudgingly admitted but positively welcomed. Essentially these reasons fall into two categories. In the first place, it is argued that the efficient running of a modern enterprise cannot be carried out exclusively on the basis of the carrot and the stick. . .

284 This line of argument can . . . be readily distinguished from the argument which is based not on efficiency but on democracy. The master and servant relationship, the relationship of subordination, cannot easily be reconciled with the substance of equality. . . . That freedom and responsibility go together is a real reflection of the circumstances in most places of work. Whether the emphasis is placed on greater freedom or on greater responsibility is therefore in this sense immaterial. The case for a measure of industrial democracy on these grounds is not one that can be proved. It rests on the assertion of rights, and on assumptions about the aspirations of working people. . . .

32 Radical forms

32.1 Unofficial Reform Committee, *The Miners' Next Step, Being a Suggested Scheme for the Reorganisation of the Federation*[1] (Tonypandy, Robert Davies & Co., 1912), pp. 25–30

POLICY

I. The old policy of identity of interest between employers and ourselves be abolished, and a policy of open hostility installed.

· · · · · · ·

X. Lodges should, as far as possible, discard the old method of coming out on strike for any little minor grievance, and adopt the more scientific weapon of the irritation strike by simply remaining at work, reducing their output, and so contrive by their general conduct to make the colliery unremunerative.

· · · · · · ·

XIII. That a continual agitation be carried on in favour of increasing the

[1] The Miners' Federation of Great Britain, transformed into the National Union of Mineworkers in 1945.

minimum wage, and shortening the hours of work, until we have extracted the whole of the employers' profits.

XIV. That our objective be, to build up an organisation that will ultimately take over the mining industry, and carry it on in the interest of the workers.

It will be seen that the policy is extremely drastic and militant in its character, and it is important that this should be so. . . . The main principles are as follows:—

DECENTRALIZATION FOR NEGOTIATING

The Lodges . . . take all effective control of affairs, as long as there is any utility in local negotiation. With such a policy, Lodges become responsible and self-reliant units, with every stimulus to work out their own local salvation in their own way.

CENTRALIZATION FOR FIGHTING

. . . So soon as the Lodge finds itself at the end of its resources, the whole fighting strength of the organisation is turned on. We thus reverse the present order of things, where in the main, we centralize our negotiations and sectionalize our fighting.

THE USE OF THE IRRITATION STRIKE

. . . The Irritation Strike depends for its successful adoption on the men holding clearly the point of view that their interests and the employers' are necessarily hostile. Further that the employer is vulnerable only in one place, his profits! Therefore if the men wish to bring effective pressure to bear, they must use methods which tend to reduce profits. One way of doing this is to decrease production, while continuing at work. . . .

. . . .

THE ELIMINATION OF THE EMPLOYER

This can only be obtained gradually and in one way. We cannot get rid of employers and slave-driving in the mining industry, until all other industries have organized for, and progressed towards, the same objective. Their rate of progress conditions ours, all we can do is to set an example and the pace.

NATIONALIZATION OF MINES

Does not lead in this direction, but simply makes a National Trust, with all the force of the Government behind it, whose one concern will be to see that the industry is run in such a way as to pay the interest on the bonds, with which the Coalowners are paid out, and to extract as much more profit as possible, in order to relieve the taxation of other landlords and capitalists.

. . . .

INDUSTRIAL DEMOCRACY THE OBJECTIVE

To-day the shareholders own and rule the coalfields. They own and rule them mainly through paid officials. The men who work in the mine are surely as competent to elect these, as shareholders who may never have seen a colliery. To have a vote in determining who shall be your fireman, manager, inspector, etc., is to have a vote in determining the conditions which shall rule your working life. On that vote will depend in a large measure your safety of life and limb, of your freedom from oppression by petty bosses, and would give you an intelligent interest in, and control over your conditions of work. To vote for a man to represent you in Parliament, to make rules for, and assist in appointing officials to rule you, is a different proposition altogether.

Our objective begins to take shape before your eyes. Every industry thoroughly organized, in the first place, to fight, to gain control of, and then to administer, that industry. The co-ordination of all industries on a Central Production Board, who, with a statistical department to ascertain the needs of the people, will issue its demands on the different departments of industry, leaving to the men themselves to determine under what conditions and how the work should be done. This would mean real democracy in real life, making for real manhood and womanhood. Any other form of democracy is a delusion and a snare.

Every fight for, and victory won by the men, will inevitably assist them in arriving at a clearer conception of the responsibilities and duties before them. It will also assist them to see, that so long as shareholders are permitted to continue their ownership, or the State administers on behalf of the shareholders, slavery and oppression are bound to be the rule in industry. And with this realization, the age-long oppression of Labour will draw to its end. . . .

32.2 National Federation of Building Trade Operatives (London Section), *Prospectus of Guild of Builders (London) Limited* 2nd edition (London, N.F.B.T.O., 1920), pp. 1–5

INTRODUCTION

The London Guild of Builders was set up by the unanimous vote of the National Federation of Building Trade Operatives (London District Council) on April 28th, 1920. The Federation and the Guild are really the same people organised for different purposes: the Federation regulates industrial conditions, the Guild does the work, the control in each case being in the hands of the rank and file of the organisations concerned.

Although launched independently of the Building Guild Limited, which has its headquarters in Manchester, the Guild of Builders (London) Limited has declared that its objects are the same, and that it intends to join hands in a National Guild, a great industrial combine for the public service, with full democratic control by all the workers by hand or brain engaged in that service. . . .

The London Guild of Builders believes that Guild organisation will develop smoothly and naturally by means of three distinct types of Committees, each with a clearly defined function to discharge.

1. *The Area Guild Committees* (*e.g.*, Walthamstow and District), represent-

ing the Trade Union branches and approved groups in each area and concerned mainly with the organisation of the labour for each local contract, and with the social development of the Guild movement.

2. *The Regional Guild Committees* (*e.g.*, London), representing the Trade Unions, the groups and the Area Committees in each Region, registered as legal entities on a standard code of rules and acting as contractors, with all the necessary technical and administrative services for estimating contracts and carrying them through.

3. *The National Guild Committee* . . . representing the National Trade Unions, the approved Functional Organisations and the Regional Guild Committees, and concerned mainly with the purchase, manufacture and supply of materials, the co-ordinated use of plant and equipment, the arrangement of credit, and the central reserve funds for continuous Guild pay, Technical Research and Insurance.

.   .   .   .

With the signature of the first Guild contract now secured, the curtain rings up upon one of the greatest adventures of our time. It is a deliberate attempt—by men who believe that it is more important to build than to destroy—to set up a new industrial system based upon service instead of gain, and enlisting for its high purpose all the best that science and skill can provide.

THE MEANING OF THE GUILD

.   .   .   .

A Guild is a self-governing democracy of organised public service. It is the very embodiment of the "team spirit." In its full development it means a whole industry cleared for action, with all sections united for a common purpose—inspired by a new incentive—the organised service of the community, instead of the attainment of profits.

It boldly challenges the industrial traditions of a century, and makes its appeal solely to the best instincts and creative impulses of men. For it is the first industrial organisation in history that is set up to *give* service rather than to *get* it. . . .

.   .   .   .

THE STRUCTURE OF THE GUILD OF BUILDERS (LONDON) LIMITED

The final voice in the control of the Guild rests with the people who do the work.

The Guild Committee, therefore, consists of representatives elected by the following Trade Unions or approved groups within the District:—

(*a*) The Trade Unions affiliated to the District Section of the National Federation of Building Trade Operatives.

(*b*) Any other Trade Unions or groups of Building Trade Workers within the District, whether Administrative, Technical, Clerical or Operative, that may be approved by the Committee.

Each Trade Union or approved group elects One Member.

Approved groups, under this clause, have already been formed by the Architects and Surveyors, and groups of Civil Engineers, and of Sculptors and Decorative Artists, are under consideration.

Approved Area Guild Committees are also represented on the Guild Committee. In this way we secure an elected Executive responsible both to the Trade Unions and to the Area Committees, and the Trade Union Ticket becomes the Certificate of Guild Membership.

THE LEGAL ENTITY

Each member of the Guild Committee holds One Shilling Share in a Society registered under the Industrial and Provident Societies Acts, 1893–1913,[1] and entitled THE GUILD OF BUILDERS (LONDON) LTD. He also deposits with his electors a signed open transfer, thus giving them power to replace him at any time. The Guild Committee thus becomes a legal entity with power to enter into contracts, and yet the whole of its members are under the control of the industrial democracy they represent. The shares are for registration purposes only and carry no dividend. The whole Committee forms the Board of Directors.

OBJECTS OF THE GUILD

The first and immediate duty of the Guild is to mobilise the necessary labour to build the houses so urgently needed by the nation, and to build them in the best possible manner at the lowest possible cost.

The objects, as stated in the Rules, are:—

1. To carry on the industry of Builders, Decorators and General Contractors.
2. To undertake all branches of supply, whether as Merchant, Manufacturer or Transporter.
3. To carry on any other work which the Society may think necessary or desirable in connection with the above objects.

From this it will be seen that the Guild is designed ultimately to undertake every branch of the Building Industry, and to provide its customers with the services of skilled architects and engineers, to purchase and manufacture the materials, to transport them to the site, erect the buildings, and furnish them.

DEMOCRATIC CONTROL IN PRACTICE

The Guild Committee is responsible for the appointment and removal of Managers and General Foremen, and for the fixing of their salaries. General Foremen are nominated by the Area Committees and ratified by the Guild Committee. Departmental Foremen are elected by the Guildsmen of the Trade concerned.

It is important to notice here the difference between the Guild practice and that of the self-governing workshops which have so often been set up without

[1] Industrial and Provident Societies Act 1893, Industrial and Provident Societies (Amendment) Act 1895, Industrial and Provident Societies (Amendment) Act 1913.

conspicuous success. The manager of a self-governing workshop is responsible to his own staff. The Guild Manager, however, is responsible—through the Guild Committee—not only to his own staff, but to the whole of the organised Building Trade Operatives in the District. This gives him security without weakening the full democratic control by the workers.

REMUNERATION OF THE BOARD OF DIRECTORS

All Members of the Board (*i.e.*, the whole Committee) are entitled to subsistence allowances, and compensation for lost time and expenses.

POWERS OF APPOINTED MANAGERS

The duty of Managers is to carry on the work of the Guild in accordance with the policy laid down in the Prospectus and Rules, and in the Minutes of the Board, and to keep the Board properly informed on all points.

The Board having all power, and being responsible to the rank and file, can afford to trust its Managers and give them that freedom of initiative which is so essential to rapid development.

THE NEW STATUS OF THE GUILD WORKER

The labour of Guildsmen will no longer be regarded as a commodity like bricks or timber, to be purchased, or not, as required. *As soon as the necessary financial reserve can be created*, the Guildsman will be "on the strength," and will draw Guild pay in sickness or accident, in bad weather or in good, at work, on holiday, or in reserve.

The minimum Guild pay will never be less than the full standard rate as fixed for the industry in the district, but there is no doubt that the Guild will be able to increase the purchasing power of its members' pay by the scientific organisation of production.

THE GUILD CONTRACT

The Guild will undertake work for every type of building owner, whether public or private.

The Guild form of Contract as approved by the Ministry of Health for Municipal Housing Schemes creates a great triple alliance under which the Guild carries out the whole of the work, the Co-operative Wholesale Society undertakes to supply the materials, and the Co-operative Insurance Society guarantees the due performance of the contract, the liability under this head being, however, limited to twenty per cent. of the estimated cost. The price paid by the Local Authority is the prime cost of material and labour at standard rates, with the addition of the sum of £40 per house to enable the Guild to guarantee continuous pay to its workers in all contingencies, and six per cent. calculated upon the estimated cost, to provide for plant, for Head Office administration, and, if necessary, for interest upon hired capital. The estimate of cost is given by the Guild and approved by the Ministry for each

P

195

contract. The initial cost of plant and equipment is covered by an advance from the Co-operative Wholesale Society's Bank, secured against payments due under the contract. All other problems of finance are reduced to manageable proportions by the provision of payments weekly by the Local Authority, both for labour and materials delivered, and for the authorised Guild charges.

ORGANISED PUBLIC SERVICE

This is the watchword of the Guild. It means that its surplus earnings will under no circumstances be distributed as dividends. This is a fundamental rule. Surplus earnings will always be used for the improvement of the service, by providing for increased equipment, for reserve, for technical training and research, and for the elimination of hired capital.

OWNERSHIP OF PLANT AND MATERIAL

It is intended that all plant and material shall be transferred to the properly constituted authority to be set up in connection with the National Guild of Builders.

33 Co-operation and co-partnership

33.1 Co-Operative Productive Federation Ltd, *General Rules for an Industrial and Provident Productive Society* (Leicester, C.P.F. Ltd, 1966), pp. 6, 10, 12–13, 15–18, 22–25

CHAPTER III—MEMBERSHIP

6. *Membership*—The society shall consist of . . . such persons or societies as shall hold not less than the minimum number of shares as required by these rules, and as may be admitted to membership by the committee.

. . . .

9. *Application by an Employee*—Every employee shall complete an application for membership within twelve months of joining the society and the qualification shares shall be paid for either in cash or by allocation of bonus earnings or share of profits as hereinafter provided.

. . . .

CHAPTER IV—CAPITAL

SECTION I—SHARE CAPITAL

15. *Value of Shares*—The value of the shares of the society shall be the nominal value of £1. Each member shall hold at least five shares, and no member (other than a society) may hold more than £1,000 in shares.

16. *Payment for Shares*—In the case of members who are not employees, shares shall be paid for by direct contribution, and in the case of employee members, shares may be paid for either by direct contribution or by allocation of bonus earnings or share of profits as provided hereafter.

17. *Description of Shares*—Shares shall be transferable, but not withdrawable.

. . . .

SECTION 2—LOANS AND CHARGES

. . . . . .

20. *Deposits: Power to Receive*—The committee may receive from any persons whether members or not, on deposit, withdrawable on such notice as they may fix from time to time, being not less than seven clear days, any sums . . . not exceeding £2 in any one payment, nor £50 for any one depositor.

. . . . . .

CHAPTER VI—GOVERNMENT AND ADMINISTRATION

SECTION 1—MEETINGS OF THE SOCIETY

36. *Meetings*—Meetings of the society shall be either ordinary meetings, or special meetings. Every member who under these rules has a vote shall be entitled to attend such meetings on the production of such evidence as the committee may from time to time determine.

. . . . . .

49. *Votes of Members*—Each member shall have one vote and, in order to be entitled to a vote, a member must hold five fully paid shares, and must not be otherwise disqualified by these rules.

. . . . . .

SECTION 2—THE COMMITTEE OF MANAGEMENT

53. *How formed, Number of* . . . The business of the society shall be conducted by a committee of management, which . . . shall consist of the president, and of six committeemen . . . The number of the committeemen, unless fixed by a special rule, may be altered from time to time by any general meeting . . .

54. *Retirement of Committee:*—

(*i*) One-third of the members of the committee . . . shall retire, and a like number shall be elected at each ordinary general meeting. . . .

. . . . . .

64. *Powers of the Committee*—The Committee shall have full power to conduct the business of the society and to exercise on behalf of the society for the purpose of accomplishing its objects all the powers of the society not specifically prescribed by these rules or otherwise required to be exercised by the society in meeting. Without prejudice to the generality of the foregoing the committee shall have power in particular from time to time to engage, remove, or discharge a manager, a secretary of the society and commercial travellers and fix their duties, salaries, or other remuneration and to require them to give security.

. . . . . .

SECTION 3—OFFICERS OF THE SOCIETY

69. *The Manager:*—

(*i*) The committee shall appoint a general manager or chief executive officer (hereinafter called "the manager") who shall have such remuneration, powers and duties, as the committee may determine, and for the due performance of these duties he shall give such security as the committee may require.

(*iii*) The manager shall have power to engage, suspend, or discharge all persons employed by the society except the secretary, assistant manager and commercial travellers appointed by the committee.

SECTION 4—EMPLOYEES

74. *The Co-partnership of Labour*—The employees of the society shall be entitled to have a *bona fide* share of the profit distributed among them as a dividend upon their wages or salaries. No employee of the society over the age of 16 years shall be refused membership except on the ground of personal unfitness.

CHAPTER VIII—PROFITS

96. *Application of Profits*—The profits of the society shall be applied as follows:—

(*a*) Firstly, in paying interest on the share capital at such rate (not exceeding £5 per cent. per annum) as may be recommended by the committee and approved by the Annual General Meeting;

(*b*) Secondly, in setting aside to a General Reserve Fund such proportion of the profits as may be recommended by the committee and approved by the Annual General Meeting;

Thirdly, in setting aside to an Interest Guarantee Fund such proportion of the profits as may be recommended by the committee and approved by the Annual General Meeting, until such time as this Fund shall amount to the sum required to pay interest at £5 per cent. per annum for period of three years on the share capital of the society. Any amount standing to the credit of this Fund may be transferred to the general funds of the society for any purpose, including transfer for the purpose of paying interest on the share capital at the rate recommended under Clause (*a*) of this rule.

(*d*) Fourthly, in any or all of the following ways in such proportions and in such order as may be recommended by the committee and approved by the Annual General Meeting:—

(*i*) To the employees of the society in proportion to their earnings during the year to which the allocation relates.

(*ii*) To a Provident Fund.

(*iii*) To an Education Fund.

(*iv*) To customers of the society in proportion to their invoiced purchases from the society during the year to which the allocation relates.

(*v*) To a dividend on shares, provided that the aggregate of share interest and share dividend distributed in any one year shall not exceed 7½ per cent. on the share capital.

(*vi*) To the creation and building of a Capital Reserve for the maintenance of working capital.

(*vii*) To the making of payments for any lawful purposes whatsoever, whether within the objects for which the society is formed or not, provided that no distribution of net profits to the members shall be made, except as is expressly provided for in this rule.

(*viii*) To be carried forward to the accounts of the following year.

97. *Employees' Share of Profits:*—

(*i*) The proportion of profits due to an employee under Rule 96 (*d*) (*i*) shall be credited to the recipient as share capital, until he holds five fully paid up shares, whereupon he may withdraw half of any further allocation, while the remaining half will be credited to him as share capital, until such time as the share holding in the case of a female employee is £25, and in the case of a male employee is £50, when any future allocation under this rule may be withdrawn in full.

(*ii*) If an employee to whom a proportion of profits would normally be due under Rule 96 (*d*) (*i*) has applied for membership of the society but has been refused, his allotted proportion shall be paid to him in cash.

(*iii*) If any employee to whom an allocation of profits would normally be due under Rule 96 (*d*) (*i*) has not already applied for membership of the society, the amount due shall be held in suspense against receipt of such application. If he does not apply for membership within 12 months from the date when the first distribution of profits was made after the commencement of his employment, he shall, subject to the discretion of the committee, forfeit all claim to a proportion of the profits under Rule 96 (*d*) (*i*).

(*iv*) Any employee leaving his employment in the society before the end of any year, unless it be by retirement or sickness, shall forfeit his proportion of profits for the period dating from the time up to which the last balance sheet was made up to the time of his leaving.

(*v*) Any proportion of profits due to employees of the society under Rule 96 (*d*) (*i*) that have been forfeited under paragraphs (*iii*) or (*iv*) of this rule shall be transferred to the Provident Fund.

CHAPTER IX—DISPUTES

98. *Determination of Disputes*—Any dispute arising between a member or any person aggrieved who has for not more than six months ceased to be a member, or any person claiming through such member or person aggrieved,

or under these rules, and the society, or an officer thereof shall be decided by the three arbitrators to be chosen for this purpose . . . and any decision made by such arbitrators shall be binding and conclusive on all parties without appeal and application for the enforcement of such a decision may be made to the County Court.

33.2 *Profit Sharing: A Summary of the I.C.I.[1] Employees' Profit-Sharing Scheme* (I.C.I., 1966)

The payment of bonus under the Scheme is entirely at the discretion of the Company. The Scheme shall not form any part of any contract of employment, and it shall not confer on employees any legal or equitable rights whatsoever against the Company, directly or indirectly, or give rise to any cause of action in law against the Company. An employee's participation in the Scheme is sufficient authority for the Company to place his name on the Register of Members without it being necessary for him to sign a Transfer Deed or any other document before stock can be registered in his name.

The benefits to employees under the Scheme do not form any part of their wages or remuneration or count as pay or remuneration for pension fund or other purposes.

1 What is the Employees' Profit-Sharing Scheme?
It is a scheme designed to give eligible employees the opportunity to become Ordinary Stockholders of I.C.I.
2 What does the Scheme provide?
The Scheme provides in certain circumstances for a bonus to be paid for the benefit of eligible employees. The bonus is paid in respect of a "Bonus Year," which is the calendar year and corresponds to the financial year of the Company.
3 Who administers the Scheme?
The Scheme is administered by Trustees appointed by I.C.I. and these include Staff and Works Payroll employees.
4 How do I become eligible?
If you are employed by the Company on the Permanent Staff or Works Payroll in the United Kingdom you are eligible under the Scheme and qualify for bonus when you satisfy the necessary conditions of service.
5 What conditions do I have to satisfy to qualify for bonus for a particular year?
(*a*) You must have completed 12 months' continuous employment with the Company by the end of the "Bonus Year".
(*b*) You must have been in the employment of the Company throughout the "Bonus Year."

For your first "Bonus Year" you will qualify for bonus only for the period from the date on which you complete 12 months' service to the end of the of the year (31st December).

. . . .

[1] Imperial Chemical Industries Limited.

7 What determines whether the bonus is paid for a particular "Bonus Year"?
First the Company has to decide that a bonus shall be paid. Second the total
rate of dividend paid on the Ordinary Stock of the Company must not be
below 5%.
8 How is the rate of bonus determined?
Starting with the bonus payable in respect of the year 1966 the rate of bonus
will be fixed by the Company each year and announced at the same time as
the final dividend for the year.

In fixing the rate of bonus annually the Company will take into account all
relevant factors but will have regard mainly to the profits of the Company and
of those subsidiaries whose employees participate in the scheme in relation
to the capital employed in earning those profits. Other matters which will be
taken into account include:

(a) any factors outside the Company's control which affect the amount of
    money available for distribution to stockholders
(b) changes in the structure of the I.C.I. Group and in those companies whose
    employees participate in the scheme.

It is intended that the rate of bonus will range from a minimum of 6d. in the
£ in a year of low return on capital up to about 2s. in the £ in a year of high
return. However, no bonus will be paid for a year in which the total rate of
ordinary dividend is below 5%.
9 On what is the bonus calculated?
It is calculated on the total remuneration paid to you by the Company in the
tax year ending on 5th April following the "Bonus Year" except for your first
"Bonus Year," when it is calculated on the total remuneration paid to you in
respect of the period from the date on which you qualified to participate in the
Scheme to the end of the "Bonus Year" (31st December).
10 What is meant by total remuneration?
It is the gross amount received by you from the Company which is used for
P.A.Y.E. purposes but excludes profit-sharing bonus. It includes overtime,
bonuses of any kind other than profit-sharing bonus, all taxable allowances,
etc., and is after any deductions from your remuneration in respect of State
sickness or injury benefits.
11 Is the profit-sharing bonus taxable?
Yes; income tax is deducted from the bonus and paid over to the Inland
Revenue in accordance with the P.A.Y.E. procedure as if it had been your
income of the tax year referred to in 10 above. . . .
12 To whom is the bonus paid?
The bonus, after deduction of tax, is paid to the Trustees of the Scheme.
Payment is made not later than sixteen weeks after the Annual General
Meeting of the Company, which is normally held in April.
13 How do the Trustees use the cash bonus paid over to them?
They use it to take up I.C.I. Ordinary Stock on your behalf. This stock
is not purchased on the Stock Exchange but is new stock issued by the
Company.

If however your bonus is less than the value of five stock units, the amount
of bonus will be credited to you and carried forward on your account to the
following year. It will be added to any bonus you may receive for that year

201

and, provided that the total amount of bonus is then not less than the value of five stock units, it will be used to take up stock as indicated above.

14 At what price is this stock issued to the Trustees?

The price is fixed each year by the Company, and it is the intention that the price will be either:

(a) the average price of the Ordinary Stock on the London Stock Exchange during January following the Bonus Year, or

(b) the price on the last business day of that month, whichever is the less.

. . . .

16 When is the stock handed over to me?

All stock acquired in a particular year will be handed over to you in that year, usually in September. Once you receive a stock certificate you will be in the same position as any other holder of I.C.I. Ordinary Stock. This position will be explained to you when you first receive the stock certificate.

17 Can I sell or transfer the stock handed over to me?

Once the stock has been registered in your own name you can sell or dispose of your stock in the same way as any other stockholder of the Company.

18 Will I receive a statement of my bonus account?

Yes; each year in May you will receive a detailed statement.

19 Are there any circumstances where an employee's entitlement under the Scheme can be liable to forfeiture?

The Company has the right to instruct the Trustees to forfeit an employee's entitlement under the Scheme in the following circumstances:—

(a) If he is dismissed for misconduct or resigns to avoid dismissal for misconduct; or

(b) If he assigns or charges, or attempts to assign or charge, his interest in the Scheme, i.e. if he attempts to transfer stock or cash standing to his credit or promises it as security for a loan before it is handed over to him; or

(c) If he is adjudicated bankrupt.

20 What happens if I leave the service of the Company?

If you leave the service of the Company on or after 5th April any stock which may be due to you for the previous bonus year will be handed over to you at the usual time in September. It is not possible to issue it before that time.

Any cash balance held by the Trustees on your behalf is paid to you when you leave.

. . . .

25 If I die, who would receive the stock and cash to which I am entitled under the Scheme?

Your legal personal representative, who is normally either the person you name in your Will or, if you do not make a Will, your next of kin. . . .

26 Can the Company alter the Scheme?

The Scheme remains fully under the control of the Company. Although changes will not be made without good reason, the Company may make any alterations which changed circumstances may render necessary or desirable.

When announcing the changes effective from 1st January 1962 the Board stated:

"The experience of other firms with profit-sharing schemes, and the Company's own experience too, has shown that keeping rigidly to a scheme which does not fit changing circumstances is fatal. All successful profit-sharing schemes have had to be flexible, and this was one of the reasons why, from the first, the Board retained complete discretion in the operation of the I.C.I. Scheme. Hence, further amendments to the Scheme are likely to be required from time to time."

34 Nationalisation

34.1 General Council of the Trades Union Congress, *Report to Congress: Trade Unionism and the Control of Industry* [*Trades Union Congress Report* 1932 (London, Trades Union Congress, 1932), pp. 217–219]

SUMMARY
GENERAL

(i.) The modern tendency is for public ownership or control of industry and trade to increase.

· · · · · · ·

CONTROL

(xii.) The position of the workers in relation to the control of industry should be as follows:—

(a) *In Industry as a Whole.* A National Industrial Council constituted in accordance with the recommendations of the Melchett-T.U.C. Conference,[1] or on some other basis, should be established for the discussion of the general problems of industry.

(b) *In entire Industries or Services.* Boards of management of socialised industries or services should consist of persons appointed by the Government solely on the ground of their fitness for the positions, not excluding persons from any class but not selected as representing particular interests. Advisory Committees should be constituted to represent particular interests, including trade unionism.

(c) *In Individual Undertakings.*
(1) As regards labour questions, including recruitments, dismissals, discipline, working conditions, etc., the Trade Unions should assume more responsibility in this sphere.
(2) As regards technical, commercial, and financial matters, ultimate responsibility should be in the hands of managers

[1] See Document 24.6.

203

satisfying proper standards of fitness, including fitness to work successfully with large bodies of workers, and appointed solely because of their competence to fill the positions.

(3) Works Councils, the workers' side to be organised by the Trade Unions, might be established for regular consultation on all internal matters not coming within the scope of the ordinary negotiating machinery.

34.2 General Council of the Trades Union Congress, *Interim Report on Post-War Reconstruction*[1] 1944

SUMMARY

GENERAL

1. The main objectives of the Trade Union Movement include the maintenance and improvement of wages, working conditions and living standards, the assurance to workpeople of adequate opportunities for suitable employment and the implementation of their right to share in the control of industry.

2. These objectives . . . can only be adequately fulfilled within a system of public control.

. . . .

Public Ownership

5. Certain industries are of such vital importance to the life and well-being of the community that their immediate transfer to public ownership is essential. They are notably the transport, fuel and power, and iron and steel industries.

. . . . . .

7. The form of organisation for all publicly owned industries should be that of a public corporation, established by Act of Parliament to take over all the undertakings in the industry. Responsibility to the public should be maintained by the appointment of the Governing Boards by a Minister responsible for the industry to Parliament. Those appointed should be selected solely on the basis of their competence and ability to administer the industry efficiently in the public interest, but statutory provision should be made for the adequate representation of the viewpoint of the workpeople engaged in the industry.

. . . .

The Organisation of Industry
. . . . . .

13. There are, however, a large number of important industries which immediately require some measure of direct public regulation. In general this should be secured by the setting up of industrial boards in these industries.

[1] Published as Appendix D of the *Trades Union Congress Report* 1944 (London, Trades Union Congress, 1944).

The boards should be composed of representatives of workpeople and employers in equal proportion and an impartial chairman and other independent members appointed and paid by the Government.

. . . .

15. The broad purpose of the industrial boards would be to interpret the industry's requirements to the Government and to apply the Government's requirements to the industry, in order to secure the general planning of the industry and maximum efficiency of production in a manner which adequately safeguards the public interest. Specifically their functions might usefully include:—

(a) The concentration and specialisation of production;
(b) The standardisation and specification of equipment and products;
(c) The development of technique by common research organisation, the pooling of methods and patents, the planning of technical education;
(d) The collection and pooling of costing and commercial information;
(e) The setting up of common marketing and purchasing agencies; and
(f) The promotion of welfare services for the industries' employees.

The boards would be empowered to register and levy producers for the purposes of administration. Wages and other conditions of employment should continue to be negotiated separately by the trade unions.

. . . .

Trade Union Participation

18. The extension of public control must mean an increasing democratisation of economic life. It will be essential for the Trade Union Movement to participate in the determination of all questions affecting the conduct of an industry and the well-being of its workpeople, as well as in the operation of all economic controls.

19. Central machinery will be required to ensure that detailed industrial experience, including that of workpeople, is drawn upon in the formulation and administration of the Government's economic policy. For this purpose a National Industrial Council should be set up representative of all responsible for economic and industrial development, including the trade unions.

20. In publicly owned industries the right of the organisations of workpeople to be represented on the governing boards should be recognised by statute. This could be secured by the selection of a number of the board's members from nominations submitted on behalf of the appropriate trade unions by the T.U.C. In addition there would be consultative councils at national, regional and sectional levels to advise the governing boards and their responsible officials on the formulation and administration of policy, and on these the trade unions would be directly represented by persons appointed by and responsible to them.

21. In private industry there should be equal representation of the employers and the trade unions on industrial boards or other organisations established for the regulation of industry.

22. In the individual undertakings works councils, representative of

management and workpeople, should be established to deal with matters other than those covered by established negotiating machinery. The workers' side of these councils should be organised by the trade unions.

35 Joint consultation

35.1 Union of Post Office Workers, *National Rules and Standing Orders* 1968

2 1. The objects of the Union shall be:

. . . .

To pursue joint consultation with management at all levels of the Service in order to secure the greatest possible measure of effective participation by the Union in all decisions affecting the working lives of its members. To encourage the amalgamation of organisations catering for Post Office workers into one industrial Union.

35.2 Sub-Committee on Relations between Employers and Employed, *Interim Report on Joint Standing Industrial Councils* (Cd. 8606) 1917

2. The terms of reference to the Sub-Committee are:—
   "(1) To make and consider suggestions for securing a permanent improvement in the relations between employers and workmen.
   "(2) To recommend means for securing that industrial conditions affecting the relations between employers and workmen shall be systematically reviewed by those concerned, with a view to improving conditions in the future."

. . . .

5.

. . . . . .

In the interests of the community it is vital that after the war the co-operation of all classes, established during the war, should continue, and more especially with regard to the relations between employers and employed. For securing improvement in the latter, it is essential that any proposals put forward should offer to workpeople the means of attaining improved conditions of employment and a higher standard of comfort generally, and involve the enlistment of their active and continuous co-operation in the promotion of industry.

To this end, the establishment for each industry of an organisation, representative of employers and workpeople, to have as its object the regular consideration of matters affecting the progress and well-being of the trade from the point of view of all those engaged in it, so far as this is consistent with the general interest of the community, appears to us necessary.

. . . .

7. With a view to providing means for carrying out the policy outlined above, we recommend that His Majesty's Government should propose without delay to the various associations of employers and employed the formation of Joint Standing Industrial Councils in the several industries, where they do not already exist, composed of representatives of employers and employed, regard being paid to the various sections of the industry and the various classes of labour engaged.

. . . .

9. The Council should meet at regular and frequent intervals.

10. The objects to which the consideration of the Councils should be directed should be appropriate matters affecting the several industries and particularly the establishment of a closer co-operation between employers and employed. . . .

. . . .

13. In the well-organised industries, one of the first questions to be considered should be the establishment of local and works organisations to supplement and make more effective the work of the central bodies. It is not enough to secure co-operation at the centre between the national organisations; it is equally necessary to enlist the activity and support of employers and employed in the districts and in individual establishments. The National Industrial Council should not be regarded as complete in itself; what is needed is a triple organisation—in the workshops, the districts, and nationally. Moreover, it is essential that the organisation at each of these three stages should proceed on a common principle, and that the greatest measure of common action between them should be secured.

14. With this end in view, we are of opinion that the following proposals should be laid before the National Industrial Councils:—

(a) That District Councils, representative of the Trade Unions and of the Employers' Association in the industry, should be created, or developed out of the existing machinery for negotiation in the various trades.

(b) That Works Committees, representative of the management and of the workers employed, should be instituted in particular works to act in close co-operation with the district and national machinery.

As it is of the highest importance that the scheme making provision for these Committees should be such as to secure the support of the Trade Unions and Employers' Associations concerned, its design should be a matter for agreement between these organisations.

Just as regular meetings and continuity of co-operation are essential in the case of the National Industrial Councils, so they seem to be necessary in the case of the district and works organisations. The object is to secure co-operation by granting to workpeople a greater share in the consideration of matters affecting their industry, and this can only be achieved by keeping employers and workpeople in constant touch.

. . . .

207

16. Among the questions with which it is suggested that the National Councils should deal or allocate to District Councils or Works Committees the following may be selected for special mention:—

(i) The better utilisation of the practical knowledge and experience of the workpeople.

(ii) Means for securing to the workpeople a greater share in and responsibility for the determination and observance of the conditions under which their work is carried on.

(iii) The settlement of the general principles governing the conditions of employment, including the methods of fixing, paying, and readjusting wages, having regard to the need for securing to the workpeople a share in the increased prosperity of the industry.

(iv) The establishment of regular methods of negotiation for issues arising between employers and workpeople, with a view both to the prevention of differences, and to their better adjustment when they appear.

(v) Means of ensuring to the workpeople the greatest possible security of earnings and employment, without undue restriction upon change of occupation or employer.

(vi) Methods of fixing and adjusting earnings, piecework prices, &c., and of dealing with the many difficulties which arise with regard to the method and amount of payment apart from the fixing of general standard rates, which are already covered by paragraph (iii).

(vii) Technical education and training.

(viii) Industrial research and the full utilisation of its results.

(ix) The provision of facilities for the full consideration and utilisation of inventions and improvements designed by workpeople, and for the adequate safeguarding of the rights of the designers of such improvements.

(x) Improvements of processes, machinery and organisation and appropriate questions relating to management and the examination of industrial experiments, with special reference to co-operation in carrying new ideas into effect and full consideration of the workpeople's point of view in relation to them.

(xi) Proposed legislation affecting the industry.

.   .   .   .

20. It has been suggested that means must be devised to safeguard the interests of the community against possible action of an anti-social character on the part of the Councils . We have, however, here assumed that the Councils, in their work of promoting the interests of their own industries, will have regard for the National interest. If they fulfil their functions they will be the best builders of national prosperity. The State never parts with its inherent over-riding power, but such power may be least needed when least obtruded.

.   .   .   .   .   .

23. It may be desirable to state here our considered opinion that an essential condition of securing a permanent improvement in the relations between employers and employed is that there should be adequate organisation on the part of both employers and workpeople. The proposals outlined for joint co-operation throughout the several industries depend for their

ultimate success upon there being such organisation on both sides; and such organisation is necessary also to provide means whereby the arrangements and agreements made for the industry may be effectively carried out.

. . . .

APPENDIX

The following questions were addressed . . . to the Sub-Committee on the Relations between Employers and Employed in order to make certain points which appeared to call for further elucidation. The answers given are sub-joined.

. . . .

Q. 3. *Is it understood that membership of the Councils is to be confined to representatives elected by Employers' Associations and Trade Unions? What is the view of the Sub-Committee regarding the entry of new organisations established after the Councils have been set up?*

A. 3. It is intended that the Councils should be composed only of representatives of Trade Unions and Employers' Associations, and that new organisations should be admitted only with the approval of the particular side of the Council of which the organisation would form a part.

Q. 4. (*a*) *Is it intended that decisions reached by the Councils shall be binding upon the bodies comprising them? If so, is such binding effect to be conditional upon the consent of each Employers' Association or Trade Union affected?*

A. 4. (*a*) It is contemplated that agreements reached by Industrial Councils should (whilst not of course possessing the binding force of law) carry with them the same obligation of observance as exists in the case of other agreements between Employers' Associations and Trade Unions. A Council, being on its workmen's side based on the Trade Unions concerned in the industry, its powers or authority could only be such as the constituent Trade Unions freely agreed to.

35.3 Committee on Relations between Employers and Employed, *Supplementary Report on Works Committees* (Cd. 9001) 1918

2. . . . there are . . . many questions closely affecting daily life and comfort in, and the success of, the business, and affecting in no small degree efficiency of working, which are peculiar to the individual workshop or factory. The purpose of a Works Committee is to establish and maintain a system of co-operation in all these workshop matters.

. . . .

5. . . . We look upon successful Works Committees as the broad base of the Industrial Structure which we have recommended, and as the means of enlisting the interest of the workers in the success both of the industry to which they are attached and of the workshop or factory where so much of their life is spent. . . .

6. Works Committees, in our opinion, should have regular meetings at fixed times, and, as a general rule, not less frequently than once a fortnight. They should always keep in the forefront the idea of constructive co-operation in the improvement of the industry to which they belong. Suggestions of all kinds tending to improvement should be frankly welcomed and freely discussed. Practical proposals should be examined from all points of view. There is an undeveloped asset of constructive ability—valuable alike to the industry and to the State—awaiting the means of realisation; problems, old and new, will find their solution in a frank partnership of knowledge, experience and goodwill. . . .

7. We recognise that, from time to time, matters will arise which the management or the workmen consider to be questions they cannot discuss in these joint meetings. When this occurs, we anticipate that nothing but good will come from the friendly statement of the reasons why the reservation is made.

8. We regard the successful development and utilisation of Works Committees in any business on the basis recommended in this Report as of equal importance with its commercial and scientific efficiency; and we think that in any case one of the partners or directors, or some other responsible representative of the management, would be well advised to devote a substantial part of his time and thought to the good working and development of such a committee.

35.4 Upper Clyde Shipbuilders Limited, *Joint Consultative Scheme* 1968

INTRODUCTION

It is recognised by Upper Clyde Shipbuilders Limited and by the signatory Trade Unions that Management and Employee representatives alike shall be free to discharge their duties in an independent manner without fear that their individual relations with the Company may be affected in any way by any action taken by them in good faith when acting within the remit of the Joint Council Scheme.

It is recognised that joint consultation generally, and the Joint Council Scheme in particular, will succeed only if everyone concerned believes in it and acknowledges that it requires good faith and trust from every person taking part.

Upper Clyde Shipbuilders Limited and the signatory Trade Unions recognise the value of consultation in the successful operation of the business and intend to act, and train their officials and representatives to act, in this spirit.

THE JOINT CONSULTATIVE SCHEME

1. Definition of Joint Consultation and General Principles

1.1 The term "joint consultation" is intended to cover all means whereby management involved in taking decisions, and the representatives of employees affected by those decisions, may consider together matters affecting their joint or several interests. Subject to the reservations in 1.3 and 1.5 below, no matter affecting management or employee interest shall be proscribed from discussions in Joint Councils.

1.2 Joint consultation is an advisory and consultative process, resulting in advice, expression of view or recommendations to management. The responsibility for all policy and executive decisions rests with management. From time to time, management may delegate to joint consultative bodies the authority for executive decision(s) in some functions—on each occasion these functions shall be clearly defined and responsibility specifically allocated.

1.3 Matters which are the subject of an operative agreement between U.C.S. and any Trade Union(s) may not be discussed in the Joint Council Scheme without the consent of the Company and the Trade Union(s) concerned.

1.4 Joint consultation shall, wherever possible, take place before a decision is made on matters affecting employees and in reaching a decision management shall take into account any discussion or recommendations arising from joint consultation.

1.5 From time to time situations will arise because of commercial and competitive considerations, which may preclude the possibility of joint consultation before decisions affecting employees are made. In such cases management shall raise the matter through the Joint Council Scheme as soon as possible, giving reasons for the inability to implement 1.4.

1.6 Joint consultation may be either informal or formal.

2. Objects of the Scheme

The objects of the Joint Council Scheme within Upper Clyde Shipbuilders Limited are:

.   .   .   .

2.2 To provide the means whereby employees may be given an opportunity to influence the conditions under which their work is performed, and the prosperity of the Company.

2.3 To promote throughout each Department, Yard, Division, Subsidiary Company and throughout the Company as a whole, a spirit of co-operation in securing the efficiency of every part of the Company, and the contentment of all employees.

2.4 Supplementary to the normal line of management, to provide a recognised and direct two-way network of communication between employees and management on matters affecting their joint or several interests.

3. Informal Consultation

3.1 Wherever possible, informal means, i.e. normal discussion between employees, employee representatives, foremen and managers concerned, should be used to resolve day-to-day matters requiring consultation before referring them to the formal Joint Council Committees.

3.2 It shall be open to management or employees involved in informal joint consultation to raise any matters so discussed through the formal joint council system by means of their respective representatives.

4. Formal Joint Consultation—the Joint Council Scheme

The basis of formal joint consultation is the Joint Council Scheme. There shall be four levels of council for formal consultation, *viz.*:

Trade Group Councils (T.G.C.)
Yard Councils (Y.C.)
Upper Clyde Shipbuilders Joint Council (U.C.S.J.C.)
The Bi-Annual National Council (B.N.C.)

5. Trade Group Council

5.1 Trade Group Councils shall be established in each Division/Subsidiary Company. The actual numbers and composition of Trade Group Councils shall be appropriate to each Division/Subsidiary's circumstances and shall be discussed and agreed once per year by the Yard Councils. If the Yard Council is unable to agree, the matter shall be referred to the U.C.S. Joint Council for final decision.

5.2 As a guide, there shall be four Trade Group Councils for each Division/ Subsidiary Company, to cover:

Steelwork Trades
Finishing Trades
General Trades
White Collar Trades

and each Trade Group Council shall consist of:
—A Chairman appointed by the Local Director
—An equal number of management and employee representatives
—A Secretary appointed by the Local Director from the management representatives.

5.3 The management representatives will be appointed by the Local Director and will be selected from the various levels of management concerned. The Employee Representatives will be elected from members of the Trade Unions in the Trade Groups concerned.

· · · · · ·

6. Yard Council

6.1 For each Division/Subsidiary Company there will be established a Yard Council.

· · · · · ·

6.3 The Yard Council shall consist of:
—A Chairman, normally the Local Director, who will be appointed by the Company
—Four management representatives, appointed by the Local Director
—The Division/Subsidiary Company's Personnel Manager
—Up to 17 representatives from the Trade Unions signatory to the Employment Charter (i.e. up to 3 representatives from the A.S.B.S.B. & S.W.[1] and one each from the other Unions). The names of the Trade Union

[1] Amalgamated Society of Boilermakers, Shipwrights, Blacksmiths and Structural Workers.

212

representatives will be sent in writing to the Division/Subsidiary Company Personnel Manager by the local Trade Union officials concerned. Persons nominated as employee representatives shall not be under 21 years of age and must have had at least 6 months continuous service with Upper Clyde Shipbuilders Ltd., prior to nomination. To facilitate reporting back, the employee representatives should include a member from each Trade Group Council

—A Secretary appointed by the Local Director.

The Personnel Director may attend ex officio any meetings of Yard Councils.

. . . .

6.7 Each Yard Council shall meet at least once per month. Special meetings may be convened by the Chairman and/or at the request of one half of the employee representative members of the Council.

6.8 Local Directors of Divisions/Subsidiary Companies, other than those appointed as management representatives, shall be ex officio members of their own Yard Council.

. . . .

7. Upper Clyde Shipbuilders Joint Council (U.C.S.J.C.)

7.1 For the Company as a whole there will be established an Upper Clyde Shipbuilders Joint Council (U.C.S.J.C.).

. . . .

7.3 The U.C.S. Joint Council shall consist of:

—The Chairman/Managing Director of the Company, who will be Chairman of the Council

—The Personnel Director, who shall be Deputy Chairman of the Council

—The Production Director

—The Technical Director

—One Non-Executive Director

—The Local Director in charge of each Division/Subsidiary Company

—Four management representatives, one of whom shall be Joint Secretary

—Five National Executive Officers, as follows:

1 representing the Steelwork Trades
2 representing the Finishing Trades
1 representing the General Trades
1 representing the White Collar Trades

—up to 17 full-time local officials of the Trade Unions . . . (i.e. up to 3 representatives from the A.S.B.S.B. & S.W. and one from each of the other Trade Unions). One of the local T.U. officials will be appointed Joint Secretary

—Six employee representatives from the Yard Councils as follows:

2 representing the Steelwork Trades
2 representing the Finishing Trades
1 representing the General Trades
1 representing the White Collar Trades

213

(The six employee representatives shall retire every two years but shall be eligible for re-appointment).

. . . .

7.5 The U.C.S. Joint Council shall meet not less than four times annually. Special meetings may be convened by agreement.

. . . .

8. *The Bi-Annual National Council of Upper Clyde Shipbuilders Ltd.* *(B.N.C.)*

8.1 At national level there will be established a Bi-Annual National Council of U.C.S. (B.N.C.).

. . . .

8.3 The Bi-Annual National Council shall consist of:
—The Chairman/Managing Director of the Company, who shall be Chairman of the Council
—The Financial Director
—The Marketing Director
—The Personnel Director
—The Production Director
—The Technical Director
—One Non-Executive Director
—Four management representatives, one of whom shall be Joint Secretary.
—Up to 17 officials with Executive Authority from the Trade Unions signatory to the Employment Charter (i.e. up to 3 from the A.S.B.S.B. & S.W. and one from each of the other Trade Unions). One of the Trade Union Officials with Executive Authority will be a Joint Secretary.
—Five full-time local officials of the Trade Unions signatory to the Employment Charter, as follows:

    1 representing the Steelwork Trades
    2 representing the Finishing Trades
    1 representing the General Trades
    1 representing the White Collar Trades

8.4 The B.N.C. shall meet twice each year. Additional meetings to discuss issues considered by the management or the Trade Unions to be matters of grave importance may be convened by agreement.

. . . .

9. *General*

. . . .

9.5 Separate meetings of employees' representatives reporting back

On request, the Local Director in charge of each Division/Subsidiary Company shall accord reasonable facilities during working hours for separate meetings of the employees' representatives on his own Yard Council and Trade Group Councils.

At least annually each Yard Council shall review the arrangements within

214

its own Division/Subsidiary Company for separate meetings of employees' representatives, and for reporting back, to ensure that they are not only effective but also reasonable and do not overlap.

9.6 Payment to Employees' Representatives

Employee members of all Councils, and of all recognised sub-committees thereof shall be paid reasonable travelling expenses incurred owing to meetings of the Councils or Sub-Committees and shall also receive their normal day-shift rate of earnings in respect of time spent on Council business.

No payment shall be made in respect of time spent in travelling outside the individual's normal working hours.

9.7 Administration

Administration for the Trade Groups and Yard Councils shall be the responsibility of the Division/Subsidiary Company Personnel Departments.

Administration for the U.C.S. Joint Council and for the Bi-Annual National Council shall be the responsibility of the U.C.S. Personnel Department, which will maintain a functional line with Division/Subsidiary Company Personnel Departments.

The Personnel Director will attend each Yard Council at least once each year.

35.5 *Constitution of Colliery Consultative Committees*[1] [*Guide to Consultation in the Coalmining Industry* 3rd edition (London, National Coal Board, 1968)]

1. PREAMBLE

In a publicly owned Coalmining Industry the concern of managements and workmen should be identical. It is expedient, therefore, to set up a consultative body at each colliery with the object of securing the closest co-operation amongst all those concerned in the operation of the colliery.

. . . .

3. TERMS OF REFERENCE

The Committee shall be the recognised means for the regular consideration of, and the making of recommendations on, questions relating to:—

(*a*) the safety, health and welfare of all workpeople engaged in or about the colliery, and

(*b*) the organisation and conduct of the operations in which the workpeople are employed together with any other colliery matters of mutual interest to the management and the workpeople, but excluding wages questions, or like subjects which are normally dealt with through Trade Union negotiating machinery.

[1] A slightly amended form of a Constitution reproduced in the 1st edition of the *Guide*, published in 1948.

4. FUNCTIONS

. . . .

(b) *Subjects for Consideration.* . . . . the functions of the Committee shall include keeping under constant review and making recommendations on such matters as—

(i) the accident and sickness trends at the colliery and measures for reducing them;

(ii) the Colliery Welfare arrangements, including the canteen, washing accommodation, sanitation, safety appliances, first-aid equipment, protective clothing and safety footwear, etc.;

(iii) the training and educational activities associated with the colliery;

(iv) the technical efficiency of the colliery, for which purpose the committee shall be required to examine the colliery's business objectives, performances and initiate effective measures to improve production in close co-operation with the workmen and the Trade Union Lodge;

(v) the development of arrangements designed to secure the active support of the Committee's activities by the workmen;

(vi) the scrutiny of current and future development plans of the colliery, shortages, equipment lost and salvaged;

(vii) any other appropriate matters referred to the Committee by the Area Consultative Council,[1] or raised by any of its members.

5. CONSTITUTION

(a) *Committee Membership*
The Committee shall consist of—

(i) the colliery manager who shall be Chairman of the Committee. The Committee shall appoint a Vice-Chairman from amongst its members;

(ii) the Area Agent and the Colliery Lodge Secretary of the National Union of Mineworkers, the Area Agent of the National Association of Colliery Overmen, Deputies and Shotfirers and the Production Manager as ex officio members. . . .

(iii) four members appointed by the manager, one of whom shall be a deputy, two of whom shall be other underground officials and the other a surface official;

(iv) one member appointed by N.A.C.O.D.S. who shall in Scottish North, Scottish South, Northumberland, North Durham and South Durham Areas be a deputy;

(v) six other members appointed by the N.U.M. These members shall be representative of the five main grades or workers, viz. face worker, underground haulage worker, contract worker not employed at the face, surface worker (including checkweighman), and

---

[1] A Council based on an administrative area of the National Coal Board.

216

tradesman. Two of the six members so appointed shall be face workers.*

. . . .

(b) *Secretary*

The Committee shall appoint a Secretary from outside their number, to keep records of the proceedings and business of the Committee, and to deal with the secretarial duties arising therefrom. . . .

. . . .

(c) *Assessors*

Colliery officers responsible for matters relating to personnel, training, safety, health or welfare shall be required to attend meetings to which they are officially summoned by the Committee. Such officers shall submit reports on the particular subjects for which each is responsible as and when required by the Committee.

The Committee shall also be empowered to invite any other person or persons having a special knowledge of any matters under discussion to attend meetings of the Committee in the capacity of assessors.

. . . .

6. ELIGIBILITY OF CANDIDATES FOR APPOINTMENT

Candidates eligible for appointment to the Committee under section 5(a) (iv) and (v) shall be members of a Trade Union generally recognised in the industry as being appropriate for their particular grades, and shall have served for a period of not less than twelve consecutive months at the colliery immediately preceding their appointment.

7. TERM OF OFFICE

(a) *Term of Office*

. . . members appointed under section 5(a) (iv) and (v) shall hold office for a period of three years. One third of those members appointed under section 5(a) (v) shall retire each year. The appropriate Trade Union shall nominate members to fill the vacancies.

(b) *Retiring Members*

Retiring members shall be eligible for reappointment.

. . . .

8. MEETINGS OF THE COMMITTEE

(a) *Frequency*

The meetings of the Committee shall be held fortnightly, and additional meetings shall be held where it is agreed by the Committee to be necessary.

. . . .

(d) *Payment*

The Board will either pay 8s. 6d. as an expense allowance when meetings

---

* *Face worker includes any workman normally employed at the face, e.g. a power loader man, a coal-getter, coal-cutter, filler or stripper, pan-turner, ripper or brusher, or waste-man.*

are held outside normal working hours, or make good any loss of earnings incurred by members when meetings are held during their normal working hours. . . .

.   .   .   .

(e) *Right to attend Meetings*
Any duly authorised official of the National Coal Board shall have right of access to any meetings of Consultative Committees.

36 Worker directors

36.1 Trades Union Congress, *Trade Unionism*[1] 2nd edition (London, Trades Union Congress, 1967)

REPRESENTATION AT DIFFERENT LEVELS OF MANAGEMENT

286 Although the most obvious level at which workpeople's representatives play a part in the running of an enterprise is at the level of the establishment, there are a number of different levels of management which can be identified and at which the possible role of workpeople's representatives needs to be examined. Judgment on this question will depend on the nature of the enterprise involved, taking account of . . . its overall size, the size of the establishment in relation to the size of the enterprise, and the diversity of the enterprise in terms of products manufactured or services provided. . . .
287 What has to be decided over the next few years, first in the case of the nationalised industries, is how best to relate the purpose of trade union representation at the very top level with workpeople representation at the level of the establishment. The key to the examination of this whole range of issues is clear recognition of different sorts of functions which are carried out at different levels of management.
288 Depending on the size of the enterprise and establishment, the form which this representation should generally take at works level is the acceptance of a workpeople's representative, who would normally have been elected for his other duties, for example as a shop steward, to sit on whatever is the normal body which regularly meets at plant level to take decisions on the running of that plant. Likewise, again depending on the industry and enterprise in question, there should be trade union representation at the higher level, whether this be the regional level or at a level which represents the functional authority for the particular product within the enterprise.

REPRESENTATION AT BOARD LEVEL

289 Arising out of this, there is the further question of representation at the top level which is generally in Britain not differentiated between boards of

[1] See footnote to Document 4.2.

218

directors with an executive or functional bias and boards of directors with a bias towards outside appointments, presumably of persons with qualifications of a more general character. . . . There is an obvious conceptual difficulty, given existing company law, in envisaging how the appointment or election of a trade union representative or representatives to the board of the company would affect the rights of shareholders through the annual general meeting to elect whoever they wish to the board. However, in view of the somewhat farcical nature of most annual general meetings, farcical not being too strong a word when it is noted that the annual general meeting is ostensibly the ultimate authority in the enterprise and is analogous to the annual debates in Parliament on the reports of nationalised industries, this is probably more an apparent difficulty than a real one.

290 . . . Legislation of a discretionary character would be widely welcomed. . . . For a substantial measure of progress to be achieved, the CBI[1] would have to take a strong lead in encouraging its members to follow the spirit of the proposal. Prior discussion between the Government, the TUC and the CBI would clearly be called for. Compulsory legislation on a question of this character would prove very difficult to draft and . . . it should be remembered that the real object is to encourage companies to recognise and take advantage of the mutual benefits to be obtained from more active participation by trade union representatives in company policy and day to day practice.

36.2 National Executive of the Labour Party, *Industrial Democracy*[2] 1968

The traditional socialist critique of private enterprise is based upon our opposition to the concentration of ownership and control of the means of 'production, distribution and exchange' in a few powerful private hands. . . .

. . . .

THE TECHNOLOGICAL IMPERATIVE

The growing size of industrial units; the increasing remoteness of higher levels of management from the workers whose economic lives hang by their decisions; the emergence of tiers of salaried professional managers interposed between the owners of industry and their employees—all of these factors have dramatically altered the environment within which workers and their trade unions operate.

These changes have called for the intervention of government and an increasing measure of social control or supervision of industry. . . .

At lower levels, however, evolution has been slower. Managerial power remains arbitrary and untrammelled. The influence of workers and their representatives tends to be negative or remote. Change and insecurity leads to tension and dispute. An extension of industrial democracy, and the effective

---

[1] Confederation of British Industry.

[2] A statement to the Annual Conference, published as Appendix 5 of the *Labour Party Conference Report* 1968 (London, Labour Party, 1969).

participation of workers in decision making in individual industries and firms, is therefore urgent and essential if the nation is to meet the human needs of those confronted by the major structural changes that are now taking place. It is no longer enough for workers and their representatives to treat management defensively; waiting for them to act and then protesting; asking but rarely achieving some measure of consultation in advance.

They must be involved in planning change and in the decisions that are now taken arbitrarily by management, if the alienation and resentment workers feel when an upheaval of their lives arrives without warning is to be avoided. . . .

The aim is to extend into the workplace the constructive power the unions now have in national economic planning. It will mean a new positive role for the shop steward or plant official. It will require the closer integration of shop stewards into the unions' chain of command.

· · · · · · ·

THE NEED FOR INDUSTRIAL DEMOCRACY

· · · · · ·

. . . We are trying to restate, in terms of principle appropriate to modern conditions, our commitment to the extension of the rights and power of organised labour—and our conviction that this alone will enable us to build a society which is at once humane and dynamic.

We therefore endorse the following principles:—

(1) That the growth of industrial democracy must be firmly based on the general and effective recognition of the *right* of workers to organisation, representation and participation in major matters affecting their working lives.

(2) That the development of industrial democracy should be pursued through the creation of a *single channel* of communication between workers' representatives and management. The scope and subject matter of collective bargaining should be extended so that all the elements of management (dismissals, discipline, introduction of new machinery, forward planning of manpower, rationalisation and so forth) are within the sphere of *negotiations* at plant and national level.

(3) That workers' representatives should have the *right* to adequate information covering all aspects of their company's affairs, provided only that this does not seriously jeopardise the firm's commercial interests.

The aim of this approach would be to extend democracy in industry, not by evolving new and complex (and perhaps alien) structures, but by gradually increasing involvement in a development of existing machinery—which is already known and used because it deals with fundamental questions like pay and conditions. . . .

· · · · · · ·

THE LEGISLATIVE FRAMEWORK

In order to achieve for workers an effective voice in the control of policy and administration, the Government will be required to act in a number of ways. First and foremost; the Government must accept the right of workers to representation. This will lead to the acceptance of a wider subject matter for collective bargaining. Second, the Government must improve by law the availability to workers of information on their firm and its prospects, which is essential to make bargaining effective. . . .

．　．　．　．　．　．　．

There must also be dramatic improvements in education and training for participation through the development of special new courses for worker representatives, and through co-ordination of the present scattered provision made by unions, firms, technical colleges and extra-mural departments. Special efforts must be made to coax people with suitable experience into this sector of teaching, and day release for workers must become much more common.

．　．　．　．　．　．　．

THE TRADE UNION RESPONSIBILITY

The effect of the measures discussed above would be to provide the community, and to put into the hands of worker representatives and the trade union movement, several new defences and potentially powerful weapons for winning a wide measure of democratic control over the growing concentrations of industrial and economic power. But before the trade unions can take full advantage of this situation and play their part in a developing pattern of wider social accountability, there are several steps they must take.

Unions must improve the range and quality of their services to members; through the recruitment and training of more full-time officers, and more "specialist" officers, and improvements in the training and servicing of shop stewards and other shop floor representatives. At the same time, there must be a continued and growing willingness to overhaul union structures, extend the internal representation of membership interests, and to press on with rationalisation by amalgamations, inter-union agreements, joint servicing and so on.

．　．　．　．　．　．　．

Unions should investigate areas where workers could assume unilateral executive responsibility under the terms of a bargained agreement, e.g. the administration of welfare funds, regulation of overtime or in appropriate circumstances some aspects of selection and promotion.

The unions might also increase their influence through the agencies of social accountability (both those on which their members serve, e.g. the Economic Development Councils,[1] and others, e.g. Prices and Incomes Board,[2] Select Committee on Nationalised Industries) by submitting evidence in the course of enquiries and making sure they are closely and actively involved in the follow-up to their reports.

[1] Usually called Economic Development Committees. See *supra*, p. 16.
[2] National Board for Prices and Incomes.

· · · · · ·

We favour experiments in placing representatives of the workers in a nationalised industry on the board of that industry. This representation should not be confined to union officials; nor should it divert attention from the need to involve worker representatives in decision making at every level in an industry, and especially at the various points of production.

Public industries should also consider "model agreements" on the provision of adequate information to unions to enable them to bargain effectively over the whole range of matters of concern to their workers.

36.3 British Steel Corporation, *Group Boards and Employee Directors* (Press announcement, 28th March 1968)

GROUP BOARDS AND THEIR MEMBERS

The British Steel Corporation's Report on Organisation 1967, published as a White Paper (Cmnd 3362) in August 1967, defined the functions of Group Boards and their members as follows:—

"Each Group will have a board appointed by the Chairman of the Corporation after consultation with the Group Managing Director. These boards may include part-time as well as full-time members. The Chairman of each board will be the Group Managing Director and the board's function will be to assist him in his responsibilities for directing the affairs of the Group, including the preparation and implementation of the annual operating plan and of schemes for new capital expenditure. The boards will also have a special role in advising the Group Managing Director on issues involving regional or social factors peculiar to the Group. They will not be statutory boards under the Companies Acts."

EMPLOYEE DIRECTORS

The scheme for the appointment of employees to serve as part-time directors on the Group Boards of the British Steel Corporation was devised by the Corporation with the co-operation of the Trades Union Congress. It is the first national scheme of its kind in industry.

Three employees have been appointed to serve on each of the four Group Boards. Their appointments are for three years from the 1st May, 1968. Employee directors will be paid the same salary as other part-time directors, and expenses, and will receive compensation for loss of earnings, where appropriate. They will continue to do their existing jobs, but will, of course, attend Board Meetings and fulfil any other responsibilities as part-time board members. Employee directors will serve in a personal capacity and not as representatives of trades unions, and will (where applicable) relinquish union office for the period of their directorships.

The appointments cover a wide range of employees. They include men of works grade, non-supervisory and supervisory staff, and management staff.

The employee directors are appointed by the Chairman of the British Steel Corporation and were chosen after consultations with the TUC and within the industry. In preparation for their new responsibilities they will be given up to five weeks leave of absence to attend a voluntary introductory course arranged jointly by the TUC and the Corporation.

37 Contemporary views

37.1 Confederation of British Industry, *Evidence to the Royal Commission on Trade Unions and Employers' Associations* (London, C.B.I., 1965)

POSITION OF THE WORKER IN THE UNDERTAKING

103. Radical changes in the structure of the undertaking involving the position of workers have been suggested in order to obtain the all-important co-operation between worker and management. These include co-ownership and workers' participation in management. However, the British trade union movement has never adopted a policy of pursuing these aims, and many firms which have experimented with them have found only limited support for them among their workers. The Confederation does not believe that the limited number of successful schemes which exist suggest that general developments on these lines is possible. It considers that the aim of producing a satisfying job for the individual and general recognition of the workers' role within the undertaking is best furthered by ... policies ... covering:

—the development and application of sociological research of the factory situation;
—the allocation in the management structure of responsibility for labour matters;
—managerial, supervisory and shop steward training;
—the development or revival of joint consultative machinery;
—the improvement of communications; and
—the development of programmes covering sickness, pensions and redundancy.

37.2 *In Place of Strife: A Policy for Industrial Relations* (Cmnd. 3888) 1969

APPOINTMENT OF WORKERS' REPRESENTATIVES TO BOARDS OF UNDERTAKINGS

49. There are various ways in which workers can participate in manage-

223

ment. The most effective is through membership of a trade union which negotiates with management on all questions affecting conditions of employment including, for example, the introduction of new machinery, manpower planning and deployment, and disciplinary and dismissals procedures. There are other forms of participation, for example through the appointment of workers' representatives to the boards of undertakings. The Government favours experiments in this method, and will have consultations on how they may best be facilitated. Any changes in the law which the consultations show to be desirable will be included in the Industrial Relations Bill.[1]

POLITICAL ACTIVITIES

38 Purpose and methods

38.1 Trades Union Congress, *Trade Unionism*[2] 2nd edition (London, Trades Union Congress, 1967)

VOICE IN GOVERNMENT

107 ... Workpeople's right to a view on matters which affect their interests applies ... at the level of Government as well as at the level of firm or industry. The trade union claim to a voice in Government rests on the wide-ranging scope of modern Government. If trade unions are at arms length from Government, there is a lack of influence in both directions: trade unions are in a poor position to state their views and Government also does not have the facility to take account of trade union experience or to prepare the ground for new policies which will affect the interests of working people. ...

· · · · · · ·

INFLUENCING GOVERNMENT

147 ... the relationship between trade unions and the state ... is one of some complexity. The influence which trade unions exert on the Government ... occurs within the context of this relationship as a whole. At the same time as trade unions influence Government, they are influenced by Government. It may broadly be said that the measure of influence in both directions is a measure of trade union involvement in Government. This involvement arises from trade unions' responsibilities in advancing and protecting the interests of their members.

· · · · · · ·

149 One distinct aspect of trade union influence on Government, and an aspect which fits most readily into the classification of trade union methods, is pressure on the Government to enact a particular piece of legislation, which

[1] See footnote to Document 6.3.   [2] See footnote to Document 4.2.

will strengthen, or fill a gap in, the scope of collective bargaining or workers' participation. ... Acts of Parliament are not exclusively, or even mainly, the object of trade union influence on the Government. Insofar as the Budget, for example, is enacted through the Finance Act, Government action over a wide field can be equated with legislation, yet in this field of economic policy it is the continuing or day-to-day influence, based on clearly formulated trade union economic policy, of which Government can be expected to take some account.

POLITICAL ACTION

150 At the turn of the century there was no party in Parliament prepared to look after the interests of working people, so one had to be established. The creation of the Labour Party as the political arm of the trade union Movement is clearly of immense historical significance; its roots in the community find their strength, in common with those of the trade union Movement, in the experience of working people, and this common approach to practical problems means that the Labour Movement does not get out of touch with the realities of everyday life. Trade unions and political parties do, however, perform quite distinct functions and their pre-occupations can often be quite different. The growth of the Labour Party to the point where it became the Government of the country has entailed a significant divergence of function. The existence of common roots yet distinct functions is therefore the most important feature of the relationship between trade unions and the Labour Party. It is in this context that political action as a method of securing trade union objectives should be examined.

. . . .

152 The main way in which trade unions influence the policy of the Labour Party as a method of furthering trade union objectives is by formulating broad policies on industrial matters which are then debated generally within the Movement. The sponsoring of candidates for Parliament is of secondary and quite limited importance. ...

. . . .

TRADE UNION CONSULTATION WITH GOVERNMENT

. . . .

172 ... The TUC General Council is a representative body and not purely a federation of sectional interests. Questions considered by the TUC, and often put subsequently to the Government, fall into two broad categories. There are those which concern all trade unions equally, and there are questions which are of special concern to only a small number of unions, though perhaps nevertheless of general concern to all trade unions. A good example of this is transport policy. First, there are unions with membership in transport and second, there are unions whose members have a considerable interest in transport policy, not just as users of public transport, but also as employees of companies whose prosperity depends on the quality of transport services available for the transport of goods. The TUC is the only forum for the discussion of all the questions involved from a trade union standpoint. Whilst the

committee of the General Council which considers transport policy comprises all the members of the General Council whose unions have a direct interest, the composition of the committee is much wider than this. Furthermore, when this committee meets the representatives of all unions engaged in transport, members of the committee representing the General Council are in a position to promote agreement on policy between the various separate interests. The results of such deliberations are therefore at the same time authoritative and broadly based, and can offer the Government a clear picture of trade union policy.

39 Legal conditions

39.1 Trade Union Act 1913[1]

3. (1) The funds of a trade union shall not be applied, either directly or in conjunction with any other trade union, association, or body, or otherwise indirectly, in the furtherance of the political objects to which this section applies (without prejudice to the furtherance of any other political objects), unless the furtherance of those objects has been approved as an object of the union by a resolution for the time being in force passed on a ballot of the members of the union taken in accordance with this Act for the purpose by a majority of the members voting; and where such a resolution is in force, unless rules, to be approved, whether the union is registered[2] or not, by the Registrar of Friendly Societies, are in force providing—

(*a*) That any payments in the furtherance of those objects are to be made out of a separate fund (in this Act referred to as the political fund of the union), and for the exemption in accordance with this Act of any member of the union from any obligation to contribute to such a fund if he gives notice in accordance with this Act that he objects to contribute; and

(*b*) That a member who is exempt from the obligation to contribute to the political fund of the union shall not be excluded from any benefits of the union, or placed in any respect either directly or indirectly under any disability or at any disadvantage as compared with other members of the union (except in relation to the control or management of the political fund) by reason of his being so exempt, and that contribution to the political fund of the union shall not be made a condition for admission to the union.

(2) If any member of a trade union alleges that he is aggrieved by a breach of any rule made in pursuance of this section, he may complain to the Registrar of Friendly Societies, and the Registrar of Friendly Societies, after giving the complainant and any representative of the union an opportunity of being heard, may, if he considers that such a breach has been committed, make

[1] For minor changes proposed in the Industrial Relations Bill 1970, see Appendix, p. 571.

[2] See footnote to Document 2.1.

such order for remedying the breach as he thinks just under the circumstances. . . .

(3) The political objects to which this section applies are the expenditure of money—

(*a*) on the payment of any expenses incurred either directly or indirectly by a candidate or prospective candidate for election to Parliament or to any public office, before, during, or after the election in connexion with his candidature or election; or

(*b*) on the holding of any meeting or the distribution of any literature or documents in support of any such candidate or prospective candidate; or

(*c*) on the maintenance of any person who is a member of Parliament or who holds a public office; or

(*d*) in connection with the registration of electors or the selection of a candidate for Parliament or any public office; or

(*e*) on the holding of political meetings of any kind, or on the distribution of political literature or political documents of any kind, unless the main purpose of the meetings or of the distribution of the literature or documents is the furtherance of statutory objects within the meaning of this Act.

The expression "public office" in this section means the office of member of any county, county borough, district, or parish council, or board of guardians, or of any public body who have power to raise money, either directly or indirectly, by means of a rate.

(4) A resolution under this section approving political objects as an object of the union shall take effect as if it were a rule of the union and may be rescinded in the same manner and subject to the same provisions as such a rule.

(5) The provisions of this Act as to the application of the funds of a union for political purposes shall apply to a union which is in whole or in part an association or combination of other unions as if the individual members of the component unions were the members of that union and not the unions; but nothing in this Act shall prevent any such component union from collecting from any of their members who are not exempt on behalf of the association or combination any contributions to the political fund of the association or combination.

4. (1) A ballot for the purposes of this Act shall be taken in accordance with rules of the union to be approved for the purpose, whether the union is registered or not, by the Registrar of Friendly Societies, but the Registrar of Friendly Societies shall not approve any such rules unless he is satisfied that every member has an equal right, and, if reasonably possible, a fair opportunity of voting, and that the secrecy of the ballot is properly secured.

39.2 Trade Disputes and Trade Unions Act 1927

4. (1) It shall not be lawful to require any member of a trade union to make any contribution to the political fund of a trade union unless he has at some time after the commencement of this Act and before he is first after the thirty-first day of December, nineteen hundred and twenty-seven, required to make such a contribution delivered at the head office or some branch office of the trade union, notice in writing in the form set out in the First Schedule to this Act[1] of his willingness to contribute to that fund and has not withdrawn the notice in manner hereinafter provided; and every member of a trade union who has not delivered such a notice as aforesaid, or who, having delivered such a notice, has withdrawn it in manner hereinafter provided, shall be deemed for the purposes of the Trade Union Act, 1913, to be a member who is exempt from the obligation to contribute to the political fund of the union, and references in that Act to a member who is so exempt shall be construed accordingly:

Provided that, if at any time a member of a trade union who has delivered such a notice as aforesaid gives notice of withdrawal thereof, delivered at the head office or at any branch office of the trade union, he shall be deemed for the purposes of this subsection to have withdrawn the notice as from the first day of January next after the delivery of the notice of withdrawal.

For the purposes of this subsection, a notice may be delivered personally or by any authorised agent and any notice shall be deemed to have been delivered at the head or a branch office of a trade union if it has been sent by post properly addressed to that office.

(2) All contributions to the political fund of a trade union from members of the trade union who are liable to contribute to that fund shall be levied and made separately from any contributions to the other funds of the trade union and no assets of the trade union, other than the amount raised by such a separate levy as aforesaid, shall be carried to that fund, and no assets of a trade union other than those forming part of the political fund shall be directly or indirectly applied or charged in furtherance of any political object to which section three of the Trade Union Act, 1913, applies; and any charge in contravention of this subsection shall be void.

(3) All rules of a trade union made and approved in accordance with the requirements of section three of the Trade Union Act, 1913, shall be amended so as to conform to the requirements of this Act, and as so amended shall be approved by the Registrar of Friendly Societies (in this Act referred to as "the Registrar") within six months after the commencement of this Act or within such further time as the Registrar may in special circumstances allow, and if the rules of any trade union are not so amended and approved as aforesaid they shall be deemed not to comply with the requirements of the said section.

. . . .

(6) Section sixteen of the Trade Union Act, 1871[2] (which provides for the transmission to the Registrar of annual returns by registered[3] trade unions), shall apply to every unregistered trade union so far as respects the receipts, funds, effects, expenditure, assets and liabilities of the political fund thereof.

---

[1] Effectively reproduced in *Trade Union Act 1913: Model Rules For Political Fund*, published by the Chief Registrar of Friendly Societies. See Document 39.3.

[2] This section is not included in extracts from the Act reproduced in this book.

[3] See footnote to Document 2.1.

5. (1) Amongst the regulations as to the conditions of service in His Majesty's civil establishments there shall be included regulations prohibiting established civil servants from being members, delegates, or representatives of any organisation of which the primary object is to influence or affect the remuneration and conditions of employment of its members, unless the organisation is an organisation of which the membership is confined to persons employed by or under the Crown and is an organisation which complies with such provisions as may be contained in the regulations for securing that it is in all respects independent of, and not affiliated to, any such organisation as aforesaid the membership of which is not confined to persons employed by or under the Crown or any federation comprising such organisations, that its objects do not include political objects, and that it is not associated directly or indirectly with any political party or organisation:

Provided that the regulations made in compliance with the provisions of this section shall not prevent—

(*a*) any person who is at the commencement of this Act an established civil servant from remaining a member of any trade union or organisation not composed wholly or mainly of persons employed by or under the Crown of which he had, at the commencement of this Act, been a member for more than six months, if under the rules thereof there had on the fourth day of April, nineteen hundred and twenty-seven, accrued or begun to accrue to him a right to any future payment during incapacity, or by way of superannuation, or on the death of himself or his wife, or as provision for his children; or

(*b*) any person employed at the commencement of this Act by or under the Crown who thereafter becomes an established civil servant from remaining, so long as he is not appointed to a position of supervision or management, a member of any trade union or organisation, not composed wholly or mainly of persons employed by or under the Crown, of which he is a member at the date when he so becomes an established civil servant, if under the rules thereof there has at that date accrued, or begun to accrue, to him a right to any future payment during incapacity, or by way of superannuation, or on the death of himself or his wife, or as provision for his children; or

(*c*) a person who in addition to being an established civil servant is, apart from his service as such, also engaged in some other employment or occupation from being a member, delegate, or representative of any trade union or organisation, of which the primary object is to influence or affect the remuneration or conditions of employment of persons engaged in that employment or occupation.

(2) Subject as hereinafter provided, any established civil servant who contravenes the regulations made under this section shall be disqualified for being a member of the Civil Service:

Provided that, in the case of a first offence, a civil servant shall forthwith be warned by the head of his department, and the said disqualification shall not take effect if within one month after such warning the civil servant ceases to contravene the said regulations.

229

39.3 Chief Registrar of Friendly Societies, *Trade Union Act 1913: Model Rules For Political Fund*

NOTE.—These model rules comprise the statutory requirements of the Trade Union Act, 1913, with regard to the political fund. Subject to these statutory requirements, the Chief Registrar will consider in each case any modifications or additions which a union may desire to make for the purpose of its own political fund.

.... Union.

RULES FOR POLITICAL FUND

1. The objects of the
Union shall include the furtherance of the political objects to which Section 3 of the Trade Union Act, 1913, applies[1] ...

.   .   .   .

2. Any payments in the furtherance of such political objects shall be made out of a separate fund [hereinafter called the political fund of the union].

3. The executive committee, as soon as practicable after the adoption of a resolution of the union approving the furtherance of such political objects as an object of the union, shall cause a notice in the following form to be given to each member of the union:—

Trade Union Act, 1913.

Union.

A resolution approving the furtherance of political objects within the meaning of the above Act as an object of the union has been adopted by a ballot under the Act. Any payments in the furtherance of those objects will be made out of a separate fund, the political fund of the union, but every member of the union has a right to be exempt from contributing to that fund. A form of exemption notice can be obtained by or on behalf of any member either by application at, or by post from, the general office or any branch office of the union or from the Chief Registrar of Friendly Societies, 17 North Audley Street, London, W.1.

Such form, when filled in, should be handed or sent to the secretary of the branch to which the member belongs.

Such notice shall be published in such manner, whether in the union's journal or report or otherwise, as notices are usually given by the union or its branches to its members, and shall also be posted up and kept posted up for at least twelve months in a conspicuous place, accessible to members, at the office or meeting place of each branch of the union, and the secretary of each branch shall take steps to secure that every member of the branch, so far as practicable, receives a copy of such notice, and shall supply a copy to any member at his request. The executive committee shall provide the secretary of each branch with a number of notices sufficient for this purpose.

[1] See Document 39.1.

230

4. The form of exemption notice shall be as follows:—

Union.

Political Fund [Exemption Notice].

I hereby give notice that I object to contribute to the political fund of the Union, and am in consequence exempt, in manner provided by the Trade Union Act, 1913, from contributing to that fund.

Signature
Name of Branch
Address

....

Date   day of   , 19 .

.   .   .   .   .   .

5. Any member of the union may at any time give notice on such form of exemption notice or on a form to the like effect that he objects to contribute to the political fund of the union. Such notice shall be sent to the secretary of the branch to which the member belongs and, on receiving it, the secretary shall send an acknowledgment of its receipt to the member at the address appearing upon the notice, and shall inform the general secretary of the name and address of the member.

6. On giving such notice, a member of the union shall be exempt, so long as his notice is not withdrawn, from contributing to the political fund of the union as from the first day of January next after the notice is given, or, in the case of a notice given within one month after the notice given to members under Rule 3 hereof or after the date on which a new member admitted to the union is supplied with a copy of these rules under Rule 12 hereof, as from the date on which the member's notice is given.

.   .   .   .   .   .

8. A member who is exempt from the obligation to contribute to the political fund of the union shall not be excluded from any benefits of the union, or placed in any respect either directly or indirectly under any disability or disadvantage as compared with other members of the union [except in relation to the control or management of the political fund of the union] by reason of his being so exempt.

9. Contribution to the political fund of the union shall not be made a condition for admission to the union.

10. If any member alleges that he is aggrieved by a breach of any of these rules for the political fund of the union, he may complain to the Chief Registrar of Friendly Societies, and the Chief Registrar, after giving the complainant and any representative of the union an opportunity of being heard, may, if he considers that such a breach has been committed, make such order for remedying the breach as he thinks just in the circumstances; and any such order of the Chief Registrar shall be binding and conclusive on all parties without appeal and shall not be removable into any court of law or restrainable by injunction, and on being recorded in the county court, may be enforced as if it had been an order of the county court.

231

11. Any member may withdraw his notice of exemption on notifying his desire to that effect to the secretary of his branch, who shall thereupon send such member an acknowledgment of receipt of the notification and inform the general secretary of the name and address of the member so withdrawing.

12. The executive committee shall cause to be printed, as soon as practicable after the approval and registration of these rules for the political fund of the union, a number of copies thereof having at the end copies of the certificates of approval and registration sufficient for the members of the union, and a further number for new members, and shall send to the secretary of each branch a number of copies sufficient for the members of the branch. The secretary of each branch shall take steps to secure that every member of the branch, so far as practicable, receives a copy of these rules, and shall supply a copy to any member at his request. A copy thereof shall also be supplied forthwith to every new member on his admission to the union.

13. A return in respect to the political fund of the union shall be transmitted by the union to the Chief Registrar of Friendly Societies before the first day of June in every year prepared and made up to such date and in such form and comprising such particulars as the Chief Registrar may from time to time require, and every member of the union shall be entitled to receive a copy of such return, on application to the treasurer or secretary of the union, without making any payment for the same.

40 Finance

40.1 Chief Registrar of Friendly Societies, *Report for the year 1968, Part 4: Trade Unions* (London, H.M.S.O., 1969), p. 10

POLITICAL FUNDS

Industrial Group	Number of Unions (a)	Membership Total 000's	Membership Number Contributing 000's	Contributions £000's	Average Contribution per contributing member s. d.	Other Income £000's	Expenditure £000's	Average expenditure per contributing member s. d.	Funds at end of year £000's
				Unions of Employees					
1. General Labour Organizations	3	2,275	2,059	221	2 1	1	166	1 7	307
2. Agriculture, Forestry, Fishing	1	113	112	8	1 2	(c)	6	1 0	9
3. Coal Mining	12	505	361	81	4 6	20	79	4 5	408
4. All Other Mining and Quarrying									
5. Food, Drink and Tobacco	3	73	48	7	2 9	(c)	5	1 11	11
6. Chemicals and Allied Industries	1	16	11	1	1 1		(c)	0 10	2
7. Metal, Engineering, Shipbuilding, Vehicles, etc.	23	2,117	1,532	262	3 5	17	231	3 0	404
8. Cotton, Flax, Man-made Fibres	14	76	63	9	3 2		10	3 4	18
9. All Other Textile Industries	12	81	73	7	1 10	1	5	1 5	23
10. Leather, Leather Goods, Fur	3								
11. Clothing, other than Footwear	3	113	81	5	1 2		5	1 2	10
12. Footwear	1	76	70	11	3 0	(c)	7	1 11	25
13. Bricks, Pottery, Glass, Cement, etc.	2	30	27	3	2 4		(c)	(d)	9
14. Timber, Furniture, etc.	2	61	40	4	2 11	(c)	3	1 6	5
15. Paper, Printing, Publishing	4	341	152	21	2 9	(c)	13	1 8	48
16. Other Manufacturing Industries	4	4	3	(c)	1 1	(c)	(c)	1 8	(c)
17. Construction	4	310	196	20	2 0		17	1 9	38
18. Gas, Electricity, Water	1	4	4	(c)	1 1	(c)	(c)	1 1	(c)
19. Railways	3	302	281	58	4 1	10	51	0 7	257
20. Other Transport and Communication	5	374	301	42	2 9	2	32	2 7	58
21. Distributive Trades	2	311	281	71	5 0		38	2 9	209
22. Insurance, Banking and Finance	3	17	9	1	2 9		1	2 5	14
23. Educational Services									
24. All Other Professional and Scientific Services	2	162	130	17	2 7	(c)	14	2 2	29
25. Cinemas, Theatres, Radio, Sport	3	63	34	4	0 11	1	(c)	1 3	8
26. All Other Miscellaneous Services	1	1	(b)	(c)			(c)	2 5	(c)
27. National Government Services									
28. Local Government Services	2	314	292	52	3 6		48	3 3	87
TOTAL 1968	108	7,741	6,160	903	2 11	52	733	2 5	1,979
1967	110	7,802	6,194	923	3 0	47	725	2 4	1,758
1966	113	7,997	6,423	941	2 11	41	1,192	3 9	1,494
1965	116	8,112	6,615	909	2 2	41	685	2 1	1,707
1964	117	8,013	6,457	891	2 9	34	1,003	3 1	1,444

(a) *Number of unions . . . that include among their objects the furtherance of political objects as defined in Section 3(3) of the Trade Union Act, 1913.*
(b) *Less than 500.* (c) *Less than £500.* (d) *An insignificant amount*

41 The individual union and political activity

41.1 Transport and General Workers' Union, *Report and Balance Sheet for the year ended December 1966* (London, T. & G.W.U., 1967), pp. 215–217

POLITICAL

There were some additions to the Union's Parliamentary Group during 1965. In January, 1965, Bro. Frank Cousins was elected as M.P. for Nuneaton and in the following May Bro. J. Dunn (Liverpool-Kirkdale) and Bro. M. MacPherson (Stirling and Falkirk) also joined the Group. At the dissolution of Parliament early in 1966 Bro. F. McLeavy, M.P. for Bradford East, retired. The General Election of March, 1966 brought the membership of the Group to 27 with the addition of three new members, Bro. J. Ellis (Bristol North-West). Bro. R. Hughes (Newport) and Bro. J. Lee (Reading). The constituencies of Bristol North-West and Reading had both previously been held by Conservatives.

On December 5, 1966, Bro. Cousins . . . gave up his seat at Nuneaton. With the resignation of Bro. Cousins the Parliamentary Group consisted of 26 members . . .

. . . .

. . . Changes in January, 1967 resulted in the following Government posts being held by members . . .

BRO. G. BROWN, P.C., M.P.	Secretary of State for Foreign Affairs.
BRO. A. GREENWOOD, P.C., M.P.	Minister of Housing and Local Government.
BRO. R. PRENTICE, P.C., M.P.	Minister of Public Building and Works.
BRO. J. SILKIN, M.P.	Parliamentary Secretary to the Treasury and Government Chief Whip.
BRO. M. FOLEY, M.P.	Under-Secretary of State for the Royal Navy.
BRO. R. MELLISH, M.P.	Joint Parliamentary Secretary, Ministry of Housing and Local Government.
BRO. J. BRAY, M.P.	Joint Parliamentary Secretary, Ministry of Technology.
BRO. P. SHORE, M.P.	Joint Under-Secretary of State, Department of Economic Affairs.

In addition to the quarterly meetings a number of special meetings of the Parliamentary Group were held on topics ranging from redundancy in the car industry to industrial diseases.

In November 1965, Bro. Bray succeeded Bro. Probert as Chairman of the Parliamentary Group and when Bro. Bray was appointed Parliamentary Secretary to the Minister of Power in April, 1966, Bro. Park took over as

Acting-Chairman and was re-elected as Chairman at the Annual Meeting in November, 1966. At the same meeting Bro. Bennett was elected Vice-Chairman.

Members of the Group have been active in raising matters of concern to the Union, both by tabling questions and in correspondence and interviews with Ministers.

Amongst the measures passed in 1965 a number were of particular interest to the Union such as the Covent Garden Market Act,[1] on which Bro. Mellish spoke for the Government, the Control of Office and Industrial Development Act and the Trade Disputes Act which dealt with the Rookes *v.* Barnard decision. During 1966 Bro. Mellish introduced two important Housing Bills— on slum clearance compensation and on subsidies. A considerable amount of Parliamentary time was taken up by the Government's economic measures, in particular the Prices and Incomes Act. Bro. Frank Cousins resigned as Minister of Technology on July 3, 1966 and took a prominent part in the debates on the Prices and Incomes Bill. He was also a member of its Standing Committee. Other members of the Group who spoke on the Second Reading were Bros. Brown, Hughes and Park. Bro. G. Brown also wound up the debate on economic affairs which took place on July 27. On October 25,1966 an important debate on the implementation of Part IV of the Prices and Incomes Act took place and Bro. Frank Cousins made a substantial contribution voicing the Union's policy. In the two day debate on economic affairs at the end of November Bro. Park also spoke critically of the Government's policy.

A number of members have been appointed to committees. Bro. Jeger served on the Standing Committee on the Trade Disputes Bill, Bro. Doig was on the Standing Committee on the Rent Bill and on a number of committees relating to Scotland. Bros. Bray, Carter-Jones, Dunn, Shore and Mrs. Short served on the Estimates Committee. In addition, Bros. Bray, Dunn, Mahon and Oakes were on the Committee which give the Second Reading to the Criminal Law Bill. More recently Bro. Oakes was appointed to the Standing Committee on the Criminal Justice Bill and Bro. Probert made Chairman of Standing Committees. Bro. Park was appointed to the Select Committee on Nationalised Industries.

Ireland continued to feature in the Group's activities. A deputation saw the Home Secretary concerning the closure of the Joint Anti-Submarine School in Londonderry. The matter of Government contracts with Monarch Electric Ltd. was taken up with the Postmaster-General and the Department of Economic Affairs. Bros. Jeger and Probert have continued to press the question of British Rail Shipping Services on the Southampton-St. Malo route and the Waterford-Fishguard crossing.

The General Secretary and the National Organiser of the Malta General Workers Union met Bros. J. Bennett and J. Ellis to discuss the crisis there. Other matters raised by the Group included the question of investment allowances for dumb barges[2] in the Port of London, anomalies in the Redundancy Payments Act, vehicles for the disabled, Government assistance to the Industrial Therapy Organisation, and industrial diseases.

[1] In fact, passed in 1966.   [2] Barges without independent motive power.

Members of the Group continued to contribute monthly articles to the *Record*.[1] Parliamentary Information, providing news of important activities in Parliament, circulated at regular intervals while Parliament was in session. Constituency reports were received regularly.

41.2 Royal Commission on Trade Unions and Employers' Associations, *Minutes of Evidence 24, Witness: Amalgamated Engineering Union* (London, H.M.S.O., 1966)

17. THE POLITICAL FUND AND CANDIDATE SELECTION

... The Political Fund pays expenses incurred by a candidate or prospective candidate for election, including the holding of meetings and distribution of literature in support of a candidate. $33\frac{1}{3}$ per cent. of the money raised for the Political Fund is allocated to District Committees for the payment of expenses for candidates for public offices, other than Parliamentary candidates. The Political Fund is used also to meet the cost of affiliation to the Labour Party and to provide certain grants to the Party. A member can at any time give notice of withdrawal from paying towards the fund. Contributions are at present 1s. per member, payable quarterly.

We therefore encourage our members to pay the levy, in order that our influence at the Conference, and in the Labour Movement as a whole, be as strong as possible. Branches usually affiliate to their local Labour Party. Affiliation fees to the Constituency Party are paid from the Fund. Number of representatives depends on the size of the membership.

... Affiliation to the Labour Party means that the extent of the contribution of funds is made public knowledge, because voting strength of the delegates is related to numbers contributing to the fund. The AEU sends 26 rank and file delegates, and eligible members of the Executive Council, the President and General Secretary to the Labour Party Annual Conference.

We would urge the same requirements for contributions to the political funds of any other political party. At present, Boards of Directors do not make public any details of the contributions of their companies towards the funds of a political party or any organisation existing for political purposes.

The selection of Parliamentary candidates follows a regular procedure. Firstly, members are selected for the Parliamentary Panel, which is the equivalent of a list of suitable candidates. For this, nominations are called for from Branches through their respective District Committees, who are constantly aware of members' activities within the Labour Movement and take note of members who might be suitable for candidates. All nominations received by the District Committees must be forwarded to Executive Council. Each one is either recommended for inclusion on the panel, or not recom-

[1] The Union's Journal.

mended. In the case of the latter, reasons for rejections must also be forwarded. All candidates are interviewed by Executive Council.

Candidates must be less than 60 years of age by the closing date for nominations, unless they are already members of Parliament. If candidates are included on the Panel but not adopted by a constituency before reaching the age of 60, their names are removed when they reach the limit.

The Executive Council selection panel consists of three stages, modelled on the group selection technique. It lasts for a period of two days, and is a procedure which has evolved over years of experience.

Candidates first have a private interview with the selection panel. Marks for this are awarded in two parts; firstly for the candidate's appearance and speaking ability, and secondly for the accuracy of his replies to the questions which relate to knowledge of the history and present development of the AEU, past and present policies of the Labour Party, its history and its development, knowledge of current international events, and knowledge of current domestic and social problems.

Candidates are secondly required to deliver an address for ten minutes on a major policy issue of the Labour Party. The subject for the address is not disclosed to the candidates until ten minutes before it is to be delivered. Thirdly, candidates participate in a discussion led by an AEU M.P. Marks for this are awarded for clarity of expression, knowledge, and participation, with reference to their approach. The aim is to test the debating skill of candidates.

Finally, candidates are required to write an essay for two hours, under examination conditions. Subjects for the essays are made known ten days before their attendance, to allow them to make any research they may feel necessary. The essays are marked by a National Agent of the Labour Party and the writer's name is not disclosed to the adjudicator.

The final result of the selection procedure is obtained from the average percentage mark, which at present must be 80 per cent. The Executive Council also take into account candidates' qualifications and experience before making a final choice for the panel.

The Executive Council prepare a report on the successful nominees; this is submitted to the National Committee for its approval. The report also includes details of the rejected candidates. The number of members on the Panel is limited by the number of members paying the Political Levy; the union is allowed one candidate per 30,000 levy-paying members.

The names of nominees chosen are then forwarded to the Labour Party for inclusion on the list of suitable candidates. Members of the Panel are required to accept nominations for any constituency which might reasonably be offered. Candidates from the Panel may be chosen by District Committees at any time for recommendation to the Executive Council; only when Executive Council approve does it become an actual nomination and the Labour Party's Nomination Form is then completed by the Union and signed by the General Secretary, or an appropriate member of the Executive Council. The Labour Party receive, with the nomination, details of the candidate.

If the Labour Party accept the nomination, Branches within the constituencies are asked to support the candidate at the selection conference.

237

42 Relationships with the Labour Party

42.1 Labour Party, *Constitution and Standing Orders*[1] 1968

CLAUSE II. MEMBERSHIP

1. There shall be two classes of members, namely:—
    (*a*) Affiliated Members.
    (*b*) Individual Members.
2. Affiliated Members shall consist of:
    (*a*) Trade Unions affiliated to the Trades Union Congress or recognised by the General Council of the Trades Union Congress as *bona fide* Trade Unions.
    (*b*) Co-operative Societies.
    (*c*) Socialist Societies.
    (*d*) Professional Organisations which, in the opinion of the National Executive Committee, have interests consistent with those of other affiliated organisations.
    (*e*) Constituency Labour Parties and Central Labour Parties in Divided Boroughs.[2]
    (*f*) County or Area Federations of Constituency Labour Parties, hereinafter referred to as Federations.

· · · · · · ·

CLAUSE III. CONDITIONS OF MEMBERSHIP

1. Each affiliated organisation must
    (*a*) Accept the Programme, Principles, and Policy of the Party.
    (*b*) Agree to conform to the Constitution and Standing Orders of the Party.
    (*c*) Submit its Political Rules to the National Executive Committee

· · · · · · ·

3. Each individual Member must
    (*a*) Accept and conform to the Constitution, Programme, Principles, and Policy of the Party.
    (*b*) If eligible, be a member of a Trade Union affiliated to the Trades Union Congress or recognised by the General Council of the Trades Union Congress as a *bona fide* Trade Union.

· · · · · · ·

CLAUSE IV. PARTY OBJECTS
NATIONAL

1. To organise and maintain in Parliament and in the country a Political Labour Party.
2. To co-operate with the General Council of the Trades Union Congress,

---

[1] Published as Appendix 3 of the *Labour Party Conference Report* 1968 (London, Labour Party, 1969).
[2] Boroughs containing more than one Parliamentary Constituency.

or other Kindred Organisations, in joint political or other action in harmony with the Party Constitution and Standing Orders.

3. To give effect as far as may be practicable to the principles from time to time approved by the Party Conference.

4. To secure for the workers by hand or by brain the full fruits of their industry and the most equitable distribution thereof that may be possible, upon the basis of the common ownership of the means of production, distribution, and exchange, and the best obtainable system of popular administration and control of each industry or service.

5. Generally to promote the Political, Social, and Economic Emancipation of the People and more particularly of those who depend directly upon their own exertions by hand or by brain for the means of life.

INTER-COMMONWEALTH

6. To co-operate with the Labour and Socialist organisations in the Commonwealth Overseas with a view to promoting the purposes of the Party, and to take common action for the promotion of a higher standard of social and economic life for the working population of the respective countries.

INTERNATIONAL

7. To co-operate with the Labour and Socialist organisations in other countries and to support the United Nations Organisation and its various agencies and other international organisations for the promotion of peace, the adjustment and settlement of international disputes by conciliation or judicial arbitration, the establishment and defence of human rights, and the improvement of the social and economic standards and conditions of work of the people of the world.

. . . .

CLAUSE VI. THE PARTY CONFERENCE

1. The work of the Party shall be under the direction and control of the Party Conference which shall itself be subject to the Constitution and Standing Orders of the Party. The Party Conference shall meet regularly once in every year and also at such other times as it may be convened by the National Executive Committee.

2. The Party Conference shall be constituted as follows:—

(*a*) Delegates duly appointed by each affiliated Trade Union or other organisations to the number of one delegate for each 5,000 members or part thereof on whom affiliation fees, by-election insurance premiums and any levies due were paid for the year ending December 31 preceding the Conference.

(*b*) Delegates duly appointed by Constituency Labour Parties (or Trades Councils acting as such) to the number of one delegate for each 5,000 individual members or part thereof on whom affiliation fees, by-election insurance premiums and any levies due were paid for the year ending December 31 preceding the Conference; where the individual and affiliated women's membership exceeds 2,500 an additional woman delegate may be appointed; where the membership of Young Socialists Branches

239

within a constituency is 200 or more an additional Young Socialist delegate may be appointed.

(c) Delegates duly appointed by Central Labour Parties or Trades Councils acting as such in Divided Boroughs not exceeding one for each Central Labour Party provided the affiliation fees, by-election insurance premiums and any levies due have been paid for the year ending December 31 preceding the Conference.

(d) Delegates duly appointed by Federations not exceeding one for each Federation provided the affiliation fees and any levies due have been paid for the year ending December 31 preceding the Conference.

. . . .

CLAUSE VII. APPOINTMENT OF DELEGATES TO THE PARTY CONFERENCE

1. Every delegate must be an individual member of the Labour Party . . . except persons resident in Northern Ireland who are duly appointed delegates of affiliated trade unions and who individually accept and conform to the Constitution, Programme, Principles and Policy of the Party.

2. Delegates must be *bona fide* members or paid permanent officials of the organisation appointing them, except in the case of Members of the Parliamentary Labour Party or duly-endorsed Parliamentary Labour Candidates appointed to represent Constituencies . . .

. . . .

CLAUSE VIII. THE NATIONAL EXECUTIVE COMMITTEE

1. There shall be a National Executive Committee of the Party consisting of 25 members and a Treasurer, elected by the Party Conference at its regular Annual Meeting in such proportion and under such conditions as may be set out in the Standing Orders for the time being in force. The Leader and Deputy Leader of the Parliamentary Labour Party shall be *ex officio* members of the National Executive Committee. The National Executive Committee shall, subject to the control and direction of the Party Conference, be the Administrative Authority of the Party.

. . . .

CLAUSE IX. PARLIAMENTARY CANDIDATURES
. . . . .

3. The selection of Labour Candidates for Parliamentary Elections shall not be regarded as completed until the name of the person selected has been placed before a meeting of the National Executive Committee, and his or her selection has been duly endorsed.

4. No Parliamentary Candidature shall be endorsed until the National Executive Committee has received an undertaking by one of its affiliated organisations (or is otherwise satisfied) that the election expenses of the Candidate are guaranteed.

. . . .

7. No person may be selected as a Parliamentary Labour Candidate by a Constituency Labour Party, and no Candidate may be endorsed by the National Executive Committee, if the person concerned:—

(a) Is not an Individual Member of the Party and, if eligible, is not a member of a Trade Union affiliated to the Trades Union Congress or recognised by the General Council of the Trades Union Congress as a *bona fide* Trade Union; or

(b) is a member of a Political Party or organisation ancillary or subsidiary thereto declared by the Annual Party Conference or by the National Executive Committee in pursuance of Conference decisions to be ineligible for affiliation to the Labour Party; or

(c) does not accept and conform to the Constitution, Programme, Principles, and Policy of the Party; or

(d) does not undertake to accept and act in harmony with the Standing Orders of the Parliamentary Labour Party.

· · · · · ·

CLAUSE X. AFFILIATION AND MEMBERSHIP FEES

1. Each affiliated organisation (other than Federations, Constituency and Central Labour Parties) shall pay an affiliation fee of 1s. per member per annum to the Party.

· · · · · ·

STANDING ORDERS

· · · · · ·

STANDING ORDER 3. VOTING

Voting at the Annual Party Conference shall be by cards on the following bases:—

(a) National and Constituency Organisations: One voting card for each 1,000 members or part thereof on whom affiliation fees were paid for the year ending December 31 preceding the Conference.

(b) Federations and Central Labour Parties: One voting card each.

· · · · · ·

STANDING ORDER 4. ELECTION OF THE NATIONAL EXECUTIVE COMMITTEE

1. For the purpose of nomination and election the National Executive Committee shall be divided into four Divisions:—

Division I shall consist of 12 members, to be nominated by Trade Unions from among their duly appointed delegates and elected by their delegations at the Annual Party Conference.

Division II shall consist of one member, to be nominated by Socialist, Co-operative, and Professional Organisations from among their duly appointed delegates and elected by their delegations at the Annual Party Conference.

Division III shall consist of seven members to be nominated by Federations, Constituency Labour Parties, and Central Labour Parties from among their duly appointed delegates and elected by their delegations at the Annual Party Conference. A Constituency Labour Party may nominate its Member of Parliament, or duly endorsed Candidate attending the Conference as an *ex-officio* member.

Division IV shall consist of five women members, to be nominated by any affiliated organisation, and elected by the Annual Party Conference as a whole. A Constituency Labour Party may nominate its woman Member of Parliament or duly endorsed woman Candidate attending as an *ex-officio* member of Conference.

2. The election for each Division shall be made by means of ballot vote on the card bases as provided in these Standing Orders.

3. Nominations for the National Executive Committee shall be made in accordance with the following conditions:—

. . . . . .

(*d*) Members of the General Council of the Trades Union Congress are not eligible for nomination to the National Executive Committee.

42.2 National Executive Committee of the Labour Party, *Report*[1] 1970

MEMBERSHIP[2]

		Trade Unions		Total Membership
		No.	Membership	ship
1918	...	131	2,960,409	... 3,013,129
1919	...	126	3,464,020	... 3,511,290
1920	...	122	4,317,537	... 4,359,807
1921	...	116	3,973,558	... 4,010,361
1922	...	102	3,279,276	... 3,311,036
1923	...	106	3,120,149	... 3,155,911
1924	...	108	3,158,002	... 3,194,399
1925	...	106	3,337,635	... 3,373,870
1926	...	104	3,352,347	... 3,388,286
1927	...	97	3,238,939	... 3,293,615
1928	...	91	2,025,139	... 2,292,169
1929	...	91	2,044,279	... 2,330,845
1930	...	89	2,011,484	... 2,346,908
1931	...	80	2,024,216	... 2,358,066
1932	...	75	1,960,269	... 2,371,787
1933	...	75	1,899,007	... 2,305,030

[1] Reproduced in *Labour Party Conference Report* 1970 (London, Labour Party, 1971).

[2] The Table given is an edited version of one covering the years 1900–1969 and containing also data on Constituency Parties, individual membership, and Socialist and Co-operative Societies, etc.

| | | *Trade Unions* | | *Total* |
		No.	*Membership*	*Membership*
1934	...	72	1,857,524	...	2,278,490
1935	...	72	1,912,924	...	2,377,515
1936	...	73	1,968,538	...	2,444,357
1937	...	70	2,037,071	...	2,527,672
1938	...	70	2,158,076	...	2,630,286
1939	...	72	2,214,070	...	2,663,067
1940	...	73	2,226,575	...	2,571,163
1941	...	68	2,230,728	...	2,485,458
1942	...	69	2,206,209	...	2,453,932
1943	...	69	2,237,307	...	2,503,240
1944	...	68	2,375,381	...	2,672,845
1945	...	69	2,510,369	...	3,038,697
1946	...	70	2,635,346	...	3,322,358
1947	...	73	4,386,074	...	5,040,299
1948	...	80	4,751,030	...	5,442,437
1949	...	80	4,946,207	...	5,716,947
1950	...	83	4,971,911	...	5,920,172
1951	...	82	4,937,427	...	5,849,002
1952	...	84	5,071,935	...	6,107,659
1953	...	84	5,056,912	...	6,096,022
1954	...	84	5,529,760	...	6,498,027
1955	...	87	5,605,988	...	6,483,994
1956	...	88	5,658,249	...	6,537,228
1957	...	87	5,644,012	...	6,582,549
1958	...	87	5,627,690	...	6,542,186
1959	...	87	5,564,010	...	6,436,986
1960	...	86	5,512,688	...	6,328,330
1961	...	86	5,549,592	...	6,325,607
1962	...	86	5,502,773	...	6,295,707
1963	...	83	5,507,232	...	6,358,436
1964	...	81	5,502,001	...	6,353,317
1965	...	79	5,601,982	...	6,439,893
1966	...	79	5,538,744	...	6,335,612
1967	...	75	5,539,562	...	6,294,614
1968	...	68	5,364,484	...	6,086,625
1969	...	68	5,461,721	...	6,163,882

42.3 *Labour Party Conference Report* 1968 (London, Labour Party, 1969)

STATEMENT OF ACCOUNTS FOR THE YEAR ENDING 31 DECEMBER 1967

GENERAL FUND

1966 £	INCOME	£	£
	AFFILIATION FEES:		
273,716	Trade Unions	276,902	
39,201	Labour Parties	37,848	
1,059	Socialist and Co-operative Societies ...	972	
313,976			315,722
	PUBLICATIONS:		
28,218	Sales	19,300	
5,556	Subscriptions	6,180	
33,774			25,480
	SUNDRY SALES AND FEES:		
3,036	Bookshop—Sales	2,372	
3,349	Summer Schools—Fees	2,991	
40	Study Courses—Fees	58	
10	Rents Receivable	10	
55	Royalties and Copyright Fees	230	
61	Membership Subscriptions—Overseas Residents	7	
6,551			5,668
	INVESTMENT INCOME (Gross):		
9,193	Interest on Investments	22,752	
22,854	Local Authority and Temporary Loan Interest	8,620	
597	Bank Interest	406	
32,644			31,778
£386,945			£378,648

42.4 Trades Union Congress, *Trade Unionism*[1] 2nd edition (London, Trades Union Congress, 1967)

THE STATE AND TRADE UNION FUNCTION

174 ... It is where trade unions are not competent, and recognise that they are not competent, to perform a function, that they welcome the state playing a role in at least enforcing minimum standards, but in Britain this role is recognised as the second best alternative to the development by workpeople themselves of the organisation, the competence, the representative capacity, to bargain and to achieve for themselves satisfactory terms and conditions of employment. In general, therefore, because this competence exists, the state stands aside, its attitude being one of abstention, of formal indifference.

175 ... Virtually all the traditional activities of the Ministry of Labour in the field of industrial relations can be described as complementary to free collective bargaining .... The difficult issues which arise regarding the role of the state concern the definition of what is complementary; in other words, which function trade unions should welcome the state performing and which functions if performed by the state would detract from the independence of the trade union Movement. Whether seeking legislation in a particular field is the most advantageous way for trade unions to proceed is a question which cannot be answered in the abstract. However, the considerations outlined above are relevant to every particular issue, for example, to the examination of such questions as trade union recognition, developing trade union membership, workers' rights in regard to dismissals procedure, equal pay, minimum wages, and the furtherance of industrial democracy.

176 The attitude of abstention which has become traditional in Britain still remains largely true. Yet a significant change has come about over the past five years, a change which is in the direction of statutory intervention. In brief, this change can be seen to arise from what may be termed an overall Government view of labour market policy as a key element in its economic policy. ...

177 ... These recent developments point in the direction of the Ministry of Labour itself becoming an economic Ministry. A rather different distinction is between functions which are alternative to bilateral regulation through bargaining and functions which are broadly complementary to bargaining, or strengthen bargaining as such. There are also functions which lie right outside the field of collective bargaining. The third distinction is between legislation broadly favourable to trade unions, and legislation which may be termed restrictive or unfavourable. Between these two there are statutes which are in this sense neutral.

178 In connection with this third distinction it should be pointed out that legislation favourable to unions does not logically strengthen the argument for unfavourable legislation as a sort of quid pro quo. Improving terms and conditions of employment and enhancing the freedom and dignity of workpeople is essentially a one way process, just as improving social security

[1] See footnote to Document 4.2.

arrangements is a continuing process. The TUC is careful not to make demands on the Government without considering this argument, but statutes such as the Industrial Training Act[1] and the Redundancy Payments Act[2] which are undoubtedly of benefit to working people are developments which from the Government's own point of view were absolutely necessary if, as part of its economic policy, it wished to see greater adaptability and mobility in the labour force.

179 A fourth distinction therefore is between Government action arising from its role as conciliator and that arising from its role as economic manager. The new interpretation of this latter role is one which trade unionists have some sympathy for, yet they have definite views about how Government should play this role. For Government to say that such and such action is necessary arising from the Government's role as economic manager and co-ordinator of the economy is to beg all sorts of questions. The way in which the Government should play its role will obviously reflect the great extension of responsibilities it now assumes. There can be no doubt, however, that the Government's new responsibilities in this field, and in particular the Government's preoccupation with productivity, prices and incomes, raise very difficult questions of conflicting function. In this general field, these new functions currently being debated concerning productivity, prices and incomes are predominantly "alternative" functions, as opposed to "complementary" ones, and the trade union Movement is naturally looking at them with some misgivings.

180 The main problems which affect current relations between trade unions and the state are not therefore connected with industrial conflict, or the law affecting trade disputes. . . . The difficulties stem from the increasingly positive role being played by the Government as economic manager. These problems are currently confused with the crisis in the British economy which makes the task of distinguishing short-term from long-term considerations especially vital. . . .

42.5 Trades Union Congress, *Incomes Policy* [Report of a Conference of Executive Committees of Affiliated Organisations held on 2nd March 1967 (London, Trades Union Congress, 1967), pp. 21–23, 25]

STATEMENT FOR GENERAL COUNCIL

· · · · · · ·

Mr. George Woodcock (General Secretary)

· · · · · · ·

So we want this policy and we want you to give us the right to go on with this constructive policy. . . . This is not an attempt, believe me, to pick a fight with the Labour Government or with any Government. Indeed, far from

[1] 1964.　　　　　　　　　　　　　　　　[2] 1965.

246

being an attempt to pick a fight with the Government, it fits in exactly with what I believe to be an inevitable relationship in these days between the trade union Movement and the Government of a democratic country.

In the 19th century we could and indeed we had to keep the Government at arm's length because of the way governments operated in those days. They were governments which believed as a matter of principle that it was wrong and would be futile in practice if the Government were to attempt to interfere in industry. They left industry severely alone—*laissez faire*, if you like, though this is perhaps too glib a description of the general attitude. At the most they came in to remedy the worst defects of industrialisation in the sense of bringing in a Factories Act to protect special classes like women and young persons. . . . They accepted no responsibility for the general level of activity. In our field in particular they offered us nothing—if they did not offer hostility at least they offered indifference. . . .

This is not the position today, as you know. Governments today, whether they like it or not, and whether we like it or not (and I like it very much) are in industry, are concerned with economic development and not simply concerned with a few safety measures in industry. They are concerned with economic growth and with the balance of payments. . . . It is not therefore surprising in my view that with all these responsibilities the Government also want to have an interest in wages. I do not consider this to be wrong on the part of the Government or vicious at all. I think it is natural, necessary and inevitable that they should want to be in on this question of wages. I believe they must be in on this question of wages. We are not trying to keep them out altogether. We must co-operate with governments these days.

These are two questions that arise. To what extent does the Government interfere? Where do the Government's interests in the field of wages stop? They have a right to a view, they have a right to point out how wage movements affect their ability to deal with these problems which we insist they shall undertake. The question is, where do they stop? Apart from the question of where they stop, there is the further question: on what terms do they seek our co-operation? We are not going to be told by governments just what we should do, and then do nothing but say, "Yes, sir, we will do it." We will not be made the agents of government, not because we are arrogant and conceited, but because we cannot be the agents of government and it would be wrong and not even in the interests of government if we were simply their agents. So we want to discuss all these problems with them, and put our views and let them put their views. Doing it in that way we can, we hope, get some kind of agreement both as to the area in which the Government operate and the means whereby they shall operate and the area in which the main responsibilities will be ours and the means by which we shall operate . . . But we will not enter into discussions under the limitation that we have to agree, which would mean that in many cases we find agreement in words even when we disagree or differ about real intention. That is not a way of going on. It is much better to discover the extent to which we genuinely agree and the points upon which we genuinely differ, than to paper over the cracks and give the appearance of agreement when in fact there is no such agreement.

The point is, that we want to work with governments. There can be no question about it; you could get rid of the whole of the General Council tomorrow and collect all the brightest and most militant lads from these executives to fill their places and they will have to work with government the day after you do it. The Government can say what they like to us. It is not a question whether we should talk to governments or not, it is a question of what weight you bring to bear in your discussions with government. We have to work with them, and we want to work with them. We are not seeking to fight the Government. Let me make this absolutely clear. . . . Their scheme involves sanctions. I think this is a pity. . . . I do not believe, to begin with, that at this stage, at any rate, whatever may happen as the years go by and things develop, legal penalites have any place in an incomes scheme when you are dealing with these problems of industrial relationships. Legal penalties could come in if you were adopting what I suppose would be popularly thought of as a Communist system where everything was regulated—profits, prices, raw material allocations, a whole host of things. In a tightly controlled system of that kind you might say, "We will have a similar tight control of labour." I would not like that, and I do not think it would work anyhow. But apart from the fact that we are not in this situation, our nature itself makes it impossible for us to envisage this as a contribution, and I believe that in so far as the Government seek to rely upon legal sanctions, they will find they come to a dead end with their policy.

42.6 *Trades Union Congress Report* 1960 (London, Trades Union Congress, 1960), pp. 396, 442–444

DISCUSSION ON THE REPORT OF THE GENERAL COUNCIL

WORLD PEACE

Mr. F. Cousins (*Transport and General Workers' Union*) moved the following motion:—

This Congress, believing that the great majority of the people of this country are earnestly seeking a lasting peace and recognising that the present state of world tension accentuates the great danger of an accidental drift into war, is convinced that the defence and foreign policies of the future Labour Government should be based upon:—

1. A complete rejection of any defence policy based on the threat of the use of strategic or tactical nuclear weapons.

2. The permanent cessation of the manufacture or testing of nuclear and thermo-nuclear weapons.

3. Patrols of aircraft carrying nuclear weapons and operating from British bases ceasing forthwith.

4. The continuation of the opposition to the establishment of missile bases in Great Britain.

5. A strengthening of the United Nations Organisation, including the admission of representatives of the Chinese Peoples Republic, with a

view to the creation of a new world order and the avoidance of a return to the methods of the cold war period.

6. Pressing for the re-opening of discussions between nations at the earliest possible moment as the means by which world disarmament and peaceful co-existence can be most readily achieved.

· · · · · · ·

PUBLIC OWNERSHIP

Mr. W. E. Padley, M.P. (*Union of Shop, Distributive and Allied Workers*) moved the following composite motion:—

This Congress reaffirms its belief in the principle of the common ownership and democratic control of those sections of industry which are vital to the well-being of the country and, recognising the vital contribution that public ownership has to make to the solution of many problems facing the nation, calls for the extension of that principle on a selective and progressive basis. It therefore calls upon the General Council to prepare a comprehensive report on the subject . . . Congress also calls upon the General Council to conduct a vigorous campaign to explain the moral and material benefits that would accrue to all sections of the community as a result of the application of the socialistic principle of control of the means of production, distribution and exchange in the national interest.

· · · · · · ·

Mr. F. Cousins: (*Transport and General Workers' Union*): . . . We are asking Congress to reaffirm a principle which it has held all the time. That is, that we believe in the public ownership of the means of production, distribution and exchange, and we know that the overwhelming feeling at Congress is in support of that line.

In fact, it might not have been necessary, even at this time, to have made reference to it, except for a growing development in certain parts of the Labour Movement to try to talk down the value of public ownership. You will be aware of the considerable controversies that have been going on within the Movement since the speech at the Conference of the Labour Party in November of last year, when references were made to the possible consequences on the election result of the beliefs we had expressed in public ownership.

· · · · · · ·

The control of power is vested in the control of many sections of industry. We cannot develop fully the economic forces of the country under a Socialist system without also having control of those means of production of wealth. But we do not want anyone to get the idea that we are seeking a modernised shopping list or a new edition of *Industry and Society*.[1] We want it to be clearly defined that we believe firmly in the principles of ownership on behalf of the public and that our endeavours will be to use and exercise that principle as and when we get the opportunity. . . .

· · · · · · ·

[1] *Industry and Society: Labour's Policy on Future Public Ownership* (London, The Labour Party, 1957).

249

... But what we want to reaffirm is that we cannot apply socialism fully without control of large sections of industry. Let us reaffirm our belief in that and let the world—and some of our comrades who may have different views in another conference chamber—know that that is where we stand because that is what we believe.

SERVING AS AGENCIES FOR COMMENTARY ON CONTEMPORARY ISSUES

43 The individual union

43.1 *Electron*[1] July 1961, p. 97

EDITORIAL OPINION

BRITAIN MUST NOT *JOIN THE COMMON MARKET*

Great Britain refused to enter the Common Market, except on her own conditions. When these proved unacceptable she joined in forming ... the European Free Trade Association—the Outer Seven. EFTA, as it was called, never became and could not become an effective answer to the European Common Market. This ineffectiveness led to demands that Britain should leave the European Free Trade Association and join the Common Market.

Insistent Demand

In recent months this demand has become more and more insistent. Its inspiration has come from two sources: the U.S.A. and the monopoly groupings inside Britain, some of whom are already established within the tariff ring of the Common Market.

The motives of the United States are clear: it wants the economy of Britain to be more closely integrated with the economy of the Common Market, which would allow American capitalism the more easily to penetrate the markets of the Commonwealth. The British monopolies want to share what it considers to be the not inconsiderable benefits to be derived from membership of the Common Market.

But membership of the Common Market means much more than economic integration. ...

Economic integration is to be the prelude to political integration. Western Germany, already the strongest economic and military partner of the Common Market, is bound to become its dominant political force. It is a frightening prospect and fraught with serious consequences.

It is already admitted that if Britain is to enter the Common Market, she

[1] The monthly journal of the Electrical Trades Union.

250

will have to sacrifice not only much of her economic independence, but also much of her political sovereignty. *She would become an exceedingly junior partner in a bloc dominated by Western Germany.* Vital economic and political decisions would be taken out of her hands. Her people would have no voice in the determination of the country's domestic and foreign policies.

. . . .

Good Reason to Stay Out

. . . Cut off from the reciprocal markets of the Commonwealth, her foreign trade with other countries restricted by the necessity imposed upon her to adapt her economy to the requirements of the Common Market, Great Britain could well become the economic backyard of Western Europe.

But there are other, more urgent and compelling reasons why the trade unionists should oppose Great Britain's entry into the European Common Market. We should be denied the right to determine our own living standards. We should be negotiating with employers whose powers of ultimate decision would not wholly reside in them. Finally, our autonomy as free and independent organisations would be seriously undermined because our policies would have to have relevance to the policies of other Common Market trade unions.

TO THE QUESTION SHOULD GREAT BRITAIN ENTER THE EUROPEAN COMMON MARKET, WE RETURN AN EMPHATIC "NO."

43.2 Cannon, L.,[1] *Automation* (*Electron*[2] October 1968, p. 162)

One aspect of the rapid technological advances of recent years has been the way in which the increased use of automation and computers has thrown up new problems of industrial relations.

By introducing automation and computers it is hoped to increase productivity and improve efficiency, which in turn will raise the living standards of us all.

Any discussion, therefore, on the subject of attitudes towards computers should be against this background of their ability to be used to increase national wealth. If this is not the object of their installation then their existence has no meaning for a country. This does not mean, however, that we should avoid or ignore the social consequences which arise when an industrial nation such as our own re-energises its machine by the introduction of a more advanced technology. Whole industries are declining and new ones such as electronics, automation and computers are springing up in their place.

As many people have said, we are in the throes of a second industrial revolution and just as the first transformed society so the impact of this one is creating difficulties for all of us who are involved in it.

[1] The then President of the Electrical Trades Union.
[2] The monthly journal of the Electrical Trades Union.

FEAR OF CHANGE

Most human beings react fearfully to any change in their established pattern of living; they generally have formed habits and routine which govern their behaviour at work and in their leisure time and which, since they are known, give them security and confidence. Any attempts to alter these routines are resisted not because the alternatives are in themselves unacceptable, but simply because they force people to create new patterns. So we must recognise immediately that the introduction of a computer into a factory or an office will generate opposition not of a reasoned kind which evaluates the useful and harmful aspects of such a product but the instinctive fear of reorganisation and the effects on the individual.

Contrary to ideas held by many people, the trade union movement does not oppose modernisation simply because it creates difficulty and does not want to see technical improvements suppressed or opposed on the grounds of fear of change. We feel that the impact of this new equipment should be strong and since it must increase productivity and efficiency will assist in convincing our members of its necessity if we are to go on being a major industrial power.

44 The Trades Union Congress

44.1 *Trades Union Congress Report* 1937 (London, Trades Union Congress, 1937), p. 266

DISCUSSION ON THE REPORT OF THE GENERAL COUNCIL

SITUATION IN SPAIN

. . . .

Sir Walter Citrine ... moved the following Composite Resolution:—

This Congress expresses its deep abhorrence of the murderous attacks on defenceless men, women and children in Spain by Franco's Fascists, aided by German, Italian and Moorish forces. It further deplores the fact that the British and other Governments continue to deny the legal Government of Spain the right under international law to purchase necessary arms and equipment, thus affording support to the Fascist rebels.

The Congress declares its complete solidarity with the Spanish Government in its new appeal to the League of Nations. The presence of a regular Italian army on Spanish soil is now officially and defiantly avowed by the head of the Italian Government. Acts of aggression against Spanish merchant ships and ships of other nations have been committed recently in different parts of the Mediterranean by ships of the Italian Navy. It should be obvious that armed foreign intervention in Spain, which now endangers the freedom of shipping in the Mediterranean, threatens to disturb international peace. It is therefore the duty of the Council of the League of Nations to examine this problem in all its aspects and to propose measures, including the withdrawal of foreign troops from Spain, which will effectively safeguard the peace of nations and enable the Spanish people to recover their political and territorial independence.

44.2 General Council of the Trades Union Congress, *The International Situation*[1] 1939

DECLARATION

1 Under the leadership of its Nazi Dictators, Germany has destroyed the peace and order of the world. By an appalling act of injustice and ill-will it has once more broken faith with the civilised nations and has deliberately provoked armed conflict in Europe to further its aims of domination and conquest. Its invasion of Poland by overwhelming military forces, beginning with the pitiless bombing of open towns, reveals the Nazi Government as the destroyer of the ordered life of mankind.

2 No opportunity was given to the Polish Government, or the Governments that were striving with its sincere co-operation and goodwill, to preserve peace, even to consider the demands of the German dictators. . . .

. . . .

4 Nor would compliance with these demands have satisfied the insane ambition of Germany's rulers. It would not have saved the peace of Europe. Congress places upon them the supreme responsibility for this war. . . .

5 This Congress believes that the Nazi Government, having chosen for its people the way of war, must be resisted to the utmost. . . . Congress, with a united and resolute nation, enters the struggle with a clear conscience and steadfast purpose.

6 Finally, Congress renews its most earnest appeal to those of the German people who are conscious of the dreadful crime their rulers have committed in forcing this war. . . .

7 We make a renewed appeal to the German workers who, violently torn apart from the International Trade Union Movement, have, we believe, never lost their sense of comradeship and loyalty to the principles upon which the cause of the organised workers is founded. We recall to them the efforts made by our Trade Union and Labour Movement to secure justice and fair play for the German people at the end of the tragedy of 1914–1918. . . . We declare that our efforts are directed solely against the destroyers of freedom and the enemies of peace. The organised millions of Trade Unionists, in whose name this Congress speaks, will carry on our struggle until aggression has been eliminated from the adjustment of international relations, and until the principles of democratic order and justice have been established upon an unassailable foundation.

[1] Published as Appendix B of the *Trades Union Congress Report* 1939 (London, Trades Union Congress, 1939).

44.3 *Trades Union Congress Report* 1933 (London, Trades Union Congress, 1933), pp. 261–263

DISCUSSION ON THE REPORT OF THE GENERAL COUNCIL
UNEMPLOYMENT AND INDUSTRIAL RECOVERY

Mr. Walter M. Citrine (General Secretary)... moved the following resolution:—

This Congress records its strongest protest against the continued failure of the present Government to take effective measures against unemployment, to support the proposal for the 40-hour week and the construction of useful public works, and to produce a positive policy for promoting the recovery of industry and trade.

Whilst reaffirming belief that social ownership and control furnishes the only adequate and lasting solution to the problems, Congress appreciates the significance of the vigorous efforts now being made by President Roosevelt towards the stimulation and regulation of industry by means of the Industrial Recovery Act and allied legislation; it welcomes the recognition given in that legislation, and in the "codes of fair practice" promulgated thereunder, to the trade union policy of reducing working hours as a means of diminishing unemployment, and of raising wages as a means of increasing purchasing power.

Congress congratulates the American trade unions upon their energetic assertion of the workers' right to bargain collectively through their own independent organisations. Congress expresses the earnest hope that with the co-operation of the trade unions President Roosevelt will be able to overcome the difficulties involved in this decisive departure from the traditional individualism of American industry.

Congress further trusts that the present British Government will pursue a similar policy by taking immediate steps to initiate useful schemes of public works, financed by the use of the national credit; to enact a maximum working week of 40 hours without reductions of wages; to prohibit child labour under 16 years of age, and to raise the school-leaving age to 16.

Further, that the Government will set an example to employers by raising wages in the public services, beginning with the restoration of the "economy" cuts in wages, salaries, and social services; to make more liberal provision for pensioning aged workers; and generally to take all possible measures for increasing the purchasing power of the masses, and for planning the economic life of the nation in the interests of the whole people.

He said the resolution commenced, as would be observed, by a perfectly justifiable and well-merited protest against the failure of the present Government to apply some effective remedies for the desperate situation that now existed. ... No Government, of recent days at least, had been faced with an opportunity at once so great and a responsibility so heavy. ...

... The British Government believed quite firmly in a policy which had been described as deflationist, but which might be described as contractionist. They believed that somehow or other, prices having fallen, wages and the standard of life generally at some stage must be adjusted to that fall in prices; that social activity of almost every kind must be curtailed, and that public and private expenditure must follow the line of economy in order that stability at the lower levels should be reached. At all events, that was the policy they had pursued since they were returned as a Government in 1931. This Congress, however, had protested continuously and steadfastly against that policy. They believed it was entirely misdirected, and...could only lead to an intensification of the depression. ... The expansionist policy which was now being pursued in the United States and which in a greater or lesser degree had been advocated by this Congress through its reports and resolutions, was receiving a much greater measure of support than at any period in the post-war history.

Members of the present Government did not quite know where they were.... Their declarations were expansionist but their actions were deflationist. They were now producing the hoary and discredited device of trying to raise prices, not by increasing purchasing power, but by curtailing supplies. They were not aiming at stimulating demand and increasing purchasing power, which would inevitably be reflected in a recovery in the home market, but they were pursuing a national form of ca' canny which, if pursued industrially by any of the trade unions, would be denounced upon all sides. Of course they did not call it ca' canny, they called it quantitative restriction, but its effects were the same. Far from trying to stimulate social activity they declined absolutely to invest in a scheme of public works such as ... had been advocated by this Congress as part of the T.U.C. policy, despite the fact that to-day it would be true to say that nearly every reputable economist in this country was convinced that the moment had arrived when public expenditure of that kind should be undertaken. Similarly they declined internationally to reduce working hours, and yet they complained of international competition which they said prevented them from making any attempt along those lines. ... They preached international co-operation but they practised economic self-sufficiency. They erected tariff barriers, while at the same time they denounced tariff barriers as one of the causes of the depression.

Now they were claiming credit for the slight improvement in trade which had taken place in many parts of the world. The causes of that improvement were as yet very vague and ill-defined. He would be a bold man who would say that the improvement would be continued. One hoped for the best while fearing the worst. They were told by the economists that the trade cycle was responsible for this improvement and that now the trade cycle was on the upward grade. If that was true now was the time to help that trade cycle by a bold policy of expansion such as was being followed in the United States. But the only policy adopted by the British Government was to send up prices by creating an artificial scarcity. It was the well-worn device of an inefficient and discredited capitalism.

44.4 General Council of the Trades Union Congress, *Report to Congress: Promotion and Encouragement of the Arts* [*Trades Union Congress Report* 1961 (London, Trades Union Congress, 1961), pp. 197–198]

THE SCALE OF PROVISION OF CULTURAL FACILITIES

. . . .

There can be little doubt . . . that public support for the arts is at present totally inadequate. . . .

. . . .

The inadequacy of public financial support for the arts has inevitably limited the scale of provision of non-commercial cultural facilities and has thus restricted access to such facilities by workers (and by members of the community generally). This situation has been to some extent accentuated by the failure of public authorities to provide adequate facilities to meet the distinctive leisure-time needs of certain groups within the population which include substantial numbers of members of workers' families. The neglect of the Youth Service over a period of many years, the failure to make adequate provision for the interests of old people, and the limited provision of leisure-time facilities for housewives, have in themselves deprived many members of workers' families of wider opportunities for cultural activities.

. . . The numerous local voluntary societies concerned in all areas with the arts and cultural activities . . . provide many workers with opportunities to pursue cultural interests which would otherwise be denied them. The degree to which such societies can thrive is therefore a significant factor affecting the extent to which workers can participate in cultural facilities. . . .

. . . .

The facilities available to workers for participation in cultural activities are . . . inadequate, particularly in the localities, both in scale and quality. . . .

That the trade union Movement has an interest and responsibility in this matter is not in question. "The function of trade unionism," stated the General Council in 1946[1] . . . "does not end with securing the worker improvements as regards his conditions of work. . . . Beyond day-to-day questions it is concerned with seeing that the worker has the widest opportunity for a full life, and if there are respects in which facilities available to him for the use and enjoyment of his leisure can be improved, in pursuing such improvement. There is another sense in which the Movement has a direct interest in leisure. In so far as it relies for its strength on a conscious community of interest and aspiration, it is concerned that the mass of the population shall not be merely passive recipients of provided entertainments and pastimes. Mental inertia is the greatest enemy of trade unionism, as of democracy generally. We are, therefore, concerned that people should be alive and critical in their appreciation of and participation in social activities of all kinds."

[1] General Council of the Trades Union Congress, *Report to Congress: Leisure* [*Trades Union Congress Report* 1946 (London, Trades Union Congress, 1946), p. 125].

"At the same time," continued the General Council, "we would not consider it any part of our business to pass judgment on the way in which people spend their leisure . . . our main interest is that there shall be available to the worker the fullest possible facilities for a satisfying use of leisure, and that good standards by which people may judge for themselves the use to which their leisure shall be put, shall be encouraged."

These views concerning the problem of leisure generally hold good today.

INTERNATIONAL ACTIVITIES

45 Purpose

45.1 Trades Union Congress, *Trade Unionism*[1] 2nd edition (London, Trades Union Congress, 1967)

INTERNATIONAL ACTIVITIES

153 The broad objectives of trade unionism are similar throughout the world, but the methods employed to achieve them are conditioned by national circumstances of great variety. From the early days of the Movement there has been a genuine sense of international fraternity amongst trade unionists. This has been given a new emphasis by the steady increase in the number of enterprises which operate on an international basis and also by the recent growth of regional and world-wide institutions . . .

154 In general, international trade union activity brings about a very wide interchange of experience and ideas and is an important element in trade union competence at the national as well as the international level. At national level, it widens both the conceptions of trade union objectives and the methods employed to attain them. At international level, it makes possible the development and expression of trade union views on matters of broad social and political interest as well as on more immediate practical issues. . . . As far as the British trade union Movement is concerned, the overall effect of its international experience has probably been to strengthen its characteristic reliance on flexibility of method in a great variety of circumstances.

[1] See footnote to Document 4.2.

46 The individual union

46.1 Amalgamated Engineering Union, *Rules* 1965

MEMBERS OVERSEAS

RULE 42[1]

AUTONOMY

Notwithstanding any conditions stipulated in these rules respecting the powers of the Commonwealth Council and Branches, the Executive Council shall have power to enter into negotiations with such Council with a view to making arrangements to grant the Commonwealth Council complete autonomy and to make financial arrangements mutually satisfactory. If the circumstances warrant, the Executive Council shall also have power to completely sever connection with the Commonwealth Council or all or any branches abroad.

RULE 43[2]

COMMONWEALTH COUNCIL

1. There shall be a Commonwealth Council vested with authoritative and administrative powers sufficient to enable them to protect and advance the interests of the Union in the Commonwealth. Their duties shall be as hereafter set forth, subject generally to the rules of the Union and to the Executive Council.

2. The Commonwealth Council shall consist of three members and a Chairman and Secretary, who must possess the qualifications applicable to other General Officers ...

.   .   .   .

5. The Commonwealth Council shall be located in such place as the majority of members voting in the Commonwealth shall decide.

6. For the purpose of electing Commonwealth Councilmen the branches shall be grouped to form three divisions ...

7. There shall be eight Organisers for the Commonwealth, nominated and elected under the rules governing General Officers ...

.   .   .   .

8. The Commonwealth Council may consult their members whenever they deem it necessary on the propriety of raising or replenishing a Fund for the following purposes: for making grants to members in distressed circumstances, for the payment of additional full-time Officers, for the supplementing of the salaries of General Officers, for granting assistance to our own and other trades, for the provision of motor transport for organising staff ... They may

---

[1] After the formation of the Amalgamated Union of Engineering and Foundry Workers in 1967, the Rules of the A.E.U. continued to apply to the Engineering Section. In 1968, Rule 42 was replaced by a version reading: 'The Executive Council shall have power to sever connections with all or any branches abroad'.

[2] Severance was effected in 1968, and this Rule deleted.

open new branches and shall have power to issue a quarterly report and an abstract of the financial reports of their respective branches, and shall purchase all stationery and books that may be required for the purposes of the Union in the Commonwealth. . . . They shall also arrange to register travelling cards and regulate the nomination and election of delegates. They shall have power to decide on disputed points of rule in all branches under their jurisdiction, and publish the same, subject to the members' right of appeal to the Executive Council and Final Appeal Court. They may also authorise the registration of any of their members going to a State or territory where there is no branch of the Union.

In the Commonwealth, District Committees shall have power to direct branches under their jurisdiction to summon meetings to take a ballot vote of members upon the desirability of raising a levy of the district for the assistance of other trade unions, or towards the election expenses of direct Labour candidates to Parliament; but no such levy shall be in force for a longer period than 13 weeks without a further vote of the members in the district being taken, and separate levies shall be raised for each and all of the objects herein mentioned, and the votes of the members shall be taken separately upon each portion.

. . . .

10. The members of the Union in Australia shall be a section of the Union under the jurisdiction of the Commonwealth Council, which section shall consist of all the branches in Australia, and shall be subject to the general and special rules of the Union.

11. The members in the Commonwealth shall have power from time to time to adopt any rules to enable the Australian section of the Union to comply with the conditions prescribed by any Labour Legislation enacted in the Commonwealth, and to repeal and alter any such rules or any existing rules for the purpose of complying with such conditions, but shall have no power to abrogate any of the benefits of the Union, and any rules so adopted or altered shall be binding on the members of the Union in the Commonwealth.

46.2 International Transport Workers' Federation, *Constitution* 1968

PREAMBLE

The International Transport Workers' Federation, founded in 1896, is an international organization which aims to embrace transport workers' trade unions of all countries, irrespective of colour, nationality, race or creed.

It is a free trade union body, established to defend and further internationally the economic and social interests of transport workers of all kinds, and their trade unions. It stands for the defence of democracy and freedom and is opposed to colonialism, totalitarianism and aggression in all their forms and to any discrimination based on colour, nationality, sex, race or creed.

Its activities shall be governed by the following Constitution, in which the term "the ITF" shall be understood to mean the International Transport

T

Workers' Federation. . . . For working purposes, the affiliated organizations' declared membership is divided into the following industrial sections:

Railwaymen's Section
Road Transport Workers' Section
Inland Navigation Section
Dockers' Section
Seafarers' Section
Fishermen's Section
Civil Aviation Section
Allied Industries and Services Section

RULE I—AIMS AND METHODS

1. In all aspects of its work the ITF subscribes fully to the principles of the world free trade union movement and the aims and ideals of the International Labour Organization (ILO) in particular as stated in its Declaration of Philadelphia[1] of 1944.

2. The aims of the ITF shall be:

a) to promote universal recognition of Conventions No. 87 and 98[2] of the International Labour Organization, concerning respectively Freedom of Association and Protection of the Right to Organize and to Bargain Collectively and other relevant instruments of that Organization;

b) to support the work of the United Nations, its agencies, other inter-governmental and non-governmental organizations in those activities promoting peace based on social justice and economic progress;

c) to assist affiliated organizations to defend and promote, internationally, the economic, social, occupational, educational and cultural interests of their members;

d) to assist affiliated organizations by developing research activities on problems and trends affecting their members, on working conditions, labour legislation, trade union organization and education, collective bargaining and other matters related to the achievement of the ITF's aims.

3. The ITF shall seek to achieve its aims by the following methods:

a) establishing and promoting close relations among trade union organizations in transport and allied services and foremost among its affiliates nationally and internationally;

b) assisting affiliates in their drives to organize the unorganized, in their educational and legislative efforts in general and in particular in those countries where economic development and nation-building call for special efforts in the spirit of international brotherhood and solidarity;

c) promoting and co-ordinating schemes of mutual assistance among affiliates in different countries and supporting, by appropriate means, affiliates engaged in disputes;

d) seeking and using the right to represent its affiliates in and to co-operate with, the International Labour Organization and inter-governmental agencies and other bodies concerned with transport;

[1] See Document 47.4.   [2]See Documents 6.1 and 6.2.

260

e) collaborating, wherever possible and conducive to the attainment of its objectives, with other international trade secretariats and with the International Confederation of Free Trade Unions (ICFTU);

f) disseminating information to affiliates and other interested parties through its publications or documentation as appropriate and by initiating and co-ordinating activities on an international scale.

RULE II—MEMBERSHIP AND OBLIGATIONS

1. Trade union organizations or, where appropriate, Federations or Associations of such organizations are eligible for affiliation to the ITF, provided that:

a) they subscribe to the aims of the ITF and undertake to uphold its Constitution and to promote the interests of the ITF in general;

b) their constitution and practice ensure democratic conduct of their affairs;

c) they undertake to fulfil the obligations arising from affiliation.

. . . .

3. Affiliates of the ITF are required:

a) to pay affiliation fees at the rates and under the conditions laid down by the appropriate bodies of the ITF ...

b) to send to the ITF relevant publications and reports on activities and to furnish any other information which may be of interest to the work of the ITF;

c) to co-operate in carrying out the decisions of the governing bodies of the ITF, and to report to the ITF on the action taken to that end and its results, or on the reasons why no action has been taken;

d) to report to their governing bodies on the activities of the ITF and to inform constituent bodies and rank and file members of the work and purposes of the ITF;

e) to encourage the establishment of advisory committees of affiliated organizations at national level to discuss and co-ordinate ITF activities;

. . . .

4. In assuming these obligations, an organization admitted to membership shall retain its full autonomy.

. . . .

RULE IV—CONGRESS

1. There shall be a Congress which shall have supreme authority. An Ordinary Congress shall take place every three years at a time and place to be decided by the Executive Board.

. . . .

RULE V—GENERAL COUNCIL

1. There shall be a General Council which shall be next in authority to the Congress. . . .

. . . .

RULE VI—EXECUTIVE BOARD

1. There shall be an Executive Board which shall consist of twenty-two members, elected by Congress from among the members of the General Council, and the General Secretary. . . .

. . . . . .

RULE XII—REGIONAL AND OTHER ORGANIZATION

The Executive Board shall have authority to establish regional and other offices or bodies of the ITF and determine their terms of reference.

RULE XIII—INDUSTRIAL SECTIONS AND SPECIAL DEPARTMENTS

1. There shall be industrial sections, as defined in the Preamble of this Constitution, to deal with matters concerning individual branches of transport and allied activities. The Executive Board shall have authority to set up such further sections or special departments as deemed necessary to improve the services of the ITF to its affiliates . . .

. . . . . .

RULE XIV—ASSISTANCE IN DISPUTES

1. Affiliated organizations may call upon the ITF for assistance in disputes of major importance.

2. Such assistance may consist of organized moral support of the affiliate and its stand on the issues involved in the dispute, of approaches to national governments and inter-governmental organizations, of financial help or a combination of these or any other steps deemed appropriate in the circumstances.

3. The ITF shall be given as much notice as possible of the likelihood of such a dispute and as much information as possible on the issues involved and on the attitude to the dispute of other affiliates and important trade union organizations in the country where the dispute takes place.

4. An affiliate facing an important dispute which may involve the ITF shall not call upon affiliates of the ITF outside its own country for assistance without having first consulted with the General Secretary of the ITF. The same applies to calls to non-affiliated organizations abroad for assistance or support. Contraventions of this provision shall absolve the ITF from any obligation to give or continue to give support.

47 The Trades Union Congress

47.1 International Confederation of Free Trade Unions *Constitution* 1969

AIMS

The International Confederation of Free Trade Unions declares its aims to be:

(*a*) to maintain and develop a powerful and effective international organisation at world-wide and regional levels, composed of free and democratic trade unions, independent of any external domination and pledged to the task of promoting the interests of working people throughout the world and of enhancing the dignity of labour;

(*b*) to seek the universal recognition and application of the rights of trade union organisation;

(*c*) to further the establishment, maintenance, and development of free trade unions, particularly in economically under-developed countries;

(*d*) to weld international trade union solidarity by giving succour to the victims of all kinds of oppression, by giving token assistance to those suffering from the consequences of natural and industrial disasters and by providing support in all other cases where workers should stand shoulder to shoulder;

(*e*) to undertake and coordinate the defence of the free trade unions against any campaign aiming at their destruction or at the restriction of their rights or at the infiltration and subjugation of labour organisations by totalitarian or other anti-labour forces;

(*f*) to assist in providing peoples who have been victims of war and subjugation with all practicable means for the speedy rebuilding of their economies and in promoting international measures of aid for them, with full respect for their political and economic independence;

(*g*) to strive for the establishment of full employment, the improvement of working conditions, the introduction, maintenance and extension of social security for all, and the raising of the standard of living of peoples of all countries of the world;

(*h*) to encourage the development of the resources of all countries in order to further the economic, social and cultural progress of the peoples of the world, and particularly of economically under-developed countries and non-selfgoverning territories;

(*i*) to advocate, with a view to raising the general level of prosperity, increased and properly planned economic cooperation among the nations in such a way as will encourage the development of wider economic units and freer exchange of commodities and to seek full participation of workers' representatives in official bodies dealing with these questions;

(*j*) to protect, maintain and expand the system of free labour and to eliminate forced labour everywhere;

(*k*) to represent the free trade union movement in all international agencies

263

which exist or may be set up to perform functions affecting the social and economic conditions of working people and to further the implementation of their decisions whenever desirable;

(*l*) to establish and extend association with international organisations, both governmental and non-governmental, in work which will further the aims of the International Confederation of Free Trade Unions in protecting and advancing the interests of the peoples generally and guaranteeing human rights;

(*m*) to support the establishment of a world system of collective security, but pending its attainment to further and support within the Charter of the United Nations all measures that are necessary for assuring the defence of world democracy and the freedom of nations against any totalitarian or imperialist aggression;

(*n*) to carry out a programme of trade union and workers' education as a necessary adjunct to the Confederation's organisational activities in those countries where trade unions do not yet exist or are still weak and also as a means of promoting better understanding of the tasks of the free trade union movement everywhere;

(*o*) to engage in and foster publicity work which will increase the knowledge and understanding of national and international problems confronting the workers, so as to enable them to make their struggle more efficacious and so as to realise the widest support for the Confederation's activities;

(*p*) to maintain and develop an international clearing-house of information and research on the problems of trade union organisation, wages and working conditions, labour legislation, collective bargaining and any other matter related to the implementation of the Confederation's aims.

MEMBERSHIP

ARTICLE I

(*a*) All bona fide national trade union centres accepting the aims and Constitution of the Confederation shall be eligible for membership.

(*b*) Individual bona fide trade union organisations which accept the aims and Constitution of the Confederation may be admitted into affiliation provided that the Executive Board, following consultation with the affiliated national centre or national centres of the country concerned, is satisfied that such affiliation is desirable. The decision to accept such applications shall in every case require a three-quarters majority of the Executive Board members present.

(*c*) The autonomy of affiliated organisations is guaranteed.

. . . .

(*i*) The Executive Board shall have the right to suspend, and the Congress shall have the right to expel, after charges have been preferred, a member organisation for action deemed by those bodies to be in contravention of this Constitution, or against the interests of world labour. Provision shall be made for a hearing of charges before a decision is rendered. The procedure for such hearings shall be laid down by the Executive Board.

. . . .

CONGRESS

ARTICLE II

(*a*) In the determination of the programme and policy of the organisation and in the interpretation of this Constitution, the supreme authority shall be the Congress.

(*b*) The regular Congress shall be convened at least once every three years.

. . . .

ARTICLE IV: REPRESENTATION

(*a*) The Congress is composed of delegates of the affiliated organisations . . . on the following basis:

(i) representation of national trade union centres:

Up to 100,000 members	1 delegate
Between 100,001 and 250,000 members . .	2 delegates
Between 250,001 and 500,000 members . .	4 delegates
Between 500,001 and 2,000,000 members . .	6 delegates
Between 2,000,001 and 5,000,000 members . .	8 delegates
Between 5,000,001 and 7,500,000 members . .	12 delegates
Between 7,500,001 and 10,000,000 members . .	15 delegates
Over 10,000,000 members	20 delegates

(ii) representation of individual trade unions:

Up to 100,000 members	1 delegate
Over 100,000 members	2 delegates

Delegates shall have the right to speak and to vote.

. . . .

(*c*) The International Trade Secretariats, associated with the Confederation in accordance with Article XXIII of this Constitution, are entitled to send representatives having the right to take part in the debates but not to vote, on the following basis:

Up to 1,000,000 members	1 representative
Between 1,000,001 and 2,000,000 members .	2 representatives
Between 2,000,001 and 4,000,000 members .	3 representatives
Over 4,000,000 members	4 representatives

. . . .

ARTICLE XI: VOTING

(*a*) The endeavour of the Congress shall be to secure the widest possible measure of agreement rather than the carrying of simple majorities. When a vote is called for, however, the decision of the Congress shall be by majority, except in the case of proposals for the amendment of the Constitution, the expulsion of an organisation or the suspension of Standing Orders, which must secure two-thirds of the votes cast.

(*b*) Voting shall, as a rule, be by show of hands, but, at the request of any two or more delegations representing at least 25% of the Congress membership, a roll-call vote shall be taken, in which each delegation shall cast its vote as a unit on the basis of the membership it represents.

. . . .

EXECUTIVE BOARD
ARTICLE XIII: COMPOSITION

(*a*) There shall be elected by the Congress an Executive Board having twenty-nine members nominated by the respective areas as follows:

Africa.	3
Asia	5
Middle East	2
Australia and New Zealand	1
Britain	2
All other countries of Europe	6
Latin America	3
North America	6
West Indies.	1

Furthermore, a representative elected by the ICFTU/ITS[1] Advisory Committee on Women Workers' Questions shall be entitled to take part in Executive Board meetings on a consultative basis.

. . . .

(*f*) Representation of International Trade Secretariats shall be in accordance with arrangements made under Article XXIII.

. . . .

ARTICLE XIV: MEETINGS

(*a*) The Executive Board shall meet not less than twice a year. . . .

. . . .

ARTICLE XV: COMPETENCE

(*a*) The Executive Board shall have the authority to act on behalf of the Confederation. It shall be responsible for directing the activities of the Confederation and giving effect to the decisions and recommendations of the Congress.

. . . .

ARTICLE XVII: SUB-COMMITTEE

(*a*) At its meeting immediately following the Congress the Executive Board shall elect a Sub-Committee composed of the President, the General Secretary and up to nine members of the Board. This Sub-Committee shall be consulted whenever questions of urgency or importance arise between meetings of the Executive Board.

. . . .

REGIONAL ORGANISATIONS
ARTICLE XIX

(*a*) Regional organisations shall be established as organic parts of the Confederation for such areas as may be determined by the Executive Board.

. . . .

[1] International Trade Secretariats.

(*c*) It shall be the task of the regional organisations to deal with problems affecting the workers and the trade unions in their respective areas and to further the aims and objects of the Confederation as set out in this Constitution.

. . . .

(*g*) The regional organisations shall be answerable for their actions to the Confederation, and shall submit annual reports on their activities to the Executive Board. All questions involving modifications in the general policy of the ICFTU shall be referred to the Executive Board.

FINANCE

ARTICLE XX

(*a*) The activities of the Confederation shall be financed out of income deriving from:
    (i) regular affiliation fees;
    (ii) special levies;
    (iii) voluntary contributions.

(*b*) Affiliated organisations shall pay regular affiliation fees at the rate of BFR 1,900 or US $38 or £ sterling 15.16.8 per thousand members or part thereof.

(*c*) The Congress may decide to empower the Executive Board to levy affiliated organisations to an amount to be fixed by the Congress which shall also decide the nature, duration and purpose of such levies.

(*d*) The Congress or the Executive Board may decide to organise fundraising campaigns based on voluntary contributions towards a well defined programme. Funds thus collected shall not be used for other purposes, unless the contributors so agree.

. . . .

COOPERATION WITH INTERNATIONAL TRADE SECRETARIATS

ARTICLE XXIII

Arrangements shall be made for the most effective cooperation between the Confederation and the International Trade Secretariats in the performance of their functions.

47.2 International Confederation of Free Trade Unions, *Report on Activities 1965–69* (Brussels, I.C.F.T.U., 1969), pp. 29–31

COOPERATION WITH INTERNATIONAL TRADE SECRETARIATS

. . . .

ITS *GENERAL CONFERENCES*

. . . .

The main topic on the agenda of the 1966 and 1967 general conferences was the so-called "Milan agreement" adopted at the second world congress (Milan, 1951) summarising the relationship that existed between the ICFTU and ITS at that time.

At the 1966 conference, the ICFTU general secretary introduced proposals for adapting the agreement to the changed circumstances and further proposals were put forward in the discussion. . . .

. . . .

The text of the new agreement incorporating all these changes was submitted anew to the ICFTU executive board at its 43rd meeting (Brussels, October 1967), which recommended its ratification by the 9th ICFTU world congress. The full text is now as follows:

"(i) The ICFTU recognises the autonomy of the ITS; the ITS and the ICFTU will cooperate in all questions of common interest. The ICFTU recognises the ITS general conference as giving collective representation, but this recognition does not prevent the ICFTU from having individual relations with the ITS.

(ii) The ICFTU and the ITS recognise that they are in fact part of the same international trade union movement. This implies the adoption by the ITS of the general policy of the ICFTU.

(iii) So as to keep the ITS regularly informed on the general policy of the ICFTU and to afford them the opportunity of expressing their opinions on this subject, and in order to be able to discuss together all the problems of common interest, it is decided that:

(a) the ITS shall be invited to send up to two representatives to the meetings of the ICFTU sub-committee of the executive board, and up to four representatives to the meetings of the ICFTU executive board. These representatives shall have consultative status;

(b) the ITS shall be invited to participate in the congress of the ICFTU, their representation to be fixed on the following basis:
Up to 1,000,000 members . . . . 1 delegate
1,000,000–3,000,000 members . . . . 2 delegates
Over 3,000,000 members . . . . . 3 delegates;

(c) on the other hand, the ITS shall invite the ICFTU to take part in their general conference, whilst the ITS shall individually invite the ICFTU to their general conferences and to other important meetings of common interest with consultative status;

(iv) In order to discuss major questions, including divergences of opinion on subjects of common interest, a joint council shall be set up, composed of the representatives of the ITS and a delegation from the ICFTU executive board. This joint council shall meet upon the request of either of the parties.

(v) This agreement shall replace the Milan agreement of 1951 after ratification by the ICFTU and the ITS."

. . . .

NEW ARRANGEMENTS FOR ICFTU/ITS COOPERATION
. . . . . .

An agreement whereby the ICFTU would provide the services hitherto furnished by the Geneva liaison office[1] was negotiated in January 1966 . . . According to this agreement the ICFTU would provide liaison between the ITS and intergovernmental agencies (notably the ILO) and information services covering important trade union developments including those taking place behind the iron curtain. . . .

47.3 International Labour Organisation, *Constitution* 1968

PREAMBLE

Whereas universal and lasting peace can be established only if it is based upon social justice;

And whereas conditions of labour exist involving such injustice, hardship and privation to large numbers of people as to produce unrest so great that the peace and harmony of the world are imperilled; and an improvement of those conditions is urgently required: as, for example, by the regulation of the hours of work, including the establishment of a maximum working day and week, the regulation of the labour supply, the prevention of unemployment, the provision of an adequate living wage, the protection of the worker against sickness, disease and injury arising out of his employment, the protection of children, young persons and women, provision for old age and injury, protection of the interests of workers when employed in countries other than their own, recognition of the principle of equal remuneration for work of equal value, recognition of the principle of freedom of association, the organisation of vocational and technical education and other measures;

Whereas also the failure of any nation to adopt humane conditions of labour is an obstacle in the way of other nations which desire to improve the conditions in their own countries;

The High Contracting Parties, moved by sentiments of justice and humanity as well as by the desire to secure the permanent peace of the world, and with a view to attaining the objectives set forth in this Preamble, agree to the following Constitution of the International Labour Organisation:

[1] Of the ITS. The office was closed in 1966.

CHAPTER I—ORGANISATION

ARTICLE 1

1. A permanent organisation is hereby established for the promotion of the objects set forth in the Preamble to this Constitution and in the Declaration concerning the aims and purposes of the International Labour Organisation[1] adopted at Philadelphia on 10 May 1944 . . .

2. The Members of the International Labour Organisation shall be the States which were Members of the Organisation on 1 November 1945, and such other States as may become Members in pursuance of the provisions of paragraphs 3 and 4 of this article.

3. Any original Member of the United Nations and any State admitted to membership of the United Nations by a decision of the General Assembly in accordance with the provisions of the Charter may become a Member of the International Labour Organisation by communicating to the Director-General of the International Labour Office its formal acceptance of the obligations of the Constitution of the International Labour Organisation.

4. The General Conference of the International Labour Organisation may also admit Members to the Organisation by a vote concurred in by two-thirds of the delegates attending the session, including two-thirds of the Government delegates present and voting. Such admission shall take effect on the communication to the Director-General of the International Labour Office by the government of the new Member of its formal acceptance of the obligations of the Constitution of the Organisation.

. . . .

ARTICLE 2

The permanent organisation shall consist of—
(*a*) a General Conference of representatives of the Members;
(*b*) a Governing Body composed as described in article 7; and
(*c*) an International Labour Office controlled by the Governing Body.

. . . .

ARTICLE 7

1. The Governing Body shall consist of forty-eight persons—
Twenty-four representing governments,
Twelve representing the employers, and
Twelve representing the workers.

. . . .

4. The persons representing the employers and the persons representing the workers shall be elected respectively by the Employers' delegates and the Workers' delegates to the Conference.

5. The period of office of the Governing Body shall be three years. If for any reason the Governing Body elections do not take place on the expiry of this period, the Governing Body shall remain in office until such elections are held.

. . . .

[1] See Document 47.4.

ARTICLE 10

1. The functions of the International Labour Office shall include the collection and distribution of information on all subjects relating to the international adjustment of conditions of industrial life and labour, and particularly the examination of subjects which it is proposed to bring before the Conference with a view to the conclusion of international Conventions, and the conduct of such special investigations as may be ordered by the Conference or by the Governing Body.

. . . .

ARTICLE 19

1. When the Conference has decided on the adoption of proposals with regard to an item on the agenda, it will rest with the Conference to determine whether these proposals should take the form: (*a*) of an international Convention, or (*b*) of a Recommendation to meet circumstances where the subject, or aspect of it, dealt with is not considered suitable or appropriate at that time for a Convention.

2. In either case a majority of two-thirds of the votes cast by the delegates present shall be necessary on the final vote for the adoption of the Convention or Recommendation, as the case may be, by the Conference.

. . . .

5. In the case of a Convention—

. . . .

(*b*) each of the Members undertakes that it will, within the period of one year at most from the closing of the session of the Conference, or if it is impossible owing to exceptional circumstances to do so within the period of one year, then at the earliest practicable moment and in no case later than 18 months from the closing of the session of the Conference, bring the Convention before the authority or authorities within whose competence the matter lies, for the enactment of legislation or other action;

(*c*) Members shall inform the Director-General of the International Labour Office of the measures taken in accordance with this article to bring the Convention before the said competent authority or authorities, with particulars of the authority or authorities regarded as competent, and of the action taken by them;

. . . .

(*e*) if the Member does not obtain the consent of the authority or authorities within whose competence the matter lies, no further obligation shall rest upon the Member except that it shall report to the Director-General of the International Labour Office, at appropriate intervals as requested by the Governing Body, the position of its law and practice in regard to the matters dealt with in the Convention, showing the extent to which effect has been given, or is proposed to be given, to any of the provisions of the Convention by legislation, administrative action, collective agreement or otherwise and stating the difficulties which prevent or delay the ratification of such Convention.

271

6. In the case of a Recommendation—

. . . .

(b) each of the Members undertakes that it will, within a period of one year at most from the closing of the session of the Conference, or if it is impossible owing to exceptional circumstances to do so within the period of one year, then at the earliest practicable moment and in no case later than 18 months after the closing of the Conference, bring the Recommendation before the authority or authorities within whose competence the matter lies for the enactment of legislation or other action;

(c) the Members shall inform the Director-General of the International Labour Office of the measures taken in accordance with this article to bring the Recommendation before the said competent authority or authorities with particulars of the authority or authorities regarded as competent, and of the action taken by them;

(d) apart from bringing the Recommendation before the said competent authority or authorities, no further obligation shall rest upon the Members, except that they shall report to the Director-General of the International Labour Office, at appropriate intervals as requested by the Governing Body, the position of the law and practice in their country in regard to the matters dealt with in the Recommendation, showing the extent to which effect has been given, or is proposed to be given, to the provisions of the Recommendation and such modifications of these provisions as it has been found or may be found necessary to make in adopting or applying them.

. . . .

8. In no case shall the adoption of any Convention or Recommendation by the Conference, or the ratification of any Convention by any Member, be deemed to affect any law, award, custom or agreement which ensures more favourable conditions to the workers concerned than those provided for in the Convention or Recommendation.

47.4 General Conference of the International Labour Organisation, *Declaration concerning the Aims and Purposes of the International Labour Organisation* 1944[1]

The General Conference of the International Labour Organisation, meeting in its Twenty-sixth Session in Philadelphia, hereby adopts, this tenth day of May in the year nineteen hundred and forty-four, the present Declaration of the aims and purposes of the International Labour Organisation and of the principles which should inspire the policy of its Members.

[1] Published as an Annex to the International Labour Organisation, *Constitution* 1968.

The Conference reaffirms the fundamental principles on which the Organisation is based and, in particular, that—

(*a*) labour is not a commodity;

(*b*) freedom of expression and of association are essential to sustained progress;

(*c*) poverty anywhere constitutes a danger to prosperity everywhere;

(*d*) the war against want requires to be carried on with unrelenting vigour within each nation, and by continuous and concerted international effort in which the representatives of workers and employers, enjoying equal status with those of governments, join with them in free discussion and democratic decision with a view to the promotion of the common welfare.

II

Believing that experience has fully demonstrated the truth of the statement in the Constitution of the International Labour Organisation that lasting peace can be established only if it is based on social justice, the Conference affirms that—

(*a*) all human beings, irrespective of race, creed or sex, have the right to pursue both their material well-being and their spiritual development in conditions of freedom and dignity, of economic security and equal opportunity;

(*b*) the attainment of the conditions in which this shall be possible must constitute the central aim of national and international policy;

(*c*) all national and international policies and measures, in particular those of an economic and financial character, should be judged in this light and accepted only in so far as they may be held to promote and not to hinder the achievement of this fundamental objective;

(*d*) it is a responsibility of the International Labour Organisation to examine and consider all international economic and financial policies and measures in the light of this fundamental objective;

(*e*) in discharging the tasks entrusted to it the International Labour Organisation, having considered all relevant economic and financial factors, may include in its decisions and recommendations any provisions which it considers appropriate.

III

The Conference recognises the solemn obligation of the International Labour Organisation to further among the nations of the world programmes which will achieve:

(*a*) full employment and the raising of standards of living;

(*b*) the employment of workers in the occupations in which they can have the satisfaction of giving the fullest measure of their skill and attainments and make their greatest contribution to the common well-being;

(*c*) the provision, as a means to the attainment of this end and under adequate guarantees for all concerned, of facilities for training and the transfer of labour, including migration for employment and settlement;

(*d*) policies in regard to wages and earnings, hours and other conditions of work calculated to ensure a just share of the fruits of progress to all, and a minimum living wage to all employed and in need of such protection;

(e) the effective recognition of the right of collective bargaining, the co-operation of management and labour in the continuous improvement of productive efficiency, and the collaboration of workers and employers in the preparation and application of social and economic measures;

(f) the extension of social security measures to provide a basic income to all in need of such protection and comprehensive medical care;

(g) adequate protection for the life and health of workers in all occupations;

(h) provision for child welfare and maternity protection;

(i) the provision of adequate nutrition, housing and facilities for recreation and culture;

(j) the assurance of equality of educational and vocational opportunity.

IV

Confident that the fuller and broader utilisation of the world's productive resources necessary for the achievement of the objectives set forth in this Declaration can be secured by effective international and national action, including measures to expand production and consumption, to avoid severe economic fluctuations, to promote the economic and social advancement of the less developed regions of the world, to assure greater stability in world prices of primary products, and to promote a high and steady volume of international trade, the Conference pledges the full co-operation of the International Labour Organisation with such international bodies as may be entrusted with a share of the responsibility for this great task and for the promotion of the health, education and well-being of all peoples.

V

The Conference affirms that the principles set forth in this Declaration are fully applicable to all peoples everywhere and that, while the manner of their application must be determined with due regard to the stage of social and economic development reached by each people, their progressive application to peoples who are still dependent, as well as to those who have already achieved self-government, is a matter of concern to the whole civilised world.

47.5 General Council of the Trades Union Congress, *Report to Congress: Section F International* [*Trades Union Congress Report* (London, Trades Union Congress, 1967), pp. 275–277]

(247) CO-OPERATION WITH OVERSEAS UNIONS

The General Council have continued to co-operate with overseas unions by providing information, publications and correspondence courses, and by making the facilities of the T.U.C. Training College available to visitors and students, especially those studying at residential colleges in this country and participants in the courses conducted by the Ministry of Labour under government technical assistance agreements. By arrangement with their unions, a grant was made to enable the president of the Industrial Union of Commercial, Clerical & Allied Workers, West Cameroon, to attend a one-year course at Plater College, Oxford, and courses of training with the T.U.C. were provided for the vice-president of the Nigerian Tobacco General Workers' Union and for the chairman of the Malta Customs Federation.

The General Council made the first of three annual grants of £500 to the Trade Union Education Institute in Jamaica and also made available the first of three annual grants of £500 to be used for bursaries tenable either at the Institute or at the Cipriani Labour College, Trinidad, by students from the smaller islands in the West Indies. The General Council have invited the Ghana T.U.C. to send a small delegation to this country as their guests later this year.

At the invitation of the Minister of Overseas Development the General Council have taken part in discussions on the possibility of young trade unionists participating in voluntary service overseas.

During the year the Guyana Labour Union and the Union of Commercial Workers, Trinidad, completed repayment of interest-free loans made to them for organising purposes in previous years.

(248) SWAZILAND

It was reported to Congress in 1966 that the General Council had agreed that plans should be made for a T.U.C. representative to visit Swaziland to assist the unions there, with the aim of establishing a firm basis for future trade union development. A member of the T.U.C. staff went to Swaziland in February and spent four months there on organising and educational work, mainly with the Swaziland Pulp and Timber Workers' Union and with the Citrus Plantations and Agricultural Workers' Union. It was necessary to give assistance to various unions on issues arising out of trade union law and its application, since the law in Swaziland bears little relation to the prevailing standards of literacy or industrial experience of the workers, or to the state of development of the trade unions, all of them comparatively recently established. . . .

. . . .

(249) NATIONAL INDEPENDENCE

A message of congratulation was sent to the Prime Minister of Barbados in November, when Barbados became independent. The message referred to the status and respect enjoyed by Barbados through many years of responsible government, to the noteworthy contribution made by trade unionists to its democratic way of life, and to the association between the T.U.C. and the pioneers of trade unionism in the Barbados Workers' Union, and before that with the Barbados Progressive League. The General Council were represented

275

by Mr. F. Hayday at the twenty-fifth anniversary celebrations of the Barbados Workers' Union, immediately preceding independence.

In March, Antigua, St. Lucia, St. Kitts, Grenada, and Dominica became independent states in association with Britain. Messages conveying the good wishes of British trade unionists were sent to their Prime Ministers and trade union organisations.

(250) MALTA

In January 1967 the Government announced that the military establishment in Malta was to be reduced by two-thirds in stages between 1967 and 1970, halving expenditure by the forces there. The Malta Government accused the British Government of failing to observe the Anglo-Maltese agreement on defence and assistance, 1964, and at the end of January asked Britain to stop using the rights and privileges and facilities enjoyed in the island and ordered oil firms to stop deliveries to the British services until customs duty on aircraft fuel was paid at the normal rate. A similar line was adopted over other supplies. These developments and the circumstances surrounding them were brought to the attention of the General Council in February, when they were informed that an approach had been made by the General Workers' Union and the Confederation of Malta Trade Unions emphasising the serious consequences that would ensue for their members, and for the economy of the islands generally, if the rundown took place as proposed. The view was expressed that both governments had been somewhat imprudent, the British by appearing not to consult the Maltese Government and the Maltese by summarily suspending privileges and facilities. It was argued that Britain had a moral obligation to help Malta, since the economy of the island had been distorted by previous British military requirements, and in view of the rising level of unemployment which the General Workers' Union estimated might reach 18 per cent of the labour force if the proposal was carried into effect. Existing Maltese plans for economic development were in any case inadequate and a greater effort would be required in Malta, bearing in mind that the country received a considerably higher level of aid per head of population than any other Commonwealth country. The principal needs were for a new development plan and for interim measures which would enable Malta to avoid the worst consequences of the defence cuts.

Representatives of the General Council met Lord Beswick, Parliamentary Under-Secretary of State at the Commonwealth Office, early in February and discussed these views with him. A further meeting with Lord Beswick took place on February 21 when the General Council's representatives were informed that revised proposals had been put to the Malta Government rephasing the rundown in forces over five years instead of four and making further provision for redundancy payments. The General Council's representatives were also informed that the possibility of sending a mission to Malta which would make recommendations to both governments on retraining and the creation of new job opportunities was under discussion. Throughout this period the T.U.C. was in contact with the unions in Malta.

Negotiations eventually took place between the two governments as a result of which the Malta Government was finally offered various revisions of the original proposals, including a guarantee that in the first 18 months of the revised rundown period the number of posts abolished would not exceed 850, and the appointment of an economic mission was proposed. These proposals were initially rejected by the Malta Government but finally proved to be acceptable to them.